SAM McKELVIE—*Son of the Soil*

SAM McKELVI

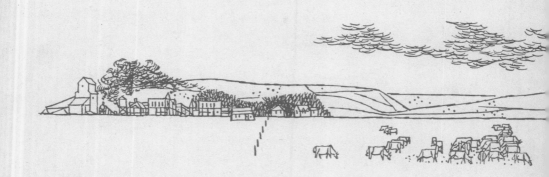

Nebraska Heritage Series

n of the Soil

Sketch of a self-reliant American
who cheerfully fought his own battles

By Bruce H. Nicoll and Ken R. Keller

with a foreword by
Clarence Budington Kelland

Johnsen Publishing Co., Lincoln, Nebraska · 1954

A TERM OF ADMIRATION has appeared in the last few years which is expressive and which must be very welcome to those upon whom it is bestowed. Certain adept and efficient men have come to be spoken of as "Ball Players' Ball Players," or as "Golfers' Golfers," or as "Lawyers' Lawyers." It is a term which signifies that these men have earned the accolade of men who are most able to judge of their abilities and their skills; they are men who have proven to their fellow competitors, as distinguished from the less knowing applause of mere spectators, that they are of the elect.

Samuel Roy McKelvie has won for himself a finer title than any of these. He is a man worthy to be called an Americans' American.

Sam was born into a different world than we see today. It was a world characterized by integrity, industry, frugality and self-reliance. It was a world that lifted but did not lean. It was a world, at least where Sam was born in Nebraska and I was born in Michigan—in the same year of our Lord, 1881, when folks were willing to help but did not ask to be helped; and where the muscles of their arms and the will in their souls were strengthened by the exercise of tightening their belts when evil days came along. Men of those days knew they could fight it through and were calmly willing to fight it through. It might mean a lengthening of the hours of toil, and self-denial, such as is rare in this day. It was a time when folks thought it was better to put a dollar in the savings bank at the end of the week than to answer the ring at the door announcing the arrival of the man come to collect the installment on the piano. If you could afford a piano you bought it with cash, and if you couldn't afford one you contented yourself with a mouth organ. It was a day when you stood on your own feet and resented anyone who tried to prop you up; and when no other thought came to you than that there was only one way to get anything—which was to earn it.

These matters were not considered to be virtues. They were just normal behavior. And at the root of them was proper pride and self-respect.

These things became a part of Sam McKelvie on the Nebraska farm of his magnificent parents. He did not have to learn them because they were born in him, and as he grew up in that farmhouse they were so firmly embedded in him by the life he led, and by the examples by which he was surrounded, that even an atom bomb could not have blasted them out of his character.

Today, after nearly seventy-three years of living they are as much a part of his make up as the bones of his framework.

Because of this, it is well that there has been set down simply and with truth the simple story of Sam McKelvie, and some hints of the sweet story of Martha who has been by his side for so many wonderful years. It is a story that no boy can read without profit and that no adult can read without envy. The sorry world today would have been sorrier had not Sam McKelvie and his kind lived in it.

If you wish to know the definition of a good citizen, read this little story about how Sam lived and what he has done.

Clarence Budington Kelland
Phoenix, Arizona, 1954

Samuel R. McKelvie

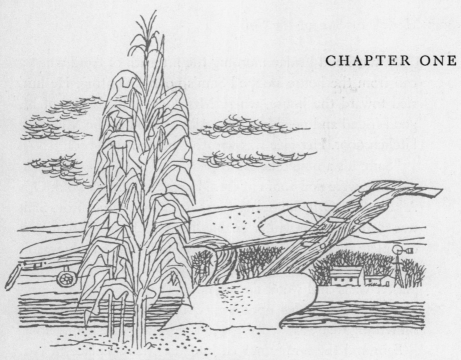

CHAPTER ONE

THE ROOTS GO DOWN

APRIL OF 1881 was a bright month, and full of promise, for Sam and Jennie McKelvie.

Generous spring rains filled the banks of little Sandy Creek to the brim. Buds loaded the branches of thicket lining the creek's banks, promising a bountiful harvest of wild plums in the summer. The dark green prairie was speckled with tiny isles of blossoms.

This was the month that Sam sank the steel plowshare into the prairie's tough sod and broke out the first sixty of his one hundred twenty-acre homestead.

This was the month too that Sam and Jennie moved into their new Nebraska home which stood atop a little rise overlooking Sandy Creek in the almost flat Clay County prairie.

3

It was Good Friday morning the fifteenth of April when a call from the house stopped Sam's potato planting. He hurried toward the house, where Mrs. Celia Albee, wife of his good friend and neighbor John Albee, stood at the McKelvie kitchen door. Her face was wreathed in smiles.

"Sam, it's a boy," she said.

There were now four children, Homer L., six years old; Otis Albert, five; Othello, nearly four; and now Samuel Roy. Sam was glad the open winter enabled him, and his neighbors, to complete the house. The old Massey sodhouse simply wasn't large enough for his growing family. Besides that the white plaster walls and wood floors and glass windows of the new place gave Jennie her opportunity to really keep a tidy place, something that was denied her in the soddy with its dirt floor.

Sam and the family moved into the Massey place in November, 1879, soon after they arrived on a B. and M. railroad immigrant train from Schuyler County, Illinois. The Massey place was just a short distance from Sam's homestead, four miles north of Fairfield in southern Clay County. In the spring of 1880 Sam's first crop planted on rented land had turned out well despite a dry winter and a terrible, almost suffocating dust storm in March which engulfed the prairie. His wheat, which nearly perished in the dust, made ten bushels to the acre. Five acres of buckwheat planted in June flourished and made fifty-five bushels, forty of which he sold for a dollar a bushel—enough to pay the rent. He held the rest for pancakes and seed.

But the corn, Sam was elated about that. It made a fine crop, a handsome dividend for the extra-hard work of preparing a field from wheat stubble by burning, plowing and

4

then rolling with a heavy elm log to hold the moisture. The crop matured early, escaping an early frost which ruined most of the other corn in the vicinity. Travelers often stopped to view the field and Sam was told he had the finest corn in the county. This pleased him greatly for when Sam came to Nebraska he had in mind growing corn, rather than spring wheat which was the main crop thereabouts. He planted some wheat, of course, for cash and flour. But corn was best to fatten hogs. When you market corn in fat hogs you just naturally stand to get more, Sam maintained.

But what pleased Sam as much as the corn was the fine litter of pigs. He got seven males and one female from a purebred Poland China he had brought from Illinois.

One thing that delighted Sam and his father back in Illinois was taking their hogs to fairs. There is something thrilling about that. But as Sam's father often said there was a practical side to showing at fairs too. First of all there's a man's pride. When you show your hogs against other exhibitors' you naturally want to win, and if you're going to stand up to the competition you've got to work hard at raising and breeding better hogs. But besides this, going to fairs gives you a chance to pick up a lot of good information from other breeders.

This was why Sam was so pleased to hear there would be a fair in Hastings in mid-September. When he came home from that fair, his pockets were lined with $105, the price received for the litter of seven little male "wind splitters," the best of show.

There was some trouble at the hog judging though. It began with a breeder from Gage County, whose tent was pitched

5

near Sam's wagon. On the day of the hog show two of the judges went to the tent and Sam saw them passing around a jug of the breeder's whisky. Sam found the third judge, a man by the name of Dan Nettleton, a tall, slim, shy fellow. Dan assured Sam the judging would be fair. So, after the judges had examined the litters, Sam saw Dan call his fellow judges aside. A heated discussion followed. Then Dan walked over to Sam's pen and hung the blue ribbon. This was an act of fair play Sam never forgot. It led to a strong friendship between them. Dan reminded Sam for all the world of Abe Lincoln. Sam often visited Dan at his cattle farm near Spring Ranch in the eastern part of the county. Dan was known to many as Uncle Dan, but Sam called him "The Tall Cycamore of the Blue."

There were other things to cheer Sam and Jennie in the fall of 1880. All summer, wagons brought new homesteaders to the county, and this meant more neighbors, a fact given substance by Sam's old friend Leander Brewer who was Fairfield's postmaster. Mr. Brewer told Sam he figured the county's population was now about 11,000, nearly four times larger than when Sam had first visited it six years earlier to claim his homestead.

Fairfield itself was getting to be quite a place, especially since its incorporation as a village two years earlier. It now had a population of about eight hundred. Sam marveled at the way main street had grown. Each side of the street was now lined with about a dozen narrow frame buildings and several of them were painted. The street was wide but badly rutted, a condition resulting from wet weather when it became an almost bottomless quagmire.

The merchants, largely in deference to the womenfolk, had built sidewalks of rough planks. The walks were slightly elevated, and extended for a full block on each side of the street, ending in a downward slope to the mud or dust, where the ladies were on their own. Hitching posts lined the walks. They reminded Sam of good fence posts set too close together. He was surprised to find that one of the general stores was being operated by J. E. Hopper, the former agent for the St. Joseph and Denver City Lines who had sold him his land. Indeed, times were changing. No longer was it the St. Joe and Denver. The old St. Joe and Denver was now part of the Union Pacific and called the St. Joseph and Western.

The fact was, Sam surmised as he surveyed the bright blue sky over the prairie that April day of 1881, it looked like this was to be his permanent home. Any notions he had of returning to Schuyler County, Illinois, and resuming his role of a rural school teacher had faded.

Sam liked his new country, the new frontier which was drawing hundreds of families from east of the Missouri to its prairieland. It was pretty country. Big, thousands of square miles, big. Exciting. Strange. Taming this raw land called for sweat and toil. There were disappointments. But there was hope and promise. And plenty of elbowroom for a man who wanted to grow up.

Yes, Sam knew why he—and his neighbors—wanted to stay in Nebraska. It was the land; good land, millions of acres. Cheap land. Land that smelled sweet in the spring thaw. Land that thrust stems of grain or stalks of corn towards the summer sky. Land that rested beneath the yellowed grass in autumn and the soft blanket of winter's snow. Land that strained

7

backs, gave riches, denied existence. Land was the beginning, the life, and the end.

Sam loved the land, and worked at its tending diligently. Jennie had heard Mrs. Albee, and her other neighbors, say Sam was one of the hardest working farmers in the county. Of course, when they said that Jennie would blush shyly. But later when she was alone she admitted her pride to herself because she believed passionately that good things came to those who worked for them.

Good things came to the McKelvies in the rush of ten years on the prairie. By 1890 the little homestead of one hundred twenty acres became six hundred and forty. Cattle and hogs and rich prairie grass and corn paid off if you knew how much of each you wanted and when. Sam did.

The Osage hedge on the north and south borders of the original homestead stood six feet tall. The trees Sam and Jennie loved so well had been planted, dozens of them, but only a few cottonwoods and boxelders survived the caprice of Nebraska weather. A rich lawn spread itself generously about the house.

The little white frame house had grown too. A three-room addition clung to the north side. A second story was added. There were now seven rooms. All were needed. Besides Homer, sixteen, Otis, fourteen, and Othello, or "Oley" as everybody called him, thirteen, five other children had "climbed the board"—Samuel Roy, nine, Maude, seven, Claude, six, Pearl, four, and Florence, two. Floyd, born in December, 1889, died the following June 6. "Climbing the board" was Jennie's way of telling when a baby became a youngster. The board was a heavy plank about 18 inches wide. Jennie propped it

8

securely in the doorway between the kitchen and the parlor. When a toddler was able to climb over the board and get underfoot as Jennie busied herself in the kitchen, out the child went into the great wide world of the front lawn.

For Jennie life moved swiftly. She was well aware of it as she pulled her hand from the bread dough and wiped her forehead with the back of her wrist one hot July afternoon in 1890. Bake the bread. Peel potatoes. Scrub floors. Sew underwear from flour sacks. Can fruit. Render lard. Churn butter. Make soap. Sweat in the summer. Shiver in the winter. Work. Laugh. Cry. Let the worry for tomorrow erase the unhappy memories of yesterday.

All about the homestead the tough Nebraska sod was being shaped to the ways of the plow. Land seekers, tens of thousands of them, crossed the Missouri and spread westward. The new country was hard, a moody land. It could pour forth its riches one season and in the next cruelly withhold the fruits of labor in a battering hail when the wheat was dead ripe, in a horde of hungry grasshoppers out of a clear sky when the corn was in the silk, or in an endless procession of searing days that killed crops in withered fields. You never knew. Some despaired and headed back East with bitterness in their hearts. Some stayed, like the McKelvies, and deepened their roots in the good black soil. You never knew. You hedged against tomorrow.

Sam came in the kitchen and dropped his stained straw hat on a chair. His forehead, glistening with beads of water, was white. Below the line of his hat band spread the deep red of a face, fringed with a black, sweat-soaked beard. His faded blue cotton shirt was muddied where dust had clung to sweat spots.

He walked to the sink and pumped cool water over his hands. Then he cupped them and dashed water over his face before taking down the big tin cup for a drink.

Sam said it was awful hot for a young lad to be hoeing weeds so he filled the cup again and took it out to Roy. At the hedge Sam saw the hoe. His glance moved to the shade of a nearby cottonwood. There Roy was sound asleep. Sam strode over and shook him.

"Roy," Sam said sternly, "everybody works around here. There's no place for laziness. Laziness is for the wicked. When I ask you to do a job, get it done." And he jerked the boy across his knee and added, "Here's a warm reminder to remember."

Sam's anger was stirred quickly when the children failed to measure up to his expectations. It cooled just as quickly. That night when the family sat down for supper, Sam looked at Jennie and said, "Roy's going to be a lad who's not afraid of work. I found him lying down asleep right beside it." Everybody laughed. Even Roy flushed and smiled.

The spankings were but a small part of Sam's philosophy of farm life. Jennie had seen him stamp his philosophy on the boys, on Frank Kowalk, the hired man, on the neighbors, and even on the banker in Fairfield. Many times she nodded in agreement when Sam said it took a smart man to be a good farmer. Farming, he would say, is a big risk. What you do today may not be any good tomorrow. Usually at this point he would run a rough hand over the bald spot where he parted his hair on the left side. Then he would say you can't keep regular hours on a farm. It may be twelve hours. Maybe longer, especially if you've got livestock. The main thing is that farming's hard work for both your hands and your head.

Sam believed his philosophy and lived it fully as the head of his family. At night he would push his chair from the supper table, walk into the parlor, light the kerosene lamp beside the big creaking rocker with the hard shiny leather bottom, and begin reading the Breeder's Gazette from Chicago, or The Iowa Homestead, or The Nebraska Farmer, or The Twentieth Century Farmer. His favorite was the Breeder's Gazette, every line of it from cover to cover. Nothing like the Gazette. It gave a man everything he needed to know about the livestock business. In fact, Sam was so devoted to the Gazette that a couple of years earlier he had rounded up so many subscriptions in the neighborhood that the grateful magazine sent him a handsome clock in a mahogany case. The clock sat on the roll-top desk in the corner where Sam kept his records. Unerringly he knew when an hour of reading had passed but by habit he glanced at the clock, and his judgment confirmed, he would stand up, stretch, turn out the lamp, and head for bed. This ritual signaled bedtime for the entire family and the end of a McKelvie day.

CHAPTER TWO

SCHOOL DAYS

IT WAS A HOT mid-summer afternoon. The sun had just passed its overhead position in the pale blue sky. Heat waves rose shimmering from the stubble of the freshly harvested wheat field. The corn stalks stood waist high. The cattle switched beneath the trees at the far end of the pasture. The lengthening shadows on the north side of the barn invited rest and a young man, straw in his mouth, lay there squinting idly at the tranquil scene.

This was a time for contemplation for Samuel Roy McKelvie, age fourteen. It was a time to ponder the world and things. He had received his diploma in April and now the time for decision had arrived. Was it more school? Or work on the farm? Or adventure in the world that lay beyond his prairie horizon?

13

It was a time for introspection; a time for summing up. His experiences were simple but they were those of all other young men in his neighborhood, and Roy had many things to remember.

He remembered the romps with his mother. Despite her five feet two and about 90 pounds, she was an extremely active woman who loved the out-of-doors. Many afternoons, when the house work was done, Jennie joined Roy and the others to play pump-pump-pull-away, or run-sheep-run, or crack-the-whip. Jennie excelled at all of them. For these occasions she would take off her shoes and fly after the youngsters. Only once was her fleetness challenged. That was the time she caught Homer, a confident sixteen-year-old, up to some mischief in the barn. Homer took one look at the angry flush in his mother's face and fled through the barn door. Jennie was right at his heels. Twice around the barn and she caught the panting youngster, promptly turned him over her knees, and gave him a tanning.

And the apples. He brushed half-heartedly as a fly buzzed his ear. Yes, the apples. He could glimpse the edge of the orchard where, as in other summers, the young fruit hung. Many times he had stood a watchful guard there while Homer had climbed to reach the shining green of a couple of apples. It was hard to wait for the crispness of autumn to change the green to yellows and reds. Autumn and apple butter time. And a little later Jennie would supervise them as they dug little pits for storage. Into each would go two dozen of the finest to be covered with straw and dirt against freezing. And then the cold winter nights when they would pull away the protective covering and carry the treasures to the warmth of the kitchen, fragrant with popped corn and hot butter. Even in the heat of late July, his mouth watered with the thought of the chill of a winter apple against his teeth and the pop of the first bite.

But life on the farm was not all rosy red apples. Roy shared his burdens of assigned chores. Still, even the chores had their light moments. There was the evening of Old Pied's accident. Roy and Claude were milking. The mosquitoes were thick and Old Pied kept switching her tail in Roy's face. Claude grabbed and held the tail. His next idea was better. He tied the tail to Blackie's in the next stall. That ended the switching. When the milking was finished, Claude gave Blackie a customary wallop. She jumped and took the better part of Old Pied's tail with her. Their quick laughter ebbed with the thought of their father's wrath. Together they ran to retrieve Pied's tail and hid it in the feedbox. By the next morning the boys had their plan. Much earlier than usual they milked and while Claude kept watch, Roy used string to reunite Old Pied with her tail and drove her out to pasture. Out of sight of the house the boys removed the tail and hung it on a fence wire. That evening Oley brought the cows back to the shed and reported Old Pied's unusual accident. No questions were asked.

Roy recalled the thrill of his first trip to Lincoln on the train, and the excitement of the state fair, and the prizes his father's hogs always won. He pondered the confidence Sam and Jennie had placed in him more recently when they allowed him to go to Fairfield with Roy and Herman Briggs. That trip to town for him was free adventure. He wondered at many things, especially the dank, sour odor as he passed the saloon. He remembered that his father touched neither liquor nor tobacco. Jennie's voice came to him, rising with evangelism as 15 she recalled the splendid work done at Hastings and Harvard and Fairfield by John B. Finch who had come all the way from New York City to further his labors against rum. Jennie called him a delivering angel for those who had succumbed to the demoralizing rum power of the saloons. Why, Jennie would exclaim, Mr. Finch in one year pledged 50,000 persons to total abstinence and raised in different localities where he had spoken $20,000 for the establishment of reading rooms for those who proved themselves rid of this evil by wearing the "red ribbon," proud symbol of the Grand Lodge of Good Templars of Nebraska. And while Jennie was not one of the 450 ladies in the Fairfield area who had joined the Temperance Alliance and who sang hymns at the doors of the saloons, yet she believed fervently that their efforts rescued many a fine man from the clutches of drink. And so it was Roy quickened his steps as he passed the saloon.

But clearest among all his memories was Catfight. Catfight school. Now that it was over, and his diploma rested safely in his father's roll-top desk in the parlor, Roy thought of school.

He remembered the obvious pride with which his father—a school board member for many terms by virtue of his experience as a teacher—told and retold how the little white school of District 40 got its name. It was the first spring that his father had settled in Nebraska and one morning, looking across the prairie, he discovered the schoolhouse had been moved a quarter of a mile from its familiar location. A half-dozen men and several teams of horses were rolling it on logs across the prairie. Roy's father threw himself on a horse and hurried with the news to John Albee, the school district director.

16

More than a week later Mr. Albee returned to the McKelvie farm with his report. It was, he opined, another typical example of the ruthless enterprise of the Clay Center crowd. The new county-seat town needed a schoolhouse. Part of the town was in District 40 and the little school on the prairie seemed to be an easy and inexpensive answer to its problem. Just move it into town. Mr. Albee would have no part of it. He got the sheriff to serve papers to halt the removal. He appealed to the county superintendent, a battling Baptist preacher, who called a meeting of the two factions. After much heated argument the school district gave Clay Center one and one-fourth sections of land in exchange for the little white schoolhouse. From then it was known as "Catfight School" despite the later efforts of some of the housewives to rename it "Harmony School."

For Roy the real joy of school days at Catfight came every two weeks when the Literary Society met of an evening in the little school. The Literary Society was the occasion when the students recited poetry, gave orations, took part in debates, and held spelling bees. Most of the families of the neighborhood came. The little room was always packed. It was upon these occasions that Roy realized his boyish ambition to stand before an audience and recite.

Roy's first appearance came when he was in the third grade and the teacher gave him two weeks in which to memorize a poem. He rushed home to announce his assignment. Jennie told him she had saved a poem for just such an event, a poem by John J. Ingalls called, "Opportunity." Night after night, and even after school, Jennie helped him get the poem so well in mind that nothing could dislodge it.

17

The big night arrived and Roy, scrubbed and confident, faced his audience. The glow of the kerosene lamps on either side of the teacher's desk caught the sheen of his blond hair, and the valley of the side part. The big black bow that Homer had tied so carefully all but hid the corners of his wide, white collar. His snug, gray jacket sleeves were respectfully short of his white cuffs. His knee pants were neatly pressed; his black stockings smooth where they entered the tops of his polished boots. His round face shone and he delivered his poem, ramrod stiff, but without a hitch, a poem he was to find himself repeating many years later:

> Master of Human Destiny am I.
> Fame, Love and Fortune on my footsteps wait.
> Cities and fields I walk:
> I penetrate deserts and fields remote, and passing by
> Hovel, mart and palace, soon or late
> I knock unbidden once at every gate!
> If sleeping wake; if feasting, rise before
> I turn away. It is the hour of fate
> And they who follow me reach every state
> Mortals desire, and conquer every foe
> Save death; but those who doubt or hesitate,
> Condemned to failure, penury and woe,
> Seek me in vain and uselessly implore.
> I answer not and I return no more.

The applause opened a new world for Roy and he soon became one of the star performers at the Literary Society meetings. Most of all, as his school years drew to a close, he liked debate best. The debate teams comprised three pupils each.

The Sam McKelvie family about 1890. Back row, left to right
Homer, Otis, and Othello. Seated in front, left to right, Maud, Roy.
Pearl, Florence seated on her mother's lap, and Claude.

Of all the debate questions Roy remembered these, "Resolved: Fire is more hazardous than flood," and, "Resolved: The country is a better place to live than town."

Yes, Roy reflected, the Literary Society days came to an end all too soon. But with the end of school came an end to the drudgery of fractions and history, neither of which he recalled with fondness. And the end of school also freed him from the winter's routine of going upstairs and studying each night until Sam finished reading the papers.

It was father's ironclad rule that Roy and the other children study in silence. So much as a giggle and his voice boomed up from the parlor with a final warning, "You boys quit that fooling around or I'm going to come up there!" One night, however, his warning was unheeded. Roy and Oley were tussling. Roy crashed to the floor. It was then they heard his footsteps. Lamps were quickly doused. Silence blanketed the room. When Sam stomped in, he groped for the lamp, found it, and angrily struck a match on the wall. It failed to light. He struck another, and still another. At that moment Jennie arrived with a lighted lamp. She stared at the three black streaks on the white plaster wall. Sam's gaze followed hers. Momentarily he faced her and then, without a word, turned and retreated down the stairs. Jennie followed him, unmindful of the titters in the darkness.

Something besides the Literary Societies, and trips to Fairfield and Lincoln, stirred young Roy McKelvie's musings that hot summer afternoon in the shade of the barn. The new thought was fresh in his mind. Only recently he had listened as his father and the neighbors talked politics. They always talked politics when they got together. At first politics and

21

the men who made them seemed far away and unreal. But now he had heard and seen real-life politics.

For weeks the neighborhood talked of the two political rallies to be held in Clay Center. The first night Senator John M. Thurston addressed a Republican rally. The following night the Democrats presented Thurston's opponent for the U. S. senatorship, Congressman Williams Jennings Bryan.

The McKelvies attended the Democratic rally. When the big night arrived the whole family climbed into the buggy and drove to Clay Center. Roy was proud and pleased. He sat on the front row because high up there on the stage with its bunting and flags was his father, Sam McKelvie, Democratic candidate for the state legislature, a nomination Sam had reluctantly accepted. Next to his father sat Mr. Bryan. Mr. Bryan's speech, loud and clear, stirred the packed hall with cheers and stomping. He paused at the end of a statement and reached for a glass of water. As he did so, somebody yelled, "Rats!" Mr. Bryan flashed his answer, "Rats leave a sinking ship!" The crowd whooped with glee. Roy loved it.

He remembered the long ride home and his father's repeated praises of Mr. Bryan's speech. But father seemed to dislike his own campaign for the legislature. For one thing he had deep respect and friendship for his opponent, Uncle Dan Nettleton. And for another, there was Jennie's disapproval of politics. Father lost the election.

But now, as Roy rested in the shade contemplating the shimmering horizon before him, he wondered about the strange thrill of politics, and the colorful men who swayed the emotions and stirred the imaginations of people who came to hear them. There was something fascinating about it.

CHAPTER THREE

NEW HORIZONS

THE SUMMER OF 1895 was bitter for many Nebraska families who had broken the sod of the rolling prairies in the previous decade. A dry spell had lengthened into a drouth. The once bountiful soil dried hard in the glaring sun and hot winds. The crops shriveled. Grasshoppers ate their way across the land, leaving it bare.

The following year adversity still plagued many Nebraska farms. But for the McKelvie family, and especially for father Sam, it was a time of opportunity—an opportunity born of the thrift and hard work of fifteen years. Sam had stored a considerable quantity of wheat from previous years. Now he fed it to the cattle which desperate farmers were willing to sell at low prices. It was a time when Sam was able to purchase 2,000 acres of good grassland to the west in Chase County.

23

Young Roy McKelvie, with the boyhood days of Catfight school behind him, considered the prospects of the "grown-up" world about him. And that world appeared to be casting him as a full-fledged hand on father's farm. Yes, it looked that way. Homer had married and started farming on his own place nearby. Roy wasn't sure he liked the way things were going. He began to have his doubts about the farm. He liked the livestock end of the business—raising hogs and cattle. But field crops were another matter. He hated to plant. He hated to cultivate. He hated to harvest.

It was possible, of course, he reasoned, he might go on to school. Homer and Oley had. He wondered why father or Jennie didn't mention it. The opening day of high school in the county passed. Still no mention of school. September dragged into October. Still no school. Then one evening after dinner, Sam looked up from the pages of the Breeder's Gazette. Without preliminaries he announced abruptly that Roy would enroll in the high school at Harvard.

The last Sunday in October, Sam bundled Roy and a heavy suitcase into the family buggy and off they rolled on the rough prairie road toward Harvard, nine miles to the north.

The house was big and white, two-storied with a gabled roof. A high iron fence surrounded it. This was the home of Mrs. Jerushia Soule, Mrs. Susan Perkins and Miss Annetta Buck, three sisters who provided rooms for young boys from the country who came to Harvard for high schooling.

Roy was impressed with the high ceilings, the bright flowered paper on the walls, the varnished oak floors and woodwork, and the lace curtains of his room. But he was alone. Miss Buck came to his door and said the other boys were on their

24

way to supper at a boarding house nearby. She seemed to understand when he said he wasn't hungry. Annetta Buck had seen homesick boys before.

In the dusk he lit the kerosene lamp and then stretched out on the bed. He stared at the bright circle of light on the ceiling above the lamp. His eyes moved to the lamp's reflection in the blackness of the windows. A dreary ending for a bright October day.

At home now they would be eating supper. The familiar picture of the McKelvie kitchen was vivid in the soft yellow light of the table lamp. Sunday evening at home. The odor of popcorn. The apples that were red and chilled. Jennie at the organ. The hymns. The contentment. The ticking of the Breeder's Gazette clock. This room had no clock. No ticking. The memories rushed upon him and with them came tears.

The melancholy of the first night away from home faded in the following days of school. Roy won friends quickly. Despite his diminutive build, he was a sturdy lad; fair-haired, blue-eyed, and easy with laughter. He had a flair for self-expression uncommon to other youths in his class, a flair which both the students and the teachers noted.

Because of his late start Roy found himself far behind his class. It was hard work catching up. He never caught up in algebra. But in civil government he soon stood at the head of his class.

It was in this subject that he came to the attention of the school superintendent, Mr. Samuel Arnot. He whetted Roy's interest in government at every opportunity. Mr. Arnot suggested that Roy's knowledge of local government might be improved if he subscribed to a daily paper and read about the

25

doings in the state legislature which had convened in January of 1897. Roy's father agreed and the expenditure paid an unexpected dividend. One night Roy noticed an item about a bill being introduced which would outlaw the sale of school lands but permit their continued use on a lease basis. An important part of Sam's farm was leased school land. The next week end Roy took the paper home and showed the item to his father. Sam promptly bought his school land at $2.00 per acre. The bill was passed later in the session. (In later years Roy reflected that the money his father saved on the school land reimbursed him for every cent he spent for Roy's education.)

Winter passed and as the sunny, windy days of March rolled around, Roy's interest in the monotonous routine of the classroom steadily diminished. He was homesick. The week ends when he walked the nine miles home sharpened his appetite for the out-of-doors. One warm day late in March Roy packed his suitcase and headed home. This, he thought as he trudged down the dusty prairie road, is the end of high school at Harvard for me. And it was.

After a summer on the farm, Sam persuaded Roy that he should try once more to finish his schooling. But this time it was to be at the University of Nebraska in Lincoln. Not the University exactly; its preparatory school.

There were several things that appealed to Roy. For one thing, it would give him his first ride in a passenger train, a luxury which had thus far been denied him. His trips to the state fair in Lincoln had been in the cattle car with his father's prized swine and cattle. For another thing, going to school in a city like Lincoln would be thrilling.

But when he reached there Roy was an utterly bewildered young man who would have been completely lost had it not been that a friend of Sam's met him at the station. Together they found a room which Roy shared with another student.

The room cost them $3.50 apiece. This left Roy $6.50 of his monthly allotment of $10.00. That was plenty for board per month, but not much else. So the boys got jobs waiting on tables. The cafe left much to be desired. But it had food, and plenty of it.

The first day convinced Roy that the cafe's customers were the roustabouts who worked around Hay Market Square. Roy had worked just three days when it happened. One of the usual customers came in at the close of the noon hour about the time Roy was ready to leave for class. Impatiently he took the order and when it was ready he hustled the big plate of steak through the swinging doors of the kitchen. He saw the meat slide to the floor. Avoiding the eye of his customer at the end of the counter, Roy picked it up. Carefully he wiped it off on his apron, and carried it with a flourish to the man. But his customer had been an interested witness. He shouted for the manager. Roy slipped through the front door. He did not return—ever.

Though his allowance paid for his board, there were other things he wanted. He had always envied the boys who could dance. He was determined to have dancing lessons. He paid for them by washing dishes in another cafe nearer the campus.

Roy enjoyed the companionship his student rooming house afforded. He experienced a comradeship he had not known before. There was a delightful lightheartedness about it. When one of his fellow roomers looked in and said, "Come on, Roy, 27 let's rush the growler," Roy sensed a new adventure. He had no idea what a growler might be. His companion carried a pitcher and that aroused his curiosity. Together they swung down the street, Roy matching his friend, stride for stride. Only when they passed through the swinging doors did Roy stop. The dank, sour smell struck his face. Wide-eyed he watched his companion march toward the long bar. In one awful moment he caught the picture: men drinking from bowls, the yellowish light tossed back by the giant mirror, the floor of sawdust, the spittoons, and the bald, aproned man behind the bar. Roy turned and fled.

It was as though the evil of rum that Jennie had so often described had suddenly become a creature of reality, a thing that reached for him as he ran. In two bounds he was up the porch steps. The stairway to his second-floor room was the homestretch to safety. With one sweep he closed his door and snapped the lock. His roommate looked up from the study table, startled and bewildered.

"Quick," Roy commanded, "under the bed."

He doused the light and together they lay prone in the darkness.

"Not a word," Roy whispered. "No matter what, not a word."

Forever passed before he heard the clump on the stairs. Then the voice of his growler friend, "Hey, McKelvie." He tightened his grip on his roommate's arm. Their room was dark and still. Roy heard the doorknob turn and the raps. "What'sa matter, McKelvie? Lose your nerve?" Stillness again and then the diminishing sound of footsteps. Finally silence. The temperance lectures of Jennie McKelvie had prevailed.

28

The lustre of the University classes soon began to dim. Around mid-December Roy withdrew from the preparatory school. He had another educational venture in mind. The University was beginning, in January, a three-month's short course for country boys. Roy registered along with eight others. Besides the training, they were offered Saturday jobs at a dollar a day if they wanted them. And all of them did. But when March rolled around and the course ended, Roy heard the call of the farm and answered it.

The following fall Sam again urged Roy to take some additional schooling, this time in law. This seemed utterly remote to Roy. In an unusual spirit of compromise, his father suggested a term in the Lincoln Business College. So Roy again returned to Lincoln and school. This time classroom life was brighter. He especially liked the debating society. But once more mathematics proved his undoing. He flunked the semester examination. Discouraged with failure, Roy quit school and headed for Iowa to visit his uncle. The winter weather was severe and the train drafty. Roy came down with a bad cold. He spent several days in bed at his uncle's home. Still weak from illness he was helped aboard a train for Fairfield.

When he arrived at the farm without advance notice, the reception he got from Sam was less than cordial. But Jennie saw a sick boy. Under her expert care, Roy rapidly recovered. Then came the evening when Sam sternly reviewed the ups and downs of Roy's schooling. He concluded with an ultimatum, "You can go back to the Business College now and stay until you get your diploma, or you can stay here and work—and I mean work."

Roy took the train the next day. The closer he got to Lin-   29 coln, the more he dreaded the ordeal of facing the college boys and girls to whom he had said good-bye with such airy finality only a couple of weeks before.

Roy attacked his studies with a new intensity and with considerable extra assistance from one of his teachers, he finished the course. The Business College diploma was his.

It was not the business world, however, which beckoned to young Roy McKelvie that spring commencement day in 1901. It was the farm back in Clay County. And it was back on the old home place that a series of events which had taken place over the years were to rapidly crystallize in his mind and direct him into his principal life-long career.

The McKelvie family—especially Sam and Jennie—were hardworking people who had come to understand thrift as a fortress against the uncertainties of farm prices and Nebraska weather. Thrift demanded work, and work on the McKelvie place left little time for social life. But the welcome sign was always out for a special group of visitors. They usually came in August or September. They were the field men for the farm papers.

The main job of a field man, of course, was to sell his farm paper to influential farmers and in turn try to get these hand-picked customers to sell subscriptions to the neighbors. For the field man the cattle breeder was always, in addition, a prospective advertiser.

But the thing that interested Roy—and his father—most was the information the field men brought to the isolated farms. All of them were prepared and willing to discuss new methods of farming, new machinery, new crop varieties, new cattle or hog raising practices, and of course, news of the markets, the

30

The photo the farm paper field man took of Roy in the doorway of the McKelvie barn caught the fancy of scores of editors across the nation and was given wide circulation.

state of the nation, and general condition of the world. Their reports and opinions were sources of amazement to Roy. He dogged their steps around the farm.

Sam's farm was always a stopping place for all the field men because he was a nationally-prominent breeder of Poland China hogs and was making quite a name for himself as a breeder of Red Polled cattle. When Sam decided to disperse his herd of cattle at auction, one of the field men came with a camera to take pictures of the top animals. The field man noticed Roy in straw hat standing in the door of the barn. He came over and said, "Kid, sit down in that door. Put a straw in your mouth and hold this pitchfork in your hand." Roy did. The camera snapped. The picture was printed a few days later on the front page of The Omaha Bee and appeared in many other papers across the nation.

Sam remained faithful to the Breeder's Gazette published in Chicago. He subscribed to two of the Nebraska farm papers, The Nebraska Farmer and The Twentieth Century Farmer, but considered the Nebraska publications second-rate. "Nebraska needs a better farm paper," he often remarked to Roy. "The ones we've got now just don't start to fill the bill."

In the winter of 1901–1902 Roy discovered a new interest in the farm papers. He found himself frequently discussing their contents with Sam. By spring he was convinced that a field man's life must be interesting. Roy imagined the thrill of traveling around the state, visiting the livestock breeders, seeing their herds, and selling them ads.

Soon after his twenty-first birthday, Roy heard that a field man's job was open on The Twentieth Century Farmer in Omaha. He wrote to the publisher, Charles Rosewater, and   33 applied. Mr. Rosewater invited him to come to Omaha the following day. Roy promptly packed two bags and took the train. Once aboard he found his enthusiasm mounting. It was a feeling different from that he had experienced when he left the farm for school. The prospect of becoming a field man gave him a sense of well-being and importance.

The train was late into Lincoln. Roy's appointment in Omaha was set for four o'clock that afternoon and he began to wonder whether he would make it. The train was later still when it left Lincoln and Roy decided to take drastic action. He would send his first telegram. At Ashland he hurried into the station to send the message. Should it read, "Train delayed will be forty minutes late," or should it be more impressive, something like, "Regret train is behind schedule. Sorry I will be forty minutes late"? No. He would stay within ten words.

Mr. Rosewater was ready to leave the office when Roy finally arrived. He asked Roy to ride the streetcar home with him for supper. Getting the job was easier than Roy anticipated. Long before their streetcar ride was over, Mr. Rosewater simply told him he would start at $65 a month. Sixty-five dollars! Here was real wealth, enough wealth to make him feel almost at ease as he walked into the Rosewater house, bigger and more elegant than any he had ever seen.

The next day he was assigned to the south central Nebraska area as a "hog man." He worked hard and successfully, thanks to a welcome lift from his father who knew most of the other breeders in the region. Several months later when he returned to the office in Omaha, the treasurer of the paper stopped him and asked testily, "McKelvie, where the devil are your expense accounts for the last three months?"

Roy gulped. Was this the way The Twentieth Century fired its failures? "Expense accounts," he repeated foolishly. What in samhill was the fellow talking about? Had he neglected some responsibility?

"You know," the treasurer was saying, "bills for travel and hotel. I haven't had a swindle sheet from you since you've been on the payroll."

Roy was relieved. Unbelievable as it seemed, he had an expense account in addition to $65 per month. "Yes sir," he said, "I'll get them in right away."

In 1903 Roy made his headquarters in Lincoln and it was then that his social life became something of a reality. One warm summer evening he visited the home of a young lady he had been calling on, and found another young lady was a guest at the house. Roy soon discovered that the pretty blonde-haired, green-eyed girl of sixteen was Martha DeArnold whose parents had brought her to Lincoln to study piano at a conservatory. Somehow Roy's attention focused more and more on Martha. When it came time to leave, he asked to walk Martha home. She accepted. Never, Roy thought, had the moonlight been so beautiful.

A year later, in June, 1904, he and Martha felt they could afford to be married. He had received an unsolicited increase which boosted his salary to $100 per month. For six months they lived with Martha's parents in an apartment in the conservatory building at Thirteenth and L Streets. Both of them wanted a house and had found one at Twenty-sixth and N Streets which overlooked the gentle slope of Antelope Valley. At first the $4,000 purchase price seemed out of their reach. They talked about it a great deal. The more they talked the 35 more certain Martha was that they could manage it. Her parents, she knew, would be glad to help. They could make their home there too. And she would get a job teaching piano in the conservatory. Roy hesitated but eventually agreed. "All right," he grinned, "can't tell I might even get another raise."

The following year an event transpired which was to profoundly change Roy's career in the farm paper field. Frank O. Edgecombe, publisher of several weekly Nebraska newspapers but notably the one at Geneva, purchased The Nebraska Farmer then being published in Omaha. Shortly after (Roy suspected that his good friend Tom Callahan, the auctioneer, had put in a good word for him) Mr. Edgecombe offered Roy the editorship of The Nebraska Farmer. Two facts led to the removal of the paper to Lincoln. One was that Mr. Edgecombe wanted it nearer his home at Geneva. The other was that Roy wanted the job but not at the sacrifice of leaving their new home and moving to Omaha. So an office for the paper was opened on North Eleventh Street and Roy with some fear in his heart assumed the editorship.

Being an editor, he discovered, was vastly different from serving as a field representative. Sheer determination drove him through the many tasks and decisions incident to getting the paper out on schedule, but for the life of him, he could not maintain his interest in writing the editor's column. He convinced Mr. Edgecombe that someone else should carry on this task and free him to do his best as an editor-field man. Under such an arrangement he was in a position to do much to increase the number of subscribers and advertisers.

Roy liked the new set up. It gave him the chance to be with people; to talk, to sell. His flair for public speaking won him

36

invitations to address farmers institutes and meetings of commercial clubs in many communities. He had two favorite topics, one on the necessity for the farmer and the businessman to cooperate for the betterment of the state, and the other on the evils of the mail-order business. It had not taken Roy long to recognize the mail-order houses were hurting the advertising business of farm papers.

When he had made the decision to leave The Twentieth Century Farmer for The Nebraska Farmer, Roy had weighed the futures that both might offer. He considered Mr. Edgecombe more of a dealer in publications than a publisher. This had influenced his decision. Now, after three years as the virtual manager of The Nebraska Farmer, he felt he was ready to talk to Mr. Edgecombe about selling the paper. Roy's father had agreed to put $5,000 into the venture. Mr. Edgecombe agreed to sell.

So at the age of twenty-seven, Roy McKelvie became publisher of a fifty-year-old farm paper. But it was a business property which had made little profit. Roy was sure he could make it pay. He was determined to make it go. There were compelling reasons. Besides the big debt to pay off before he became owner of The Nebraska Farmer, there were the payment of a mortgage on his home; and a wife to support.

A lawyer who officed in the same building met Roy on the street soon after the purchase had been made and asked him how he was getting along. "Fine, just fine," Roy beamed. "That's right, Roy," the lawyer said. "I know you're broke, but don't ever admit it, and don't ever give up."

And he didn't. He was about to turn a new corner.

CHAPTER FOUR

POLITICAL STIRRINGS

ROY MCKELVIE DIVED into politics when he was twenty-seven years old. The decision to become a candidate for the Lincoln City Council was, as he admitted later, ill-considered. Only two years earlier he had come to Lincoln. For less than a year he had lived in the neighborhood he sought to serve. Most of his close friends in Lincoln were University students, not men in a position to be of much help in a political campaign. Moreover, McKelvie, when he thought about it, could not conclude logically that he was genuinely interested in civic affairs. He was not even genuinely interested in politics.

There were, however, certain motivating factors and at the time these seemed to outweigh the more realistic considerations. First, there was his background. For years political talk   39 had been the protein base of family conversational diet in the McKelvie farm home in Clay County. Of course, his mother always made clear that in her opinion men who ran for public office were likely to be very low citizens indeed. At the same time it was she who frequently stimulated discussions of a political nature. Though she abhorred the thought of a member of her family as a candidate, still she recognized the importance of politics.

Second, there was young Roy's nature. He liked people; liked to meet and talk. And when he did, people liked him. His conversation sparkled and his eyes sparkled and his quick laughter was infectious. His outward qualities were those of the natural salesman. He sensed that the step from popularity in the field of selling to popularity in the field of politics must be a short one.

But there were many young men in 1907, who came from farm homes where politics were talked and many who also were gregarious. What prompted Roy McKelvie to plunge into the pool of politics while others did not was the same basic ingredient that caused Sam and Jennie to stick to the farm in those early years when so many others turned back. It was an insatiable desire to progress, to get ahead. To Sam, getting ahead meant securing land, producing fine stock, and being respected and looked up to by the people who knew him. To Roy, getting ahead now meant building a successful farm publication, encouraging better agricultural practices, and being respected and looked up to by the people who knew him.

Roy had been a field man and an editor long enough to learn that you do not get better results by doing exactly as your competitors do. On The Twentieth Century Farmer, for example, he had not been content to sell advertising alone. He made notes as he traveled, little observations about farm and livestock practices. These he wove into a readable column of high interest to farmers and stockmen. The column served two purposes. It made the name of Roy McKelvie familiar and it gave him prestige, at least enough to meet new prospects with ease.

Now that he was editor of The Nebraska Farmer he expected more of himself. He had no doubt of his ability to serve as a public office holder. That, however, was not the point. The holding of public office would afford him the opportunity to demonstrate ability and integrity. Such performance, of course, would reflect well on Roy McKelvie, but more important, it would enhance the reputation of The Nebraska Farmer.

The invitation to seek election to the city council came from a neighbor, a man who had no desire to be a candidate himself but who followed political campaigns in much the same spirit that some men maintain an interest in baseball. Little did the neighbor realize the fertility of the soil upon which his advice was falling. He assured the young editor that his filing for the council would be virtually the same as winning the election. It was only a matter of obtaining a few petition signers, holding a meeting or two, and stepping into office. There would be no opposition. The neighbor was certain of that.

Characteristically, Roy brushed aside any thought of opposition. It would make no difference to him whether he had no opposition or faced twenty other contestants. If you wanted something, you went after it. Nobody was going to hand it to   41 you. The only question was, did he want to launch into politics in a city election? Answering the question was not difficult. Some fifteen years earlier, when he had spoken from the little stage of the Catfight schoolhouse, Roy had sometimes imagined himself a candidate. Just being at the political rallies in Clay Center generated a surge of excitement. At Harvard he had caused Mrs. Jerushia Soule and her sisters no end of worry on the November night in 1896 when the McKinley-Bryan election returns came in. He left the house early in the evening. The fears of the sisters mounted as the dining room clock ticked on into the suspicious hour of ten, then eleven, and finally into the alarming zone of midnight. Their admonishments, their scoldings, the outpourings of their anxieties scarcely reached his brain when he finally returned. He had witnessed the excitement and fervor of a newspaper office on election night, and he loved it.

He was half aware during all those years that someday he would enter politics. The idea had been with him almost as long as he could remember. Once, he recalled, he told his mother he would be governor. He could not have been more than six at the time. Jennie had silenced him with a look. He wondered idly what his mother would think when she heard her son was a candidate for a city office. As for himself, it was not quite what he had imagined. He had supposed it would be a state office he would first seek. There was little reason to speak of farm measures on the city council. He had figured on including some farm talks in his first campaign. Well, a man had to get his feet wet sometime and here was the opportunity.

As his neighbor had said, getting petition signers to qualify as a candidate was no trouble at all. Shortly after the filing was official, the neighbor called a ward caucus. A total of four responded, counting Roy and his adviser. Roy had not expected a large gathering. But three! He told Martha about it the next morning and in doing so he made the most of the humor of his first "mass meeting." These were times when he tried his utmost to say something, to recount some incident, that would bring a smile to Martha's lips. The sudden, tragic loss of their baby had been a bitter blow. She had lived only six weeks. The sense of loss, they both knew, was something they would never out-live.

He was pleased to see that Martha appeared interested in his campaign. Unlike his mother, she saw nothing in politics that need tarnish a man.

"If you want to be elected," she told him, "I want you to be elected."

The affairs of The Farmer kept Roy so busy during the next few weeks that he gave little thought to his campaign. Even when two other candidates filed, he paid little heed. He had doubted his neighbor's assurances that victory would come by default anyway. When election day came, Roy hired an automobile and a driver. The use of an automobile in 1907 was an event worth remembering, regardless of the outcome of the election. Moreover, the driver knew his business. The trouble was that Roy did not know where to direct him.

Together he and the driver crossed and re-crossed the ward. Now and again Roy remembered where another of his neighbors worked and to that office or store they would speed. The end result was always the same. The reasons, however, varied. Some had already voted. Others were too busy to leave at the moment. One was in court. Another was away for the day.

43

Late in the afternoon one of Roy's friends told him of a railroad worker who was reputed to have said that McKelvie was a nice fellow and that he would vote for him. Here was the best prospect of the day! The race to the roundhouse had its rewards. He found not only his prospective constituent, but the fellow had a co-worker who would as soon vote for McKelvie as anyone else. Neither could leave the job, however, until quitting time. When that golden hour finally came, the four men hurried to the car and sped to the firehouse polling place on O Street. Just as they reached the entrance, the election judge stepped to the door and shouted in a stentorian voice, "Hear Ye! Hear Ye! the polls are now closed!" And he shut the door.

Paying the driver ten dollars for a service that had failed to net a single vote would have chilled the Scotch blood of Roy McKelvie had no lesson been involved. As it was, he felt it worth the money.

What was done, was done. Roy wasted no time brooding about it. He went home, hungry and tired. The next morning's papers carried the outcome. He was a poor third in the three-man race.

The defeat, Roy knew, was of his own doing. He had refused to recognize that odds were against him. He had turned away from any thought of attempting to equalize those odds. He had planned not at all. But he had had a good time. He had learned something, too. Next time it would be different.

Next time, indeed, it was different. There was no election. Within six months after his defeat, the growth of Lincoln demanded the revision of its wards. The man who had won Roy's race urged the Democratic mayor, Frank M. Brown, to appoint

Republican Roy McKelvie. Mayor Brown agreed and Roy attended his first council meeting as an office holder on the Monday evening of July 6, 1908.

During the months he served on the council, Roy was dogged by two factors. First, there was his youthful appearance. He did not mind being repeatedly called "The Baby," yet he knew that his boyish looks might become a serious problem. It was obvious that his colleagues liked him. They enjoyed his company. It was difficult, though, to command serious attention when he spoke on complicated subjects. Well, he could not change his face. Perhaps he could convert his very boyishness into an asset. It was something to sell. He would remember that.

Second, there was the matter of time. He was now publisher of The Nebraska Farmer. Out-of-town trips were frequent. He put in long hours at the office. City business required time, too. And, finally, there were social demands. Both he and Martha enjoyed the companionship offered by their Little Dinner Club. Martha's broad interests in music, writing, and painting also attracted visitors to the McKelvie house at Twenty-sixth and N Streets. Roy recognized that sociability was his avocation. More than that, it gave him an opportunity to meet people. Meeting people was part of his business.

More and more frequently he found it difficult to get to council meetings on time. He avoided absences as much as he could, but his lack of punctuality became a tittering subject for the city hall reporters. Often they would record Councilman McKelvie's late arrival at a meeting as a vital item to be inserted in the agenda.

The city elections were held in May, 1909. There was little

45

time for campaigning. Roy, who was now becoming known as "S. R. McKelvie," turned to the printed word. His advertisement in the Lincoln papers placed stress on his experience and his Republican affiliation. It read:

"I believe every intelligent voter appreciates that after a ten-months' service and education in the City Council, I am in a position to do more for the Sixth Ward during the next two years than any inexperienced person. . ."

Lincoln voted dry in that municipal election of 1909. There was far more interest in that result than in the fact that a Democrat defeated S. R. McKelvie in the Sixth Ward. The liquor question was a bitter one, not only in Lincoln, but all over Nebraska. McKelvie had taken his stand with the local option forces. He let it be known that his vote in a local option contest would be with the Drys. He felt no sense of discouragement at losing a council race for the second time. He had showed real strength in the voting. His name had become familiar to Lincoln. Instead of regretting the loss, he felt he was ready for bigger things.

The legislative elections of 1910 proved his judgment correct. He filed for the House of Representatives and won the Republican nomination easily. And the general election campaign was simple enough, too. There was but one big question: county option. Lincoln had already voted dry. The anti-saloon forces were determined to have state-wide county option. To young Publisher McKelvie, county option seemed logical. Let each county settle the question. He was certain that the sooner the liquor question got out of politics, the better. So he stood for county option. He never wavered from it when questioned on tours he made with other Republican candidates throughout the county. He made no speeches. On the tours he was happy to be seen and unheard.

His political experience, shallow as it had been, had taught him that voters are like customers. They want to be sold. The question was how. McKelvie recognized that in this election— as in the legislative session to follow it—party lines would mean nothing. You were not a Republican or Democrat. You were a Wet or a Dry. He was aware that there was little chance of changing the vote of either a Wet or a Dry. The only fertile field to cultivate was that inhabited by the marginal few whose votes would be decided by factors other than the clear split on liquor.

He had every confidence in the power of advertising via the printed word. He devised a two-pronged attack. First, he supplied his friends with an ample stock of endorsement postal cards. The printed message on the card recommended S. R. McKelvie for the legislature. The friend's signature appeared at the bottom of the card. It was an inexpensive way to advertise. It carried the flavor of a personal message. And in 1910 it was much more novel than it is today.

The second prong of the attack came directly from the candidate in the form of newspaper advertising. McKelvie wanted something that would carry with it the thought that he and the voter had a mutual interest; something in common. The result was a "Let's Get Acquainted" message.

"To advertise my candidacy for the Legislature is to court the Acquaintance of Every Voter in the County," his introductory line read.

47

"I most regret that I cannot go amongst the voters and meet and shake the hand of each one. But I'm too busy for that. In fact, I'm too busy to make any sort of a personal canvass. I am a business man, not a politician. At first thought, this may not interest you. You're wrong—it should interest you. You should know something about the man for whom you cast your vote. That's why I want to get acquainted with you. Ask about me. Ask about my business. Ask anyone who knows me. *That's All I Ask!*

"I stand for and believe in County Option; direct legislation; and selection of the U.S. Senators by a direct vote of the people. Let's Get Acquainted. Sincerely, S. R. McKelvie."

The psychological wisdom of bluntly telling a prospective voter, "You're wrong," is undoubtedly open to debate. So is the thought, "I'm too busy." McKelvie himself was later to comment on his own "lack of diplomacy" as a weakness, but somehow the electors got the idea that here was a candidate who was giving it to them straight. One of his friends commented it probably was the fact that he made no speeches rather than the advertising that accounted for the flattering vote he received. He won handily.

In the legislature, however, he soon learned that any laws he worked to make would come from the pens of others. None of the four bills he introduced, all of them agricultural measures, ever got out of committee. One of these would have inaugurated a county agricultural extension agent program, very similar to the system now in use.

His seatmate in the House, H. Clyde Filley, who later became widely known as a farm leader and professor at the University of Nebraska College of Agriculture, shared McKelvie's

48

disappointment on the death of his bills. "You're ahead of your time, Roy; you're ahead of your time," Filley would say again and again.

The legislative experience was considerably different from what McKelvie had expected. He had hoped that his boyishness would not attract the same kind of comments it had when he was on the council. That hope, however, was dashed the first day when a veteran solon from Hall County took one look at him and cried, "A babe in swaddling clothes!"

Members of the farm bloc with whom McKelvie had fancied he would crony, kept their distance. They chuckled at his humor. The enjoyed his outbursts of hearty laughter. Yet they made it clear they considered him "a city kid."

Amid such shocks to his confidence, McKelvie suddenly realized the day would soon come when he would be asked to take his turn at presiding over a general session of debate. The thought terrified him. He knew nothing of parliamentary procedure.

"They'll laugh me out of the chamber," he told Martha.

"No they won't," she said firmly. "You're going to study."

And study he did. He enrolled, almost secretly, in a parliamentary law course at the Lincoln Business College. At home, Roberts' Rules of Order prevailed. Long after the supper dishes were done, Martha would pose the motions and Roy would rule on them. It proved a concentrated education that was to serve him well. To the astonishment of the House, his first turn as presiding officer went smoothly. It gained a new respect for him, but not unqualified acceptance.

Representative McKelvie marveled at the ingenuity of the men who opposed enactment of a state-wide county option.   49

The Lancaster County delegation, firmly in favor of county option, and for the most part representing Lincoln which had already voted dry, detected the skillful hand of the liquor lobby in a bill to move the state capital from Lincoln to Kearney. Apparently the strategy was to scare the Lincoln votes out of the county option corner. There were other evidences of the plan also. Each time the subject of adequate financial support for the state institutions located in the Lincoln area came up, there was talk of budget cuts. Cut the University. Cut the Penitentiary. Cut the State Hospital.

The sound of the threats carried beyond the walls of the old capitol to the Lincoln business district. Lincoln business men were first uneasy, then alarmed. The Commercial Club called a meeting and invited members of the Lancaster County delegation.

One of Lincoln's prominent citizens, obviously in a high state of agitation, advised the legislators: "Forget this business of opposing legislation in which members from other parts of the state are interested. Forget it! Work for Lincoln. Let the other fellows have what they want. Subordinate everything to the interests of our institutions here at home."

McKelvie never forgot the reply of the delegation's dean, John H. Mockett. Mockett, small of stature, seemed to grow to a tower of strength as he answered quietly, "I will desert no principle in which I believe. I am going to stand for the things that I think are right, regardless of the effect on the state institutions located in Lincoln."

There was nothing more to say. The meeting adjourned. From it young Representative McKelvie walked with a light heart and a deeper understanding of integrity.

He made his principal speech in the legislature on the subject of removing the capital from Lincoln. The removal act was never passed but Representative McKelvie admitted the result did not stem from his speech.

Despite the disappointments of the session, McKelvie drew one assignment which was to affect his entire political career. He was appointed as a member of the House Finance Committee. The committee's principal function was to hear budget requests from the various state agencies. McKelvie's instinctive Scotch business sense revolted as day after day the committee listened to requests for funds. The agencies seemed endless. Each spokesman talked as though his agency, and only his, was important to the welfare of Nebraska. There was no certain method to check the claims of need, the boasts of accomplishments.

In the final days of that, the Thirty-Second Session of the Nebraska Legislature, he reached two conclusions. If he ever had the opportunity he would strike hard to install a business system at the state house, one in which the governor would be made the accountable and responsible head of Nebraska government. And second, he was finished with the legislature. He wanted something bigger. The governorship.

Whether he would, or would not be governor, was a question S. R. McKelvie, Publisher of The Nebraska Farmer, wasted no time considering. He concentrated only on the method. What would be the best way?

He could file at once. Did he know enough people for that? Certainly, he knew far more than he had known two years earlier. And far more knew him. He had seen to that. He worked out a forty-minute talk on the need for cooperation   51 between town and rural people. In it he poked at the mail-order houses and stressed the importance of a local market to the farmers. It was ideal for farmer-business men's affairs sponsored by commercial clubs. To increase his audience; to reach more people, he prepared on an almost-weekly schedule a short column in which he preached the same doctrine and envisioned a speedily-developing Nebraska. It was too good for ad-hungry weekly editors to omit. It was the same text they used in trying to sell advertising to their local merchants.

All of these activities, without question, had brought him new acquaintances. Perhaps 15,000, maybe 20,000 altogether. But what was that when between 250,000 and 300,000 could be expected to vote in a gubernatorial election? No. He still did not know enough people to jump directly into a race for governor.

There were other routes to the governorship. He gave serious consideration to two of them. He could run for congress; serve a term and then shoot for the governorship. In a normal year that might be the way. But his sharpened political sense told him this was not a normal year. This was 1912. The Taft-T. R. Roosevelt storm clouds were already emitting lightning which might well strike and split the G.O.P. He had no desire to get in the middle of a party split.

The best course, he decided, was through the lieutenant governor's office. He could campaign easily, keep making his non-political talks and turning out his columns. He would be helping The Nebraska Farmer and his candidacy by a single effort. The thought of a single effort was appealing. Not that he was lazy. Not that. Rather it was the shock he had received when he was turned down for a life insurance policy. The

52

doctor did not advise golf; he ordered it. McKelvie must stop desk work at four o'clock each afternoon. The more he thought about golf, the better he liked it. A new way to meet people. Fun and exercise at the same time. More than one return from a single effort.

McKelvie campaigned for the lieutenant governorship almost exclusively by mail and by farm magazine and newspaper advertising. It was easy. He breezed to the nomination in April, and won the general election in November by more than 15,000 votes over his Democratic opponent. This success appeared a real accomplishment because the same voters elected John H. Morehead, a Democrat, to the governorship.

Two months after taking his new office, Lieutenant Governor McKelvie received a summons from Governor Morehead.

The Governor came to the point at once. "Mac," he said, "I am going to Washington to attend the inauguration of President Wilson. Some of my friends tell me I should not chance leaving the state and placing the office in your hands, since you are a Republican. They seem to fear that you might make some appointments in my absence. I don't believe it, but I thought we should have a talk."

For a fleeting instant, Roy felt his temper mount. Did some people give him no credit for decency and integrity? Why must there be those who always thought in terms of partisanship? But his impatience died in a burst of his own laughter.

"Governor," he said, "The people elected you to this office; not me. The responsibility is yours. Even if I wanted to, I could render no service by attempting to thwart your plans."

His own duties as presiding officer of the senate permitted   53 full use of his parliamentary training. The senators appreciated it. Throughout the session he was aware of a growing warmth and respect from Republicans and Democrats alike. For the most part, his afternoons were free and he used each warm spring day to improve his golf. He loved the game and was good enough to enter tournament play. The papers made a small fuss over that. With his picture, one of the Omaha sportspages carried this headline: "Nebraska's Lieut. Governor Is a Golfer—Look at Him," and the cutline, "S. R. McKelvie would rather play golf than politics. He's playing in the state tourney, entering from Lincoln."

Publicity like that, he knew, might help his campaign for governor. Before the year was out, however, his gubernatorial plans received a stunning blow. The first hint of trouble came from one of his lawyer friends. There was, it seemed, a constitutional provision which stated in rather clear language that an incumbent executive state officer could not seek election as governor. McKelvie could not believe it. What better training for the governorship could a man have than service first as lieutenant governor?

The story leaked to the press shortly after McKelvie made what he thought was discreet inquiry of the secretary of state to learn whether that officer would honor his filing for governor if he made it. The answer was firm. The secretary would seek an opinion from the attorney general's office before accepting the filing. Further inquiry revealed the attorney general would advise the secretary of state to refuse the filing.

Roy McKelvie, the up-and-coming publisher of The Nebraska Farmer and former lieutenant governor, looks confidently ahead to the Nebraska governorship.

McKELVIE LOSING NO SLEEP
OVER CLAUSE IN THE CONSTITUTION

That was the headline. And as far as the Lieutenant Governor was concerned, it was true. He wasn't. Great as was this threat to his plans, it simply was not his nature to worry about something he could not help. What was done, was done.

As McKelvie saw it, there was but one course open. Fight the thing through. He engaged W. H. Thompson of Grand Island—a Democrat, incidentally—to handle the case. Let Thompson do the legal work. S. R. McKelvie would handle the salesmanship.

In January of 1914 he formally submitted his filing to the secretary of state. And, just as formally, the secretary of state rejected it. A mandamus action followed. McKelvie's attorney sought an order in the Lancaster County district court to compel the secretary of state to accept the filing.

All of that was expected, of course. What was not expected was the simultaneous blooming of an item in virtually every paper in the state, reporting the modest willingness of S. R. McKelvie to be "the goat" in this test case. Readers who had never remembered McKelvie before, would not forget him now. He was the young fellow who was willing to risk his political future just to get things straightened out.

The Lieutenant Governor, indeed, was losing no sleep over the contest. He was representing Nebraska in the Panama-Pacific International Exposition in San Francisco. The Exposition planners envisioned a building for each state in the Union, or at least, as many of them as were interested. Mc-

57

Kelvie's job, along with others of a small Nebraska delegation, was to lay the cornerstone of the Nebraska building.

Without question, the young official from Nebraska was having the time of his life. He and other members of the delegation rented formal attire, complete with silk hats, to participate in the ceremony. The coup was complete. Their friendly rivals from Iowa, also charged with the responsibility of laying a cornerstone, appeared in street clothes.

Back at the Palace Hotel, S. R. McKelvie got the word from Attorney Thompson. They had lost in District Court. Without hesitation he wired back, "Justice prevails. Appeal at once."

The appeal, however, like the plans for Nebraska's building at the Exposition availed nothing. McKelvie learned later that the cornerstone he had so carefully laid, was not stone at all. It was a wooden frame filled with sand. And funds for the building were never forthcoming. Neither was the Supreme Court's permission for him to run for governor. By the end of April the case was closed.

True to form, McKelvie issued a pleasant statement.

"The court's finding is absolutely satisfactory to me," his quotation ran. "I realized that it was an open question and had not built up my plans to such an extent that I feel any personal disappointment or vexation. I did have an ambition to be governor, as I hoped to be able to work out some things I have in mind, but at the same time it would have meant considerable personal sacrifice to me in my business and from that standpoint I am not at all displeased that the decision went the way it did.

58   "I am glad to have tested out this question and given the

people of Nebraska the benefit of having it judiciously settled for all time. If the ruling of the court had been otherwise I should have made the race, but as it is I have enough to do to keep me busy without engaging in politics. I shall not be a candidate for re-election as lieutenant governor. At the end of my present term, I will step out and devote myself exclusively to business affairs."

Significantly, S. R. McKelvie did not say he was abandoning his intention to someday be governor of Nebraska.

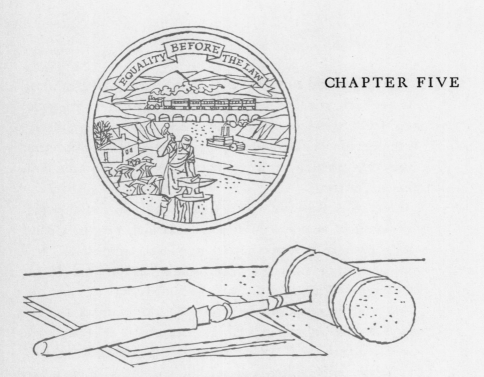

CHAPTER FIVE

SAM McKELVIE: GOVERNOR

No PHYSICIAN WAS NEEDED. Publisher McKelvie was fully capable of diagnosing his own case. He had the habit. He could not forsake politics now if he wanted to. The originally pleasant dream of someday being governor was, now in 1915, an obsession. Business interested him and The Nebraska Farmer was prospering. Golf interested him and he was expert at it. He had a thirst for travel and enjoyed quenching it. His friends were legion and he loved them. But above all was this gnawing political passion. There was, he knew, but one cure. He must win the office.

In less than a year after he forsook the lieutenant governorship he was back in the swim. This time he struck out directly for his goal. The experience afforded by his tenure as lieuten-

61

ant governor had matured his political thinking a great deal. He planned carefully. A well prepared, eighteen-page booklet was ready to announce his candidacy. His friends outstate were alerted. On December 14, he announced for governor "subject to the Republican Primaries, April 18, Nineteen hundred and sixteen."

Four other Republicans contested with him in the primaries. It might be argued that none beat him. For the second time, he was to be tripped up by an unexpected obstacle. Not the constitution this time. The prohibition question. In his pre-campaign thinking, he had concluded that his most difficult point would again be his youth and youthfulness. He marshaled his arguments well. He was almost thirty-five. He was also experienced. Look at the record. Before he was thirty-six, Alexander Hamilton was, as McKelvie put it, "a big figure in American history." Thomas Jefferson was author of the Declaration of Independence at thirty-two. In Nebraska, Albinus Nance became governor at thirty, and George L. Sheldon, "one of the best governors Nebraska ever had," was elected at age thirty-six.

McKelvie considered his record on the liquor question clear. He had been identified with the Dry forces throughout his political career. This, he felt, was sufficient. Moreover, he recognized that Nebraska had other problems to solve. He talked of efficiency, rather than the old saw of economy, in state government. The state must have better roads. Agriculture needed to heed the problem of distribution of its products. And the schools. He proposed the inauguration of strong agricultural training courses in grade and high schools. He asked the voters to remember that the great majority of farm youngsters did not go on to the College of Agriculture. If Nebraska's agricultural progress was to be rapid, the schools should be giving their pupils an opportunity to learn about farming and ranching.

The vision and depth manifested in his campaign messages attracted a great deal of editorial and conversational support. During the closing days of the campaign he made a whirlwind tour of the North Platte Valley and the response both then and at the polls in that area was remarkable. He carried each community in which he spoke.

But he underestimated the single-track determination of the Prohibitionists. For them there was but one issue. They wanted a candidate who spoke of nothing but ridding the state and the nation of liquor. Their support—all of it—was given to one of the other Republican candidates, Judge A. L. Sutton of Omaha.

Judge Sutton finished the race a scant 800 votes ahead of McKelvie. McKelvie actually carried sixty-one of the state's ninety-three counties.

As usual, he entertained no regret over the outcome of the primary. And, in fact, he had no cause for regret. For in the general election, the skillful campaign of President Woodrow Wilson with the slogan, "He Kept Us Out of War," swept Nebraska and tugged in a complete slate of Democratic state officers. The successful gubernatorial candidate, Keith Neville, was, indeed, a "boy governor." Neville was a year younger than McKelvie. McKelvie knew he was at long last finished with the political bugaboo of his boyishness.

The heat from Europe's fire was beginning to affect Nebraska. With other thoughtful men, McKelvie sensed the urgency of the time. Unlike some, he wasted no energy doubting the loyalty of any segment of Nebraska's population. He knew these people. He knew where they would take their stand, when they understood the issue. He had always believed in the inherent wisdom of the public. As he saw it, the perennial problem was to make sure the public understood.

One thing was certain, they did not understand now the vital importance of food production. Through The Nebraska Farmer's columns and in public speeches, he cried out for speedy adjustment of the state's agricultural economy. He intensified his efforts to encourage better farm and livestock practices. He preached against profiteering by the "middle men," who, as he saw them, were growing fat on the efforts of the men and women who sweated out their lives on the farm. He urged support for farm co-operatives. Had anyone warned him that his earnest effort to improve Nebraska agriculture would one day be twisted into accusations against him, he would have stared at his adviser in bewilderment. Yet that day was not far off.

The weeks following the formal declaration of war brought a confusion of emotions. There was apprehension. There was excitement. There was a wild, false gayety. There was the awful silence of dread. There was evidence of selfishness. And, too, there was a wave of derring-do bravado, a cyclonic force which pulled men to the colors. There was an evangelism about it. Almost like wanting to be saved. If you enlisted, you were saved.

Though he was but nine days short of thirty-six years old when the United States declared war with Germany, Publisher McKelvie felt the power of the pull. A few short months ago he almost resented his youth. Now he feared he was too old. That, and the knowledge that his health was not the best. His desire to be governor paled in the grip of this new desire. The desire to enlist. Without confiding in anyone, he left his office one afternoon and consulted his doctor.

The old physician waited for his patient to dress following the examination.

"Well?" McKelvie asked.

"Mac," the doctor said, "you'd never be accepted. What's more, you had better have that hernia taken care of right away. You won't be well until you do."

McKelvie went to Chicago for the operation. His stay in the hospital, away from Lincoln friends, gave him time to put his thoughts in order. In the quiet of his room, he concluded that service can be where you perform it. His mind was made up when he returned to Lincoln.

Had it been his nature to concern himself about the strength of his opponents, he might have interpreted as a good omen a visit he received almost as soon as he returned to his office. The visitor was Adam McMullen, a Republican state senator from Beatrice. McMullen was a man of no mean political stature. He came to find out whether McKelvie intended to be a candidate for governor in the elections of 1918.

"If you are not interested in the governor's race," McMullen told him, "I think I'll have a try at it. Otherwise I'll run for congress."

"I'm going to be a candidate," McKelvie said.

And as soon as McMullen left his office, he went to the state house and filed.

In the summer primaries of 1918, McKelvie eventually faced   65 a single Republican opponent. R. B. Howell, a well-known Republican figure, announced his candidacy but withdrew later to enter naval service. There was little doubt who would receive the nomination. Even McKelvie was surprised at the number of McKelvie-for-Governor clubs that popped up, mushroom-like, across the state. The beginning of the club movement, of course, was not entirely spontaneous. It was conceived and nourished by a nucleus of young professional men who had supported McKelvie in his previous political efforts.

Long before voters went to the polls on August 20th, his Republican supporters could see the light of the nomination. They were not the only ones who saw it. The men who formed the hard core of the Democratic leadership saw it too.

Desperation drives men to actions they might not consider under less pressure. But the Democratic kingpins were under pressure. The Wilson slogan, "He Kept Us Out of War," which had shone so brightly and effectively a year earlier, was now a heavy, thorny crown. War was here. Nobody had kept it away. In the eyes of thousands of Nebraskans that slogan had become a deception, a fraud.

The Democratic Party leaders in Nebraska could sense hostility in the air. If voters distrusted them, they realized, the best defense was to induce the electors to distrust their opposition even more. They needed a target, a defendant. He must be one closely identified with Republicanism in Nebraska. McKelvie? Certainly he would be nominated. He could be fired upon all summer and in the autumn weeks prior to the general election. Who else but McKelvie?

The attack opened in early summer. It started as a guerrilla action. In several newspapers throughout the state there appeared in the letters-to-the-editor columns brief references to McKelvie as a champion of The Non-Partisan League.

The League, regardless of the intentions of the men who had put life in its lungs as early as 1914, was now a suspect organization. In the beginning it had grown to great strength in North Dakota. Its original goal included speedy growth for farm co-operatives. The Scandinavian farmers of the Dakotas were familiar with co-operatives. The co-operative system had done much to improve farm conditions in the homelands of their fathers.

In Nebraska, McKelvie and The Nebraska Farmer had spoken kindly of farm co-operatives. McKelvie saw co-operatives as a means to concentrate the power of agriculture. Some method, surely, was needed to weld the tiny murmurings of individual farmers into a clear, articulate voice. Agriculture needed a voice that could be heard in the market places, and one strong enough to command attention in the fixing of freight rates.

By the time the League was active in Nebraska, the movement in North Dakota had already won substantial victories at the polls. Once in power in North Dakota, the League's leaders had pushed through such radical measures that sober-minded Nebraska farmers began to wonder whether the League was interested in co-operatives or socialism. Moreover, some of the League spokesmen in Nebraska assailed the entry of the United States into the World War. The noisy wave of patriotism running across Nebraska had, it seemed, finally washed the glitter from the League and revealed it as a subversive organization. Pro-Kaiser. Pro-Central Powers. Yellow.

McKelvie's Scotch blood neared the boiling point. He and his supporters tried in vain to locate the writers of the letters. They suspected, of course, that the names of the purported authors were fictitious. They were never able to find any such people.

His political sense warned him not to snap at the bait too vigorously. He must not let the campaign become a ridiculous floundering. He could not ignore the innuendo completely, but his campaign must be a great deal more than a repeated answering of it. He recognized, too, that among the Nebraska followers of the League were sincere and well-intentioned men. The League members were a minority. Yet some were men of principle, men who were conscientiously concerned, not with subversion, but with the improvement of Nebraska agriculture. He would not bring himself to forget their feelings. He would not denounce them as slackers, or as unpatriotic. Even if it cost him the election, he would not do that.

He kept his replies moderate to inquiries about his opinion of the League. In June and July of 1918, he was to write many letters in the following vein:

"You have asked what I think of The Non-Partisan League and whether I denounce it as being disloyal and pro-German. I shall answer you in the same frank manner in which you have put these questions. . . .

"I would preface my remarks by saying that I have many personal friends in the League—men for whom I have a very high regard—and the opinions that I shall express here regarding the League are intended as no reflection upon their motives or integrity of purpose.

"First, the League, in my opinion, is not non-partisan, but

highly partisan. Judged by its principles and platform it is a socialistic political party that is extremely radical in its economic aims.

"Second, the program of the League is intended to injure and retard the healthy development of farmers' co-operative organizations and societies. There is nothing in common between your plan of state socialism which contemplates state ownership of industrial enterprises, and pure cooperation which provides for an equitable distribution of benefits among the members of co-operative societies. The former will eventually destroy the latter.

"In this state, farmers have made splendid progress with their co-operative enterprises and I would regret very much to see any movement encouraged that would annul or delay this work. . . ."

The primary elections went by, a casual incident to the general election campaign which for all practical purposes was already under way. As the head of the Republican state ticket, McKelvie began to talk more and more of governmental reorganization. He insisted that the greatest need of Nebraska government was the inauguration of a businesslike system of departmental organization. To keep attention centered on this issue, he knew, would be difficult. Party chiefs of the opposition would never cease their efforts to tie him solidly to the ugliest rumors associated with The Non-Partisan League.

Even his natural buoyant optimism threatened to fail him. First, there had been the insurmountable barrier of the constitution. That, of course, was something his inexperience had kept him from seeing. Next, the single-mindedness of the Drys had kept him from realizing his ambition. And now, this: the trumped-up League and socialism bogey. Not only could it block his path to the governorship once more but—and this

69

became an even more regrettable prospect—it could keep him from focusing the attention of Nebraskans on the urgent need to end the chaos in which their government was attempting to function. Well, what was done, was done. He would fight as best he could.

He launched his tour early in September with a meeting at Seward. The applause that followed his introduction seemed to dispel his doubts. It rang down the curtain on the pee-wee discussions of the strategy sessions. It signaled the beginning of the attack. Let them fling their mud. This was action and he loved it.

He made as many as twelve speeches a day and he was pleased by the way they were received. Still more pleasant and heart-warming, however, was the conduct of his opponent, Governor Keith Neville. McKelvie had been on tour less than three days when he realized that Neville was remaining coldly aloof from the innuendoes and distortions that the pumps of his party bosses were dredging daily. It was clear that Neville had no intention of stooping to a smear campaign. He might be powerless to halt the practices of his more unscrupulous boosters, but it was evident he would not cooperate with them.

McKelvie had never had reason to dislike Neville. Now he felt a warm respect for the young man from North Platte. He said time and again that in either party, "I never had a fairer opponent."

The two nominees met, quite unintentionally, at Scottsbluff. They were scheduled to speak at different halls one early October evening. Having both candidates in town on the same night was too much for community leaders to resist. Both Neville and McKelvie were willing that the meetings be joined, but each declared he had no wish to engage in a debate. Who should speak first was decided by a drawing of straws. Governor Neville won the dubious honor.

As he listened, McKelvie appreciated the burden his opponent carried. He was an "in," an officeholder. He had a record to defend and explain. In a time of war shortages and restrictions, this was a cross of considerable weight. He smiled at the way Neville went about his task. He was known as "Nebraska's Wartime Governor." He made the most of patriotism. Figuratively, he waved the flag fore, aft, and sideways.

When he rose to take his turn, McKelvie was glad to be an office seeker rather than an officeholder. There was nothing he need sidestep. He covered the field. The need for better roads. Agricultural training in the public schools. Curb profiteering. Reorganize the state government for efficiency. But mostly that night he talked about high taxes. High taxes would keep "the boys" from home ownership when they returned from France unless something was done. A complete overhaul of the state's administrative machinery could help cut taxes. He intended to overhaul that machinery. He was determined to have efficiency in state government.

Obviously, the crowd contained more Republican supporters than Democratic. The applause was gratifying. When it subsided a little, Governor Neville stood up and addressed his opponent.

"Mind if I have a couple of minutes for rebuttal, Mac?" he asked.

"Of course not," McKelvie answered, "but I hope you haven't mistaken this for a debate."

"No," said Neville, "I haven't. I thought it was an old-time   71

Indian medicine show, the kind where one bottle has a cure for everything. You're that bottle, Mac. You're the greatest cure-all for everything I've ever seen."

That was the extent of Neville's "rebuttal." The house roared with good-natured laughter and some of the heartiest came from S. R. McKelvie.

From Scottsbluff, his campaign turned eastward again. As he entered the territory of the opposition's Omaha newspaper, the tempo of the attacks against him increased. One morning in mid-October, the Omaha paper carried a cartoon depicting "Slippery Sam" McKelvie as a multi-headed serpent. It gave the viewer ample reason to believe "Slippery Sam" was not the man for governor.

McKelvie saw the paper at Albion. His political experience told him that here was opportunity. That afternoon he addressed a large crowd—large considering the size of the town.

"Slippery Sam," he told his listeners, "is a good name for me. I accept it. I accept it because I will *slip* into office and I will *slip* the skids under this political machine that too long has abused our people."

The response began with a ripple of laughter. Then, as if walls confining pent-up feelings had suddenly given way, the laughter became a roar of delight and excitement. The crowd stamped its feet and shouted out its devotion and encouragement.

"Sam" McKelvie was born that afternoon at Albion. In the exuberance of the occasion he promised to carry his fight to the very shadows of the newspaper office building from which his sobriquet had come.

72   His adoption of the "Slippery Sam" title proved profitable

Youthful Governor Sam McKelvie in 1919 found his duties included those of host to dignitaries who visited the state, including former President William Howard Taft.

politically. Many weekly editors had little use for the big Omaha daily. They were pleased to see somebody talk back. They spread the story. The rural readers, particularly, chuckled with delight. Sam McKelvie had had a chance to test his theory that it is often to the campaigner's advantage to have "the big city press" against him. He had never trembled before the editorial onslaughts of the daily press. He knew now he had no reason to.

The great influenza epidemic of 1918 caused him to cut his campaign short. In six weeks he had given more than 150 speeches. He had shaken thousands of hands. By October 20, however, he noticed the crowds were dwindling. Many people were afraid to risk their health in public gatherings. Many others had sickness at home. He announced cancellation of all remaining rallies; all, that is, except a finale to be held in Omaha. It would, as he had promised, be within a few feet of the newspaper office from which had come the most vitriolic criticism of him.

Whether the things he said at that final rally, held the Saturday night before the election, harvested any votes is doubtful. But by all odds it was the best rough-and-tumble speech of his career. The influenza epidemic was on the wane. People were free to congregate again. His repeated promises to make this talk in Omaha had whetted political appetites.

The November air was cold and crisp. The voices of the preliminary speakers—all Republican candidates for local offices—carried well. The crowd was in the high, good humor of anticipation. Sam McKelvie was introduced amid a tumult of applause. His first few phrases he delivered with confidence and aplomb.

75

Suddenly, from not more than 50 feet away, came the blare of a jazz band. The opposition had forsaken paper and ink for the raucous beat of "The Bunny Hug." Here was competition that Sam McKelvie had not expected. Momentarily the humor of it made him laugh. In the next instant, however, he was downright angry. The trick was so typical of the bosses who had heaped personal insults upon him. If they could not silence him, they would try to drown him out.

His audience seemed to catch something of his mood. Its instinctive desire for fair play told it that here was a circumstance which made Sam McKelvie the underdog. He was past caring, however, what the crowd thought. He hurled his answers and taunts at the editorial powerhouse of the political machine that had opposed him. The fact that his shouts were mingled with strains of "I'm Forever Blowing Bubbles," bothered him not at all. And the crowd was delighted. It screamed, almost in cadence, "Go it, Sam! Pour it on 'em, Sam!"

Martha had told him long ago, "You make the best talks when you're mad." If this were true, Sam McKelvie had reason to believe that his final address on the night of November 2, 1918, was a jewel. The words went unrecorded, but the story of what had happened spread over the state before the following Tuesday, election day. The opposition had misjudged the cuteness of its trick. The Nebraska voters did not like it.

He was chock full of the campaign. He had no desire to see another new face, or shake another hand. He waited for the election returns in the company of a few of his closest friends. They played poker. By the time two hands had been played, Sam found himself almost more interested in the game than in learning the outcome of the election. It would be past midnight, he surmised, before the result could be determined. But it wasn't. By ten o'clock the answer was unmistakable. He was the new governor of Nebraska. He telephoned Martha.

"Looks like we made it," he said.

"How do you feel?" she asked.

"If I could turn the job over to somebody else, I'd be happy," he answered.

There were many times during the next two years when Governor McKelvie recalled his response to Martha's question. At the time he had not realized how right he was. He had led the Republican state ticket to a sweeping victory. His victory over Neville was by 23,000 votes. Not as wide as the margin by which a test on woman's suffrage carried, but substantial.

Immediately following the election, Sam headed east. He had three reasons for the trip. He wanted to cement some business affairs as solidly as possible. He had pledged himself that he would devote his full energies to the governorship and let The Nebraska Farmer run as best it could without him. Second, he needed a rest. And third, he could escape temporarily the demands for political appointments that were sure to come.

In Chicago he met Sam Arnot, the former Harvard high school superintendent who had whetted his interest in politics. Arnot was jubilant. His former pupil Governor! Arnot was not the only man in Chicago who was jubilant. The news—later proved a few days premature—that the War was over had just come in. One of Arnot's friends, whose son-in-law was in France, was celebrating. "Meet the new governor of Nebraska," Arnot shouted. The friend took a long, unsteady look   77 at Sam McKelvie, and said, "Misser Arnot, I may be drunk but I'm not that dam' drunk." At thirty-seven, Sam knew, he still looked more like twenty-nine or thirty.

He anticipated a mad whirl of work and activity at the beginning of the term. He had not, however, imagined that the rush would go on and on. First there were the appointments. It seemed that every elector who had voted for him, and many who had not, wanted a state job. Originally, he had supposed he would choose about six key department heads and turn lesser appointments over to them. Soon he saw the futility of that hope. He divided his day—a day that began at 7 A.M. and ran until 6 P.M.—into ten- and fifteen-minute periods to interview as many appointment-seekers as he could. In the end, he shocked Republican wheelhorses by retaining a few Democrats in their old jobs. They were men whom he considered capable, conscientious public servants. He saw no reason to replace them.

On the afternoon of January 9, 1919, Retiring Governor Keith Neville could well have been forgiven if he recalled the good-natured jibe he had given his debonair successor that night in Scottsbluff. It was apparent that Sam McKelvie intended to sell this Thirty-Seventh Session of The Nebraska Legislature the biggest single dose of improvement medicine in the history of the state.

Neville, like his predecessor, Governor Morehead, in his retiring message had admonished the legislators on the need for a businesslike system for state administrative offices. It was not a new problem. He had reminded them of that. But listen to Sam! Scarcely governor an hour now and he was fairly bursting with recommendations for new legislation. Recommenda-

78

tions? To hear Sam go, you might think this was a sales meeting. Almost as if those representatives and senators were working for him. He was recommending, sure. But there was a snap to it that sounded mighty akin to an order. Well, Mac had never been one to boast about his diplomacy. One thing, a retiring governor need not worry about how his successor would get along with the legislature.

And, indeed, Governor McKelvie was firing with rapidity. In addition to the customary references of an inaugural message, his contained subjects that seemed downright radical to those status-quo solons who viewed their legislative service as a kind of biennial exercise.

First there was the Civil Administrative Code. That had been the feature of McKelvie's campaign and they expected it. But Sam was not content to just mention it. He kept pounding away on why they should enact it at once. It would exchange eleven boards and commissions and ten other subdivisions and departments for six departments. Each department would be headed by a secretary. It would be a cabinet form of government, fashioned after the federal system. Illinois had only recently pioneered with a similar plan. Why, he was even giving them the pro and con arguments. He was serious about this Code.

The Code was not all Governor McKelvie requested. He wanted legislative machinery for an executive state budget. The governor should be the chief state officer in fact as well as in name. Fix it so the governor submitted budget recommendations to the legislature. Don't rely on the departments only. The governor has that responsibility. Let the governor help paint the picture of the state's financial needs.

And there was more. Clear the track for farm co-operatives. Relieve farm credit: give farmers the right to form credit co-operatives so they can borrow money at moderate rates of interest. Enact laws to encourage farm ownership; the tenancy rate is now about half. Too many tenants on the farm won't help the land. And when you enact the Code Law, put the state's hog serum plant under the Department of Agriculture. It doesn't belong at the College of Agriculture. If farmers can't get the serum they need at decent prices from private industry, make it clear that the state plant will supply them.

Roads. You know the last session of the legislature agreed to match funds with the Federal government for road building. Nebraska probably will need about two and a quarter million dollars a year for that program during the biennium. Don't put the burden on the land. Enact a tax on motor vehicles. Their owners will benefit most from the roads. Start with about $10 for automobiles weighing less than a ton, and graduate the tax upward. Such a system could raise two million dollars a year!

Put out a call for a state constitutional convention. The voters have approved it. And ratify the national prohibition amendment at once. Memorialize congress to speed enactment of woman's suffrage. The last election let you know how our people feel.

And finally, a new capitol. You know we need a new state house. Let's get one. If we do it now, it can be a fine memorial to the boys who lost their lives in the service.

The inaugural message had the legislators buzzing. So did the inaugural ball that followed. Nebraska had never seen such a formal party. There was Sam in full dress and most of the

80

state constitutional officers too. The dance at the mansion lasted until well after midnight. But, as one representative remarked later, it did not disturb anybody because nobody but the caretaker lived in the mansion. The Governor and Mrs. McKelvie had made it clear they would continue to reside in their home at Twenty-sixth and N.

But if Sam McKelvie played hard, he worked hard, too. The farm program, the executive budget, and action to build a new capitol, came through without too much difficulty. But the Code. His political opposition was far from dead. The newspapers that had fired upon him throughout the campaign now aimed their guns at his Civil Administrative Code bill. The very title was something to arouse suspicion. McKelvie wished over and over that he had labeled it a "Cabinet Form of Government" instead.

To kill two birds with one stone, as they expressed it, his legal advisers had suggested revising a number of laws along with the Code amendments. It would be a simple way to chop out obsolete provisions and deadwood language. The suggestion appealed to Sam. The working result, however, was a five hundred-page bill. Opponents immediately cried, "Shenanigan!" Why would the Governor need a five hundred-page bill to "simplify" government? Something must be afoot here! In all those pages and all those words somebody was attempting to pull the wool over the eyes of an unsuspecting public. That was the nature of the attack.

Senators C. Petrus Peterson of Lincoln, and John Cordeal of McCook, successfully piloted the cumbersome bill through the senate. But the house consideration of the Code bill was delayed time and again throughout the session.

Not all the ammunition, however, was being fired by the opposition. Sam McKelvie was busy, too. He prepared several different booklets describing the intent and method of the Code legislation. These he scattered over the state and personally thrust into the hand of every office caller. If the people understand, they will act! He was sure that if they understood the Code, they would support it.

Now that he was governor, Sam McKelvie appreciated more than ever the urgent need for the administrative reorganization that his bill would bring. His own office, when he assumed it, contained no records of value. This, he knew, was no fault of Neville's; it was merely the result of the system, or lack of system. Furthermore, the gubernatorial appropriation was exhausted. Many other offices were in a similar state of disruption.

His salary as governor was $2,500 a year. McKelvie had to use some of his own money for a few weeks to keep his office running. He was determined, too, to exercise his position as governor to every advantage in attracting national attention to Nebraska. He wanted new industry. He wanted responsible people around the nation to know that Nebraska was a member of the Union, a state worthy of note and investment. He had no intention to abandon his plans for advertising his state. If he considered a trip advisable, he went. Often he paid his own way.

He had preached against government by board and bureau, but not until he held the governorship did he fully grasp the confusion of the system he had condemned. It seemed that he was forever being scheduled for a meeting: the Banking Board; the Board of Charities and Correction; the State Insurance Board; the Board of Irrigation, Highways and Drainage, to name a few. Usually he knew nothing of the agendas. There was no time to probe the facts surrounding a question presented at a meeting. You voted as a clerk suggested, and you hoped for the best.

A few days before the end of the session he received alarming news from the house. The representatives, tired and with tempers frazzled, were in a mood to quit and go home without acting on the Code bill. The committee charged with guiding the bill through the house could only suggest that the Governor appear and make a personal plea to the house membership. McKelvie told the committee members to schedule his appearance.

Though he had received the committeemen with an outward show of confidence, Sam McKelvie dreaded his appearance before the one hundred members of the house. His political enemies there were eager to spring any trap that might embarrass him. His whole program for administrative reform might be sunk by the slip of his own tongue. At that meeting the success or failure of his major political effort would hang in a balance. Well, he had more cause than ever now to fight for the Code. But how should he fight? What should he say? It came to him that state representatives also wear pants. Collectively from a governor's viewpoint, they might be a cantankerous organization, but individually they were citizens. Good, affable men. The same kind of men he enjoyed appearing before during a campaign. Why, then, should not they too respond if they understood?

Governor McKelvie spoke to the house membership as he would have spoken to a farm audience. He had brought along

83

a series of simple charts to illustrate his points. His manner was informal. Patiently he pointed out on an organization chart how a row of boards and agencies stood between the people and their elected officials. A barrier of impersonal but powerful boards between the people and their servants! That was poor business, certainly. But even more, it was undemocratic. That was not the kind of government the men of Valley Forge had envisioned. That was not the self-government that the patriots had fought to establish. It was a foolish, dangerous, expensive result of neglect. It should be corrected. It could be corrected by this House of Representatives!

His victory came too easily. The house passed the Code bill with ten votes to spare. Had he known, he could have gathered his strength at that last moment and pushed the measure through with the emergency clause and thereby the Code would have gone into operation at once. As it was, the new system could not be officially inaugurated until ninety days after the close of the session.

Within those ninety days the opposition made a final drive to kill the Code. Petitions were circulated to bring a referendum vote. The Governor knew that obtaining signatures was no problem. With a half-smile he recalled how easily he had obtained signatures when he first ran for the Lincoln council. He was determined, though, to make the path of the opposition a rough one. He stepped up his educational campaign. He pounded home in pamphlets and talks to Nebraskans that the Code which the legislature had enacted cleared the way for, as he put it, "A Responsible Form of Government."

But the opportunity to test the effectiveness of his efforts never came.

84

In their haste, or in their desire to keep the issue clouded in confusion, the petition-backers failed to state adequately the nature of the repeal they were proposing. Secretary of State D. M. Amsbury refused to accept the petition filings on the ground the explanatory statement they carried was too fragmentary to enable a signer to know what he was signing.

In a rage, the Code opponents stormed into District court for a mandamus which would compel Amsbury to accept the petitions and put in motion the action necessary to have a popular vote on the repeal of the Code. The District court agreed with Amsbury. On appeal, the Supreme court eventually did also.

The Governor received the news on the telephone in his office. He replaced the receiver carefully. Then he startled his secretary with a sudden burst of laughter. He did not bother to explain. The very court that a few short years ago had told him he could not run for the governorship had just now handed him a precious victory. The Code, he knew, would stand through the years as perhaps the greatest accomplishment of his gubernatorial service. But the part that had triggered his laughter was this: he knew the court was correct both times.

His battle for the Code had been longer and more bitter than he had expected. The struggle had swayed back and forth for the better part of a year, from January into August. Strange it should have been so. Every citizen, certainly, should have welcomed a plan to bring order and sound fiscal practices into his state government. Perhaps in his zeal he had appeared too undiplomatic. Maybe it was his bluntness that had made the road so rough. Still, he felt he had been fair. He had, he felt, 85 explained the plan accurately and well. Why, then, had the accomplishment been so difficult? No doubt it was simply the way of politics.

Politics. He could not say he was sorry he was in it. Yet, he understood more fully now the attitude his mother had held. He could appreciate more deeply her unwillingness to have a member of her family engaged in an occupation that dealt in distortions, innuendo, and, he must admit, sometimes deliberate vilification. When one was required to fight in such a bog, was the triumph worth it? At the moment he felt it was. How would his mother weigh the value of the Code against the price of its achievement? Little Mother Jennie. How would she view it?

His musings carried him back to the twilight of that late February evening. Again he sat alone on a rail of the orchard fence. He looked at the familiar sweep of fields and trees and barren thickets. The scene swam before him. Every outline burned out in the surge of his emotion and in the golden burnish of the sunset. Jennie was home. Home from the long journey across the dusty prairies. Home from the trials of motherhood; the drudgery of homemaking. Drudgery? No, not drudgery. The glory.

It had come so unexpectedly. He had caught a glimpse of her as he read from the rostrum on inauguration day. A somber, but trim little figure there in the crowded chamber. He had tried to send a private little message to her; a special twinkling from his eye that she would recognize and understand. A momentary thing, but something that she would sense in the fleeting pause between his phrases to these others.

Had she received it? He searched the tiny face, the bright

eyes. He sought, in that instant, the trace of a smile at the corners of her lips: some token of understanding. If it was there, he failed to see it. Jennie McKelvie was intent upon what the Governor of Nebraska had to say.

Even then, he knew now, she must have been tired out; ill. He had received the word some six weeks later. Mother was sick. Pneumonia. Could he come? He had carried her, he remembered, from her bed to a cot near one of the south windows. The sun streamed in there, warm through the glass even in February. She had always loved the sunshine so. And she had been aware of it as he had folded back a margin of sheet over the patchwork quilt that her own busy fingers had stitched so precisely in some long forgotten winter evening. "Is the sun shining?" she whispered. "Is it shining, Roy?"

In the strength of sunshine a man could measure things. In the sunlight there was no illusion; no false beauty, no shadow to cloak a blemish of weakness. In the sunlight only the imperfection of sight could hide the truth. No doubt Jennie had found a certain satisfaction before she died in measuring the accomplishment of prohibition. She would measure it, he knew, in the bright light of motive, in the strong beam of righteousness. Mayhap the fact that he had signed Nebraska's ratification of the Eighteenth Amendment as one of his first official acts had afforded Jennie some sense of pride. Nebraska was the thirty-sixth state to ratify, and his signature had been the one that made the nation dry. Or, so it was said.

Even as he had affixed his signature to the bill, Governor McKelvie experienced his inward doubts. Nebraska had been officially dry for months. Yet in fact it was not. None knew that better than the Governor and the men charged with law enforcement. He wondered at the outcome. Perhaps national prohibition would make the local enforcement problem easier, but he doubted it. Take liquor out of politics? Ten years earlier he had firmly believed it might be done.

No, politics was not a pretty pastime. Still it had its moments; moments of greatness perhaps, and moments of heartwarming whimsy certainly. His experience with the milkman was an example of the latter.

The absence of exercise in the job of governor was a problem. He had little time for golf. To compensate for that loss, McKelvie made a practice of walking the mile from his home to the state house. It was a poor substitute, but it was better than nothing.

One morning, quite to his surprise, he was hailed by a milkman. A bright day was beginning and in the early hour of 6: 30 there was a minimum of traffic. The milkman, obviously, felt the need of companionship.

Sam disliked exchanging his walk for a ride on the seat of a milkwagon, but he, too, shared an urge for light conversation on such a morning.

"How far you goin'?" the milkman asked when his passenger was safely aboard.

"I'll get off around Sixteenth," he said, and, after a pause, "You milkmen are early risers."

"Aw, I don't know." The driver spat to the left of the singletree. "Used to be. Used to get up at 3 o'clock."

"What time do you get up now?" Sam asked.

"Not until four," the driver replied.

Sam hid his smile. The wagon neared Sixteenth and L

Streets.

"I'll get off at the next corner, if you don't mind," he said.

The driver craned his neck to survey the neighborhood. "Where do you work around here?"

"I work at the state house," Sam said.

"State house, huh," the milkman showed a mild interest. "What kind of a job have you got, Buddy?"

"I'm the governor."

The milkman's jaw dropped as he turned to scrutinize his passenger. Finally, after what Sam took to be a careful inventory, the fellow said quietly, "The hell you are."

Twice during his first two years as governor, Sam McKelvie called special sessions of the legislature. The first was to effect a resolution incident to the federal enactment of woman's suffrage. The second, following a disastrous riot in Omaha, was summoned to give county officials the legal authority they needed to meet such emergencies.

Both sessions, while satisfactory, were difficult and Sam McKelvie concluded he would never again call the legislature into special session for anything short of a vital need.

He learned, too, that not only legislative sessions try the metal of the chief executive. There was, for example, the Kirk case.

Beryl C. Kirk was sent to the state penitentiary from Omaha for 20 years for involvement in the fatal shooting of an Omaha policeman following a jewelry store robbery. Attorneys for Kirk asked the governor to review the case. A preliminary survey of the facts convinced McKelvie that the case was worthy of investigation. Kirk had not taken part in the robbery. He was in no position to have profited from the crime. It seemed that his principal offense was allowing the robbers to enter his house after they fled from the store. Kirk had been a boot-legger and his reputation was not a shining one, but there was the possibility that he had been more a victim of circumstance than an actual participant in the crime of murder for which he was sentenced. The governor promised to look into the case further.

Several weeks later Governor McKelvie returned from an official trip to Washington to learn that Kirk had been freed from the penitentiary during his absence. A so-called furlough had been granted him by the president of the state senate who had been acting in the absence of the lieutenant governor.

McKelvie was shocked and angered by the turn of events. His shock and anger, however, failed to compare with the re-action of the public when the news was presented in the full melodrama of press accounts. The Governor moved at once to rectify the error. He ordered Kirk returned to prison. It was then he got the full jolt of the seriousness of the incident. Kirk had, contrary to his promise, left the state. A period of several weeks went by before law enforcement officers were able to find the convict and return him to the penitentiary. During that time, abuse was heaped upon the governor's office. With-out doubt, here was an issue he would have to face in any campaign he might make for re-election. It was, he reflected wryly, an issue he had little part in making.

There were, however, entries on the positive side of the ledger, too. The new Code was proving its merit. The effects of the new budget system were being reflected in savings. Road construction was progressing at an encouraging rate. State parks were being improved. The farm program was roll-ing. And, in addition to all of these things, plans for a new

90

capitol for Nebraska were finally on the architect's boards with a ten million dollar pay-as-we-go finance program to back them up.

The Governor could take just pride in the progress toward the new capitol, a structure which would rank as one of the finest buildings in the world. That it should be so was more than mere happenstance.

As chairman of the Capitol Commission, Sam McKelvie had selected a bi-partisan membership to serve with him. The Commission wisely enlisted the aid of a representative of Nebraska's architectural profession to help plan its program.

By the early autumn of 1919 the call was out across the state and nation for a building design. The Commission opened wide its door. "That each competitor may feel perfectly free to solve the problem in his own way," its announcement to architects read, "no style or type of building is barred and no suggestion is offered as to the relative desirability of a single unit or group plans."

A little more than a year later, Governor McKelvie signed for the Commission a contract with Bertram G. Goodhue, one of the world's great architects, for the complete plans and specifications of a new state house, a capitol destined to inaugurate a new trend in the design of similar public buildings throughout the world.

CHAPTER SIX

A GOVERNOR STEPS DOWN

SAM MCKELVIE SUSPECTED he should feel the tenseness of this hour. Certainly the small group of men seated on the other side of his desk appeared dramatic enough. Apprehension was in their eyes; the mark of sincerity—woeful sincerity—unmistakable on their faces. They were his friends. He knew that and he loved them all. He appreciated their interest and he had no intention of hurting them.

They had just informed him that in their considered judgment, he would be unwise to file for re-election. They pointed out that he had already contributed much to his state; that he owed it to himself anyway to return to his business.

They had a point there. His personal finances could do with a bit of bolstering. It was a private little joke around the office 93 that he needed one secretary just to keep his personal notes renewed regularly at the bank. They were using the financial argument, he was quite aware, in an attempt to save his feelings. What they were really trying to tell him, he decided, was that he could not be re-elected. Their opinion was he could not make it.

He could not suppress the smile. How could they know? How could he know until he had tried? He could not help laughing. There they sat, like mourners, and there was no cause to mourn.

They accepted the laugh as his answer. All of them had heard him laugh before. Apparently they had come to recognize it as a signal that what they had said had failed to induce the Governor to change his mind. Some of the anxiety left their faces. Two or three of the younger ones grinned, and there were the resigned pledges that they would do their best. He had never doubted that. He would do his best too.

He opened his campaign in February, 1920. The primaries were to be held in April. The primary race for the Republican nomination for governor, he appreciated, would be a tough one. He knew he had offended certain elements of his party. For example, his appointment of a Democrat to the post of election commissioner in Omaha had nettled a segment of the party there. And there were other causes. He had refused to recommend state legislation to curb post-war profiteering. That had gone hard with some members of the Republican political following. But he knew that morality does not result from state or national law. He would not pretend that it might, even if such a concession might have made a good political talking point.

94

It was clear that he would have plenty of company in the ring, battling for the nomination. There were six altogether and Governor McKelvie decided to launch his battle in Omaha. He took pains to see that the meeting was well advertised. Though he would be the last to admit it, he was uneasy about this campaign. Never before had he seen so many evidences of hostility toward him displayed by members of his own party. Still, not exactly hostility either; it seemed more a desire to avoid him, to remain unlinked with McKelvie. He was too much the veteran now to be surprised when some active politicians who two years earlier had eagerly sought his company now looked the other way when he appeared. He recognized that such things happened, but they irritated him, nonetheless. He expected labels like "King McKelvie," and "The Prisoners' Friend," from the Omaha opposition papers, but to hear the same epithets whispered within his own ranks angered him.

The Omaha meeting was well attended. He spoke as candidly as he knew how. He discussed the new Code; told what he felt it was accomplishing. He talked bluntly about the Kirk case. He compared the number of prison furloughs granted under the previous administration with the smaller number granted under his. He told why he believed state statutes were not the tools with which profiteering could be stopped. He explained how the new executive budget system was working to reduce waste and inefficiency. He worked again on the assumption that if the people understood, they would support him.

If there were those who attended that meeting to see Sam McKelvie apologize for any part of his record, they left the rally unsatisfied. They also left with murmurs of approval for

95

the Governor in their ears. He had sensed that beginning his campaign in Omaha might be wise. His strongest opposition, both in and out of the party, was centered there. He had come to believe in the virtue of attack, and the most notable attacks are always in range of the enemy.

Now that he was firing his campaign guns again, he forgot all else. He scarcely noticed that some of the outstate papers spoke kindly of his Omaha appearance. The small-paper editors admired him for jumping in where the fire was hottest. They accepted it as evidence of confidence, leadership, and guts.

The late winter and early spring weather remained in his favor. He campaigned by automobile westward across the southern third of the state. He spoke seriously on the issues of his record but he usually found an excuse to twit the partisans who were shunning his presence. He was having fun and his audiences liked him for it.

At Grand Island he spoke in Liederkranz Hall. The gathering included a large number of women who were about to vote a full ticket for the first time. The Governor spoke confidently when he reached the subject of handling of prisoners. Carefully, deliberately he read off the number of furloughs allowed by the Neville administration, and next the total number of prisoners in the penitentiary when the McKelvie administration came to power. He paused. Now he reported the smaller number of furloughs his administration had allowed. He paused again to obtain full effect of his statistics.

"And how many prisoners do you think are in the penitentiary now?" he asked.

96   In the silence that followed the question, there came from

the back of the hall, a clear male voice; unhurried, calm, and matter-of-fact.

"None," it said, and the hushed hall, so serious and still a moment before, rocked with laughter.

Sam McKelvie enjoyed the joke as much as the audience. When the merriment subsided, he wiped his eyes, and grinned, "Well, anyway," he said, "I know now where one is that ought to be there." This was the campaigning he loved.

Later at Blair, in the lobby of a drab little hotel one Saturday night, he waited for the time for his rally. He was to speak at a motion picture theater but the town, it seemed, had little desire to hear the Governor. It was one of the places where the party leadership had been very busy with subjects other than McKelvie.

From where he sat, half-dozing behind the lobby's hard-coal stove Sam heard a traveling man, the only other guest, open a conversation with the desk clerk.

"Hear the governor is supposed to be in town," said the traveling man.

"That's what they say," the clerk responded.

"Don't suppose he'd stay at a dump like this," the traveler opined.

"Naw," the clerk agreed. "He's probably eatin' with the nabobs."

"What kind of a governor is he, anyway?" the traveling man yawned.

"Damndest fool governor we ever had."

"What's the matter with him?"

"Everything," said the clerk. "He's raised taxes, let everybody out of the penitentiary, and set himself up as king." 97

For a few moments the traveling man stared straight ahead. The lobby was silent save for the drumming of the clerk's fingers on the registry counter. The traveling man yawned again, stretched, stood up, and climbed the stairs.

It was then that Sam sauntered over to the desk.

"My name's McKelvie," he said. "I'm inclined to agree with your opinion of the governor but if you'll come over to the theater tonight, I'll see if I can change our minds."

In the six-way race for the Republican nomination, Governor McKelvie finished first. His closest rival, Adam McMullen, was a scant 8,000 votes behind, and from the more than 100,000 votes cast in the gubernatorial primary, Sam received one out of three. It was not an impressive victory statistically but as something which his supporters had considered impossible six months earlier, it was a great triumph.

The political air was much clearer now. At the Republican national convention, Sam again found himself the darling of the Nebraska delegation. The delegates even went so far as to back him for the vice-presidential nomination. He knew the move was nothing more than a gesture of goodwill, but such goodwill had not been his earlier in the year.

He recognized his general election opponent, former Governor John H. Morehead, as a formidable candidate. Yet he felt that the real test was already over. The national Republican ticket, Harding and Coolidge, he was certain, would romp to an easy win over Cox and the young New Yorker, Franklin D. Roosevelt.

The firm conviction that he would be returned to office, however, did not keep him from conducting a strong campaign. He concentrated on three subjects.

98

Nebraska's capitol, completed ten years after the ground-breaking
ceremony, is a magnificent structure, considered one of the world's
architectural masterpieces.

On Armistice Day, 1922, Governor McKelvie guided the plow that broke the ground for Nebraska's capitol, planned during his administration.

First, he supported the Code with all his vigor. Though it was now in operation, he knew a great many Nebraskans did not understand it. The constitutional convention had not completely fulfilled his hopes. Some of the revisions it made contemplated the permanent operation of the Code but in the main these were not as comprehensive as he had hoped they would be. So he continued to focus attention on the value of the new system and continually pointed out that more and more states were following the lead of Illinois and Nebraska and instituting reforms of their own.

Second, there was the matter of advertising Nebraska. Sometimes it seemed to him that Nebraskans must try the patience of the Almighty by refusing to appreciate the productivity of the great prairie land. He warned against the development of an habitual pessimism which would, he knew, be a very real barrier in the path of the state's progress.

Third, he was seriously disturbed by what he identified as a growing tendency to look to government for relief from any problem that appeared on the horizon. There had been demands for state laws to halt profiteering. Now there were demands for legislation to lower the prices of groceries and household goods. He believed prosperity came from hard work and careful saving, not from statute.

Good government could provide a healthy atmosphere for agriculture, for industry, for business. It could act to equalize opportunities but it could not substitute for the individual responsibility of the citizen; the responsibility to work and save. These became his watchwords: "Work and Save." To him, the boundaries of proper governmental activity appeared sharply outlined. They were boundaries to be respected: fence- 103 lines protecting the dignity of the individual from the impersonal plow of bureaucracy.

He injected some of his thinking into his second inaugural message in January of 1921.

"As a commonwealth," he said, "we are prosperous—not as much so perhaps as we have been at some times in the past, but comfortably situated, and our resources are unimpaired. We need, now, only employ the age old principles of thrift, industry and unselfishness of purpose in order that we may go forward at a rapid rate.

"Let us enact just as few laws as possible. Our statute books are encumbered now with laws that are obsolete and unenforceable. Moreover, we have legislated so much that the people have come to feel they have a never-ending source of relief from their ills through the enactment of new laws. Such a condition of reliance upon the state destroys initiative in the individual, and develops a citizenship that is dependent, flabby and discontented."

He gave the advice because he believed it important; important and timely. Everyone knew the war years and the postwar speculations had brought the bloat of inflation. It was clear there must come a day of reckoning. It was axiomatic that if you got silk shirts on credit, the day would come when you would have to sweat in your denims to pay the bill. That day, Sam McKelvie sensed, was not far off.

The financial weather remained threatening throughout the winter. The storm broke early in the spring and the fury of it was greater than Sam McKelvie or any other Nebraskan had expected. Its center was a tumult of pressure developed by credit. First, in the years immediately following the war there was an over-supply of credit. Now there was none.

The threat to Nebraska agriculture was great. Sam knew that. At the same time, he had little sympathy for those who, on the strength of pure speculation, had over-extended their operations with a gambler's desire for quick, big profits. People who gamble must expect losses as well as winnings.

Of deep concern to him, however, was the fact that this storm struck the prudent operator almost as hard as it struck the speculator. Corn prices had declined during the winter and thousands of careful farmers decided to feed hogs or cattle in an effort to market their corn as meat at a fair price. They needed money to buy livestock and they borrowed it. To meet a rising demand for cattle, ranchers expanded their operations. They, too, borrowed in many instances.

Then, almost overnight, or so it seemed, loans were called or renewals denied. Financial men said credit must be curtailed to bring a halt to inflation. Sam had no quarrel with the argument that credit must be restricted but the sudden enforcement of a rigid credit policy was, he felt, foolish and unfair. It would be different if the loans were not backed by a wealth of livestock. As it was, the policy forced farmers and ranchers alike to market their stock in a rush. Not only animals being fed for market. Basic stock was forced to market, too. Nebraska agriculture was being given a beating that was both unnecessary and undeserved.

In the summer of 1921 he wrote to every Nebraska banker. He asked for their opinions as to what might be done to gain an extension of farm credit. The overwhelming majority of the bankers laid the blame on policies of the Federal Reserve Banking system. The Reserve Bank, they said, had ordered a constriction of credit. They had no choice but to comply.

105

McKelvie wrote at once to the governor of the Federal Reserve Bank in Washington.

"I am convinced," he began, "that financial and business conditions are improving in this state, but I am also convinced that there is need for credit relief to farmers and cattlemen in this territory now."

He admitted that the federal government's War Finance Corporation loans were helping, but suggested that the Federal Reserve Board approve farm grain storage receipts, validated by Nebraska's Grain Warehouse division, as collateral for farm loans.

The reply was immediate. In fact, it reached the newspapers before it reached the Governor. The Federal Reserve chief tossed off the Governor's suggestion by saying Reserve banks were not empowered by law to make loans to individual farmers or cattlemen. Nebraska's trouble, he said, was its 10-per cent legal rate of interest. It was his opinion that member banks in Nebraska were asking 8 to 10 per cent for their money and then turning the paper over to the Federal Reserve System for 6 per cent.

The charge that Nebraska banks were profiteering on farm loans set off a bedlam of comments across the state; cries from bankers and farmers alike.

Sam McKelvie thought he saw a chance to bring a reduction in the Federal Reserve discount rate. He called a meeting of Nebraska bankers and Federal Reserve representatives in Omaha. It was a warm session. It cleared the air somewhat. The original charge of profiteering on loans by Nebraska bankers lost much of its punch when the bankers told their side of the story. The meeting, however, did not bring an immediate reduction in the discount rate.

By the end of the year the worst for agriculture was over. The experience had been bitter but there was some small comfort in knowing that an inevitable blow was struck and survived.

Without doubt his administration would be blamed somehow for the farm losses. Already the Democratic opposition, now under the loquacious leadership of C. W. Bryan, was loudly lamenting the enactment of the Code almost as though it were responsible for the curtailment of farm credit. The sagacity gained in a dozen years of political activity permitted Sam to see "Brother Charlie" Bryan as an astute political adversary. As Sam viewed it, every day was Halloween to Bryan. Bryan warned of ghosts and dangers behind every cottonwood and cornstalk from Lincoln to Scottsbluff. Before one warning had died, he was sounding another. Well, let him have his fun.

Even before he called the legislature into special session in January of 1922, Sam McKelvie had announced his retirement from office. He would not be a third-term candidate. He was finished with elective office.

Sometimes, now, he wondered why being governor had seemed so vital to him. Yet, he was proud of the accomplishment. He was proud of the Code; of the building of the new state house, the cornerstone for which he laid on Armistice Day, 1922; of the great improvement in the state's road program; of the inauguration of a state park system, and of the agricultural program. The state agricultural information service he had established was at last being recognized as a valuable agency by farmers who previously had been compelled to 107 rely upon the sometimes doubtful data issued by grain and livestock dealers. None could deny that his administration had done much to bring hog cholera under control and stamp out bovine tuberculosis. But among all of these things, the Code was first.

Basically it was the Code that enabled him to declare a dividend. He knew about special legislative sessions. He did not like them. Here, however, was a matter of importance; a harvest that would prove for all time the real worth of the Code and the executive budget system which was a part of it.

He put the issue to the legislature simply. Under the Code, business budget practices had been extended to all departments of state government and as a result, a saving of some two million dollars had been effected. He was, therefore, asking the legislature to do something no other Nebraska legislature had been asked to do. He wanted the two million cut from the current appropriations. Such action would permit a reduction of one-third in the state property tax levy.

He recommended something else, too. The inauguration of a one-cent per gallon tax on gasoline to support the road program. If this were done, it would afford additional relief to property taxpayers. Enactment of the gasoline tax would enable the legislature, if it wished, to cut another seven hundred thousand dollars from the property tax appropriations.

Tossing in the recommendation for the gasoline tax was, he decided, good insurance. He knew legislatures well enough to know that even a clear-cut and justified request to reduce taxes would be attacked by the opposition as a nefarious act. It would be unless there were some other issue to worry and snap over. Let the opposition save face by rejecting his gasoline tax proposal, but make sure Nebraskans got the benefit of the Code savings. That was his plan. And it worked.

The full effect of the budget cut, Sam McKelvie knew, would not be realized until after the general elections that fall. Not until the taxpayers got their tax bills would they appreciate the significance of the saving. It was odd, but he did not care whether they thanked him. Why should they thank him? He had asked for this job as governor. The people had enough confidence in him to grant his request. In politics you got your thanks, if you got them at all, before you performed. A queer business, politics. How could Mother Jennie have known so much about it?

CHAPTER SEVEN

BACK TO PUBLISHING

THE CHEERFUL SMILE, the buoyant optimism, the powerful drive which since his youth had assured Samuel R. McKelvie that he would never fail, all but deserted him early in January of 1923.

He stared glumly from his office at the dreary winter scene afforded by the intersection of Fourteenth and P Streets. Side-curtained automobiles chugged and slipped along in the dirty snow. Passersby picked their way carefully where shoveled paths narrowed in the drifts. Inside, steam escaping from the leaky valve in the radiator annoyed him with its spasmodic hissing.

Even the governorship, the highest political honor of the state, which he had relinquished just a few days before, seemed 111 to have lost much of its glamor. In fact, at the moment, Sam was sure he would never toss his hat into another political ring again. Four years in the governorship, it seemed now, had left him virtually without friends. Indeed, a discouraging harvest.

And there was other discouragement; more cause for bitterness. He needed $50,000. Politics had taken him away too long from his business. His prolonged absence might well prove fatal to his beloved Nebraska Farmer. The wages of his employees were four weeks past due. The banks were pressing for payment of loans. Sam was broke. Flat broke. Sell The Farmer after all the years of hard work? Impossible. Yet was it? What other course did he have?

His face drawn by dejection and melancholy, he moved slowly to his desk and slumped wearily in the chair. He stared idly at the cover of a January issue of The Nebraska Farmer on the desk before him. His mind went back to that first proud day as editor, eighteen years earlier. That first editorial! What torture to write about weed eradication. Sam permitted himself a wry smile. He still knew one thing about weeds; he was foursquare agin 'em.

Sam remembered the decision to abandon the typewriter and become a salesman extraordinary for The Farmer. Then came the decision in 1908 to purchase the paper, and the realization that the fifty-year-old Farmer needed a transfusion which only enthusiasm and hard work could give it.

There was the problem of subscribers. The paper's 30,000 were, in the main, farmers who received the publication free. When Sam, or his field men, approached a farmer with the suggestion that he pay for the paper, the reaction was always an incredulous stare. On such occasions Sam learned that even his free subscribers were not always enthusiastic about the quality of The Farmer.

Even though he spruced up the news columns and got more "down-to-earth" information in them, still paid subscriptions were hard to come by. "How in thunder," Sam exploded to Martha, "am I going to get more advertisers if I can't get the subscribers? If I don't get more advertising I'll be darned if I know how I'll keep up the payments on The Farmer."

As he recounted to a friend later, he had fairly worried himself into coming up with an answer to this predicament. His idea crystallized in 1909, and this was it: Sell individual shares of stock in The Nebraska Farmer to an unlimited, but handpicked number of well-known farmers, influential in their respective communities. Next make clear that each farmer is eligible to purchase only one share of stock. The purchase price, $100. And here Sam became enthusiastic—each purchaser could quickly get his money back by selling 100 subscriptions to The Nebraska Farmer. Each subscription pays the stockholder a dollar, and to make the offer even more inviting to these chosen ones, The Farmer would even pay them fifty cents for turning in a renewed subscription.

"And, my friend," Sam would say, "don't forget that your $100-par stock, which hasn't cost you a cent when you've sold your subscriptions, will grow and grow in value as business in Nebraska prospers."

Sam's idea caught on. Within a year The Nebraska Farmer had 5,000 new paid-up subscribers and a welcome amount of new working capital. And the plan continued to bear fruit. By 1914, The Nebraska Farmer was being delivered to 40,000 farm homes. The farmer stockholders were extolling it as the 113 finest of farm journals, and advertising revenue increased steadily.

Paid subscribers were uncommon among farm publications, but Sam had them and he knew it. He also knew that many of his competitors grossly exaggerated the size of their circulations. He needed a yardstick to measure the value of his paid subscribers to the advertisers, against the fictitious prospective customers claimed by his competitors. He found what he was looking for in the establishment of the Audit Bureau of Circulation. This was a national non-profit cooperative being organized to give the advertising clients of its members a bonafide audit of actual paid circulation. Sam became a charter member. He was sure advertisers would welcome the service. They did and proved it by buying more space than ever before in The Nebraska Farmer.

Business was looking up. Farm prices rose as war-torn Europe demanded more food from America. Boom was in the air. Sam sensed it. To his farm stockholders he reported:

"The outlook for the next twelve months is auspicious. The results of our efforts shall prove accumulative, showing greater returns with each succeeding year. That is the result of every conservative and well-directed effort. Let the winds blow what will. The Nebraska Farmer will be found safely anchored against any storm. Other publications may seek to cover the entire universe, wealthy corporations may seek to form a farm paper trust, but The Nebraska Farmer, with its splendid name and field, and its organization of farmers who stand first in the affairs of the state agriculturally will live on and on, growing in power, influence and material welfare."

114   Sam matched his bright optimism with hard work. His

hours at the office were long; his field trips many, and new responsibilities seemed to arrive daily. But he felt he was becoming a successful businessman. One day he hurried—these were days when he always hurried—to his doctor to complete an examination for life insurance. He was shocked to learn he could not be accepted for a policy. The doctor told him to take it easier. Sam did. He left his desk at four o'clock each afternoon. He played golf and became expert at it. He got more work done too, and eventually qualified for the insurance besides.

Though The Nebraska Farmer's business grew steadily, Sam was not satisfied that advertising revenue was increasing as rapidly as it should. The trouble was that advertising revenue was being split five ways. Four other farm papers were also serving Nebraska. There simply was not enough advertising business coming into the state to support all of them adequately. Looking at his competitors, it was obvious to Sam that The Twentieth Century Farmer was slipping badly, despite the lush farm prosperity of World War I.

In January of 1918, amid the rush of taking office as governor, Sam offered to buy The Twentieth Century Farmer from The Bee Publishing Company of Omaha. Its publisher was his old friend and first employer, Victor Rosewater. His bid was $92,500 and it was accepted. The deal was completed in February. The chief prize of his purchase was a new farm magazine press which Sam figured was worth the entire price.

The prosperity of the next few years enabled The Farmer to pay off most of the debt, and none too soon. In 1921 prices collapsed. Thousands of farmers went broke. Many businesses closed their doors. Sam, in the governor's chair, watched help- **115** lessly as The Nebraska Farmer's advertising revenue plummeted fifty per cent between January and April of 1922. A representative from his bank called on him regularly, each time to press for settlement of the loans it had made to The Farmer. The final blow had come only a few days ago. It was then that the bank gave him thirty days to pay up or it would foreclose.

So, on this day in January, 1923, Sam contemplated a sad ending to both his political and publishing careers. Surely no bank would loan him the money. But where else could he get the $50,000 necessary to save his business? It was then that his thoughts kept coming back to a friend in Omaha who had taken an interest in his political efforts. It was then that Sam decided he was probably his only hope. He boarded a train for Omaha that evening and the next day laid his case before his friend. The man heard him out and then began a long review of the gloomy state of business. Was he getting a polite refusal, Sam wondered. But even as he talked, his great and good friend dipped his pen in the inkwell and wrote out a check for $50,000.

"Sam," he said, "Nebraska needs a good farm paper. Let's keep The Nebraska Farmer going."

"But what about security?" Sam asked.

"I have your word on this slip of paper. That's all I need," the friend replied. He was Walter Head, president of The Omaha National Bank.

Sam, his spirits lifted from the depths of despair as he left the office, struggled to keep back the tears.

He recognized that the loan only eased the pressure of his financial plight. It had not cured it. The cure was more advertising revenue. Where would it come from? It could come only

116

from the eastern manufacturers who made things which could be sold in Nebraska. His immediate job was to convince the manufacturers that Nebraska farmers were not destitute. He had to make them understand these people who by thrift and hard work had made Nebraska a flourishing farm state. Here were good customers; the farm depression had not wiped them out. This was his first job.

But there was a larger task. On his many trips as governor, Sam had been appalled at the widespread ignorance of the midwest and of Nebraska especially. Many eastern businessmen, he discovered, still thought of Nebraska as wild-west country. The larger part of his assignment would be to reveal it in its true light: a land of opportunity awaiting only development by eastern capital. He had a job of selling to do.

Sam had sold before. He got in his car and drove east. With the zeal of an evangelist he preached Nebraska's promise along the way in every town where goods were manufactured that might be sold to farmers. His benediction was always the same. "Let's get the sellers and the buyers together. Advertise in The Nebraska Farmer!" His Amen was an advertising contract.

The pace Sam set for himself was hard. He paid little heed to mealtimes. Often he slept in his car and, when he awoke with the first light of morning, he would smooth the wrinkles from his clothes, shave in a public washroom and begin a new day. It was hard; very hard, but Sam was fighting for his business. He was determined, even eager, to fight all the way and he let no door close in his face without a full assault. If receptionists appeared the types used to brushing off salesmen, Sam stood before them not as a salesman, but as the former Gov- 117 ernor of the Sovereign State of Nebraska. It was an approach that seldom failed.

His swing through the east convinced him that the apathy there for the midwest as a market was even deeper than he had thought when he was governor. He told his readers about it in an open letter titled: "A Nebraska Farmer on Broadway":

"From a Nebraska farm to Broadway is a far cry. . . . The marked difference is this: The Nebraska farm produces the wealth; Broadway spends it. In Nebraska we buy what we need and think we are extravagant; in New York City they buy what they want and never stop to think. In Nebraska we provide for tomorrow (or try to); in New York City they recognize no tomorrow.

"In the East there are a few of the very rich, and many of the very poor, with little of the opportunity and equality found in the agricultural regions. . . .

"Mayhap you wonder just why I came to New York City. Just this: Manufacturing industries here are much ahead of the west. That is today. What they will be in the future years I cannot guess. These manufacturers sell throughout the world. One of their best territories is the corn belt. There is the base of money production. To reach the corn belt farmer these manufacturers must speak through a trusted friend. That is the reliable farm paper. Now you know why I am here. Advertising is the answer.

"One thing I find to a very marked degree amongst Eastern advertisers and agencies is a lack of knowledge of the field west of Chicago, especially west of the Missouri. . . . I cannot think of anything that would be of greater value to these men who sit at desks here in the East than an excursion through the West to be made at a time when the fields and crops may be seen in the fullness of fruition and beauty."

118

Despite the general lack of enthusiasm he had met, Sam returned to Lincoln with a pocketful of advertising contracts and promises for more. Things were looking up. Sam was too. He was ready to gamble again. There were now only two farm papers in Nebraska: his own and The Nebraska Farm Journal, published by the Arthur Capper Company of Topeka, Kansas. The two others had folded in the farm crash in 1921.

Now, in the early months of 1924, a dream of one day owning the only farm paper in Nebraska obsessed him. Sam drew upon all of his natural business acumen and his experience as he surveyed the situation. Mr. Capper's paper, he was certain, was not making the comeback that his own Nebraska Farmer was showing. The Farmer had become the dominant paper. Mr. Capper might be willing to quit the Nebraska field. He was.

In May of 1924 they closed the deal. Sam agreed to pay $100,000 for Mr. Capper's Farm Journal. Sam did not hesitate to borrow the $10,000 he needed to make the down payment. The other terms of the purchase made it an almost attractive risk. According to those terms, The Nebraska Farmer was obligated only to pay in keeping with its ability. The purchase agreement provided that on the fifteenth day of each month after July 31, 1924, the Capper Company would receive ten cents for each line of advertising published in The Nebraska Farmer in excess of the advertising lineage The Farmer had carried in the corresponding month in the fiscal year ending July 1, 1924. This arrangement was to continue until the debt to The Capper Company was paid off. The Nebraska Farmer eliminated its last rival on a pay-as-you-go basis.

The gamble paid off even faster than Sam had dared hope. 119

Sparked by the good business years of the late 1920s, The Farmer's advertising increased steadily. Instead of taking the eight years Sam had guessed it might to liquidate the debt to The Capper Company, The Farmer did it in five. Moreover, it did it while also repaying the $50,000 to Mr. Walter Head, the Omaha banker.

Sam appreciated that the remarkable recovery and growth of The Farmer was not solely of his own doing. When he thought about it he experienced a pleasant warmth. A man who spent as little actual time in his plant as he did had to have capable, loyal teammates. Sam had known that. He had insisted upon it. But the important thing was that he had them. He was proud of his employees and, though he seldom allowed himself to dwell upon it, he felt they were proud of him also.

During the twenties Sam watched with satisfaction as four of his men emerged as top-flight executives. These were Tom Leadley, his Editor-In-Chief, who had developed the news columns of The Farmer into the kind of magazine Sam was sure every farm family in Nebraska was glad to buy and read; Glenn Buck, his Advertising Manager, who had pushed the advertising lineage of The Farmer well up into the top ranks among farm papers in the country; D. E. Marcotte, his Treasurer, who kept a conservative eye on The Farmer's rapidly expanding publishing business; and Albert S. Hall, his Mechanical Superintendent, who had developed a high degree of efficiency in the printing plant.

Under Sam's direction, this management team achieved a splendid labor relations record. It became apparent that many of the men and women who came to work for The Nebraska

120

Farmer did so with intention of staying on until retirement. The Farmer also won the respect of the printers and their union by consistently paying the top local scale. Even in the face of the disastrous depression of the 1930s, The Farmer clung to this policy.

The Depression! The Drouth!

First with dismay, and then bitterness, Sam witnessed a breakdown in his contract negotiations with the unions. They collapsed in the autumn of 1934. A strike followed. The first, and only, strike in The Farmer's history temporarily silenced the presses. Somehow Sam could not bring himself to believe that his boys in the backroom wanted to go out on strike. These were the same men, most of whom he knew by their first names, who had amicably agreed to contracts year after year. But now something was changed. When the strike ended, Sam wrote his feelings into an editorial, "Our Boys Are Back":

"A month or so ago a dozen employees in the composing room of The Nebraska Farmer voluntarily quit their jobs. They did not want to leave, neither did we wish them to. They were ordered out by the Typographical Union of which they are members. The point in the controversy was wages. The union insisted on the 1929 wage scale of 91⅔ cents per hour. We held out for a reduced wage of 7½ percent, or 84¾ cents per hour. Our men were willing to take the reduction. The union was not. . . .

"Our boys are back just as they went out—voluntarily. They are to receive the 1929 wage, the highest ever paid to printers in Lincoln. There is no justification for such a wage. They knew it and admitted it, but we knew also that with our experienced and trusted employees on the outside we could not afford to fight the

121

government. With a united house, as we again have, we not only can but will resist government interference with the conduct of this business and we will have the 100 percent support of all of our employees in it.

"You inquire: Why did these men have to go out? Are they not their own bosses? Why must you pay 1929 wages in these times? . . .

"Charge it up to NRA! And take our word for it: If the people of this state vote for the continuation of such a program they may expect that industrial Nebraska with its thousands of small merchants and manufacturers will pass out of the picture. Only big business and organized labor can survive."

The editorial, in a sense, marked the end of Sam's active participation in management of The Nebraska Farmer. In the spring of 1935 he called Leadley, Buck, Marcotte, and Hall together and announced that he was appointing Mr. Buck as General Manager. What about Sam? He was "retiring" to his ranch, an enterprise which was to demonstrate once again his great capacity to see an opportunity and realize it.

"Retiring" from The Farmer, as it turned out, was not easy. Sam frequently found himself returning to his office as the paper struggled from the depression and became one of the leading farm publications in America. His bitterness over the strike had disappeared. By the outbreak of World War II it was forgotten. In 1943, Sam ordered new benefits for his employees. For a number of years The Farmer maintained a medical-hospitalization insurance plan and a life insurance program for its workers. Now Sam added profit-sharing. His plan included a trust fund for employees which gives them an opportunity to buy The Nebraska Farmer after his death.

122

Weary of the burdens of publishing, Sam and Martha in the early 1930's found contentment at their new By The Way ranch home in Nebraska's Sandhills.

Sam was sure he had done the right thing in enlarging the employee-benefit program. In the years following World War II, The Farmer's circulation extended to nine out of ten farm homes in Nebraska. Its advertising volume grew to sixth place among forty farm magazines and papers in the nation. The gross return from its job printing business, started in 1924, climbed to more than three-quarters of a million dollars annually.

Moreover, Sam saw a new opportunity to build. In 1947, he established a new paper, The Colorado Rancher and Farmer. Its editorial and advertising offices are in Denver, but the paper is printed in Lincoln and trucked into Colorado for RFD distribution. Again Sam's judgment proved correct. Within a few years after its founding the Colorado paper's audited circulation covered three-fourths of the farms and ranches in that state. Meanwhile its advertising volume increased from last to twentieth among all farm papers.

The records of The Farmer and its new sister publication were pleasing to Sam. The clean-cut appearance of The Nebraska Farmer's post-World War II home pleased him also. Each time he stepped into the office, he was impressed with the crisp efficiency; the busy but unconfused comings and goings; the steady sound of typewriters and the muffled hum of the plant's hidden, heavier machines. Perhaps it was because his visits were less frequent now, but each time he saw the office in action he experienced a little glow of excitement.

But Sam was by no means the only visitor who sensed the character of The Nebraska Farmer enterprises. Others caught it too. One visitor asked an officer of the company about it.

"This Nebraska Farmer place of yours." The visitor hesi- 125 tated as if wondering how to put his question. "It's, well, it's got a kind of personality about it. Where does it come from?"

The officer smiled. "Well," he said, "I suppose it comes from Sam McKelvie. Mr. McKelvie built this place. I'm not thinking of the brick, the steel, the glass. I'm talking about the business. He built it with principles that weren't subject to amendment. Such things as honesty and hard work are not cliches to him; they are principles. And somehow the people here have come to understand that in The Farmer you don't just work and get paid; you participate. We have come to know that Mr. McKelvie accepts a man at face value and deals openly, honestly, and frankly with him. He has made us see that it works. So I suppose some of his philosophy has rubbed off on us, and we're glad of it."

It was the officer's turn to hesitate.

"You know," he said, "I appreciate your question. I've wondered sometimes whether people notice the character of a business. From your question, I take it they do."

CHAPTER EIGHT

TWILIGHT IN POLITICS

FOR THE SECOND TIME in the eight months which had elapsed since he left the governor's office, Sam McKelvie was returning to Lincoln from an eastern trip. His heart was much lighter this time than it had been six months earlier when he had come back from his selling trip. He was still broke, but he would not be for long. Even the click of the rails seemed optimistic and sure.

Some of his buoyancy stemmed from his visit with the President of the United States, Calvin Coolidge. He had spent time with presidents before. William Howard Taft had been a guest in the McKelvie home. And as governor, Sam had been a dinner guest of the late President Warren G. Harding; had played golf with him, as a matter of fact.

127

There was something different about the visit with Coolidge. His other meetings with presidents had been primarily social. His talk with Coolidge was business and, strangely enough, it was linked in a way with his own business.

He went east on a familiar mission: to preach the virtues of Nebraska; to report to New York industrialists and business men that Nebraska farmers were not, contrary to many reports, on the rocks. They were paying off their debts. They were recovering from their losses. Over and over he told the story. Nebraska agriculture was potentially wealthy. The market should be cultivated.

He had looked forward to his stay in Washington. He enjoyed visiting the members of the Nebraska congressional delegation and his many other friends in the capital. He enjoyed meeting the men of both political faiths, and they always seemed to enjoy seeing him again. The Republicans, his colleagues, appreciated the respect with which he was held in the party at home. The Democrats appreciated his conviviality; his good humor. And it was surprising, really, to note that since he was no longer in office or a prospective candidate, the Democratic papers at home often commented with mild favor upon some of the views he expressed about agriculture.

His thoughts went back to the meeting with Coolidge. The President seemed sincerely interested in his evaluation of the midwestern agricultural situation. That situation, McKelvie admitted frankly, was still depressed. The market value of farm land was down. It was down because farm products, in more than ample supply, no longer commanded the inflated prices of the war and immediate post-war years. It was not down because it could not produce. The trouble was not in the land

Mrs. Coolidge and the President spent a day with Martha and Sam at the McKelvie summer home in the Black Hills and enjoyed an experimental panning for gold. Within a few days after this photograph was taken, President Coolidge made his famous pronouncement, "I do not choose to run."

but in the failure of those who worked the land to realize that as farmers they were more than producers. They were distributors also. They were in a business which demanded plans for marketing as well as plans for production.

The problem was a tough one, yet thousands of farmers, floored by the collapse of 1921, had picked themselves up and had begun the slow recovery. He admired their courage. It was the same kind of courage that had served his own parents so well. He never doubted for a moment its ability to bring prosperity to those who employed it. Their road was not easy. For a time their purchasing power would have to be limited to necessities, but in the end, they would win. They would have tractors and radios and milking machines, new cars and quality clothing. So, as he viewed it, the picture was not black.

Sam, however, had little patience with the few who refused to try to pick themselves up; the few who sat on their bottoms and cried for relief to be brought to them while they continued to sit. The worst of it was their wails were being echoed by certain political elements in both parties. He admitted that government had the responsibility to provide a healthy atmosphere to stimulate farm recovery. But government could not and should not try to take over the individual responsibility that belonged to the farmer. That was what some of the political criers were proposing. What provoked him most was a suspicion that some of the loudest talkers were interested first in their own political fortunes and only incidentally in the development of a sound agricultural economy.

He saw the danger of the situation. It was the same danger he had sensed when he had advised the Nebraska legislature not to try to remedy every ill with a new law. Government 131 dared not assume the role of a foolish mother who tried to forever boost and carry her children rather than have them learn to walk. Government should be like Jennie. It should see the importance of the board in the kitchen doorway and the necessity of having children strong enough to clamber over it.

Throughout the mid-twenties, Sam spoke his mind. His opportunities to speak it were more than plentiful. As a key figure in the establishment of the annual Republican Founders Day in Nebraska, his services were eagerly sought by Republicans in other states for similar celebrations. Advertising clubs wanted to hear him. He became president of the Lincoln Chamber of Commerce and an advisory official for the Boy Scouts of America. He worked hard at Republican party organization. He encouraged people who glimpsed the same threat to American democracy that he saw to become members of convention delegations: county, state, and national. His correspondence became a staggering burden; his travel schedules a complex problem.

But his message was simple and it was consistent. The words changed, but the text remained. In 1926 he wrote for *Nation's Business:*

"The disposition of the surplus is indeed an important problem for the farmer to solve, and when I say the farmer, I mean exactly that. It may be expedient for the government to try to solve it, but it certainly is not sound economically. The most the government can do is to help the sovereign citizen to help himself, bearing in mind that when the sovereignty is violated the citizen becomes a dependent, a mendicant, or what is worse, a member of a communistic state. . . .

132

"This farming is a business and the sooner we farmers find it out the sooner we will get our share of the national income."

His faith in farm co-operatives as a potent agricultural tool remained bright. A farm co-operative was run by farmers. It could be powerful and yet leave control with the farmers. He did his best to stress that essential difference between co-operatives and the government farm relief bureaus that some farm spokesmen proposed. He urged farmers to accept the necessity of changing their production and marketing methods and forget the illusion of being wet-nursed to a prosperous, productive life by federal statute.

A speech he made in Kansas City in 1927, clearly reflected his belief:

"When I was governor of Nebraska," he said, "I sponsored the enactment of a program of farm legislation drafted by representatives of 100 farm organizations. Those laws are on the books today but they did not keep the farm depression from coming into Nebraska. . . .

"I believe it is possible to apply to the farm the same methods of efficiency and control of production and distribution that are followed in the factory. A group of twenty farmers in Nebraska produced 75 bushels of corn to the acre by the applications of the principles of mass production where the farmers over a wide area were getting 26 bushels. . . . It is possible and necessary to control the total output of the farm. We must take these surplus lands out of production and conserve their fertility until it is needed."

The way Sam saw it, there was no need for farmers to consider business and industry as competitors. Some of the com- 133 mon talk then seemed predicated on a belief that business and industry were downright enemies of the farmer, seeking to strangle the life out of him. That was claptrap. He knew it and said so. The farmer, the business man, the industrialist were members of the all-American production team.

Sam could not support the McNary-Haugen legislation as it appeared in final form. It smacked too much of bureaucracy for him. He was certain it crossed the fence-line dividing the areas of responsibility that belonged on one hand to government, and on the other to the individual farmer.

Quickly he rallied to the support of President Coolidge's veto of the McNary-Haugen bill. It meant differing with some men he had come to admire; men like former Governor Lowden of Illinois. Lowden had pioneered the administrative code plan which Sam had followed zealously ten years earlier. But the question now was not one of friendships or loyalties. It was an issue of principle and it was not in Sam McKelvie to divorce himself from principles he believed in.

The climax came in early August of 1927. President and Mrs. Coolidge were vacationing in South Dakota and visited the summer home of Sam and Martha. It was then that the nation learned that Calvin Coolidge did not choose to run for the presidency in 1928. The magnitude of that news almost, but not quite, obscured other news. Between the lines of this second story the fact was revealed that Sam McKelvie had won his fight to keep the Republican administration from capitulating to the demands for farm relief handouts. Time magazine reported it:

134   "Members of the Rotary Club of Rapid City, S. Dak., took

luncheon seats one day last week, waited expectantly for onetime Governor Samuel McKelvie of Nebraska to address them on the topic of the beauty of the Black Hills. But Mr. McKelvie gave no beauty talk. Instead, he assailed onetime Governor Frank O. Lowden of Illinois for telling farmers that such federal organizations as the Interstate Commerce Commission and the Federal Reserve Banks were examples of what the government might, if so inclined, do for farmers. Mr. McKelvie was grieved to think that Mr. Lowden had supposed that farmers would like a federal commission poking into their affairs.

" 'The farmer,' he said, 'wants no governmental price-fixing on his products and he courts the minimum of state control of his affairs. . . . I can see the possibility, aye, the probability, of a system of co-operative marketing fostered by the government under which the farmer may retain his independence and initiative while working out his problems.'

"Newspaper correspondents were inclined to believe that Mr. McKelvie had become something in the nature of a White House spokesman. Last fortnight the President visited the McKelvie camp at Mystic, S. Dak., the only private invitation which President Coolidge has accepted. Mr. and Mrs. McKelvie were also the first overnight guests at the State Lodge. Also, Mr. McKelvie had been at the President's South Dakota Executive Office just before making his speech and was reported to have gone over it with Everett Sanders, Secretary of the President. . . ."

But Sam had not consulted with Sanders. After making the talk Sam feared the President might be charged with having authorized it. He hurried to the President's lodge to apologize. But Mr. Coolidge replied, "When you're wrong I'll let you know."

The months which followed telescoped into a furore of ac- 135 tivity for Sam McKelvie. He stood squarely for the nomination of Herbert Hoover. He planned and talked and traveled and wrote. He was no political novice now, but he battled not for a political faith, but for a firm personal principle. He saw the dignity of farm life, a life he knew so well, at stake. He fought to save it.

Though he had no time to think about it Sam knew it was, in a way, a lonely battle. As the tide swung his way, even before the National Republican Convention in Kansas City the following year, his name was mentioned frequently as one of the favored who surely would receive a luscious plum from the party's tree. There was talk that he would be vice president or secretary of agriculture.

Sam McKelvie was not interested in plums. He was striving to save a way of life. He said as much a few times but it was obvious his hearers either failed to understand or weighed his utterances as coming from the mouth of a smooth-operating political strategist. He did not blame them. They did not know what he knew. He knew he was sick. He knew, too, that medical treatment he had received in earlier years had, through unintentional error, worsened rather than helped his health.

The members of the Nebraska delegation at the Kansas City convention were jubilant. Herbert Hoover, whose nomination Sam had seconded as a spokesman for agriculture, wanted either Charles Curtis or McKelvie as his running mate. Curtis was refusing. He had agreed to think it over until morning; but he would refuse.

"Sam," they told him, "Sam, you're going to be Vice President of the United States!"

The next day they could not understand his good humor. Curtis had been prevailed upon finally to accept the nomination. The Nebraska delegation was dejected, but Sam McKelvie was remarkably chipper. They couldn't understand it. They shook their heads. Great campaigner, Sam.

When the election was over, Sam realized suddenly how tired he was and how miserable he felt. He and Martha went to Arizona. There he rested. It was there, too, on Valentine's Day, 1929, that he received the telephone call from President-elect Hoover. Would he accept the cabinet post? The President was asking him to become secretary of agriculture.

In the darkness he had coaxed sleep for so long that he was now too tense to expect it. Years ago sleep came almost as easily as breathing. You lay down and you slept. He remembered his father twitting him about sleeping in the corn. Didn't have to worry about Roy being afraid of work; he could sleep right beside it. Father had said that and he had felt the reproachful look of Mother Jennie. He wondered idly if Mother Jennie's antipathy for politics extended to positions in the president's cabinet. Well, no matter. He had turned it down. He was too sick to take it.

Sam spent the next several months in an attempt to rebuild his health. He and Martha had hoped that a rest in Arizona would be sufficient therapy. But Sam needed more than therapy to aid his recovery from an old x-ray burn. He went to the Johns Hopkins medical center for an operation and from there to the Black Hills to convalesce. It was there in July that he received a telephone call from Herbert Hoover. The President asked him again to accept a position this time on the Federal Farm Board as head of the grain division.

137

The President's request did not come as a complete surprise to Sam. Arthur M. Hyde, the Secretary of Agriculture, had suggested several times that Sam should seriously consider joining the Farm Board, a nine-member agency created by congress to deal with the crushing problem of agricultural surpluses and low farm prices. Repeatedly, Sam had excused himself on the grounds of frail health. The new request, however, was different. It came from the President; not only the President but from a man whom Sam respected as a great economist, statesman, and humanitarian.

Sam asked for twenty-four hours in which to decide and the next day he telegraphed his qualified acceptance. He would join the Board in September and serve until the following June.

Sam stayed with the Farm Board for two years. The assignment, sometimes discouraging to the point of frustration, nonetheless had its compensations. It allowed him to know better Herbert Hoover, an experience which deepened his respect and appreciation of the man; and it exposed him to the salty, determined Board chairman, Alexander Legg.

With his own political experience to use as a yardstick, it did not take Sam long to conclude that Herbert Hoover was no politician. Sam was inclined to agree with Henry Allen, former Kansas governor and later U. S. senator, that, politically, "The trouble with the Chief is that he always catches the ball on the second bounce."

The Farm Board, a child of Hoover's own farm program, gave the President political troubles. Its appropriation of a half-billion dollars was forever a target of private interest 138 representatives, many of them Republican, who fired at

Sam's service on the Federal Farm Board demanded his presence at the World Wheat Conference in London in 1928. He is seated second from the left.

Hoover as a "spendthrift" executive. In later years Sam recalled with some bitterness that Hoover's administration was assailed in the 1932 campaign by Franklin D. Roosevelt for irresponsible spending and that the public generally seemed not to mind at all that in the four years after Hoover left the White House expenditures and national indebtedness were more than doubled.

When Sam retired from the Farm Board in June of 1931, the federal government owned almost 200 million bushels of wheat. The Board had tried to get rid of it by any justifiable means short of dumping it on the American market. Some was sold as flour in foreign countries; some traded to Brazil for coffee; and some sent to China and Europe under plans which resulted in little, if any, financial return. Despite these efforts, however, the surplus remained a giant astride the back of American agriculture.

As he prepared to leave the Board, Sam suggested to the President that the tremendous supply of wheat be turned over to some charitable agency for distribution to the needy at home who were feeling the increasing weight of the Depression. The humanitarian aspect of Sam's proposal obviously appealed to Hoover. Eventually, however, he shook his head. Such a move, he said, would only depress prices for the producer and interfere with a recovery of the normal distribution processes. Sam threw in another argument.

"If you don't permit it now," he said, "the next congress will do it anyway and there will be no political credit in that for you."

But President Hoover was unimpressed. He remained so even when Sam tried a final argument born of desperation. 141

Sam pointed out that in effect American wheat was being given to foreign countries whose people, as he put it, were less worthy to receive the benefits than were Americans whose nation had produced the grain.

In a way, Sam was glad the President remained firm. It proved, he felt, Herbert Hoover's unselfishness of purpose and his devotion to a system of commerce which had built a great America. And also, Sam smiled, it proved again that Herbert Hoover was no politician. He simply did not understand the rules of the game.

Unlike the President, the chairman of the Farm Board, was forever alert to political implications. He understood full well that the birth of his agency in the Agricultural Marketing Act was something difficult for farmers to understand. The job of the Board, as many saw it, amounted to governmental interference with private enterprise. The Board was suspect in many minds and Alexander Legg knew it.

Sam never forgot the incident of the market ticker. The Board member heading the cotton division had found it difficult to keep up with market changes by constant use of the telephone, and, innocently enough, had ordered a ticker installed in his office. During the course of a meeting, Chairman Legg asked for information on the cotton market, and the division director said he could supply it at once. "I've got a ticker in the office," he said.

"My God!" Alexander Legg cried, "Do you want the public to think we're running a bucket shop here?"

In the early 1930s, a ticker to millions of people was the symbol of market speculation. It was removed from the Board office.

142

Sam appreciated Chairman Legg as an earnest, energetic, and sincere leader of American agriculture. He was willing to follow Legg's directions, though he was reluctant to push for performance of Legg's policy that crop acreages be drastically reduced.

"I did not concur enthusiastically in that," Sam wrote some years later. "I had been reared on the rim of the prairie where acreage was not as important as rain. Full granaries meant more to us than price. Father fed wheat to his Poland China hogs when the corn crop was short, as it frequently was."

Early in his tenure on the Board, Sam was sent by Chairman Legg on a tour of the northwest wheat country to preach the need for reduced acreages. But once he was on the circuit, Sam felt again the urge to speak sincerely of his old love, the farm co-operative movement. At meeting after meeting he ground away on the need for co-operative marketing. Somehow, it seemed there was never quite time to speak many words in behalf of acreage reduction. His words were heeded; at least by the national press services. Midway through the tour, he received a telegram from Alexander Legg. Its message was simple: "Your case is hopeless."

The Board, with its half-billion dollars to use, did aim, among other things, to encourage the growth of co-operative marketing units among farmers. But its real objective was to keep surplus farm products—wheat and cotton mainly—from reaching the glutted market until natural demand could stabilize a worthy price.

The natural demand never developed. The great economic depression of the early 1930's choked it off. The workers of business and industry—members of the two social orders which 143 some had described as enemies of the farmers—were now without so much as grocery money. The bottom dropped out of the farm market and in the rising confusion of dust and drouth, Sam McKelvie saw a way of life go down; a way of life he had loved from the top of his straw hat to the bottom of his bare toes as a boy on Sandy Creek.

He renewed the fight as best he could and participated in the 1936 campaign for Alf M. Landon but his political weather sense told him it was an exercise and no more. The 1940 campaign interested him not at all. In 1944 the spark of his old enthusiasm returned briefly. He met a fellow Nebraskan at the Chicago convention, a young, balding man, Herbert Brownell. At Brownell's request, he agreed to serve as midwestern campaign chairman with offices in Chicago. Governor Dewey, the Republican nominee, and Mrs. Dewey were guests at the McKelvie's By The Way ranch. For a few brief weeks, Sam felt that this might be it. The party at the ranch certainly was like old times. The way the ranchmen talked was encouraging. Yes, this might be it. But it wasn't.

There could be no doubt in 1948. Sam told himself that over and over again. Yet, somehow, aside from the excitement of meeting old friends at the convention, he could not generate within himself the urgency of the issue. The issue? Men spoke of many issues now. Foreign policy. Aid for Europe. Aid for Asia. Labor. Spending. Sometimes the Farm was mentioned, but only sometimes.

He did not bother to make the trip to Chicago in the summer of 1952. He watched the proceedings on television in Lincoln, first with a show of enthusiasm, then as an analyst.

144   Long before the closing sessions, Sam McKelvie quit the tele-

vision and headed for the ranch. He knew the symptoms of a
boom in the making. General Eisenhower would be elected.
He was as sure of that as he was that Highway No. 2 was the
road to the ranch. The Party would win. A Republican administration in power once more. He laughed shortly, almost
harshly. He had doubted that he would live to see the day. He
should be elated. He was a Republican. Well, he did feel
better. But he was not elated. Try as he would, he could see
nothing rising from the dust. The fields were there along the
roadside, and the cattle and the crops. They were there. But
the line that separated the individual from the crowd; it was
gone.

CHAPTER NINE

SANDHILLER AND HEREFORD BREEDER

OUTSIDE THE BIG COLISEUM of the Denver Stockyards a light January snow was drifting lazily down. Inside the big building, in a huge rising amphitheater surrounding a brightly lighted show ring, rows of interested, Stetson-hatted spectators watched intently as the judge carefully examined each of forty calves lined up before him. It was an important night in the Western National Livestock Show of 1934.

First one calf, then another, was moved from its place to the head of the line. Finally the judge came to the last calf in the line—a nicely fitted native red and white-faced Hereford. After examining it fore and aft he motioned the handler to move it to first place in the line. And there the animal stayed. He had won first in his class in one of America's foremost Hereford judging shows.

147

The owner of the calf broke into smiles as his friends gathered about him with congratulatory handshakes. It was Sam McKelvie's first victory in the purebred beef cattle show ring, but far from his last. For, as Sam told a friend later, "Boy, when that judge picked my calf for first place after all that suspense I was vaccinated for this cattle judging business for life." And he was.

Livestock judging was nothing new in Sam McKelvie's life. He had seen his father win state and national prizes many times with his swine and Red Polled cattle. But this was different. Sam was now soloing in the livestock business; his first association with it since he left the farm thirty-four years ago. And now he was in the cattle business for himself. But unlike his purposefulness in becoming a farm paper publisher, his entry into ranching was roundabout.

When Sam was governor, he and Martha bought a summer cottage near Mystic in the Black Hills of South Dakota, and used it as a retreat to escape the press of public life.

When autumn arrived each year, though, Sam's thoughts turned inevitably to Nebraska's Sandhills. It was there that ducks and grouse abounded. Sam visited the Sandhills year after year and something besides game birds began to capture his mind and his heart. Here was raw beauty. Vast stretches of rolling hills covered everywhere with a thick carpet of native grasses. Dozens of small lakes in the picturesque valleys. Here was virgin prairie, lonely, awesome. Man's presence was marked by dusty trails, by barbed-wire fences, by great herds of white-faced cattle, by windmills sentinel-like, and sometimes by a nest of ranch buildings.

148   Here, too, was loneliness. Great space which made a man

At By The Way Ranch, Sam liked to give his "white-faced bossies" considerable attention.

aware of his dependence upon his neighbors, friendly, open-faced people who accepted a man for what he is. Here, Sam understood why a man is awed by the marvels of his Creator when he tramps through the spring grass sparkling with morning dew, or smells the sweet pungence of freshly-mowed hay, or watches the pintails sweep southward against a leaden sky, or hears the moan of a blizzard.

Thoughts of the Sandhills were frequently with Sam and in the autumn of 1930 he invited other members of the Federal Farm Board to meet him there for a hunting trip. For various reasons the invitations had to be declined but Sam refused to abandon his plans.

"None of the boys on the board can come out for the hunting," Sam informed Martha one evening. "Guess who's going with me instead."

"Who?" she asked.

"You," said Sam.

Together they spent a week in the Sandhills. Sam had never had a better time. As one day melted into another, his pleasure seemed to increase instead of wane. It occurred to him, then, that perhaps this was not such fun for Martha after all. She probably was merely doing her utmost to help him enjoy an outing she thought he deserved.

At last the holiday ended, and they were enroute to Lincoln. It was on the fifty-mile trail road from the Ben Bachelor ranch to Valentine that they topped the hill. Below them spread a broad green valley. The sweep of green was broken by a lake, crystal-blue beneath the bright October sky. Near its shore a few old ranch buildings huddled before a grove of trees, alive with reds and yellows from the frost.

151

Sam slowed the car without thinking, lost in the view and the contentment he felt.

"You know, Sam," he heard Martha's voice, "I had no idea how beautiful the Sandhills can be. If we had a place as pretty as this, we could have our summer home here in Nebraska."

If the car gained speed, it was because Sam saw a green light in his mind's eye. A Sandhills home! He had dreamed of it and now Martha was saying she wanted it too.

Within a few days Sam learned that the ranch by the lake was owned by George Christopher, a Sandhiller who was willing to sell. Within three months, in January of 1931, Sam bought the place, all 3,000 acres of it.

The first year Sam rented out the hayland but during the summer he decided to start a small commercial cattle business. The summer of 1931 began the drouth which was to extend itself into six years. Cattlemen in South Dakota saw their ranges withering in the hot sun and dry winds. That was why one of them was more than interested when Sam said he had come to buy cattle for his new place in the Sandhills whose unique underground water supply kept the lakes filled and the grass green. The discouraged rancher offered Sam one hundred cows with ninety-five calves, forty two-year-old heifers, and two bulls, all registered Herefords, for $7,000. And so the drouth put Sam McKelvie in the purebred Hereford business.

During the next three years Sam and Martha began to build "By The Way." This was the name Martha suggested they give the old Christopher ranch, and also the name of Sam's column in The Nebraska Farmer. And they changed the brand, too, from Bar TW to Via. And for By The Way, they

152

built a new house, a place not far from the lake's edge, patterned after Sam's childhood home in Clay County.

Though the name of Sam McKelvie was familiar to many Sandhills cattlemen when he purchased the ranch in 1931, they soon recognized that here was an unusual neighbor. Not long after he moved in he began to tell them that the Sandhills was endowed by nature to become one of the world's greatest beef cattle producing regions. Sandhills cattlemen, he said, should work together to improve the quality of their cattle and to let the nation's markets know that their cattle are tops. The first task was to capture the interest of the feeders who, for no reason that Sam could see, favored cattle from Texas. For a man but three years in the cattle business, some said, this was big talk. But Sam persisted. And they listened.

Others listened too. In 1934 Sam was elected to a three-year term on the Board of Directors of the American Hereford Association. He was re-elected. Then he was named president. And then he served two more terms as a member of the Board. During his tenure on the Board, the Association established a $4,000,000 trust fund and built a half-million-dollar headquarters building in Kansas City. But more important to him, the Association launched a vigorous research program aimed at making Hereford cattle the best source of beef in the nation.

In 1937 Sam's ability to analyze a problem, plan a solution and get support for it, got another test. It was that year that eastern housewives went on a buyers' strike against the high price of beef. They made their protests felt in the market place. Prices dropped. Sam and his neighbors soon could get no more than six dollars per hundred-weight for their yearling steers. Good beef was worth more, and they knew it. 153

The Sandhills cattlemen were discouraged. In the spring of 1938 they met in Valentine. Again it was Sam McKelvie who had something to say.

"Dammit, gentlemen," Sam told them, "we've got the best cattle in the country. Let's blow our own horn. We've got to let everybody know that this is God's Own Cow Country!"

The cattlemen came from the meeting with a new name for their region and a new association with Sam as president, a position he was to hold for ten years.

The purposes of The Sandhills Cattle Association were set forth in McKelvie style: "The association is organizing for the purpose of advertising, popularizing, improving the quality and aiding in the sale of Sandhills feeder cattle; maintaining a code of ethics between buyers and sellers thereof; promoting a spirit of cooperation, friendship and desire to produce a mutual type of cattle in this region."

The Association's first project was publication of a bulletin which Sam took on almost singlehandedly. It listed the names of all Association members, the number of cattle each had for sale, the breed, sex, age, and brand of the cattle, and the location of every member's ranch. The bulletin was mailed to eight thousand persons who were connected in one way or another with the feeding or marketing of cattle. The results were startling. Moreover they were profitable. More buyers and feeders began to take second looks at Sandhills cattle.

The Association Bulletin was here to stay. Today, its annual edition goes to 20,000 feeders and marketers, and each Association member gets its newsletter twice a month. Scores of buyers come each summer to the Sandhills. A free guide service helps them to locate any ranch they wish to visit in the

154

20,000 square miles of the Sandhills region. The continued increase of interest from visiting buyers set in motion a competitive drive among the ranchers to produce better quality animals. Their efforts are reflected in the fact that frequently Sandhills cattle bring a premium on the market.

As the reputation of Sandhills cattle became widely known, so did Sam's reputation as a Hereford (he gives the word a Scotch inflection so that it comes out Hairford, not Hurferd) breeder. By The Way grew to a 6,000-acre layout, with five houses, twenty-three pastures, and a sales barn, complete with show ring and seats for 800 buyers and spectators. Characteristically, Sam had set a goal for himself in the cattle business, and made it.

There may have been some eyebrows raised when Sam plunged into the cattle business. Another "suitcase rancher"? It was true that a good many years had passed since Sam left the home place in Clay County. In the intervening years he had spent most of his life in the city. But to Sam buying the ranch was perfectly natural. Cattle raising was in his blood. As a youngster on his father's farm he had seen the rewards attached to the hard labor of raising purebred livestock. From the time he left the farm Sam kept hoping that someday he could buy his own place and get into the livestock business.

His opportunity had come in 1931, and he claimed it with the same enthusiasm he had shown in politics and the publishing business. He was not bashful about asking questions and learned all he could from his neighbors. He read everything he could get his hands on about cattle breeds, feeding practices and management. He traveled Nebraska, to the big national livestock shows, and to the ranches of breeders in   155 many states, exchanging ideas on cattle raising. Sam's enthusiasm bubbled at a furious rate. Cattle raising became an almost exclusive preoccupation. Publisher McKelvie had left Lincoln. Rancher Sam was at By The Way.

Sam had known all along that raising purebred cattle is hard work, patience-trying and demanding. He well remembered from his boyhood the agony of rolling from a comfortable bed to make his way to the farrowing barn to help his father. What was it old Frank Kowalk, the hired man, used to say? "I'd as well trade my bed for a lantern." When you deal in pure-breds—hogs or cattle—you can afford no risks. His father had drummed that into him and, it was, Sam knew, all too true. But dealing in purebreds paid.

The herd he purchased in South Dakota was a carefully developed purebred line. Sam appreciated that. Still, he had a choice. He could run them as high-grade commercial cattle, or he could improve the breed. The former would be easier but the pedigrees would lapse. Sam shook his head. He couldn't do it. He became a purebred Hereford breeder.

Times were tough but he went ahead. He was determined to build a herd of which he would be proud. He took the first important step in the fall of 1932. At the famous American Royal Livestock Show in Kansas City he bought for $500 a yearling Hereford. A fine animal he had selected with care. His name was Mary's Bocaldo, purchased from Robert H. Hazlett, a highly successful Hereford breeder from Oklahoma, later of Kansas. Sam was a great admirer of the Hazlett-type Herefords. They were deep and thick, exceptionally uniform in conformation, quality, and color, factors which helped give them a reputation as "the easy-feeding Bocaldos."

156

During the next two years Sam bought two more bulls carrying the Hazlett bloodlines. At the Denver livestock show of 1934 his judgment of the Hazlett line was confirmed. It was there that his calf, sired by Mary's Bocaldo, won first prize and gave him his first big thrill in the show ring.

There's probably not another occupational group in America where a man can stir up an argument quicker than among cattle breeders. A question that will keep cattlemen arguing all night is the role a good bull plays in the quality of a registered herd. Here Sam took what he called a "common sense" stand. "Sure," he said, "a bull is important to a herd, but so's the cow. When I buy I want to see the mother and father."

At about this point in the discussion Sam reminded his fellow Hereford breeders that they are mainly in business to produce economically first-rate beefsteaks for the tables of hungry Americans. And, as the discussion went on, Sam said that breeders can go too far in trying to achieve the "perfect bull"— an animal which Sam contended probably will never exist. Let's stay with basic principles, Sam said, and forget about breeding animals for the fine points of nose, neck, eyes, length, color, and the like. "The first thing we know," Sam grinned, "we will have bred ourselves right out of the market in our struggle to refine the breed."

From the start, Sam was impressed by the Hereford's ruggedness and ability to graze and make the most of whatever feed was available. He learned that Herefords were prolific because of the natural desire of the bulls to stay with the herd and the ability of the cows to bear and protect their calves in all kinds of weather. Herefords, under anything like favorable conditions, save 90 to 95 per cent of their calf crop.

157

Sam learned, too, that the coming of Herefords to western ranges had reduced the time for marketing off grass by one-half. And when Herefords leave the range they will respond readily to the fattening diets of the feedlots. There were other points. To anyone who would listen Hereford-Breeder McKelvie ticked them off. It was a Hereford, for instance, that was the first two-year-old grand champion steer at the Chicago livestock show, a victory which signaled the end of the larger, older steers and paved the way for lighter carcasses and smaller cuts of meat. Hereford superiority isn't confined to the show ring, Sam added. At all the nation's big livestock markets Herefords customarily top the market. The reason is obvious. Packers find, Sam said, Herefords second to none in losses from dressing. Well, of course, there are other breeds of cattle that are good, too, Sam admitted with a smile. But, well, those Herefords—they can really take it.

Sam was unrestrained in recommending the purebred cattle business—the Hereford kind, that is—to young men. But he mixed his words of encouragement with caution. A first requisite is an understanding interest and love for the business. A second is acceptance of the extra work involved in understanding breeds, feeds, and care in handling animals for sale or show ring. For selling, he recommended the auction ring for it is here that the stable values of the cattle are reflected and it is here where cattle, "if they are good enough will bring enough." A third requisite is breeding animals designed to do a good job of producing beef, both on the range and in the feedlot. And finally, build your herd slowly and carefully. Probably with a backward glance at the fabulous cattle prices 158 prevailing in the years following the end of World War II,

Sam admitted at the opening of his dispersion sale that he was
saddened at the thought of closing out his purebred herd.

Sam pointed out that this is not a get-rich-quick business. "If you build right you can live through the good times and the bad," he counseled.

Shortly after the end of World War II, Rancher McKelvie began reluctantly to accept the inevitability of his favorite dictum: You can't keep a registered herd and not be on the job. Sam was on the job at By The Way less and less. He had found a "second home" in the bright winter sunshine of Arizona. Near Mesa, Sam and Martha purchased an irrigated ranch, Rancho por el Camino, and it is here that they spend their winters while the snow piles deep in the Sandhills. But when spring restored the green beauty to the grasses of "God's Own Cow Country," Sam and Martha would move northward for the summer.

It became apparent to Sam that he could not stay away so much and still do justice to the management of his "White Face Bossies." But it was with some reluctance that he contemplated a dispersion sale. Finally the date was set, the handsome catalog printed, and the ranch readied for the scores of buyers, friends, and neighbors who came to the sale July 2, 1953.

Sam mounted the auctioneer's rostrum in the sale barn he knew so well, and explained, his voice choked with emotion:

"Our herd has been built for practical beef production purposes. The larger percentage of our bulls have been bought by ranchers for commercial purposes. We could not ask for a better recommendation, especially since these customers come back year after year.

"Too, our breeding herd is grown and handled on the range. Their ration is mostly grazing and hay. All but a few of the offer- 161 ing today come through the sale ring off grass. Just let 'em go on good grazing and hay, salt and minerals, plus a protein supplement and they will take care of themselves.

"It is with considerable emotion that we see our cattle leave us. We are confident that they will find good homes. That will make us very happy."

Then the familiar cry of the auctioneer's chant rang through the sales pavilion. With the final rap of the gavel, 327 Herefords had been sold to buyers from the Dakotas, Nebraska, Minnesota, Iowa, Montana, Oregon, Oklahoma, California, Kentucky and Arizona. It was one of the largest sales of its kind in the history of Nebraska's cattle industry.

It's natural for a Sandhills ranch and cattle to go together. So it came as no surprise when Sam announced later in July, 1953, that he had sold By The Way for approximately $200,000. The purchasers were Wilbur Drybread, a long-time neighbor and friend, who acquired 4,467 acres; and Ralph Baker, also a cowman neighbor, who acquired 461 acres. A provision in the sale terms was that Sam and Martha would continue to live in the ranch home as long as they wished.

"We had many opportunities to sell," Sam said, "but that was not enough. We wanted By The Way to continue to be the home of Herefords—good registered Herefords. Here at the ranch they can be produced, grown out, exhibited and marketed to the four winds as has been our tradition.

"What could be more natural than to turn over the care of By The Way to the Drybreads and the Bakers? They are genuine cattle folks. The fervent prayers of Martha and me were answered. The McKelvies will continue to live and enjoy the beauty and serenity of our wonderful Sandhills home!"

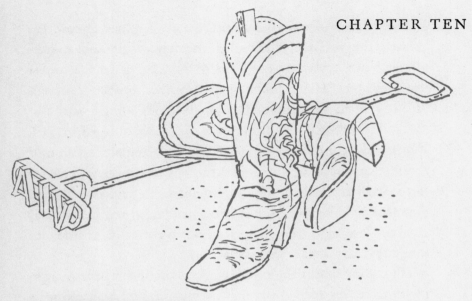

CHAPTER TEN

A SUMMING UP

THE LEATHER-COVERED DAVENPORT was comfortable and the living room with all its familiar objects remained inviting but even in combination they were no match for the September sunlight.

Sam put his magazine aside. It was a news publication and usually such papers held his interest and this one had for a time. The picture of the President fishing in Colorado stirred recollections of another President who fished in South Dakota. Idly, he had turned to a section devoted to foreign affairs and begun to read something about the struggle in the Middle East. Four times his eyes covered the words of one paragraph but only the caption, "Ingredients for Success," reached his mind. He did not want to read. He wanted to be outside. It was then that he closed the magazine and stood up.   163

The afternoon was golden in the early September sun. He crossed the veranda, descended the few steps, and walked along the concrete path, through the yard gate where the vines awaited the first touch of frost, and on toward the small lake so blue in its setting of the grassy, gently rolling sandhills.

Slowly, without demanding purpose, he continued to walk through the meadow. Across the lake he could see a dozen or so Herefords grazing, their noses to the wind. As he walked he noted with satisfaction the tufts of bluestem here and there, a sign that By The Way was in good hands and not being over-grazed. The new owner, he was certain, would handle the range and haylands successfully.

He paused where the meadow, breaking toward the margin of the lake, revealed a sloping bank of sand. The high heels of his cowman's boots submerged in the loose, white sand and he stopped to marvel as always at this strange soil which seemed so dry and yet was capable of supporting the lush grass of, as he had often put it, "God's Own Cow Country." He picked up a handful of the sand from the bank. It was clean and warm, like the light of the sun itself. He eased to a sitting position and allowed the sand to sift through his fingers.

When a man fingered sand like that he would swear it could grow nothing. It did not meet the specifications man established for productive soil. It did not adhere. It did not ball. It did not smell like good soil. And yet it was the soil of perhaps the richest cattle-producing region in North America.

Hidden somewhere in these musings, he knew, was the germ of a basic lesson he had learned. The lesson had to do with man on one hand and nature on the other: man with his instinctive desire to live and prosper, and nature with her laws which he must obey. Men excited and eager in their quest had put the plow to soil like this. If it could grow lush grasses, should it not also grow grain which they desired even more than grass? On the strength of such reasoning men had sought to substitute their will for nature's. The alchemists, not satisfied with lead, had wanted gold. The speculators, ill-content with grass, had wanted wheat. What a capricious dictator nature must seem to them; what a dull, stupid, unrelenting, vindictive, uncompromising dictator.

There had been times, Sam admitted, when he, too, had been clutched by such cynicism. There were times, during his service on the Farm Board, when he had resented the abundance of nature. Too much wheat. Too much cotton. Too much? How could there be too much in the world when some people were still hungry and others were clothed in rags? How could there be too much when next year, or the next, in the scheme of things, the grain would wither to nothing in drouth, or be washed away in flood?

For the gambler and the speculator who counted upon a few turns of the cards or the plow to bring them wealth for a lifetime, nature indeed must appear capricious: too much one year; not enough the next. Yet, it was this very uncertainty that prompted them to gamble and speculate. If they wished to try their luck, nature was willing to spin the wheel. All she asked was that the house rules be observed, rules by which only a few won while many lost. If they wished to tear her grasslands with their plows, let them try. They would learn the price by trying.

But nature's plan, as he had come to know it, was not contrived for the gamblers. It was made for the steady, humble,   165 and courageous ones; those willing to sow and reap with the seasons. The rules of nature, as he had come to understand them, operated in favor of those who, like nature herself, were more interested in the fulfillment of needs than in clever manipulations for profit.

His mind returned to the early spring day during the drouth years when he had seen from the road the modest crib of corn in the wind-swept farmyard. It was a time when Sam needed corn and was willing to pay for it. He turned into the farm. The house was small and square and white and from the kitchen door a walk of planks extended past the pump to the chicken shed. He left his car and was met at the porch door by a farmer whose face was still tanned and forehead white from last season's dusty and discouraging field work.

The corn was not for sale. The farmer was pleasant about it. He admitted he needed the money but added that he would rather have the corn.

"Kind of a principle with me," the farmer had said. "I never wipe everything off the place until I see what next year brings."

That principle, Sam knew, explained why on the farm he had seen a small flock of chickens and noted a few pigs in the lot at a time when most farms housed little but heavy mortgages. He was aware, too, he had talked with a man who not only understood that in nature's pattern adversity is almost as normal as abundance, but who also possessed a faith unknown to the speculator. The mark of toil was on him unmistakably, but his eyes were clear and deep and no bitterness was in them. He was a man who accepted nature's offer of partnership and received in return not only a share of life's physical comforts but an abiding dignity as well.

Sam marveled at, and loved, this Sandhills country whose doubtful-looking soil produced lush grasses, fine cattle, and a respect for the Almighty.

Where did such men learn their economics? Their philosophy? Their code of conduct? Not in school because there were such men in almost every wagon that pushed westward ahead of schools. Born with it? He doubted that. Born with a trust, perhaps, but a trust in the arms that held them as babes, not a faith in an unseen power whose sand might be a sterile desert or a productive cattle country.

He wished he could talk again to that farmer in the small white house, ask him where he learned his principle. In his imagination he sought to picture such a meeting. Where did I learn it? The farmer would repeat the question. Well, back home my father used to say . . .

Back home. His own first recollection was of a board in the kitchen doorway which blocked him from the wonders of the world beyond. There must have been times when he resented that board; when he sat and cried for strong arms to lift him over it; cried for hands to gently set him on the other side where again he would have had to cry for further help. But strong arms did not lift him. Help of that sort had no place in Mother Jennie's scheme of things, nor in Father's. Theirs was a code of first things first. First you proved that you were capable of climbing the board. First you worked; then you enjoyed the harvest of your effort, enjoyed it and used it to conquer new barriers. In the process you learned basic rules. The first was work. It was work to clamber over the board, and unless you worked you did not get over it. And once the lesson of work was understood, there were other rules to master. Like thrift. You did not eat all the apples at harvest time. You stored and saved some for the long winter nights. Like buckwheat, too. Some you sold, and some you saved for seed.

169

How simple the lessons of home, yet how difficult mastery of them had seemed. He recalled the shoes, the ones he had seen in the Fairfield store. Black and shiny they were with bright strips of brass across the toes. So different from the dull, heavy leather of the farm boots Father always bought for them. Momentarily he was a boy once more, pleading with Mother Jennie, pleading tearfully for the shoes and reluctantly she was yielding. He felt again the thrill of holding the treasured cardboard box on his knees during the journey from town but even clearer in his memory was Father's stern order to return the shoes and exchange them for boots serviceable in the hog lot and the corn fields . . . and bring back the difference in cash. The bitter exchange, he understood now, had not been prompted by a father's unmindfulness of a son's desire, but rather by an unpretentious, rock-like devotion to the tenets of a way of life.

And what of that way of life? What had been its dividends? Only the heartache of a young mother who longed to leave the choking dust of the prairie and return to the security of an earlier home in Illinois? Only the bone-weary stumblings through a few years of work and saving and work again? Sam shook his head. No. Out of that way of life had come a material prosperity: a dugout had become a house; a house a comfortable home. Out of that way of life a few acres had become many acres, and the harvests therefrom had helped many people build many things. But more important, out of that way of life had come young people, owners of determination and faith, and equipped to make their ways independent and unafraid.

170   Another handful of sand drifted through his fingers. Maybe

A proud moment for Sam came in 1951 when Chancellor R. G.
Gustavson on behalf of the University of Nebraska conferred upon
him the honorary degree, Doctor of Agriculture.

it was the way of life some described as rugged individualism. Perhaps. But did it have to have a label? Labels are read with such variation. Rugged individualism could be an almost fanatical desire to work and save and drive ahead without interference or help from the contrivances of other men. That concept implied a lone-wolf, predatory existence which certainly did not attach to the family life he knew. His father was no lone wolf. Other men sought his council, his friendship, and respected his judgment. Other men had paid him honor, at the University, for instance. Some of the men were old, some young, but alike they paused to pay him honor, as they had Sam himself.

No. The label was inadequate. An individual was one; a solitary figure; a lone operator. His father had not worked alone. He worked in partnership with nature. He understood that nature had her rules and habits and he was willing to respect and trust them and plan his own life accordingly. He had been willing, with nature, to husband the bounty of the good harvest, husband it wisely, for use when no harvest was to be had. He had placed his faith, not in the year-to-year outlines that men sketched sometimes on paper, but in the eternal scheme of nature whose plan manifests itself forever in the various seasons and soils.

Trust in the eternal scheme of nature. That might be the heart of the way of life that had given him his ambition, his code, his equipment, and, yes, his opportunities. It might be it. Would his farm friend in the little white house agree with that? A partnership with nature. Yes, he probably would. Knowledge of the partnership was his heritage. He would agree. And Father. Would he agree? He might. Yes, of course he would. And Mother Jennie. Certainly she would have an interest in this discussion. What would she say?

He stared at the white sand that looked so sterile but had proved so fertile. He could not recall Mother Jennie ever having said much about nature. Was she aware of a partnership with nature? Her hands were forever busy. She worked with purpose and with confidence as though she were certain of the outcome. Was it her partnership with nature that kept her from despair? Slowly Sam shook his head. Not a partnership with nature; a partnership with God. Nature to Jennie might be an agent but her partner was her God. The heart of the way of life she knew had a sweetness about it, a depth that carried beyond sowing and reaping, working and saving; it included a dignity and a soul. It explained the absence of bitterness in the eyes of those who awaited a new season as a new opportunity and prepared for its coming. It explained, too, Sam's contentment as he brushed crumbs of white sand from his hips, as he arose and walked, a little stiffly from sitting, through his Partner's meadow toward the lengthening shadows of home.

"AS WE JOURNEY THROUGH LIFE
LET US LIVE BY THE WAY."

This book was designed, printed, and bound at

The Lakeside Press, R. R. Donnelley & Sons Company

Chicago, Illinois, and Crawfordsville, Indiana

Nicoll, Bruce Hilton, 1912-
     Sam McKelvie, son of the soil: sketch of a
self-reliant American who cheerfully fought his
own battles, by Bruce H. Nicoll and Ken R. Keller.
With a foreward by Clarence Budington Kelland.
Lincoln, Neb., Johnsen Pub. Co., 1954.
     174p. illus. 25cm. (Nebraska heritage
  series)

1.McKelvie, Samuel Roy, 1881-   I.Keller, Kenneth Richt-
meyer, 1910-   joint auth   II.Title.
2.Nebraska-History.

Dear Lisa ~

Congratulations! Your name was drawn in our "Thought Leaders Book Lottery" at the PMRG AGM.

We hope this book can help you solve some market research issues you are confronting.

Karen Ahlgrin

P.S. A member of our health care team wrote one of the chapters in this book. She would be assigned as your account manager.

Branding Health Services

Defining Yourself in the Marketplace

Edited by

Gil Bashe

Chief Executive Officer
Health!Quest Global Communication Partners
Metuchen, New Jersey

Formerly
Group Company CEO
CommonHealth Worldwide
Parsippany, New Jersey

Nancy J. Hicks

Senior Managing Director
and
Co-Director of the US Health Provider Practice
Hill and Knowlton
Washington, DC

Project Editor

Amy Ziegenfuss

Marketing Coordinator
Henry M. Jackson Foundation
for the Advancement of Military Medicine
Rockville, Maryland

AN ASPEN PUBLICATION®
Aspen Publishers, Inc.
Gaithersburg, Maryland
2000

Library of Congress Cataloging-in-Publication Data

Branding health services: defining yourself in the marketplace/edited by Gil Bashe, Nancy J. Hicks; project editor, Amy Ziegenfuss.
p. cm.
Includes index.
ISBN 0-8342-1175-0
1. Medical care—United States—Marketing. 2. Corporate image. 3. Brand name products. I. Bashe, Gil. II. Hicks, Nancy J. III. Ziegenfuss, Amy.
[DNLM: 1. Marketing of Health Services—methods. 2. Names. 3. Product Line Management. W 74 B818 2000]
362.1'068'8—dc21
99-088085

Orders: (800) 638-8437
Customer Service: (800) 234-1660

About Aspen Publishers • For more than 40 years, Aspen has been a leading professional publisher in a variety of disciplines. Aspen's vast information resources are available in both print and electronic formats. We are committed to providing the highest quality information available in the most appropriate format for our customers. Visit Aspen's Internet site for more information resources, directories, articles, and a searchable version of Aspen's full catalog, including the most recent publications: **www.aspenpublishers.com**
Aspen Publishers, Inc. • The hallmark of quality in publishing
Member of the worldwide Wolters Kluwer group.

Editorial Services: Ruth Bloom
Library of Congress Catalog Card Number: 99-088085
ISBN: 0-8342-1175-0

Printed in the United States of America

1 2 3 4 5

This book is dedicated to the memory of **Jack S. Hardy**, *leader and mentor to public relations professionals across the country. His extensive experience in health care marketing and communications made him one of the most admired practitioners in the field. The compassion, intelligence, and courage that Jack demonstrated still resonate today through the work of his colleagues and throughout the pages of this book.*

Thank you, Jack, for your support and friendship.

Table of Contents

Contributors

Donna L. Arbogast
President
Crofton Communications
Crofton, Maryland

Gil Bashe
CEO
Health!Quest Global Communication
    Partners
Metuchen, New Jersey
Formerly, Group Company CEO,
    CommonHealth
Parsippany, New Jersey

Carol Bloomberg
Director of Marketing
Johns Hopkins Medicine
Baltimore, Maryland

Shirley Bonnem
Vice President, Administration
The Children's Hospital of Philadelphia
Philadelphia, Pennsylvania

Cynthia Currence
National Vice President, Strategic
    Marketing & Branding
American Cancer Society
National Home Office
Atlanta, Georgia

Steven D. Dickinson
Senior Vice President
GCI Healthcare
Atlanta, Georgia

Elaine Freeman
Executive Director
Communications and Public Affairs
Johns Hopkins Medicine
Baltimore, Maryland

Nancy J. Hicks
Senior Managing Director
Co-Director of the U.S. Health Provider
    Practice
Hill and Knowlton
Washington, DC

Neil A. Johnston
Managing Director
Enterprise IG Health
Parsippany, New Jersey

Joel G. Lee
Executive Director
Medical Center Communications
Vanderbilt University Medical Center
Nashville, Tennessee

Robin Liszewski
Director of Communications
Scripps
San Diego, California

Tony Swartz Lloyd
Special Counsel to Corporate
  Communications
CareGroup, Inc.
Boston, Massachusetts

Wayne L. Pines
President
  Regulatory Services and Health Care
  APCO Associates Inc.
Washington, DC

Hal E. Quinley
Executive Vice President
Yankelovich Partners, Inc.
Claremont, California

Joann Rodgers
Deputy Director, Media Relations Director
Communications and Public Affairs
Johns Hopkins Medicine
Baltimore, Maryland

Martin B. Rosen
Chief Communications Officer
Aetna U.S. Healthcare
Blue Bell, Pennsylvania

Deborah C. Routt
Vice President
Marketing and Branding
Scripps
San Diego, California

Lisa M. Wyatt
Vice President
Public Affairs and Marketing
Washington Hospital Center and MedStar
  Health
Washington, DC

Renée M. Zakoor
Partner
Yankelovich Partners, Inc.
Claremont, California

Amy Ziegenfuss
Marketing Coordinator
Henry M. Jackson Foundation for the
  Advancement of Military Medicine
Rockville, Maryland

Foreword

In today's health care system and with today's advanced telecommunications, branding or reputation development among health care institutions is central to continued success, financial viability, and, ultimately, survival. This book is about branding of such institutions; more than that, it is about reputation creation and protection. Reputation is hardly a new concept; the most famous quote on the topic dates back to Shakespeare.

This is an important volume because it not only focuses on the need to establish branding for health care institutions, but also explains how to establish a successful brand—what has worked in the past and why. It provides invaluable insights and reflections from people intimately involved in the process.

The concept of branding, or reputation creation and protection, as applied to health care institutions is relatively young. When traditional health care institutions—physicians and hospitals—were really in charge of the health care system, branding was less necessary. We never used to think of one hospital as superior to another in certain areas; we never thought of one insurer (or health maintenance organization) as better; we never saw lists of "best doctors" or "best hospitals"; we never even heard of most drug companies or the names of their products.

The dynamics of health care has changed radically, in part because the deliverers of health care no longer are in charge. They did not change with the times, and, as a result, failed to protect their franchises. They did not recognize the ways in which medical technology and modern pharmaceuticals would alter the delivery of health care and, more importantly, the expectations of consumers. They did not consider that, in an information-rich age, consumers no longer would accept inefficient service built around the needs of the providers rather than the patients.

Not all of these changes have been positive. We identified high costs and inefficiencies in the system and sought to correct them. However, at the beginning of the 21st century, it becomes increasingly apparent that monetary concerns are paramount. The cost-cutting concerns prevalent in today's health care environment have dictated much of our health care delivery; the result is that we are told which drugs we can take and, sometimes, even which surgeries we are allowed to undergo.

On the positive side, the revolution in information technology and the explosion of information resources have caused a shift in power. Consumers, in their guise as patients and with the benefits of information and education, understand health care to a far greater extent than any time in history. They now have the knowledge and comprehension necessary to demand proper diagnosis and treatment.

The heightened role of educated consumers creates an inherent frustration with the system. Rather than being told what's available, consumers ask their doctors about the latest drug discoveries but sometimes can't obtain the information. Consumers learn to ask about a hospital's nurse/patient ratios but have little to no recourse when the answer is unsatisfactory.

How we select our health care service providers depends increasingly on an institution's ability to communicate its capabilities and services and brand them in a way that renders insurers and consumers alike comfortable and confident. Every health care institution—hospitals, physicians, pharmaceuticals and their manufacturers, medical equipment makers—must now be concerned with reputation and branding. Those that are cavalier about how their brand is perceived in the marketplace are inevitably doomed.

However, one basic principle holds. Successful branding, or reputation building, can be achieved only in the presence of substantive performance. Above all, institutions must deliver quality care. The branding techniques discussed in this book are successful only when the subject of the branding performs well and sustains its performance over time. Even the best marketing communications cannot mask incompetence. Behind each of the excellent case studies of successful branding is a successful product or institution that has, itself, stood the test of time.

Health care professionals who remain steeped in the tradition of days when marketing of health care services was anathema might scoff at some of the ideas in this book. Traditionalists view health care branding and the competition it represents as, at worst, contrary to good health care delivery and, at best, simply a waste of money.

In fact, in today's marketplace, the necessity to create a brand leads—indeed, forces—our health care institutions to engage in a strategic thought process concerning their products and services and, much more important, their consumers' needs and their own dedication and commitment to serving those needs. It requires that organizations be reflective, community conscious, customer driven, and service oriented.

From such processes, only good can result. The best institutions and practitioners, those that understand customer needs and learn how to fulfill them, will survive. Those that fail to comprehend what it takes to create and sustain a solid reputation, a solid brand, will fall short. And perhaps they should, because their inability to recognize the fundamental themes of branding and engage actively in the thought processes and planning that underlie successful marketing render them suspect in other areas, as well.

Health care institutions and practitioners should take from this book ways in which they must change with the times. Those who want to flourish in the new millennium must understand how branding—specifically the process that leads to successful branding—ultimately leads to better health care for all.

Some things never change, despite the passage of time. The lesson of this book is that the necessity of building and maintaining a reputation for outstanding service and dedication to excellence is one of those constants.

Wayne L. Pines
President
Regulatory Services and Health Care
APCO Associates Inc.
Washington, DC

Acknowledgments

"Grateful" doesn't begin to describe my appreciation for colleagues, friends, and family who helped make this work possible. Perhaps "beholden" is more appropriate, considering their contributions.

This entire concept took form thanks to the brainstorm of my co-editor Nancy Hicks, who saw the need for this book, decided to move forward, and asked me to join the team. Nancy, you make it fun. Amy Ziegenfuss, with the Henry M. Jackson Foundation, was the smart and always-delightful taskmaster keeping us on track. Paula McAuliffe, an amazing colleague, kept us true to timelines and commitments. Andrea Strout often shaped my ideas into prose. Kelly Huegel helped to put the finishing touches on this project. Special thanks to our friends at Aspen Publishers: Kalen Conerly, who moved us from concept to reality, and Ruth Bloom, who pored over the edited manuscripts.

Thanks to the many colleagues who contributed their time, ideas, and ideals in order to make this book a first for the health care industry. They are among the best and brightest communicators in the field. Also, special thanks to Howard Paster at Hill and Knowlton, who gave us the green light and granted us the time; to colleagues within GTCR and WPP Group who gave their perspective and support; to my many clients throughout the years who shared their wisdom and, by doing so, helped shape my career.

To my late father, Jerry Bashe, whose own health battle became part of my ongoing commitment to make a difference in society through health care communications. To my mother, Lila, who rose to the occasion as devoted caregiver. Their struggle demonstrates that consumers need much more from health systems than good clinical technique and awaiting beds. In a world of great medical advances, open, caring minds will still be the providers' greatest tools.

Most important, my deepest appreciation goes to my wife Elinor and daughter Kayla. They are the ultimate inspiration for every big challenge I tackle.

G.B.

Preparing a book with contributing authors who are busy professionals is a daunting task. We were fortunate to have a superb project manager in Amy Ziegenfuss and an editor who is wonderful to work with in Kalen Conerly. My colleague Gil Bashe was a source of creative inspiration throughout this process. Leslie Whitlinger stepped in at the eleventh hour with finesse, as always. Thanks to them for being my teammates and making this so enjoyable. I would also like to thank Jim Jennings, Director of Hill and Knowlton's U.S. Health and Pharmaceutical Practice, for his support and friendship throughout this project. Finally, a special thanks to the contributing authors whose stories make this book possible.

N.J.H.

In addition to echoing the sentiments of the co-editors, I'd like to extend my heartfelt thanks to both Gil and Nancy for the opportunity to work with them on this extraordinary project. Their knowledge and enthusiasm for this subject—and for health care as a whole—are energizing and inspiring. Admiration and thanks must go to Kalen Conerly for her unfailing belief in this book, and for her tremendous energy and devotion to it. My sincere appreciation goes to the contributing authors and their teams who worked tirelessly to tell their branding tales.

I count myself lucky to have parents who have provided constant support and encouragement throughout my life, and friends and family who are continuous cheerleaders. Many thanks to Lisa Reilly and the Henry M. Jackson Foundation for encouraging and understanding my involvement in this project. And, as always, love and thanks to Kelly for endless collaboration and buttressing.

A.Z.

Chapter 1

From Ben Franklin to Branding: The Evolution of Health Services Marketing

Nancy J. Hicks

Marketing is such a recent phenomenon in health care that reviewing its development is a little like examining the space program in the context of U.S. history. To really understand the evolution of the function and to fully appreciate its accelerated development in the past two decades, it is useful to go "back to the future" for a look at health services and how the growth of this vital sector has mirrored the country it serves.

THE EVOLUTION OF U.S. HEALTH CARE

The residents of Philadelphia in 1751 would have been stunned that the "almshouse for the sick" founded by illustrious first citizen Ben Franklin would be nationally recognized 200 years later as Pennsylvania Hospital, renowned for teaching and clinical care. Most colonists were treated for illness in their homes, and until well into the 19th century only the poor went to hospitals—and that was to die. Today, heads of state and ordinary citizens make pilgrimages to the Mayo Clinic and other elite bastions of American medicine for treatments and "cures" that would have been unthinkable a century ago.

It has been a remarkable journey—one marked by breathtaking advances in technology and medical milestones that include breakthroughs at the level of cellular biology. It is indeed an achievement analogous to the moon landing. Yet it is more than a story of scientific discovery. It is about the creation of a health care delivery system that is both a testament to the practical genius of the American people in adapting to the needs of the marketplace and a reflection of great societal problems that are still unresolved.

The Early 20th Century

The fledgling hospital industry of the 19th century reached an important milestone by the century's end. In 1899, the American Hospital Association (AHA) was founded by eight hospital administrators to "facilitate the interchange of ideas." Indeed, ideas were flourishing. The Mayo brothers opened the nation's first physician group practice on the plains of Minnesota in 1888. In 1905, a researcher performed the first cardiac transplant on a dog. Both events were harbingers of developments in research and health care delivery that would by the end of the 20th century create a trillion-dollar industry that is one-seventh of the U.S. economy.

1

In the early years of this century, the advent of anesthesia, sterilization, and the technology of X-rays was transforming medical practice. Harvard biochemist Lawrence J. Hendern wrote in 1912, "A random patient with a random disease consulting a physician chosen at random had, for the first time in the history of mankind, a better than fifty/fifty chance of profiting from the encounter."

As patients fared better, so did the industry. By 1923, hospital membership in AHA had risen to 734. A few years earlier in 1919, in one of the industry's first quality control initiatives, the American College of Surgeons developed criteria for "approving hospitals."

The 1930s marked the growth of state hospital associations and medical group practices, which numbered 300 in 1933. As the nation grappled with the Great Depression, the birth of private insurance came with the Hospital Services Plan Commission, later known as the Blue Cross/Blue Shield Association. By the decade's end in 1939, Blue Shield was offering coverage of physician fees. The fledgling health insurance industry grew in response to the belief that health care coverage was vital to the security of the average American. Yet unlike Social Security, the great entitlement program born in this era, health care was seen as a privilege, not a right of citizenship. America's deep ambivalence about this issue is still evident today in the debate about universal coverage and a single-payer system.

The Postwar Years and the 1950s

World War II revolutionized American society, transforming its industrial base and thrusting the country into leadership on a world stage. Every facet of life was affected by the scope and trauma of this war. The health industry was no exception.

The development of antibiotics in the late 1930s and the surgical techniques learned on the battlefields produced great advances in medical practice. By the time victorious veterans were being cheered in Times Square, the American health care system had begun an era of unprecedented growth and prosperity.

This growth was hugely facilitated by the creation of the Hill-Burton Act in 1946. In part to compensate for the Depression and war years, the U.S. Congress distributed $4 billion (back when a billion dollars meant something) to 6,900 hospitals and other health care facilities. These monies were for facility improvement and expansion, which had been hampered for most hospitals in the war years. The caveat for the government's largesse was that any facilities receiving Hill-Burton funds would provide charity care to their community. While the hospital industry's roots were deeply nonprofit, this obligation reinforced the commitment to community-based charity care.

With funds for facility expansion, health services boomed in the postwar years and throughout the 1950s. Kaiser Permanente opened the nation's first staff model health maintenance organization (HMO) in 1945, a "way out there" idea whose brilliance would be borne out a few decades later. And the government through the Veteran's Administration (VA) spurred hospital growth by opening 150,000 beds in the VA hospital system in 1947. The locus of medical expertise had shifted from physicians to hospitals.

Poodle skirts, hula hoops, and rock n' roll defined the "Happy Days" of America in the 1950s, and the health industry clearly reflected the unbridled optimism of these years. And for good reason. The discovery of the Salk vaccine and the ability to immunize against rubella and chickenpox dramatically impacted childhood health and made the iron lung of polio a museum piece.

The increase in employer-based health insurance through third-party reimbursement such as Blue Cross afforded Americans unprecedented health care coverage. This coupled with an expansion of services drove more people to access health services than at any time in U.S. history. Health care consumerism, which so impacted the 1990s, had its genesis in the boom years of the 1950s.

It is perhaps no accident that marketing would parallel the rise of consumerism in health care. Public relations emerged in hospitals during these years, although the function largely supported human resources and fund-raising. Patients were almost entirely funneled to hospitals through physicians, a pattern that held firm until the mid-1980s. The lack of external focus in these years reflected the prevailing belief that if you kept your physicians happy, hospital beds would be full. Before managed care, this was how hospitals made money.

Internal newsletters constituted communications of the day. To the modern-day practitioner these employee pieces rife with gossip and cutesy columns like "Hatchings and Matchings" are a far cry from the sophisticated consumer magazines of major health systems. Yet early pioneers such as Marion Ramsey, a former sports writer who was the Children's Hospital of Philadelphia's public relations director from 1951 to 1954, blazed new trails in the marketing of health services.

While the 1950s may deserve their reputation in medical circles as the Golden Age of American medicine, the Eisenhower years were not without dark clouds on the horizon. Health care costs were beginning a daunting ascent that would reach crisis proportions in the late 1970s and continue unabated through the 1990s. The increasingly commercial nature of hospitals did not go unnoticed in popular culture. Comedians such as Milton Berle were making jokes about "wallet biopsy."

The 1960s

Social historians frequently note that the "Happy Days" America of the 1950s ended with the assassination of President John F. Kennedy in 1963. Ahead was a long national nightmare marked by more assassinations and the political and social upheaval of an unpopular war. Vietnam was the catalyst for the protests of the era, yet the revolutionary fervor was also fed by the Civil Rights movement and, by decade's end, the beginnings of the women's movement.

The hospital industry continued to flourish, with the number of hospital employees doubling between the mid-1950s and the mid-1960s. For the first time, more people were employed in hospitals than in the railroad or steel industries. America was beginning to turn a sharp corner from a manufacturing-based economy to one dominated by service industries.

One indicator of the growing prosperity of the health services sector was the market entry of proprietary for-profit companies. In a sector totally composed of community-based nonprofit hospitals, the advent of companies like the Hospital Corporation of America (HCA) was a milestone that would have far-reaching consequences for the industry. Suddenly health care was viewed through the prism of stock equities and "shareholder value." A business-focused approach to health services delivery was introduced with these companies, and the debate between the merits of community-run nonprofit health systems and national for-profit systems continues today.

The greatest industry change of this decade, however, occurred not in the marketplace but in the U.S. Capitol. In 1965, Congress passed the Medicare and Medicaid Acts in response to an insurance crisis among America's elderly, poor, and disabled populations. This landmark legislation not only assured medical coverage for these groups, but also significantly upped the ante of the government's involvement in the health care system. Perhaps those intrepid lawmakers would have paused had they known that the $41.6 billion health care costs in 1965 would balloon to $1 trillion in 1996, with Medicare and Medicaid accounting for 45 percent of these costs.

Marketing in the 1960s

As the health services sector flourished in these years with increased access afforded to America's aging population, the embryonic public relations function of the 1950s was in full flower. While the changes in the marketplace and in Medicare reimbursement that would force hospitals and health services companies to embrace marketing were at least a decade away, the practice of public relations was flourishing. In these years, the function was still closely allied to development, but there was a growing consciousness that a health services organization had to "keep faith" with its publics.

Preeminent among these publics were physicians and donors. Consumers were not judged to be a critical audience, since they did not directly choose hospitals but were referred by their physicians. Media relations in this era often consisted of answering reporters' questions about patient conditions. The use of media to advance strategic marketing objectives had not evolved because the market did not demand it.

Print was the medium of choice for communications throughout the 1960s in spite of the increasingly influential role that television news was playing in the lives of most Americans. Shirley Bonnem, public relations director at the Children's Hospital of Philadelphia for more than 30 years and winner of the Public Relations Society of America Health Academy's Lifetime Achievement Award, noted that from the mid-1960s to the mid-1970s "collateral was king." This was the era of slick annual reports, brochures, and community publications. If marketing was relegated to the written word, there was a growing sophistication about health care communications and a huge increase in hospitals with a formal public relations function.

The 1970s

The 1970s continued many of the trends of the previous decade, including the rise of the for-profit hospital sector. A high demand market and the stable payment system created by Medicare made health care increasingly attractive to investor-owned companies. HCA continued to flourish and was soon joined by American Medical International and other proprietary hospital companies.

Since Medicare paid hospitals directly "for services rendered" in what amounted to giving the hospital industry a blank check, there was little incentive to curb costs. With few limits on reimbursement, both nonprofit and for-profit hospitals expanded services.

In their book *From Health Services to Medical Markets*, Imersheim and Cates note: "Hospital operations could be funded under non-profit logic and at the same time—

because of funding arrangements—move significantly toward a capitalistic logic of accumulation, a transforming of medical care delivery from services to products."

The rising costs of the health care sector that were to reach crisis proportions in the 1980s and 1990s were making their way to the nation's political agenda. Presidents Ford and Carter both attempted to put caps on Medicare reimbursement. Carter's cost-containment bill was defeated by the hospital industry, which had managed to convince Congress that "voluntary controls" could keep costs in check.

In a trend that was not unrelated, the managed care industry with its emphasis on capping health costs grew in this decade, although nothing like the prairie-fire growth the industry would experience in the 1990s. A Minnesota-based pediatrician named Paul Elwood coined the term "Health Maintenance Organization" to capture the wellness orientation of this provider sector. He would later be renowned as the "father of managed competition," the linchpin of President Clinton's health care reform plan in 1993.

Twenty years before the 1993 Clinton proposal, legislation was passed that fueled the growth of HMOs. In 1973, Congress passed the HMO Law, which appropriated $375 million toward the development of HMOs nationwide. Forces were now in play that would transform the U.S. health delivery system by the end of the century.

Marketing in the 1970s

The 1970s marked the formal emergence of marketing in the health services industry. Despite the fact that Evanston Hospital claimed a vice-president of marketing in 1976, many professionals would cite the publication of Phillip Kotler's *Marketing for Non-Profits* a few years later as the advent of the marketing era in health services.

Marketing as we know it today had still not taken root in hospitals by the decade's end. Competition for patients was increasing and a higher organizational emphasis was put on public relations as a result. Consumers were targeted more directly in communications, and patient satisfaction research grew in importance. Yet marketing as the "managing of the flow of services between an organization and its customers" was not a recognized function in most health care organizations.

The resistance to marketing was born of an antipathy to "business" that ran deep among physicians in the nonprofit world of health care. In 1977, I was working at the Fred Hutchinson Cancer Research Center in Seattle in my first public relations job. I can still recall a meeting where a graphics designer was presenting logo designs to the cancer center's administrator. He said, "...Dare I mention 'marketing' as our objective here...?" Color drained from the face of the good doctor and I was sure we were going to have to call the medics. It was clear to me that neither he nor anyone else had dare mention marketing!

It would take some cataclysmic industry events to make marketing respectable in health services organizations. Those events were rapidly at hand.

The 1980s

The Reagan years may have been "Morning in America," with a renewed national optimism despite recession and conflicts abroad. The excess of the 1980s, captured so well in the television program "Dynasty," was mirrored in the growth of the hospital industry.

From 1977 to 1982, proprietary hospitals increased by 42 percent, prompting the *New England Journal of Medicine* to claim "a *new* medical industrial complex as the most important recent development in American health care." Centrally managed health systems, whether for-profit or nonprofit, were expanding during this period. By 1983, 173 hospital systems expanded operations 9.5 percent to own or manage 1,916 U.S. hospitals, foreshadowing the huge growth of multi-hospital systems in the 1990s.

If the health services sector was feeling the euphoria of unbridled growth, and maybe even a little smugness at being immune from the recession of the early 1980s, the U.S. government was about to puncture that balloon.

In a response to the dismal results of voluntary price controls, the government introduced a prospective payment system for Medicare in 1983. This marked the first time in the industry's history that a purchaser of care challenged the customary payment system. Now, hospitals were told what they would be reimbursed for based on a marvelously convoluted system called *diagnosis-related groups* (DRGs). For example, the government would reimburse hospitals for a coronary bypass DRG at $15,000. If the hospital costs exceeded this amount, the hospital would eat the difference; likewise, if the procedure cost the hospital less, it could pocket the difference.

The era of *blank check* reimbursement had ended for the hospital industry. The result was a halt to health services expansion as well as a new way of looking at those services. With DRGs, medical care had to be unbundled into individual commodity units. ***For the first time, hospitals thought of medical care in terms of product lines, a development that was to have major consequences in the marketing of health services.***

Even though the prospective payment system helped put the brakes on health care costs, the sheer velocity of rising costs could not be contained by the prospective payment system alone. It would be a little like a single matador trying to contain a field of charging bulls.

American business was gored by one of those bulls. By 1982, the cost of health insurance to companies was equal to 50 percent of pre-tax profits. In what would be the first volley aimed at market reform, businesses were organizing coalitions to control costs; by 1985, 130 business and health coalitions had formed nationwide. Many experts believe that corporate America was the engine for health care reform, advancing the issue in the 1990s far more powerfully than did the health industry itself. When Lee Iacocca announced that $800 had to be added to the cost of every new Chrysler to pay for his employees' health care costs, reform was inevitable.

While hospital-based costs were somewhat curtailed through DRGs, national spending on physician services doubled between 1980 and 1989. The growth of outpatient care, due in part to cutbacks in hospital reimbursement and spectacular technological advances in diagnosis and treatment, skyrocketed in this decade. From 1983 to 1986, outpatient centers grew from 1,000 to 2,000; by decade's end, 30 percent of medical procedures were performed in an outpatient setting.

The HMO industry grew in the 1980s, although not at the breakneck speed of the following decade. Approximately 4 percent of Americans were enrolled in HMOs in 1980; by 1992, 14 percent of Americans belonged to HMOs. The prosperity of the industry was reflected in the decision of U.S. Healthcare, founded in 1974 as a nonprofit HMO, to take the company public in 1983. This heralded a new age of for-profit medicine in this industry sector.

In a little-noticed change in the health care lexicon that would soon dominate the vocabulary of American life, someone in the late 1980s coined the term *managed care*.

Marketing in the 1980s

If marketing was born in the 1970s, it came of age in the 1980s. The health industry had evolved from a seller's market to a buyer's, a change that was to have a profound impact on the marketing of health services.

Employers and consumers had become purchasers of health care and the role of physician as "referrer" for hospital services became less important. Marketers had to look at audiences in a whole new way. The importance of consumers was heightened by the prospective payment system. The unbundling of medical services into DRGs created product lines that could be marketed by profitability. Hospitals quickly learned that direct marketing to consumers for services such as obstetrics, cosmetic surgery, and outpatient care would generate revenue that would offset "unprofitable" DRGs.

The rise of product-line marketing launched the great hospital advertising wars of the 1980s. Barely a blip on the health care marketing screen a decade earlier, the growth of advertising was nothing short of spectacular. In 1983, the year the prospective payment system was launched, hospitals spent $50 million on advertising; in 1986 that figure rose to $500 million, a tenfold increase in three years

The proliferation of hospital advertising was fueled by an increasingly competitive marketplace and a belief among marketing professionals that advertising was the key to competitive success. While the sophistication of advertising in health services has grown enormously in recent years, much of the advertising of the mid-to-late eighties was ineffectual at best and terrible at worst. Ad copy tended to be too institutionally focused, and concepts lacked the "clutter-buster" impact of advertising from the consumer product world. This was due more to the conservative, risk-aversive culture of hospitals than to a creative failure on the part of marketing professionals.

However, if marketers can be faulted, it may be for doing too much of a good thing.

There is an old saying that if all you have is a hammer, every solution demands a nail. Many marketers of the day used advertising as the hammer and neglected other tools in the communications toolbox. Once a medium of dubious respectability, advertising was now hailed as a marketing panacea for hospitals.

Whatever the problem was, advertising was the solution. Many marketing directors defined their marketing program by the size of their advertising budget. This resulted in poorly conceived strategies that might have benefited from public relations and other disciplines and an enormous waste of dollars. I remember being chagrined that a regional medical center in a rural market with literally no competition was spending more than a million dollars a year on advertising. As one of my colleagues wryly pointed out, they could have mailed each consumer in their region a $100 check to come to the hospital!

While advertising in the 1980s accelerated like an adolescent with a growth spurt, another staple of marketing thrived as well. Consumer research grew in proportion to the emphasis on consumers in health services marketing. While most hospitals conducted patient satisfaction research throughout this century, consumer research was virtually unknown until the 1970s. *By the mid-1980s, two-thirds of hospitals were conducting physician and consumer research. The latter was crucial in developing advertising messages and monitoring the success of marketing programs.*

While research was one measure of the growth of marketing in the 1980s, the overall expenditures on marketing programs were another indicator that the function had come of age. From the early to the mid-1980s, marketing expenditures had increased tenfold. The array of forces that propelled the growth of marketing in these years was enough to make the American Medical Association reverse its anti-advertising law.

Marketing may have been an ugly stepchild in the 1970s, but it was a legitimate, if not loved, member of the health services family by the end of the 1980s. As much as the function flourished in these years, it is interesting to note, however, that 30 percent of U.S. hospitals lacked marketing departments.

The 1990s

The defining political issue of the 1990s is health care. More than the economy, or war and peace or abortion, this issue persistently arouses America's passions. It has shaped and reshaped the body politic throughout the decade.

—Albert R. Hunt, *Wall Street Journal*, June 26, 1998

It is almost impossible to exaggerate the scope of change that the health services industry underwent in the 1990s. Terms like "sea change," "new paradigms," and "marketplace revolution" only begin to capture a decade that has transformed the U.S. health care delivery system.

The cost crisis that was born in the 1960s and fueled in the 1970s and 1980s had finally reached epic proportions in the 1990s. Innovations in technology creating breakthrough medical advances and an aging population of baby boomers created unprecedented demand for health services. Medicare reimbursement and fee-for-service-dominated payment systems were woefully inadequate for keeping pace with service demand. As a result, by 1992 health care costs had skyrocketed to $840 billion, representing 14 percent of the gross national product. This is roughly 33 times the amount of health care expenditures in 1960.

The health care industry was now one-seventh of the U.S. economy and as much as the gross domestic product of Italy. Health care costs were crippling American businesses and impeding their ability to be competitive in international markets.

In a 1991 issue of *JAMA* devoted to the topic of health care reform, editor George Lundberg noted that change "has an aura of inevitability." The time was indeed at hand as then Governor Clinton put health care reform on the 1992 election agenda.

In town meetings throughout the country, candidates discussed the health care system and brought issues such as managed care and the uninsured to the front page. The election of Bill Clinton assured the inevitability of change that Dr. Lundberg had predicted. Even though President Clinton's health reform proposal failed in 1994, it fueled the fire of forces already in play. Since "managed competition" was a centerpiece of the Clinton plan, providers scrambled to accommodate a marketplace that would soon be dominated by managed care.

Market-based reform replaced legislative reform as managed care spread like a prairie fire. Between July 1994 and July 1995, a record 7 million enrollees joined HMOs. Managed care presented a broader array of options, including the flexible point of service plans. As a result, employees in managed care plans surged from 55 percent in 1992 to 75 percent in 1996.

In 1988, indemnity insurance covered 72.6 percent of the market; by 1995, less than a third of the market was covered by indemnity products, and over 60 million people were enrolled in HMOs.

The growth of managed care has impacted all population segments. Once HMOs were considered the care of choice for young, healthy families. Medicare had long embraced fee-for-service medicine for seniors. One measure of managed care's vise-like grip on the health industry is the thrust from the Health Care Finance Administration (which administers Medicare) to develop Medicare HMOs. Even the American Association of Retired Persons, the leading advocacy group for the nation's seniors, endorsed HMOs for its 33 million members.

The triumph of managed care, once ridiculed by fee-for-service traditionalists, was complete. Drs. Paul Ellwood and George Lundberg in the October 1996 issue of *JAMA* referred to managed care as "the new American health system."

The transformation of the marketplace from fee-for-service medicine to managed care has caused a fundamental realignment of health care delivery with profound impact on providers and purchasers of care. The emergence of integrated delivery systems (IDSs) was a response to these market changes. Providers developed vertical and horizontal product integration that produced multisystems with "cradle-to-grave care." A consumer could now access a system for obstetrical services, home care, or hospice, as well as any level of specialty care. Hospitals and medical centers gave way to health systems as the nomenclature of health care struggled to keep pace with the evolution of the industry.

The IDS often merged provider and payer, with many systems having their own health plans. Those that did not would contract with managed care payers. This allowed providers and payers to offer an entire package of health products and insurance to employers, who in turn offered a choice of providers and health plans to employees. In one of the great paradigm shifts in health care, purchasers were not choosing individual hospitals or physician practices, but were buying an entire package of integrated health care services.

To control costs, purchasing alliances were proliferating. The Buyers Health Care Action Group in Minnesota created a program in 1996 that represented 24 employers in contracting with health providers to cover 400,000 people. This in turn spurred the development of integrated networks to secure major employer contracts. From 1991 to 1996, integrated networks grew to 504, doubling in size.

With the advent of integrated networks, the hospital industry found that bigger was better. A sole provider simply lacked the clout to secure managed care contracts and purchasing agreements with major employers. In much the same way that the Barnes and Noble "super stores" replaced mom-and-pop bookstores, it was clear by mid-decade that the era of the stand-alone hospital had come to an end.

Providers began looking in earnest for partnerships or affiliations to maintain their competitiveness in the marketplace. The great "network dance" had begun. In 1995 there were 623 hospital mergers, a 20 percent increase from 1994. This pace continued in 1996 with 768 hospital mergers and did not decelerate until the following year, which recorded 181 mergers.

The merger mania of these years produced a marked consolidation in the hospital industry. In 1974, there were 7,174 hospitals; by 1996, that number had dropped to 6,201. By the decade's end, an estimated 15 percent of American hospitals had changed hands.

The big winners in this consolidation surge were large nonprofit and for-profit health systems. Columbia and Tenet dominated merger activity in the for-profit sector. The Tenet/OrNda merger accounted for 20 percent of all mergers in that year. In 1996, Columbia acquired 17 hospitals; one year later, the company had 132 hospitals with revenues of $18.8 billion.

Nonprofit multisystems consolidated at nearly an equal pace with Catholic systems, such as Catholic Healthcare East and Eastern Mercy Health creating a 17-hospital system and Catholic Health West acquiring 26 hospitals. In 1997, the for-profit sector grew 5.9 percent while nonprofits grew by 9 percent. One hundred sixty-two systems saw their assets jump 10 percent in these years.

Regional integrated systems merged or formed alliances in record numbers, often making strange bedfellows. In markets such as Boston, Massachusetts, General Hospital merged with Brigham and Women's Hospital to form Partners Health System, and Beth Israel and Deaconess systems created CareGroup. Hospitals that were once sharp rivals in the advertising wars of the 1980s were now partners.

Consolidation in the HMO world was just as stunning. Major companies such as U.S. Healthcare and Aetna merged, as did dozens of Blue Cross plans throughout the country. The for-profit managed care sector had record profits in these years; over $1.6 billion in stock among 24 HMOs was held by investors in 1994.

By decade's end the landscape of health care delivery was irretrievably altered. National megasystems, both nonprofit and for-profit, and regional delivery systems with revenues in the billions now dominated the industry. Managed care, which had fueled much of this consolidation, was now in a corrective course with a consumers' bill of rights on the legislative agenda.

Yet the forces that transformed the industry will not turn back the clock. In the words of Regina Herzlinger, "The market forces that have reshaped much of the American economy are now working on our health care system. When they have completed their labors, the system will have lost its fat—inconvenience, lack of information, high costs—but it will have kept its muscle. A new market driven health care system will emerge." (R. Herzlinger, *Market Driven Health Care*, Addison-Wesley Publishing Company, Inc., 1997.) Many would say that day is here.

Marketing in the 1990s

As health care became market-driven in the 1990s, it was only natural that the marketing function would gain ascendancy in health services organizations. For decades the culture of health care was internally focused, with health professionals making decisions from an institutional mindset. Why else would a hospital worker wake a patient at 6:00 AM to draw blood? For the convenience of the hospital staff, among other internal considerations—certainly not for the sleep-deprived patient.

Market driven institutions have an "outside-in" way of thinking that looks at service delivery from the point of view of customers and other external audiences. The boom in guest relations programs in this decade is testament to looking at patients as "customers" and realizing that they have a choice in health services. Although health services are far from the hospitality industry in viewing services through the lens of the customer, the 1990s were a turning point in developing a real marketing perspective in health care.

Changes in the marketplace created new paradigms for marketing professionals. The rise of IDSs dictated a new approach to institutional marketing. Whereas physicians were the dominant audience in premanaged care marketing, suddenly "purchasing" audiences (such as employers) were taking center stage. Consumers as an audience became increasingly important, since most consumers had a choice of providers in their health plans.

The most crucial change in marketing, however, was the shift from product-line to institutional focus. With the advent of IDSs, purchasers were not buying individual product lines or even one hospital but rather an entire package of health services. This entailed marketing the entire health system; the whole was more important than the sum of its parts.

Hence institutional image ads replaced product-line advertising. It became more important to promote the attributes of the entire system. When a product line, such as a premier cardiac services program, was highlighted, the strategic objective was to transfer the "halo" of the clinical service to the institution.

Advertising thrived in the mid-1990s, spurred by the massive wave of hospital mergers. The hospital industry spent 33 percent more on advertising in 1997 than in 1996, for a total of $60 million. Health plans, by contrast, spent only $17.3 million in the first half of 1997.

The postmerger creation of new health systems called for new identities, and marketers responded with advertising. Just as product marketers try to create brand preference for their products, health systems marketers were now attempting to create a brand identity in their marketplace. Columbia spent $20 million dollars on a national branding campaign in 1997.

Integrated system marketing demanded more than advertising. Public relations achieved new status as the "positioning" tool of choice. To gain credibility for newly merged health systems or to reinforce positioning for established ones, the news media and other third-party vehicles gained ascendance in marketing programs. The media relations function became a strategic tool to profile clinical centers of excellence or institutional programs. Similarly, issues management and leadership profiling have become public relations vehicles that create visibility and differentiation in the marketplace.

Research, while always a cornerstone in marketing, escalated in importance in this decade. The growth of managed care, the establishment of purchasing alliances, the realignment of industry partners, and the emergence of "demand management" made market research essential.

Perhaps no single trend in the 1990s portends as much for the industry and impacts marketing more directly than the rise of the health care consumer. Today's consumers are better educated and more assertive about their health care needs than consumers of a generation ago. They have become full partners with providers and payers in reshaping the American health care system. Much of this is due to the demythologizing of medicine and a revolution in communications.

The slow fall of physicians from their pedestals is mirrored in Hollywood portrayals over the years. The Ben Caseys and Marcus Welbys were the "hero" doctors of the 1960s and 1970s. By the mid-1980s, television gave us *St. Elsewhere*, a gritty and far more realistic portrayal of doctors than those saints of preceding decades. The entertainment industry always probes the issues of the day, and it is not coincidental that eroding confidence in our medical system emerged as themes in television and film. One of the biggest laugh lines in the film "As Good As It Gets" was a diatribe about HMOs.

In a poll conducted in 1993 by the American Medical Association, the public was clearly disenchanted with medicine. Over 70 percent of respondents said they had "lost faith in doctors," and 69 percent said that doctors were too interested in money.

The rise in health care media and the interactive technology of the Internet combined to create an "informed consumer" who is more empowered with information than at any time in human history. Health care is cited consistently as one of the top three or four concerns of all Americans; this is reflected in the myriad of medical programs and media outlets that cover health care news. The *New York Times* alone has 14 reporters who cover various aspects of health care. Contrast this to the 1960s, when only one reporter at the *Times* covered health care and most newspapers did not assign any full-time coverage to the beat.

Just as developments in computer technology revolutionized medicine with imaging diagnostics such as CAT scans and MRIs, the Internet gave consumers a world of medicine at their fingertips. In 1998, 68 percent of Americans had researched a medical condition on the Internet, and 90 percent of those reported being satisfied with the information they found. Similarly, direct-to-consumer advertising, approved by the FDA in 1996, has given consumers information about prescription drugs that was previously only available through physicians. Consumers today will challenge physicians and their health plans with a confidence based on knowledge and a demand for health services that meet their needs.

Accountability is a hallmark of the new consumerism and is evident in the "report cards" issued by HMOs. Increasingly, employer groups and consumers are demanding measurable clinical outcomes data to judge the effectiveness of their health plans.

The backlash against managed care and the potential legislation of a consumer's "bill of rights" is largely consumer driven. The health industry, which for years was dominated by physicians and "special interests," must now make room for consumers at the decision table.

As consumers flex their muscles, marketing will become increasingly integrated into the operations of health services companies. The rise of marketing is apparent in the increased budgets of marketing departments. In 1992, health systems averaged $1.6 million in marketing expenditures; by 1997 that number was $2.5 million. The American Hospital Association's society for marketing professionals has changed its name over the years, and those changing names parallel the function's status in the organization. In the 1960s and 1970s, the society was named the American Society for Hospital Public Relations; the rise of marketing in the 1980s brought forth the American Society for Hospital Public Relations and Marketing; finally, in the 1990s, reflecting its operational role in health systems, it is the Society for Health Strategy and Market Development.

The function has come a long way from the internal newsletter days of the 1950s and will become even more powerful as an aging and highly informed population creates an unprecedented demand for health services. Marketing professionals will be the watchdogs for consumers within their organizations and the strategists who map the road to success in the marketplace.

BRANDING IN HEALTH SERVICES

Branding is legendary in the product world. Consumer products like "Tide," "Pepsi," or "Mercedes-Benz" have brand equity worth millions in revenue for their companies. Marketers spend careers creating brands that will translate into powerful franchises in the marketplace. Fifty-two percent of customers say that "a known and trusted brand is a reason to buy a product." A strong consumer product brand can command 30 times the earnings at the time of a sale or merger. A brand is image in a name—a distinct and enduring pledge of value that consumers instantly recognize. The power of a brand name is unmistakable. McDonald's success in franchising and AT&T's success in global expansion testify to the value of branding. Lexus can offer premium pricing because of the image its brand conveys. Martha Stewart has created her own industry with line extensions based on the power of her personal brand of the "home arts." She translated this brand into one of the most successful initial public offerings (IPOs) in market history. Even our language reflects the impact of branding. Names like "Kleenex" and "Band-Aids" have become part of the American lexicon.

It is perhaps inevitable that the evolution of health services into a market-driven industry would result in the emergence of branding in marketing programs. Branding is the first cousin of image management and health systems with marquee names have practiced institutional brand management for years. The Mayo Clinic and Johns Hopkins have "brand names" that are internationally recognized. The brand equity of these institutions translates into a loyal customer base and a name that can be franchised.

The value of these premium provider brands is just as compelling as power brands in the product world. *Modern Healthcare* came out with a headline that said "Universal adds a little 'Mayo' to its Board." A clever headline underscores the image equity that Universal Health Services, a relatively new company, hopes to borrow by adding former executives of the Mayo Clinic to its board.

BRANDING—WHY NOW?

Shifts in the purchasing of health care in the 1990s have underscored the importance of branding. As quality and price become driving forces in the industry, a brand presents the purchaser with more reasons to buy than price alone. In fact, evidence suggests that a quality brand will trump price in contract negotiations. A few years ago the Health Insurance Plan of California, one of the state's major purchasing coalitions, awarded Aetna 70 percent of its contracts. The perceived quality of the Aetna product overcame the company's higher than average price in the minds of the purchasers.

Similarly, research indicates that customers will go "out of network" for premium services. Memorial Sloan-Kettering Cancer Center is one of the world's premier brands in cancer care. It is the reason why thousands of patients a year travel to this Mecca for care from their hometowns or from across the globe. A hospital with a quality brand is the single most important criterion when consumers choose a health plan; a recent study rated this the highest attribute (9.4 on a scale of 10) for consumers in their choice of health plans.

Branding is particularly important now for providers, since consumers know little about IDSs and many merged systems have to communicate a new identity. A brand is a promise. For consumers and purchasers it is the trust and consistency that are cornerstones in their choice of health services. New systems have the challenge of building brand equity in the marketplace, and established systems must manage that brand equity and leverage it for future success. In markets rife with new players, branding helps create awareness and differentiation for an organization. The brand is the "code" that telegraphs to consumers known attributes about a system or plan. The Kaiser Permanente name communicates instantly and powerfully a brand of managed care. The Blue Cross name a few years ago communicated just as powerfully a brand of fee-for-service medicine. The Blues' brand was so established in this arena that one of their great challenges now is to transfer that brand equity to managed care products.

When brand awareness is lacking, there is little differentiation in the marketplace. This problem was recently illustrated in the Washington, D.C. market in a study by the Medstat Group and J.D. Power Associates that revealed consumers could not tell the difference among various types of health plans; of the 14 health plans cited in the study, not one stood out among consumers. Choice in health plans takes on an added weight for consumers given the narrowing of choices in managed care. A brand helps consumers make those critical choices by providing a "known quantity."

When building a brand, providers must first establish brand awareness, then brand preference, and finally brand loyalty. It is the latter that translates into brand equity, the "gold" of the marketplace. The power of brand equity cannot be overstated. It actually lowers marketing costs for an organization, since the brand can be sustained with minimal promotion.

A sustained image is one of the great legacies of brand equity. Brands that have been established 25 or more years have an 85 percent recall among consumers. It is very difficult to knock down an established brand; a competitor must work its positioning around the brand, claiming areas not associated with the branded organization in the public's mind.

The image halo of a powerful brand can be extended in the consumer mind to anything associated with the organization. In a survey a few years ago in Baltimore, consumers selected Johns Hopkins as having the best dental school. The problem was that this preeminent institution did not have a dental school. In the consumer mind, Johns Hopkins is good in everything so it seems logical that they would be the best in dentistry.

It is this halo effect of branding that presents the opportunity for brand extension. The Cleveland Clinic successfully extended its power brand a few years ago by opening clinics in Ft. Lauderdale and Naples, Florida. This brand extension is possible, however, only when you have a name that can create an instant franchise. The success of these clinics proves that consumers will buy the Cleveland Clinic brand of medicine irrespective of geography.

A successful brand can increase market value by 50 to 75 percent. With for-profit systems, a strong image will bolster price-to-earnings ratio. For nonprofit systems, a powerful brand name can be the best defense against price competition. An academic medical center such as Duke, for example, has higher costs associated with being a research and teaching facility. A for-profit provider might be more competitive pricewise in contracting, but the image of Duke could outweigh costs in preference by employers and consumers.

In a recent study, Landor Associates found that there is a high correlation between awareness and esteem. This is no secret among product managers. In a Kellogg's corn flakes taste test, approval ratings for the cereal went from 47 percent to 59 percent when consumers knew the brand name.

Provider versus Product Branding

While the power of branding is undisputed in health services, do the principles of the product world apply to providers? In other words, can you brand hospitals like Coca-Cola? The answer is yes and no.

Certain principles apply whether you are branding detergent, soft drinks, or a cancer program. You must begin with a positioning program that reflects core strengths and differentiates from competitors. The organization must understand the importance of the brand position and make organizational decisions that protect the integrity of the brand. And resources must be applied to create a distinct and memorable brand identity in the marketplace.

While the process of building brand equity is similar in both product and provider worlds, there are crucial differences based on the nature of health care services. As Jack Hardy, one of the country's foremost health marketing experts, once noted, health care is the most intimate of human services. Consumers are entrusting their health and often their lives when they choose a health service.

There are five forms of risk involved in the consumer choice of a brand: *monetary, functional (will it work), physical, social, and psychological.* Health care branding choices are more likely to involve the latter three risks. Fear for your physical well-being in particular puts health care in the "high involvement" category of consumer decisionmaking. Familiarity will drive decisionmaking for "low involvement" products like soap, gum, or paper towels; high involvement products evoke a much more complex decision-making process. A man who is faced with joint replacement surgery is going to spend more time and angst choosing a provider than he will when he chooses a new set of tires.

That same man may choose a provider within his health plan for the joint replacement surgery but jump plans to go to a "name" cancer center if he is diagnosed with prostate cancer. The more serious the condition, the more quality attributes of a brand matter and the less consequential cost and access become. Of all the "high involvement" brands, health care leads the pack. Too much is at stake for the health care consumer to make casual choices in medical services.

Because the stakes are higher in health care branding, organizations must take care not to break the "promise" implied in the brand of their organization. The integrity of the brand must be protected in organizational decisions. If the brand promotes quality, then quality must be delivered or consumers will stop believing in the brand promise.

This puts health care organizations much more at risk of damage to a brand in times of crises. When Columbia/HCA spent $26 million on an advertising campaign to develop a national brand for their hospitals, they did not anticipate that a Medicare coding issue would develop into a major crisis. Every hospital under the "Columbia brand" umbrella was suddenly tarnished by the investigation fallout.

Humana in the late 1980s launched an extensive branding campaign. A "Prime Time Live" program did an investigative report that offered a devastating portrait of excessive pricing. The image aftermath was so bad that Humana sold 18 of its hospitals to Galen and refocused its business on insurance products.

The stronger and more established the brand, the more the organization is able to withstand crises without erosion of brand equity. Columbia and Humana were hit hard because they had "young" brands, which had not yet developed a loyal franchise for the organizations. By contrast, when Dana-Farber Cancer Institute and Memorial Sloan-Kettering Cancer Center were each hit by treatment crisis stories, the centers easily withstood the temporary media storms because of the strength of their brands in the marketplace.

Health services marketers must build and manage their brands in the same way as product marketers but face challenges unknown to the product world. Price competition is a staple in consumer product wars, from gasoline price wars to MCI's "ten cents a minute." In the health service industry, price is less flexible. It would be odd if not improbable to see rival hospitals offer sharp discounts on appendectomies. Quality, access, and customer service are much more effective branding attributes for health service companies. Quality, in particular, must anchor a brand for a high-involvement product like health care.

When a consumer brand is wildly successful, brand extensions will soon follow. If you like Ralph Lauren clothes, you will love his sheets and other home products. This is the conventional wisdom of consumer marketers and usually they are right. Yet tales abound in the marketing world of failed brand extensions. Dove soap developed a dishwashing liquid but found that the "creamy quality" consumers liked in the soap was distasteful in a detergent for dishes. Gucci overextended its brand with thousands of products and as a result saw their brand equity sharply decline in the marketplace. The failure of IBM Junior affected reputation and sales of the core IBM products.

These examples are instructive for health services marketers. Brand extensions work best when they are closely tied to the core product and the favorable attributes are transferable.

Just as "creamy" was not transferable from skin to dishes, a hospital may not want to extend its brand to a health club. The issue of overextension may become a paramount concern when a health system acquires outlying clinics and wants to brand them with its name. Unless those clinics reflect the quality and other attributes of the health system brand, there is a very real possibility that the brand could be diminished by its extension. As it expanded geographically, the Cleveland Clinic Foundation developed a tiered branding strategy to protect the integrity of its core brand (see Chapter 5). Olsten Corporation took a hit to its corporate reputation when it acquired Columbia home care facilities in Florida and found itself tarred by the brush of the federal investigation of Columbia's home care division.

Branding in health services differs in other fundamental ways from branding in the product world. Most provider brands are regional in awareness. Only a few companies such as Columbia, Tenet, Aetna U.S. Healthcare, and Kaiser Permanente have national brands. The great majority of health systems—some 5,000—are known in their regions but lack national visibility. Only a handful of systems—Mayo, Johns Hopkins, and the Cleveland Clinic—have a national brand.

A national brand enables providers to franchise their services beyond their regions—hence the Mayo Clinic in Jacksonville and the Cleveland Clinic in Ft.

Lauderdale. A national brand also provides a competitive edge by differentiating the organization from local competitors that lack a national reputation. It can be a powerful "point of difference" for purchasers, particularly national or multi-state employers.

While there is undisputed power in a national brand, it is worth noting, to paraphrase a Tip O'Neill axiom about politics, that "all health care is local." Brand loyalty is developed locally, shaped by consumers' direct experience with provider services. The equity of a national brand will be reinforced or diminished by the reputation of the local provider. *For all providers, national and regional, building a brand begins at the local level.*

In consumer branding, product is king and the company often invisible. Everyone has heard of Best Foods Mayonnaise, but not many consumers know that the parent company is Beatrice Foods. For health services companies, the reverse is true. Branding is far more important for the institution than for its product lines. In fact, it is the institutional brand that lends luster to the products. The Johns Hopkins brand is so strong that any clinical program under its umbrella will flourish. Managed care has increased the importance of institutional branding, since purchasers buy the "whole" and not the parts of a system.

While institutional branding is dominant in health services marketing, product-line branding has a place. If a clinical service becomes well enough known, that product-line brand can build institutional brand equity. The Cleveland Clinic built a national reputation in part on its cardiac care services. Similarly, a superb infectious diseases program boosted Tulane Medical Center's brand regionally.

Many health companies are finding the focus of product-line branding attractive. Salick Cancer Centers and other national specialty providers have experienced rapid growth. Fortune magazine recently named HealthSouth, with its 135 rehab hospitals, one of the nation's 50 fastest growing companies.

The health services world could learn an important lesson from product branding. A product name with established brand equity is regarded as sacrosanct. Names are rarely changed even when the product is acquired by another company. Black & Decker broke this unwritten rule when they acquired the GE small appliance business. They foisted the Black & Decker name on this business and lost the consumer franchise as a result. In the current climate of merger mania, many providers are throwing out the baby with the bathwater. Providers with well-established names are at risk of losing their franchise in the marketplace by giving up the name upon which their brand equity is based. While mergers require a name reconfiguration, it is crucial for providers to think long and hard before abandoning an established name. It takes enormous resources to create brand awareness with a new name. It is much easier to build on a base of consumer knowledge about a brand. The national Blue Cross Association reports that plans that keep the Blue Cross name as opposed to adopting new names such as Trigon (formerly Blue Cross/Blue Shield of Virginia) do better in the marketplace.

Providers should also take the long view of branding that consumer marketers embrace. Branding is a process, not a program that can be created with a name and graphics. It goes beyond promoting the brand in the market to strategic decisions within the organization. *Brand management is protecting the image and value of the organization in the minds of consumers.* It may be in the province of marketing but it must be implemented throughout the organization to keep the "promise" that the brand implies.

Health care marketing, having come of age in the 1980s and 1990s, will reach its maturity in this millennium with its stewardship of branding within the organization. It has been a long journey from Ben Franklin to branding, but providers have discovered the ancient wisdom of proverbs: "A good name is rather to be chosen than great riches." Branding is the key to that good name and to riches in the marketplace.

Chapter 2

Branding and Beyond: Emotion and Reputation Management in Health Care

Gil Bashe

Not long ago, I had similar experiences from opposite ends of the brand spectrum—one with a luxury-car company, the other with an inner-city hospital—that highlight the meaning of brand.

I had brought my Audi wagon into the local dealership for its 3,000-mile oil change and, while I was there, the service personnel lent me a car and washed and vacuumed mine. They had done this at the last oil change, and the one before that, for as long as I'd owned my car. A first-time Audi owner, I was impressed—and hooked.

That same week, I went to St. Michael's Hospital for a routine physical at lunchtime. St. Michael's sits in a bleak area of tumbledown houses in Newark, New Jersey's largest city. As I sat waiting for my stress-test results, the nurse remarked, "You've missed lunch. Would you like anything sent up? Can I get you something to drink?" She went on to say she had called my wife to tell her when she could pick me up.

As an avid Internet user and the head of a health care communications company, I knew both my automotive and health care options. The Audi wagon appealed to me as much for its understated elegance as for the performance-inspiring promise behind the phrase "German engineering." St. Michael's, with its mission to meet the needs of the underserved, appealed to the side of me that had served as a young army medic.

THE BRAND IS YOU

Would I have bought my Audi if it weren't also safe? No. Would I go to St. Michael's for neurosurgery? Again, no. But the package of rational or "threshold" benefits—of safety and performance in my car example, of a well-regarded primary-care facility in St. Michael's case—was sufficiently attractive to get me to the higher-order benefits, bonding above all.

In the end, both choices were deliberate and deeply personal. They said as much about me, in a way, as a look in my medicine chest or at my curriculum vitae might. They were two of the countless choices we make each year—which television shows, Internet sites, and magazines to consume; which breakfast cereal to eat; what company to work for; which line to pursue—that make up one's personal "brand." The opposite is also true: each brand is an aggregation of the hopes, dreams, and fears with which consumers invest it.

A colleague in London, Barry Gowers, managing director of Gowers Advertising, puts it yet another way:

> What brand really represents is a shared philosophy... It's not a product's features, its logo or name... A brand is the sum of the values it represents. It doesn't actually matter what the product is at all.

Indeed, it need not even be a product. In 1997, Prime Minister Tony Blair began a high-profile campaign to "re-brand" Britain and was mocked for his use of marketing-speak to describe a policy initiative. His choice was apposite, however. Though he might have been safer talking about Britain's *image*, the concept of "brand" is both deeper and richer—rich enough to capture the culture, values, and aspirations of some 60 million people.

What brand is not, of course, is a synonym for "product." A brand is an offer, a promise, a set of expectations made tangible. It has the potential to create cadres of consumer loyalists, who bond with its package of differentiating advantages in a highly personal way.

By contrast, a product is what rolls off the assembly line or is created in the lab. It has attributes and objective benefits, such as anti-lock brakes or 24-hour dosing. What it doesn't have, yet, is a *soul*. The act of *ensoulment*, as industry colleagues at Thomas Ferguson Associates call their proprietary branding process, turns products into brands, brands into megabrands, and megabrands into franchises.

Success lies at the heart of every brand. That success may have begun to fade a little, or remain largely a promise. It might be a well-kept secret, still, as in the case of *cult* brands. But *unsuccessful brand* is an oxymoron. ***To become a brand, a product must have it all: presence, a clearly articulated promise, and delivery on that promise at every level, from the most rational to the least.***

Which begs the following question: if buying a car is an emotional experience, how much more so is the choice of a brand to treat one's depression, impotency, or infertility, or to raise one's T-cell levels? If the lure of rack-and-pinion steering is strong, how much stronger the possibility of longer time with family for an Alzheimer's patient, greater mobility for a person with multiple sclerosis, or greater protection, for someone with AIDS, from pneumocystis carinii?

This may sound flippant or, worse, callous: as if the incremental (some would say *trivial*) benefits of one kind of car ownership over another could somehow be equated with the quality of life issues that invest health care products and services. But that's precisely the point. They can't. And that is the reason so many of us have chosen the field of health care communications: for the vast potential of such communications to motivate, heal, and give hope to those who may have given up.

Not false hope, mind you, but the Real Deal; FDA and the internal regulatory functions of pharmaceutical companies and providers see to that. There is a special hell reserved for products that don't deliver on their promise, with front-row seating for medical products and services that harm rather than heal. Further—in the rare case where FDA fails to mete out punishment, preemptively or otherwise—there is the market itself and the courts. While American litigiousness is famous, if not infamous, worldwide, it too serves as a brake on the introduction of quack cures into mainstream life.

In fact, the vast majority of the medical products and devices approved each year work precisely as advertised to providers, payers, health care professionals, and, increasingly, to health care consumers. And although less than a quarter of the

$4 billion spent on health care promotion in 1997 went to direct-to-consumer (DTC) promotions, DTC advertising is the most visible and, arguably, most important development in consumer health since a whole new generation of compounds arrived on the scene more than 50 years ago.

Does that overstate the case? Possibly. Or maybe, as Holman Jenkins wrote in "Is Advertising the New Wonder Drug? (March 25, 1998, *Wall Street Journal*):

> It would not be the smallest irony if advertising turned out to be the real therapeutic miracle of our time... Companies spent millions to put [the names of cholesterol-lowering medicines like Pravachol, Zocor, Lipitor, and Mevacor] under the noses of consumers, and consumers responded by rushing to see their doctors. Some 60 percent of heart disease has typically gone untreated until somebody keels over from an attack. Ads can save lives.

With heart disease in retreat, with new breakthrough cancer therapies, and with researchers knocking at the door of immortality itself, a new "golden age" of medicine is at hand. How well consumers of the future exercise their health care options will depend, in large part, on how well informed they are—on whether we, as a society, embrace the efficiency or the effectiveness model of health care delivery—and, not least, on our ability to throw off the last vestiges of a paternalistic health care system in which everyone but the consumer had a say.

THE MIRACLE OF CHOICE

We forget how new it all is.

Not just the branding of health care products and services, but the practice of modern medicine itself. We forget that pharmaceutical giant Merck & Co. has been on these shores over 100 years, that "germ theory" dates from the latter part of the 19th century, and that the staples of modern pharmacopoeia—antibiotics and the major vaccines—have been with us only since World War II.

How quickly "wonder drugs" became the very staff of life—and captured our imaginations. Just six years after the introduction of penicillin, Hollywood gave us a brand-new villain for the brave new world of antibiosis: Orson Welles as penicillin pirate Harry Lime, a man so low he would traffic in adulterated medicine intended for children, in the 1949 classic "The Third Man."

Penicillin was followed swiftly by the isolation of streptomycin in 1944, the expansion of the sulfa class of drugs, the first chemotherapy agents in 1947 to 1949, and the first broad spectrum antibiotic, chlortetracycline, in 1949. Yet there were still so few effective therapies out there, relatively speaking, that it would have been difficult to foresee a time when multiple compounds would be available to treat a single condition. Or, for that matter, when the benefits and side-effects profiles of different molecules would require highly specialized communications to clinicians and, ultimately, their patients.

That's to say, when choice would enter the picture. And with choice, the health care consumer. And with health care consumers, health care branding. Especially as compounds with strong quality-of-life implications—the discovery in 1944 of pyrilamine, the first antihistamine, and of reserpine as a tranquilizer in 1953—began arriving on the scene.

It would be many decades before choice and quality-of-life concerns would collide with information technology to produce a vibrant health care consumerism. By contrast, the explosion in new compounds came quickly, hastened by research conducted between the wars. And a good thing, too: by 1946, hard on the heels of warnings by penicillin's discoverer, "an estimated 14 percent of the staphylococcus strains isolated from patients in a London hospital had developed resistance to penicillin," as reported by Sheryl Gay Stolberg in "Superbugs" (*New York Times Magazine*, August 2, 1998).

The expansion of the therapeutic arsenal coincided with the birth of the first real consumer society the world had ever known. America was riding a wave of prosperity in the postwar years as the sole major power with an intact industrial base. As Levittowns multiplied across the landscape to accommodate the baby boom, so did the number of prescriptions written. Professional advertising took off. Meanwhile, advertising of all kinds was having a heyday, boosted by a relaxed regulatory environment and the "new" medium of television, making its way into homes en masse.

There was a downside to it all, of course. Ads making unsubstantiated claims could and did run during commercial breaks from popular Westerns and alongside the careful print coverage of the explosive Kinsey Report. Along with the ads promising "whiter whites" and linking fresh breath to social success, at least one cigarette manufacturer used the stature of doctors to extol smoking as a digestive aid. And, while DTC advertising remained a long way off, professional advertising too was entering its "golden age," according to *Medicine Avenue* (W.G. Castagnoli, *The Medical Advertising Hall of Fame*, 1999), a history of the medical-advertising industry.

But, of course, advertising Rx products wasn't at all like promoting The Breck Girl or Doublemint Chewing Gum. In the spring of 1962, U.S. Senator and former vice-presidential hopeful Estes Kefauver held hearings aimed at regulating the advertising of prescription products. The Kefauver-Harris bill looked unlikely to pass, however, until the stories broke linking thalidomide, a sedative prescribed in Europe to combat morning sickness, to terrible birth defects.

There was no link between the legislation in question and the tragedy of thalidomide. The drug wasn't even marketed in the United States. Yet there can be little doubt that the potent mix of medicine and marketing was on legislators' minds when they passed Kefauver-Harris unanimously. As *Medical Marketing & Media* reported in September 1998 in "The Coming Showdown on DTC": "For years following the Kefauver hearings...the rule of thumb at companies and advertising agencies was, 'Don't put anything in an ad that you couldn't defend in public in Washington.'"

From where we sit at the turn of the 21st century, it's hard to remember a time when regulation wasn't our constant, if not always boon, companion. It's hard to fathom that—as recently as the 1960s—legislation requiring drug manufacturers to prove the efficacy of their products was a hard sell on Capitol Hill. And in fact, the 1960s and 1970s saw wave upon wave of new regulations enacted, from the Civil Rights Act to the Clean Air Act, followed by the inevitable deregulations of the 1980s and 1990s: airlines, telecommunications, and medical advertising.

True, the DTC-TV genie decanted in 1997 trailed a long line of "brief summaries": the mandatory disclosure of possible side effects, complications, and contraindications. True too, the FDA wasn't depending on the industry to police itself. In the first 14 months after the August 1997 draft broadcast guidelines were issued

Table 2–1 Faith in Confidence of Advice from Doctors

					A Great Deal of Confidence in Advice from Doctors TRACKING						
1989	*1990*	*1991*	*1992*	*1993*	*1994*	*1995*	*1996*	*1997*	*1998*	*1999*
%	%	%	%	%	%	%	%	%	%	%
72	60	61	61	63	53	59	59	58	58	61

Courtesy of Yankelovich Partners, Inc., Claremont, California.

allowing drug makers to link a product's brand name with its indication, the agency sent out 165 communications to 26 pharmaceutical companies concerning direct-to-consumer advertising violations, according to *Med Ad News's* October 1998 round-up issue on DTC advertising.

None of which changes the fact that something revolutionary had taken place. For the first time, consumers were being entrusted to participate in making decisions, for themselves and their families, that went to the very heart of quality of life. Even—in the case of diabetes, HIV, and hypertension drugs promoted directly to consumers—to life itself. "Put some freedom into your HIV medication schedule," an ad for Zerit capsules beckoned HIV-sufferers from subway cars and suburban bus shelters. It was a long way from the days when only hair-loss therapies dared to utter their names.

Consumers embraced the privilege with a vengeance. By 1998, DTC advertising had replaced "the advice of a friend or relative as the primary source of information" about prescription drugs, according to an IMS Health survey cited in *Med Ad News* (October 1998). This was particularly significant in light of Yankelovich MONITOR™ data that showed declining faith in the advice of doctors. (See Table 2–1.) Meanwhile, pharmaceutical manufacturers were voting for the new DTC guidelines with their advertising dollars: a projected $1.3 billion of them in 1998, a 50 percent increase over the year before.

In reality, DTC advertising is a "privilege" consumers wrested for themselves, along with so much else: the right to choose aggressive over palliative care; the right to die, to the extent possible, at the time and manner of one's choosing. And in so many ways, in the new millenium, patients continue to redefine the health care marketplace...and with it, the insurance marketplace, the legal marketplace, the marketplace of ideas. They are paving the way, for the first time, for genuine health care branding—paving the way, in time, for genuine global branding of health care products and services.

BRAND SPOKEN HERE

In the health care industry today, we talk a brave game when it comes to branding. The words *branding* and even *global branding* are on everyone's lips, it seems. But what does it mean in a business as heavily regulated as the pharmaceutical industry, for instance? As operations-oriented as the provider industry? In a world where every functioning public-health authority places restrictions on health care advertising? Indeed, in a world with as many different restrictions as names for the same product?

It would be foolish to draw too many inferences about the global market for health care products from the experience of consumer brands. It is, in so many ways, like comparing apples and Gila monsters. Yet many of the conditions that have contributed to the short, wildly successful history of U.S. consumer brands overseas inform the health care landscape, too—in particular, the relative scarcity of such products in many parts of the world, together with their manifest value to consumers.

While numerous U.S. and European health brands are marketed around the globe and some are even marketed transnationally under a single name and logotype, few, if any, have achieved the iconic status of the great consumer brands. With good reason: in Europe pre-regulatory-harmonization, drug manufacturers had little incentive to harmonize their marketing efforts. Adjoining countries might as well have been on different planets for all the "efficiencies" they offered. Elsewhere in the world, price as well as regulatory constraints have dampened consumer demand.

More daunting still is health care marketing in countries with low per capita incomes, where the $16,000 it costs to take a lifesaving AIDS "cocktail" for a year is more than most people make in a lifetime. Economics aside, few would argue that health products and services can or should be marketed like any other consumer good. So, while the lifestyle benefits of "the pause that refreshes" pale in comparison with the *quality of life* benefits of, say, an effective antihistamine to an allergy-sufferer in Bangkok, health-brand makers are still halted by the obstacle of inadequate protection of their patients.

The obstacles to a global health care marketplace are falling, though. In the European Union (EU), the London-based European Medicines Evaluation Agency now acts as a single clearinghouse for Rx products seeking entrée to EU-member countries. China has a burgeoning middle class and fierce demand for Western medicines. Prescription products and hospital systems—the Cleveland Clinic is in the process of joint venturing with hospital systems in Egypt and India—stand poised to join Tylenol and Bayer aspirin as truly global brands.

How soon they take the leap remains a question. How successfully, another. Many pharmaceutical companies are treading water in emerging markets, waiting for the day when their patience pays off. It may be a long wait: countries like China are considering strict price controls that could include Western drugs. In a November 1998 front-page story on the issue, *The New York Times* quoted Jeff Trewhitt, a spokesman for the Pharmaceutical Research and Manufacturers of America, as saying, "Virtually all companies are putting into [China] much more than they are taking out...They are investing in the future" ("West's Medicine Is Raising Bills for China's Sick," November 19, 1998).

In the meantime, in one respect at least, health-brand companies can learn from the Coca-Colas, Nikes, Kelloggs, IBMs, and McDonalds of the world. These companies, after all, invented the lingua franca of brand, using it to leap national, cultural, and gastronomic boundaries with the greatest of ease.

Captive Consumers, Borderless Brands

As long ago as the 1970s, you could quench your thirst in a Moscow restaurant—or a Bedouin encampment in the Middle East—with a Coke in its familiar bottle. Never mind that the actual legend was in Cyrillic or Arabic; the red lettering on the bottle declared it "*The Real Thing.*" However scorned by European intellectuals, Coca-Cola and a handful of other megabrands symbolized to millions around the globe The Good Life, American-style.

Perhaps nowhere was this truer than in Eastern Europe during the Cold War. Such was the power of brand that Marlboro cigarettes, Levi jeans, and Johnnie Walker Black Label became consumer icons without being for sale in the usual sense. Indeed, their availability to the happy few—mostly privileged bureaucrats called apparatchiks—was an integral part of the value equation. Sold at hard-currency stores barred to ordinary folk, often obtained on the sly, "name brands" were prized as much for their barter potential as for the pleasure of their consumption.

For Americans in those years, there was a *Through-the-Looking-Glass* quality to traveling in Eastern Europe, where American brands ruled supreme. After all, for the most part, these were radically nonconsumer societies, whose command economies might turn out women's shoes in red one year and in black the next; where cigarettes had to be smoked at just the right angle lest all their tobacco fall out; where gargantuan stores with empty shelves mocked the few shoppers who ventured in.

Quality, relevance, and mystique have a lot to do with brand appeal anywhere, but particularly where shoddy, irrelevant, and unattractive are the rule. Beyond the intrinsic value of scotch with a smooth finish, jeans with an attractive fit, or "the finest Virginia tobaccos," there was an extrinsic value to such products. In countries with nonconvertible currencies, only *brand* could hold its own. Nor could wheelbarrows full of rubles, forints, or zlotys buy East Europeans the brands they coveted. *Coveted—it should be pointed out—without a single ad dollar tossed their way.*

Things are different today, of course. While there are tens of thousands of brands, there are only tens of megabrands. Increasingly, American brands share the stage with the Filas and Absoluts, Lacostes and Lexuses of the world. While barter persists in Russia, Communism has given way to market systems almost everywhere, and ad agencies flourish in Shanghai and the former Karl-Marx-Stadt. Finally and most important, as trade barriers fall and markets become interdependent, brand access no longer depends on the right contacts so much as the necessary resources.

Yet brand lives on. As important as ever—maybe more so. As compelling in rich consumer societies as in poor subsistence ones. Today, in scenes repeated endlessly around the globe, teenagers from Amsterdam to Nanking dip into KFC for a bite, while guerrillas in the Peruvian and Congolese bush sport the Nike swoosh with their fatigues.

IN SEARCH OF "BRAND VOLTAGE"

How do we account for the transcendent appeal of brand? In what respects are health brands the same as and different from consumer brands? What brand characteristics are most predictive of consumer behavior? The WPP Group's massive study of brand equity, BRANDZ, provides some clues.

Rolled out in October 1998, the first phase of BRANDZ evaluated 3,500 corporate and product brands (including a number of Rx and over-the-counter brands) through interviews with a total of 70,000 consumers in the United States, Brazil, the United Kingdom, France, Germany, Japan, and China. Based on methodology developed by WPP Group company Millward Brown, BRANDZ analyzes the factors behind consumer loyalty using Millward Brown's proprietary BrandDynamics™ pyramid. (See Figure 2–1.)

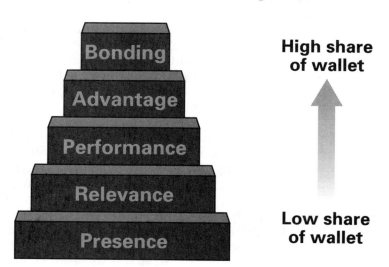

Figure 2–1 Why Should We Believe the BrandDynamics™ Pyramid? *Source:* Brand Dynamics Pyramid is a property of Millward Brown, Naperville, Illinois.

At the bottom of the pyramid is marketplace ***presence***, which researchers quantified for each brand in the study by asking respondents if they had any direct experience with the brand, whether they had formed an opinion of it, and whether it was "top of mind." One step up is ***relevance*** ("Would you want to be seen using it?," "Is it in the right price bracket?," "Can it meet your needs?"), followed by ***performance*** ("Can it deliver?") and ***advantage*** ("Does it work better than its competitors?," "Is it at a better price?," "Is it more popular?," and "Does it appeal to you more than others?").

At the very top of the pyramid is ***bonding*** ("How many other brands do you feel the same about?," "What matters in this category?"). Not surprisingly, the qualities that make consumers feel bonded to a brand are more subjective and emotional than the qualities that attach to advantage, performance, relevance, and presence. ***Bonding is also the most predictive of consumer loyalty.*** So, while a brand may score well in the presence and relevance (i.e., more rational) levels of the pyramid, if it doesn't resonate at the higher levels it will have difficulty commanding a "high share of wallet."

Assigning numerical values to a brand at each level of the pyramid, the study adds up the numbers to determine "brand voltage": a one-number summary used to compare a brand's performance to the category average and/or competitors. Brand voltage also determines whether a product or service is classified as an "Olympic" brand (one with massive presence and the ability to convert large numbers of consumers into bonded customers); a "Fading Star" (one with massive presence that has lost its emotional edge); a "Cult Brand" (one scoring low in presence and relevance but engendering high levels of loyalty among aficionados); or one of five other brand classifications.

An interesting thing happens when we look at the BRANDZ U.S. consumer segmentation map where OTCs and pharmaceuticals are concerned. The OTC and Rx brands are poised about halfway between department stores and airlines on the low ("totally price-driven") end and coffee and baby food on the high ("committed loyals") end. (See Figure 2–2, "U.S. Consumer Segmentation Map.") To me, this suggests a market environment for health brands that is more fluid and has more variables in it than that of many other brand categories.

But we knew that, you say. How many other categories must factor into the marketing mix the pressures of managed care, the complexities of FDA regulation, the unpredictability of prescriber-middlemen? Still, something about the positioning of health brands in the consumer cosmos chafes. How can consumers feel more emotionally bonded to their morning cup of joe than to the pills that ease their pain and regulate their heartbeats?

Enter the Health Care Consumer

It's a complex question that goes to the heart of health care branding. It suggests the tremendous potential of branding to elevate the pharmaceutical and provider marketplaces, to empower consumers to be better stewards of their health, and—by enriching the dialogue between patients and physicians—to enhance the patient-physician relationship, lately fallen on hard times. It speaks volumes about

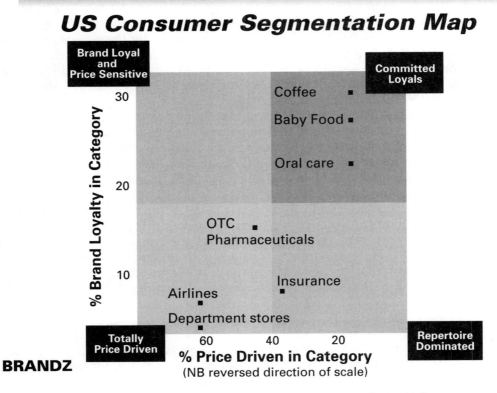

Figure 2–2 U.S. Consumer Segmentation Map. Courtesy of WPP Group, New York, New York.

how far we have come, in a short space of time, in the branding of health care products and services.

And about how far we have, still, to go.

Not so many years ago, pharmaceutical manufacturers operated in a "generic" universe of molecules and mechanisms of action. Never mind that this universe happened to have branded products; marketplace presence, physician awareness, was deemed to be enough. Drug makers were in the innovation business of producing breakthrough products, a place where consumers need not—*dared not*—tread.

With industry attention focused squarely on the person with the initials after his or her name, pharmaceutical products didn't move very far from their valuation in the lab to their communicated value to the prescriber. "Brand personality" resided largely in the drug company sales rep, who came to personify the product for the doctor through the process of personal selling.

To a lesser degree, the doctor fulfilled the same function for the patient. Except that little or no personal "selling" was required. With largely uncontested authority and, often, a longstanding relationship with the patient, the doctor merely said, "Take this," and the patient did as he or she was told. Or didn't, as the case may be, but kept quiet about it. It didn't hurt that consumer expectations were low. Then several things happened to change the balance of power forever.

Innovation "happened," first of all: the advent of CT scanners and MRIs, beta blockers and protease inhibitors, organ transplantation, immunosuppression agents, pacemakers, and the computer and digital technology that lie at the heart of today's life support systems. This knowledge explosion enabled us, suddenly, to prolong life almost indefinitely. It was then just a short step from the possibility of greatly extending life to a moral imperative to extend it, regardless of the costs.

This explosion in health care choice was mirrored by the explosion in consumer goods—Sony's Walkman, the VCR, Game Boy, and compact discs—during the boom years of the Reagan presidency. Marketing executives found themselves the cocks of the corporate walk. Business gurus preached the virtues of Total Quality Management. Consumer expectations soared.

At the nexus of the knowledge and consumer revolutions was the personal computer, making its way into American homes as the decade turned. The ultimate consumer toy of the 1980s would become, by the mid-1990s, the ultimate consumer-empowerment tool. Patients and their families were early adopters, embracing the new technology to offer and solicit support, to trade information on the latest trials, and to organize.

Meanwhile, advances in life-prolonging drug therapies and, especially, technology were sparking an altogether different movement. Squeezed by the spiraling costs of medicine in the Digital Age, payers squeezed employers and patients in turn: for higher premiums, co-pays, and deductibles. Enter managed care and a whole new lexicon of operational efficiency: formularies, capitation, independent practice association (IPA) models, and credentialed providers.

From Disease-State Management to Quality of Life

For the estimated 90 million Americans enrolled in managed-care plans in 1997, doctors became part of the operational-efficiency chain. Pressed into seeing more patients each day, they spent less time with each one. Nor did patients know their doctors as well: as employers changed insurance plans so, often, did employees change primary care physicians (PCPs). The result: less faith in doctors as all-seeing and all-knowing. More self-medicating on the part of patients. More patients seeking alternative sources of information, whether from friends, family, or one of the estimated 10,000 Internet sites offering health care information.

With two-thirds of Americans going online for health reasons, according to a June 1998 Institute for the Future-Princeton Research Associates survey("21st Century Health Care Consumers," June 17, 1998), cyberspace was reshaping health care consumer expectations. And significantly upping the ante.

Suddenly, the health care consumer was saying to his or her doctor: "I want a cure. You're offering me a disease-management solution. How far along the path to wellness and well-being are you willing and able to take me?" For the patient with Parkinson's, it was: "If you aren't going to replenish my dopamine levels long-term, what *are* you going to do for me?" For the patient with Alzheimer's: "If you can't give me back my memory, how much function can you return to me?"

Each was seeking quality of life; whether the perception of it or the reality hardly mattered. Because perception is reality when it comes to quality of life. And, increasingly, that perception is critical to what consumers buy in health brands, be they prescription or OTC drugs, acute- or chronic-care facilities, HMOs or fee-for-service plans.

As recently as a generation ago, "quality of life" was thought of—if at all—as the province of patient families. Of hospital chaplains and physical therapists. More recently, of pain specialists. And, of course, of patients themselves. Writing in the *New England Journal of Medicine* in March 1996, Testa and Simonson noted that only five key references to quality of life appeared in the Medline database in 1973 ("Assessment of Quality-of-Life Outcomes," March 28, 1996, vol. 334, pp. 834–840). By contrast, subsequent five-year periods saw 195, 273, 490, and 1,252 such mentions.

Running on a parallel track with quality-of-life concerns was the right-to-die movement. Sparked by the Karen Ann Quinlan case in the 1970s, it gathered force through the 1980s before "morphing" into the assisted-suicide movement of the 1990s. Health care consumerism had come full circle: touching every stage of the health care continuum from cradle (the advent of consumer-friendly "birthing centers" in hospitals) to grave (the state of Oregon's controversial law to permit doctor-assisted suicide).

Today, the results of this newfound health activism are as varied as patients' rights legislation and the street actions of ACT-UP. They can be as mundane—or profound—as the hospital in Perth Amboy, New Jersey that offers a money-back guarantee on the services of its emergency room. They include the fast-tracking of breakthrough therapies, the Orphan Drug Act, and increased funding for breast-cancer research.

Nor is this movement apt to burn out soon. Never mind, as *The Economist* reported in "Health Care: To the Hustings" (July 1998), that "polls constantly show that…three-fourths of Americans are happy with the reality of their managed care: a satisfaction level almost as high as [that of] Americans receiving care of the traditional sort." Few Americans would dispute that the United States is home to the world's finest health care—and a health care system with its kinks.

More and more, information is the weapon of choice of today's health care consumers, who are shedding light where bureaucratic stonewalling and professional secrecy once ruled. Prompting fertility clinics to disclose their success rates.

Making it more difficult for doctors with poor records in one system to move blithely to the next. Empowering the "end users" of health care as never before.

To truly empower, however, information has to be in the right hands, from the right source, and understood in context. Unfiltered or just plain wrong information in the hands of the underinformed can be as dangerous as giving prescribing power to your Uncle Pete. Which is why the filtering of on-line information—via services such as Medscape, Planet Rx, and the federal government's Healthfinder—remains an important development on the consumer health care front.

Important, but no substitute for guided, accurate, *consumer-specific* information. Nonetheless, with each passing year, the Internet becomes the "family doctor" of choice for increasing numbers of Americans. As reassuring as it may be to access, with a few short keystrokes, the opinions of C. Everett Koop, e-consultation should never replace the face-to-face kind.

Increasingly, it does. And by all accounts it will continue to do so, as rising education levels, falling employer-funded benefits, and mounting mistrust of anyone in a lab coat fan the flames of self-care activism.

PATENT MEDICINES: THE ROAD TO HEALTH CARE BRANDING

Things used to be simpler, of course. Before the introduction of penicillin in 1943, before the stockpiling of the vast armory of compounds available today, doctors were mostly in the palliative-care business: relieving symptoms when they could; restoring spirits when they couldn't. Doctors in practice before World War II knew all about the placebo effect. It resided in the humble, inexpensive, harmless, and indispensable sugar pills they took with them on their rounds.

These pills were largely nameless—"something to make you feel better" usually sufficed. Americans weren't as educated in those days. As "media consumers," their choices were largely limited to the local papers, whatever the corner drugstore had to offer, perhaps a well-thumbed Sears catalogue. Nor did the pill proffered by the doctor need a name. Its worth had been validated by him. End of story.

Remember, the family doctor enjoyed a relationship with his patients that was lifelong, and of an intimacy rivaled only by family and clergy. Invariably a "general practitioner" before the term was coined, the same doctor might bring your children into the world, prescribe arsenic for a sexually transmitted disease, ease your uncle's last days or hours, and stitch up a hand caught in a threshing machine.

Indeed, his duties went beyond the strictly medical. He might find a baby for a childless couple, an asylum for an "eccentric" aunt, or a place for an unmarried teenager to wait out her pregnancy. Like the doctor in Ibsen's *The Wild Duck*, he was the repository of family secrets at a time when infertility, mental illness, and out-of-wedlock births were heavily stigmatized.

No wonder his advice was obeyed.

Yet in 19th century America, professional advice of *any* kind could be damnably hard to come by. Vast swathes of the country were beyond the reach of a doctor's Gladstone bag. Where professional help was available, it could be of a highly doubtful sort: the dentist/surgeon well known to generations of Western fans. Into this vacuum rolled the patent-medicines seller in his brightly painted wagon.

His relationship with his "patients" was very different. Often itinerant and a stranger, he couldn't depend on trust. He didn't sing hymns with his customer base on Sundays; his shingle didn't hang on Main Street. Most important, he rarely had any medical training, though that fact usually went unmentioned. For him, nameless pills were out of the question. A reassuring handle, a stirring pitch, and an audience unschooled enough to suspend disbelief were needed to sell his or her brand of "hope in a bottle."

And in fact, patent medicines were sold in much the same way that bar soap, corsets, or any other consumer product was sold. Only they were far more versatile. "Dr. Heller's Elixir" could be touted to one prospective customer as a "physic," to another as a cure for gout, and to a third as a hair-restorer. Or as all three, simultaneously. It was "direct-to-consumer marketing" and "relationship marketing" of the most basic, primitive sort. The message could be, and often was, customized to fit the audience. The "sales representative" was often none other than "Dr." Heller himself.

Long before the Home Shopping Network, the public hawking of medical products was conceived as entertainment. The "medicine shows" that roamed 19th century rural America often featured minstrel, Indian, or magic acts, followed by the inevitable pitch for this or that cure-all. In an early example of franchising, the Kickapoo Indian Medicine Company had as many as 75 carnival companies fanning out across the country at one time, according to Gerald Carson, author of *One for a Man, Two for a Horse* (Bramhall House, New York, 1961), a history of the medicine-show phenomenon.

From Snake Oil to St. John's Wort

Unfortunately, the patent-medicine man's products were often worthless and occasionally harmful or fatal. Which accounted in part for the itinerant nature of the business, in which "snake-oil salesmen" sometimes stayed one step ahead of the law. Many decades before the establishment of the FDA, regulation often took the form of a swift kick out of town.

Not all patent medicines were worthless, however, nor all who sold them hucksters. Many "proprietary medicines," as they were also called, were stocked in licensed chemist shops and advertised in newspapers. Some, in altered form, even achieved lasting fame as nonmedicinal products, Coca-Cola being the prime example. Others, long a part of traditional or "folk" medicine, saw their fortunes fall in the United States as powerful new drugs were introduced, only to see them rise again as double-blind trials confirmed their effectiveness and safety, as in the recent cases of St. John's Wort and ginkgo biloba.

The case could even be made that many patent medicines, however "worthless" from an empirical vantage, actually performed a useful function—particularly when you consider the contents of the average doctor's bag of 100 years ago. Most contained no more than quinine for malaria, digitalis for heart problems, heroin to control coughing, morphine for pain, ephedrine for asthma, and the odd fever controller and sedative. Not one of these agents was effective against infectious disease, responsible for nearly half the deaths in the United States in 1900.

Couple this fact with what we now know about the "placebo effect," and the patent-medicine picture changes still more. In October 1998, in an article entitled "Placebos Prove So Powerful Even Experts Are Surprised," *The New York Times* reported that "[s]tudies have shown, time and again, that placebos...can lead to changes in pulse rate, blood pressure, electrical skin resistance, gastric function, penis engorgement, and skin conditions (S. Blakeslee, October 13, 1998).

In other words, it's possible that the "Vital Sparks" hawked—a century before Viagra—as a "restorer of manhood" by Princess Lotus Blossom of medicine-show fame actually worked as advertised in some cases. As for the ubiquitous hair-restorers of the patent-medicine chest, the same *Times* article reported that "42 percent of balding men taking a placebo either maintained or increased the amount of hair on their heads."

As Holman Jenkins concluded in *The Wall Street Journal* column, "Is Advertising the New Wonder Drug?": "Hope may be half the cure."

The Power of Hope

Lack of formal regulation conspired with the need for hope and a dearth of effective treatments to make patent medicines with secret ingredients a major force in the 19th and early 20th centuries. Of the five top-selling drugs in 1900, only Sterling's (now Bayer) Aspirin is still around in recognizable form. The other four— Dr. Carter's Little Liver Pills, Burroughs-Wellcome Beef Liver Extract, Bristol's Clinton Digestive Tablets, and Squibb's Choc-Coated Anemia Tablets—have gone the way of the Gibson Girl.

Not so their manufacturers. Burroughs-Wellcome, Bristol-Myers Squibb, and, of course, Bayer are today among the world's great pharmaceutical companies. And while regulation is often cast as the enemy of growth and innovation, there can be no doubt that the pharmaceutical industry owes some of its spectacular success (1904 industry-wide sales of $74.5 million, according to Hambrecht & Quist, versus $99.5 billion in 1998 in the United States alone) to the collateral effects of regulation: credibility, accountability, and quality assurance.

Quality assurance had become top-of-mind by the early years of the 20th century, when ordinary Americans became aware, through "muckraking" articles and the 1906 publication of Upton Sinclair's *The Jungle*, of horrendous practices in the meat-packing industry. That same year, President Theodore Roosevelt signed into law the Pure Food and Drug Act. Two years later, under the same act, the federal government sued the makers of the coyly named *Curforhedake Brane Fude*. The battle lines between patent medicines and "ethical drugs" had been drawn.

It was the beginning of health care regulation as we know it. Though most cities in the United States and Western Europe had public health authorities by the late 19th century, there was little federal regulation of food and drugs in the United States before 1906. The Pure Food and Drug Act was followed by the 1931 creation of the FDA and the Food, Drug and Cosmetics Act of 1935. Signed into law by Franklin Roosevelt, the Food, Drug and Cosmetics Act expanded the power of the FDA and coincided with an explosion of research that would lead to the postwar phenomenon of "wonder" drugs.

Secret ingredients were out; "daylight" was in. With daylight came increased efficacy, a.k.a. performance. With enhanced performance, increased relevance. And so on up the consumer-loyalty chain to bonding: the complex constellation of emotions that engenders both hope and greater compliance.

In simplest terms, the dynamic goes something like this:

Hope triggers the placebo effect, the raft of physiological changes set in motion by the patient's belief system. The placebo effect reinforces compliance as the patient "feels" him- or herself getting better and is motivated to stay the therapeutic course. Increased compliance means better performance, as the Rx or OTC product is used as directed, leading to better outcomes. Better outcomes bring us full-circle back to hope, as the healing process assumes its own momentum, aided by what Bill Moyers, in his book *Healing and the Mind*, calls the "innate healing capacities that make us nature's allies in...recovery" (Doubleday, New York, 1993).

Again, this is a gross oversimplification of the complex (and far from understood) processes at work in healing. A whole new field, psychoneuroimmunology, is devoted to the mind-body connection. What *is* clear is the important role of the patient's belief system, the expectations that—for good or ill—shape and may even determine our capacity for wellness.

Today, health care expectations are formed in many ways: through patient-physician exchanges, package inserts, waiting-room materials, Internet "chat rooms," prior personal or familial experience, and, increasingly, through direct-to-consumer advertising and the direct marketing of health care products and services. Not all these channels are equal, however. As Yankelovich MONITOR™ data show, consumer confidence in brands has risen as consumer trust in doctors has declined. (See Table 2–1.)

This invests our communications work with both meaning and responsibility—the responsibility to inform rather than distort, encourage rather than frighten. As Kathy Jenkins, chief creative officer of The Quantum Group, wrote recently in "Creating Messages That Help Heal":

> Health care communicators face the challenge of directing the minds and emotions of consumers to effectively support healing...marketers can't frighten individuals into wellness by simply emphasizing the negative. Although the amygdala gland in the brain will stimulate fight or flight on first contact with a threat, pleasurable, positive stimuli can activate chemicals in the brain to soothe and calm (*DTC Times/Pharmaceutical Executive* (August 1999).

Jenkins's challenge to health care communicators is also our tremendous privilege. The privilege of living at a time when rigorous science and post-approval surveillance has created a formidable credibility for health care products and services—credibility that can be fashioned, via consumer communications, into powerful messages of hope.

In the patent-medicine era, health care consumers had hope without performance, branding without science or surveillance. As the wonder-drug era dawned, consumers increasingly had science but no branding; performance, but not always hope. Pills were nameless, doctors all-powerful. Health care consumers weren't consulted about the most intimate aspects of their lives, nor were their hearts or minds engaged.

Did it matter? Before the miracle of health care choice, what would consultation, actually, have meant? Not a lot, perhaps. At mid-century, for a whole array of illnesses, it was penicillin or *nothing*, pyrilamine or *nothing*, reserpine or *nothing*, in effect. Substitutes, insofar as they existed, tended to be far less effective. As for side effects, they were often best left out of the picture, since the alternative, again, might be nothing.

Contrast this with the myriad products with the same indication that are available to consumers today, each with its own dosing schedule, contraindications, method of action, and side-effects profile. In such an environment, the need for disclosure takes on a whole new urgency. And with it, the need for the "shorthand" of DTC and the "longhand" of medical education, as consumers strive to become full partners in their wellness.

Not only have today's health care consumers embraced DTC communications with a vengeance, they have bonded with the products whose presence in magazines and on TV and billboards they have learned to take for granted. This act of bonding has a direct impact on the number and kinds of prescriptions written and office visits logged.

As *Med Ad News* reported in October 1998, citing Scott-Levin research data, "[S]ix of the 10 medical conditions accounting for increased office visits in 1997 were for conditions mentioned in direct-to-consumer advertising campaigns (T. Grom, "Tuned-In" October 1998). With some justification, then, we in health care communications can claim not only cadres of consumer loyalists, but a hand in increased longevity

Building Health Care "Megabrands"

Once even the ablest patients played a version of "Mother, May I?" with their doctors. No more. Information in the hands of the lay public has become part of the cure. Even many health care providers are now feeling, in a twist on the retailing come-on, that an educated health care consumer is their best patient. Indeed, for every provider irked at the second-guessing of amateurs, others are grateful not to have to explain the difference between bacterial and viral infections.

But information remains the proverbial double-edged sword. Used correctly, it is the best friend you can have. Used incorrectly—to inflate expectations, for instance—it will come back to haunt you every time.

Lately, some inside-the-beltway pundits have taken to calling this the Too-Much-Information Age. They have a point. In such an age, it is critical to have products and services worth talking about. Products and services that can rise above the clutter, withstand the klieg lights of exposé, survive the hyper-competition for consumers' attention.

How do we build brands that are distraction-, distortion-, and disillusionment-resistant? That fulfill the unique needs of today's health care consumers—the need for simplicity, above all? That have the potential for "megabrand-dom"? *In part, by adhering to the following 10 Principles of Branding:*

1. *Deliver on functionality.* Translation: Do what you say you will do. Relieve allergies. Banish toenail fungus. Prevent acid reflux. Time, after time, after time. In the BrandDynamic Pyramid, "product performance" is situated midway between "presence" at the bottom of the pyramid and "bonding" at the top—the keystone to consumer loyalty.

2. *Ace-out in the affinity department.* Have personal relevance to my life. Not just as a parent; not even as the parent of a toddler; but as the parent of a toddler with allergies, for instance. In an environment in which there is both an information glut and shrinking unscheduled time, any product, information, or service not specifically "mass customized" to fulfill my needs is one more useless distraction.

3. *Have the right window of safety.* Part of "advantage" in the BRANDZ consumer cosmos. Your product or service need not be 100 percent safe—assuming there is such a thing—as long as its parameters of safety have been well-communicated by you and well-understood by the consumer.

4. *Be right on price.* "Advantage," again. This is a value-driven, price-competitive society—a "deal-based world," as a friend of mine is fond of saying. Look for it to remain so, regardless of what the Dow is doing.

5. *Speak with one tongue.* Deliver one message to patients...and the same, bottom-line message to professionals, payers, providers, whomever. Customize that message, of course, but take care not to contradict what you said to the consumer. In an Age of Too-Much-Information, there is no such thing as privileged communications. Further, a single, compelling brand message enriches the dialogue between patient and physician, payer and provider, often leading to better compliance and outcomes.

6. *Be operationally effective as opposed to merely operationally efficient.* Hospital systems and managed-care organizations have often positioned themselves as customer-service organizations when, in fact, they were "about" operational efficiency. Operational effectiveness is the perfect way to satisfy the two, seemingly mutually exclusive, imperatives.

7. *Be "glocal."* Be transnational in your appeal while you retain your relevance to my particular household. As in Principle 2, "Ace-out in the affinity department," mass customization is key. In pursuit of glocality, explore direct-marketing solutions in addition to mass communications to achieve the optimal mix.

8. *Be an "outside-in" brand.* Fulfill a concrete need. In a mature marketplace, successful brands don't create needs, i.e., engage in "inside-out" marketing. They untap needs we didn't know we had. Who knew we needed to jog to music until Sony's Walkman came along? The test of a great "outside-in" brand: it should make you want to smite your forehead and exclaim, "Why didn't I think of that?!"

9. *Be loyal.* In a deal-based world, customer loyalty is that rarest of commodities. To engender loyalty, make loyalty to your customers reflexive, knowing it is far easier to retain existing customers than to constantly seek out new ones. Above all, seek to bond with your customers at every opportunity. Bonding translates into loyalty, which translates into ongoing compliance in turn.

10. *Franchise, franchise, franchise.* Satisfy all the foregoing requirements for brand voltage—presence, safety, price, performance, relevance, consonant messaging, and "outside-in" marketing—and you will be ready for the next and final step to megabrand-dom: franchising. The building of satellite services. Of extended families of brands. But beware: having come to expect excellence, consumers will count on you to continually sweeten the deal.

That's okay, however. Today's "show me the money" environment and street-smart, in-your-face, hyper-vigilant consumers will serve to keep health care communications honest. And in return, increased access to information—to the "truth," if you will—will give consumers a voice and power they have never had before.

Chapter 3

Consumers' Use of Brands: Implications for Health Care

Renée M. Zakoor and Hal E. Quinley

Brands continue to play an influential role linking marketers and consumers: they streamline the purchase process by providing guideposts and anchors in the selection of products and services. At the same time, the marketer-consumer relationship has changed radically over the past 50 years. While marketers once set the agenda for brands—creating products and then telling consumers why they needed them—consumers now are increasingly in charge. Today's consumers are more informed, more savvy, more proactive, and empowered.

Health care branding is emerging as a consumer-driven service under this new paradigm. Consumers are taking increasing responsibility for health care costs and decisions at a time when they are assuming greater and greater control of the marketing relationship in general. This chapter reviews how consumers today use and relate to brands, and explores the possibilities of branding health care providers.

THE ROLE OF BRANDS IN THE MARKETPLACE

Brands are the cornerstone of a consumer-driven marketplace. A brand represents a promise to the buyer—an implicit agreement, an unspoken guarantee. It is this promise that allows products and services to transcend the blur and haze of commodities, where price is the primary driver of choice, and to enter a world of distinctiveness, where consumers' beliefs, attitudes, and expectations begin to differentiate choices.

The marketplace is easier to navigate with brands to use as anchors or guideposts. Well-established brands streamline the purchase decision-making process by creating a consistent image. Consumers know what to expect when they buy Caress, they know the difference between Tone and Dial, and they know they don't need to consider Irish Spring because it doesn't meet their purchase criteria.

Brands also help manage consumer expectations of the product or service experience. Travelers know that the accommodations and ambience at a Ritz-Carlton hotel are different from those at a Holiday Inn because both brands have carefully communicated what their brand stands for through advertising, property location, and appearance. Customers are satisfied when their expectations are met and disappointed when they're not. No one checks into a Holiday Inn and expects to find the same ambience or be treated the same way as they would if they were in a Ritz-Carlton. If by some chance they did have an experience like this, it would exceed the travelers' expectations and they would leave feeling better about choosing the Holiday Inn brand. Conversely, if Ritz-Carlton guests were treated as if they were staying in a Holiday Inn, they would likely be extremely annoyed because Ritz-Carlton had failed to deliver the expectations created by their brand.

Brand creation is about developing an ownable position and a loyal, long-lasting relationship with the consumer. The relationship is forged by providing reassurance that the consumer is smart and has made an informed, well thought-out purchase decision. Trust is the foundation of this relationship. For this type of relationship to be successful, brands must make promises and consumers must trust that the brand will fulfill its promises. If the trust is broken, consumers will defect to the competition.

In thinking about this type of relationship, marriage is an obvious analogy. When a consumer buys a Ford Taurus, there is an expectation that the car will be dependable, reliable, and—at least when it is new—have sex appeal. After all, at Ford, **Quality is Job 1**. However, as with marriage, there can be divorce when a brand breaks trust with customers. If the Taurus does not deliver on its quality promise, and if Ford does not respond with appropriate customer service, the chances are that the consumer will buy from a different manufacturer the next time he or she purchases a car. And, just as everyone has heard friends' tales of wretched divorces, this unhappy customer will likely tell many acquaintances about his or her disappointment and dissatisfaction with Ford.

Simply creating a brand is not good enough for today's sophisticated consumers. The brand has to be constantly monitored to ensure that it is delivering its intended promise. Brand maintenance is critical to building a strong brand image; a strong brand image is the ultimate competitive weapon against the muddle and overload that exist in the consumer marketplace. A strong, trustworthy brand helps forge closer relationships with consumers, enhances brand equity, and opens the door for greater business opportunities.

THE EVOLUTION OF THE BRAND-CONSUMER RELATIONSHIP

The role of brands in consumers' lives has been an evolutionary one that has undergone substantial changes over the past several decades. In the first postwar decade, the 1950s, marketers took the lead in determining the terms of transactional relationships with consumers. The fact that there were actually goods to be bought was new and exciting, and if consumers wanted what a brand had to offer, the **when, where, and how** were pretty much dictated by the marketer. During this decade of conformity, the *right* brands were a way to *fit in*. Not only did brands signal one's position on the social ladder, but in significant ways they also *defined* the social ladder and, indeed, what constituted *the good life*. Consider the progression one made through the General Motors line of products: You started out with a Chevrolet. When your financial position got a little better, you moved on to a Buick, and it became clear that you had finally made it when you bought a Cadillac.

This one-way, consumer-dependent marketplace began to break down in the 1960s and 1970s. During these decades, consumers were more focused on the *experiential* than on *material* goods. Experimentation and exploration were the touchstones of this time period. Trying new brands was a way of expressing yourself, and the number of brands increased dramatically. As competition increased, brands fought to distinguish themselves from one another. Consumers used and molded brands according to their own individual designs, and marketers began to position brands that met this need for individuality.

The tea category exemplifies this experimentation movement, as well as the need to be at the forefront of brand innovation. For decades, Lipton had sold black tea in bags and faced few competitors in the marketplace. Prior to the 1970s, the biggest excitement in the category had been the introduction of "instant" iced tea. As part of the 1960s rebellion against everything associated with the *establishment*, young consumers turned away from coffee toward tea, specifically herbal tea. This coincided with the search for more natural, healthy living. Celestial Seasonings, a Colorado start-up company founded by two friends who picked herbs while hiking in the Rocky Mountains, started selling a variety of herbal teas with funky names ("Red Zinger," "Mystic Mint," "Sleepytime") and colorful graphic packaging. Celestial Seasonings became so popular that Lipton developed its own line of herbal teas ("Soothing Moments") in an effort to prevent more consumer defection to the new alternative tea brands. That Lipton failed in this endeavor reflects an oft-proven proposition: second-in usually fails.

At the same time, distribution channels also multiplied and more and more brands appeared alongside a new counterpart—store brands and private labels. Originally, these *no frills* brands were plain packaged, not advertised, cost a lot less, and were generally of inferior quality. At the start, they were put on the bottom shelf or a rack off in the corner—often a second thought, clearly not on par with the branded competition.

By the 1980s, consumers had become competitive in all aspects of life—in work, in leisure, and in consumption. Brands became symbols of status, achievement, and winning. For example, if you drove a BMW, the "ultimate driving machine," you were a winner. By the mid-1980s, however, the status of the brand was not just about owning the BMW but getting it for 20 percent less than your neighbor. Shopping, therefore, became a sport, and consumers focused on mastering the rules of consumption and the art of finding the best deal; they shopped as much to win as to own. Consumers began to develop the tools and techniques that would make them savvy and strategic shoppers. Marketers responded by rewarding these sophisticated consumers with promotions galore, which, in turn, generated consumers who were more price-loyal than brand-loyal within their consideration sets. In consumers' eyes, nationally advertised brands continued to hold the upper hand, offering a safe, easy choice inclusive of quality and performance, whereas private label brands still involved risk, inferior quality, and inferior performance, albeit at a low cost.

In the early 1990s, as the economy experienced a downward turn, attitudes regarding status symbols began to change. Status, measured by luxury or material wealth, was slowly declining. At the same time, as companies merged and corporate layoffs occurred, consumer confidence in big business and institutions began to wane. Consumers questioned who and what they were going to trust. As a result, consumers began defining themselves, not by what brands they owned but by those that they wouldn't own. When companies disappointed and broke trust, consumers were primed to consider alternatives like store brands, private labels, and the retailer as brand.

A shift had occurred and it became more acceptable to buy private brands. Seemingly, it happened at once, like some sort of sympathetic vibration across the country—but it was strongly rooted in the emerging social and economic trends. Shopping at consignment stores became popular and even desirable. Likewise, buying store brands and private labels did not have to be a hidden act. In fact, consumers bragged about their strategic buys. Quickly realizing that consumers felt they should pay less for products, retailers knew that they already had less expensive products for their shoppers on their bottom shelves or tucked away on racks in the corner. So these private brands underwent a personality makeover. Packaging and design became more attractive (often knocking off national brands); the quality got better and better; and store marketing plans became more aggressive. The choice became not which national brand to buy but whether to pick a national brand at all.

Today, the role of brands is very nearly the reverse of the 1950s. In the partnership between marketers and consumers, consumers have assumed the role of Senior Partner and they are in control. Consumers are more than ever focused on themselves and they feel strongly that they have the ability and intelligence to know what is best for them and how to accomplish it.

In this environment, manufacturers and retailers pay a steep penalty for consumer disappointment. The brand war now includes accurately setting consumer expectations and then consistently delivering upon them. Consumers have more confidence in those brands that are willing to maintain a partnership in terms of performance and truthfulness. And they quickly defect from brands that fail to make good on their promises, to a willing competition. All aspects of marketing are focused on preventing this defection and gaining new customers, as reflected in the watchwords of the late 1990s: advertisers talk in terms of direct response, database marketers talk in terms of relationships, banks talk in terms of customer satisfaction.

Nothing symbolizes and exemplifies this role reversal better than the emergence of the Internet. The power of the Internet is the freedom it gives consumers to create and control their own marketplace. Consumers are forcing marketers to expand distribution channels and include the Internet because of their need for individual customization of products and services. Yet the Internet is a double-edge sword for marketers. It allows consumers to identify companies that will work with them and for them, while also allowing consumers to quickly eliminate those who do not or will not meet their needs. This paradigm is the newest challenge facing brands.

So, what is the new role for brands today? Brands are tools that empower consumers. Brands are facilitators of access to desired ends, rather than dictators of taste or monopolists of resources. Brands are the builders of infrastructure, the teachers of competencies and skills, tutors who show consumers how to do it on their own. Brands are the facilitators that help consumers choose products and services that enhance the way they want to look and live. (See Table 3–1.)

CONSUMER TRENDS IMPACTING BRAND PURCHASES

Numerous factors are involved in a consumer's decision to purchase a particular brand. These range from the basic issue of how much it costs, to questions of trust, to perceptions about quality, to the hassles involved in making the purchase. While price remains a central factor, other dimensions are increasingly rising to the forefront as consumers seek control over their ever-more-stressful lives.

Table 3–1 Evolution of Brand-Consumer Relationship

Time Period	Role of Brand	Consumer Participation with Brands
1950s	Brands Define	Consumers go to brands to get what they provide
1960s/1970s	Brands Offer	Consumers adopt and manipulate brands to fulfill their experiences
1980s	Brands Signal	Consumers use and transform brands into symbols of their own successes
Early 1990s	Brands Seek	Consumers resist, bargain, and negotiate
Today	Brands Target	Consumers interact, receive and gain empowerment
Future	Brands Respond	Consumers practice self-invention in a marketplace they increasingly control

Courtesy of Yankelovich Partners, Inc., Claremont, California.

Stress

Coping with stress has emerged as a top concern for today's consumers. Increasingly, they are tackling stress by aggressively setting priorities and concentrating their energies on what really matters to them. What remains is either jettisoned or delegated. Indeed, a majority of all consumers agree with the statement "Sometimes I wish I could get rid of some of my day-to-day responsibilities and obligations and have a quiet, simpler life even if it meant giving up some of the things I have now."

For better or worse, today's unrelenting stress levels are forcing consumers to make choices, to prioritize what's important to them, and to search for solutions. A strong brand that truly understands its need to fit into the consumer's lifestyle will succeed. Brands that ignore this reality will be good candidates for delegation as consumers look to pare down and streamline their lives.

Trust and Confidence

Although consumer skepticism and cynicism have bottomed out in the last few years, credibility is still very hard to come by and consumer confidence in many institutions is significantly lower than it was 10 years ago. Consumers are more open to reestablishing relationships but remain to be shown that they should have more confidence in society's institutions and organizations.

Who do consumers trust more than anyone? More than anyone or anything else, themselves. (See Table 3–2.)

Table 3–2 Consumer Trust

	1988	1999
Given a choice, consumers would prefer:		
Listening to experts	38%	31%
OR		
Following own instincts	62%	69%

Courtesy of Yankelovich Partners, Inc., Claremont, California.

Today's consumers are informed and confident in their ability to look out for themselves. Their own ability is the number one thing in which consumers have a great deal of confidence. They are self-confident and self-assured.

At the same time, consumers realize the need for an occasional helping hand: It's simply too stressful to go it alone, in all circumstances, without the necessary resources or competencies. In this respect, consumers are increasingly open to brands. A known, trusted brand is now as important as price when it comes to influencing a purchase decision. To the degree that a brand is clearly defined and consistent, trusted brands can act as "editors," allowing consumers to sort through choices and reduce selection sets to a manageable number of options. Trusted brands also function as risk minimizers, providing reassurance and reducing the anxiety and uncertainty that can be associated with trying an unknown brand.

Value

The notion of value has evolved considerably over the past several decades. Whereas it was once negatively correlated with price—an inexpensive product was deemed an excellent value—factors such as quality and service began to enter the equation as consumers demanded more for their money.

Today, value is a function of both personal and marketplace conditions and can be defined as:

$$Value = f(price, quality, energy, stress, situation)$$

While the *price* component is relatively straightforward, it is important to recognize that the most expensive offering in a particular category may in fact be considered the best value *if it is worth the price paid*. For example, if Energizer batteries really do offer a longer life, they may be considered an outstanding value even at a premium price because they yield better/longer performance from your portable CD player. Conversely, an inexpensive offering may be considered a complete waste and poor value if it fails to perform. The least expensive paper towels may be of no value whatsoever if they don't absorb spills. In short, the negative correlation between value and price is no longer applicable.

Quality is perhaps the most complex variable in the equation. The ubiquitous tag to which countless retailers, manufacturers, and marketers lay claim is actually a function of three critical components: *mastery of the basics*, *consistency*, and *trustworthiness.*

The phrase *mastery of the basics* relates to performance: the product or service has to do what it's supposed to do. Among other things, a flashlight must work in a blackout. A battery has to make the music play. A car has to start every morning. A credit card has to be widely accepted. A health insurance plan must cover health care needs.

Consistency simply means the product or service has to do what it's supposed to do every time. The battery has to last. The credit card has to be accepted everywhere. The health insurance plan must cover medical emergencies.

The final ingredient of quality is *trustworthiness*. Perhaps the most important factor in trustworthiness is the level that the manufacturer stands behind its product or brand. A perfect example is Tylenol. When Johnson & Johnson learned of the tampering with Tylenol products, it pulled all Tylenol products from every shelf. By doing so, it conveyed the notion of a quality guarantee to its customers, and helped consumers to once again trust its brand.

A byproduct of trustworthiness is the perception that a product is more reasonably priced than those offered by the competition, even if in reality this product costs more.

A new component of the value mix is the effort or *energy* required to purchase or use a product/service. While money and time have long been recognized as scarce consumer resources, energy has recently been added to the list. Life today is perceived to be more complex than ever. Individuals are working longer hours while trying to devote more resources to their families. They are making every effort to be healthy and fit, yet still trying to enjoy themselves. At the end of a busy day or week, many may have the money or time to go out and let off some steam, yet few have the energy to do so. Instead, the nearest couch is the most attractive option.

Bringing the issue of energy to the marketplace, consumers place value today on purchase and use processes designed to preserve their energy reserves. Simplicity—in the form of trustworthy pricing, shorter lines or express counters, financial products (such as debit cards) designed to streamline, catalog and internet shopping, etc.—is held in very high regard. In fact, a product or service that is of excellent quality and at the right price may still be considered a poor value if it is too taxing to purchase or use.

Stress is related to the energy concept: like energy, it is negatively correlated with value. The more stressful it is to visit a particular retailer—as well as to find, purchase, or use a product—the lower the perceived value. For example, while mass merchandisers or warehouse clubs offer name brand products at less expensive prices, weaving through their aisles to pick up one or two things may be more stressful (and of lesser value) than popping into a convenience store and paying a little more money for a little less aggravation. Similarly, having to develop new physician relationships may be more stressful than paying an extra $15 a month to maintain an existing health insurance plan.

Situation is perhaps the most variable and influential element at play in determining value. As consumers' situations or circumstances change daily, hourly, or even by the minute, so too do their value needs. For example, a consumer casually looking on a Saturday afternoon at batteries for her son's portable video game is likely more interested in price and less about energy and stress than if she had to run out on her lunch hour because her watch stopped. A healthy consumer who last saw a physician two years ago will view his choice of an HMO or PPO differently than someone who has a chronic condition and sees the same physician every three months. The weight consumers place on the different conditions affecting value is thus extremely fluid. As a result, consumers look to marketers to understand their situations and respond with appropriate value propositions in accordance with their ever-changing circumstances.

In interpreting the value equation, it is critical to understand that consumers operate within the bounds of a price ceiling and a quality floor. In other words, they will only spend so much for a given product or service—regardless of its perceived quality or value. And at the same time, there is a level of quality below which they will never tread, regardless of its low price.

Value, then, is largely in the eye of the purchaser. It is a concept or perception that is not fixed or applicable across the board to a given product, service, brand, or retailer. Rather, value is dependent on each individual's set of needs and circumstances. It may be defined by one set of qualifications at one point in time, and entirely different variables the next.

Table 3–3 Factors Affecting Consumers' Purchases

Important Reasons in Deciding Where To Shop:	1994	1996	1999
Reasonable prices	83%	84%	79%
Treats customers with respect	68	70	67
Has outstanding customer service	NA	54	53
Convenient store hours	55	65	64
Convenient parking	48	56	52
Lets me shop from a catalog	11	15	17

Courtesy of Yankelovich Partners, Inc., Claremont, California.

While price is an important factor in consumers' purchase decisions, there is waning interest in going all-out to save a few dollars. Perceived value does not always mean getting the best deal. More and more, consumers are unwilling to make trade-offs involving compromise of time, convenience, and service in the name of penny-pinching. (See Table 3–3.)

Opportunities exist for brands to upsell nonprice elements of value by delivering things like top-notch service, convenience, and exclusivity. Such behavior allows a brand to be viewed as a tool and facilitator, enabling the consumer to take action more quickly and efficiently. In turn, this builds a competitive edge for the brand that is not solely built on price. The key is to make clear the value inherent in the brand and to deliver that value consistently.

All of this, of course, is much easier if we are dealing with a concrete product such as a battery, paper towel, automobile, or soap rather than with a service, with its multi-dimensionality and greater issues of consistency. Branding issues in the provision of health care services are especially complex—an issue to which we now turn.

CONSUMER ATTITUDES ABOUT HEALTH CARE

Health care is one of consumers' top public concerns—usually ranked second in importance just behind education. Most Americans think the government should guarantee health care for all citizens. Most Americans think the country should be spending more, not less, on health care programs. Most Americans favor government-mandated efforts to provide consumers with more health care choices, even if this would raise costs and increase government bureaucracy.

While Americans place a high value on health care, they have long possessed mixed views about how health care services are delivered. On the one hand, a large majority holds favorable opinions of their own doctors and feels satisfied with the quality of health care services they receive. On the other hand, Americans have often been critical of the general delivery of health care. Their chief complaints have involved cost, inequalities of access, and long office waits.

Changes in consumer values. Current attitudes toward health care have been shaped both by long-term trends in consumer beliefs and values and by recent market developments. In this first respect, the Yankelovich MONITOR™ provides a useful framework in which to understand how changing consumer values have impacted health care. It examines how consumer attitudes have evolved from the work-hard, *get-ahead belief set* of the economic-oriented 1940s–1950s; to the *do-*

Table 3–4 Evolution of Health Care Perceptions and Attitudes

Time Frame	Social Value Agenda	Agenda Core Social Values	Effect on Consumers of Health Care	Symptoms
1940s–50s	Economic	Conformity Hard Work Family Values	COMPLETE TRUST	Doctor knows best Housecalls Wellness = absence of illness
1960s–70s	Social	Doing your own thing The 'me' generation	EXPERIMENTATION	Doctor falls from pedestal Natural remedies: homeopathy, Spiritual healing Wellness = prevention
1980s	Winning	Getting Ahead Prestige Materialism	PATIENT AS CONSUMER	Malpractice as sport Early PPOs & HMOs Wellness = emotional ("shrinks")
Early 1990s	Denial	Negativism Self-doubt Anti-brand	VICTIMIZATION	HMOs = restricted medical options Malpractice excesses Victimization/lack of trust
Mid-1990s	Possibility	Self-confidence Taking a stand Openness to trust	CONFUSION	MDs get competition Working with the system No clear choices; all a muddle Wellness = moving target
Today	ME.2	Smarts Autonomy Living with paradox	SELF-INVENTION	Knowing and doing what's best for me; partnership with doctor; management of overall system

Courtesy of Yankelovich Partners, Inc., Claremont, California.

your-own thing experimentation of the 1960s–1970s; to the *getting-ahead belief system* of the 1980s; to the negativism and self-doubt of the early 1990s; to the more *self-confident possibility agenda* of the mid-to-late 1990s.

Today's consumers, as Table 3–4 shows, emphasize consumer smarts and autonomy (knowing what's best for them). We call it ME.2. Consumers today live in a world that is not built by others but is built by ME. It is shaped by ME, colored by ME, and controlled by ME. It is rooted in the realities of the 1990s, in what Yankelovich Partners sees as the fundamental paradox of the day: optimism prevails, but so do serious concerns and worries. This is the paradox with which consumers have come to live.

The social value agenda of each of these periods has influenced consumers' attitudes toward and use of health care services. The traditional model of health care is the 1950s *doctor knows best* viewpoint, with the doctor as authority and patient the subordinate. This hierarchy began to break down in the experimentation and growing emphasis on prevention in the 1960s and 1970s, and further still as patients begin to seek greater control of their health care in the 1980s and 1990s.

Undermining the traditional doctor-on-a-pedestal model is a decline in consumer trust of institutions and authorities in general, including doctors. Doctors are more often trusted than others—for example, 61 percent of consumers in 1999 said they have a great deal of confidence in doctors, compared with 27 percent for public schools, 20 percent for newspapers, 12 percent for the federal government, and only 7 percent for advertising. Nevertheless, the decline in trust and confidence in physicians over the 28-year period that Yankelovich has tracked this dimension is evident—from 81 percent in 1971 to 61 percent in 1999 (Figure 3–1).

In health care, as in other areas, consumers today are seeking partnerships based on trust and the fulfillment of their needs—not relationships that are one-sided or authoritative. This is particularly true of younger (Generation X) consumers, who believe that empowerment and entrepreneurship will be necessities for them to reach their goals.

The changeover from the traditional hierarchical doctor-patient relationship to today's partnering is illustrated by a recent study conducted by Yankelovich Partners for Pfizer Inc. A large majority of both patients and physicians described the relationship as a sharing or power or patients in charge (Table 3–5).

Changes in the marketplace. Alongside these shifts in consumer beliefs and values are fundamental changes in the marketplace for health care. Until recently, most Americans were shielded from paying the true costs of their health care. A large majority of costs were assumed by a third party—the employer, an insurance company, or the government. Until recently, moreover, most Americans received their health care in a traditional fee-for-service plan where their "health plan" was their personal doctor. A personal physician was most often chosen as a result of family tradition or the recommendations of friends, neighbors, or co-workers—not from an HMO or other managed care plan.

Under these circumstances, **brands** played a minor role in the selection of health care services. Only when the consumer faced a serious illness requiring hospitalization or specialized treatment was it necessary to think in terms of the **name** or **reputation** of a hospital or treatment center. National brands such as the Mayo Clinic and Sloan-Kettering existed, but for the most part the selection of specialized services was local or regional in nature. **Brands**—as we think of them in other consumer contexts—were largely nonoperative for health care consumers.

Much of this is changing. Managed care has developed as a marketplace response to rising medical costs and purchasers' resistance to paying continually escalating costs. Consumers have suddenly found themselves having to assume more of the financial responsibility for their health care, while seemingly having their choices restricted. Not surprisingly, many are displeased with this development. As surveys conducted by Yankelovich show, 73 percent of Americans believe there is

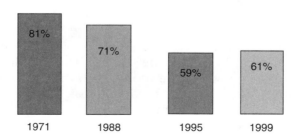

Figure 3–1 Consumer Confidence in Advice from Doctors. Courtesy of Yankelovich Partners, Inc., Claremont, California.

Table 3–5 Which Best Describes Interactions?

	Patients	Doctors
Doctors in charge	17%	9%
Authority shared	44	77
Patients in charge	33	14

Courtesy of Yankelovich Partners, Inc., Claremont, California.

something seriously wrong with our health care system; 69 percent believe the affordability of health care is not under control; 55 percent agree that the quality of health care is not as good as it used to be.

While attitudes toward the system or delivery of health care have become more negative, consumer attitudes toward their physician, the doctor-patient relationship, and the quality of their health care have changed little, if at all. Consumers continue to rate their doctors highly and to have more trust in physicians than most other institutions. The doctor-patient relationship continues to be central to the health care experience, and most patients rate their doctors highly. Similarly, a large majority of Americans, 85 percent, report a *very* or *fair* level of satisfaction with the overall quality of medical care they receive.

In sum, consumers are at an early stage of a new, evolving era in the delivery of health care services. They are assuming increasing responsibility for their health care at the same time that new delivery systems are being developed. Without question, the delivery of health services is moving toward a marketplace-driven model in which branding will play an increasingly important role.

This said, there are unique aspects of the health care delivery process that make it more complex and branding more difficult. On the provider side, these include the multiplicity of actors involved, the complexity of their roles, and problems in identifying and ensuring brand consistency. On the consumer side, they include the fact that health care costs are often unpredictable and are still rarely absorbed fully by the patient.

THE ROLE OF BRANDS IN HEALTH CARE DECISIONMAKING: LOOKING AHEAD

Consumer choice in any product category involves a series of benefit trade-offs against price. In choosing a toothpaste, you look at cavity prevention, breath freshness, teeth whitening, "natural" ingredients, and size and type of dispenser. Awareness of and familiarity with the brand are also factors. A series of mental trade-offs while standing in front of a large display area occur in a matter of seconds and a choice is made. The toothpaste's brand name helps streamline and simplify this process because it represents a promise to the consumer.

Choosing health care providers involves the same type of exercise. Consumers trade their perceptions of the quality of care they think they will receive against access and cost. Cost plays a different role in this decision than in other categories because for most consumers, medical expenses are an unknown variable. In any given year, you may be extremely healthy and have few medical expenses, or you could develop a condition that requires a series of tests and an overnight stay in a hospital, a significantly more costly experience. Additionally, most consumers have only partial choice because their employer limits the choice of providers.

Still, as in any product category, some consumers, no matter what they have to give up, always choose the lowest-cost offering. Other consumers will pay anything so that they don't have to give anything up. In health care, consumers are willing to trade some factors, such as access and choice, for lower costs (Table 3–6). They do so on the assumption that they are not sacrificing quality of care. When asked if they would be willing to trade the choice of using any doctor or specialist for lower medical expenses, many Americans willingly make that choice. However, there is a hard-core segment of Americans that will not make this trade-off and have resisted moving into any type of managed care health plan.

Meaningful brands of health care providers can help make the decision process easier. But, given the complexity of the health care delivery system, can a provider brand be created? And, considering the imperfect purchasing structure and consumers' generally passive interest in the category until they actually need the service, what will it take to make health care brands meaningful for consumers?

The essence of a brand is the promise that it makes to the consumer. It is a commitment to consistently deliver the expected service or product. Trust is at the core of the brand relationship. For consumers to trust a brand, there must be consistency. A brand represents a set of expectations, and consumers choose a brand with those expectations in mind. Unexpected surprises break the trust bond between the brand and the consumer and lead to dissatisfaction, disloyalty, and brand switching.

For consumers to believe there is equity in a brand, the brand must provide functional as well as emotional benefits and create a perceived value. The critical dimensions in health care that contribute to a brand's equity include: product features, pricing, customer service, employee behavior and appearance, the look and feel of facilities, and a distinctive identity. All of these factors must be part of the equation that defines a health care brand. Brand recognition will result from a company identifying and consistently capitalizing on those factors that are its core strengths.

Based on this definition, it is clear that some parts of the health care delivery system are well-suited to brand creation and development. Brands and brand management first emerged in packaged goods businesses, and have only recently been recognized as integral to service businesses. It is easier to brand something that is tangible and concrete, like shampoo, than it is for something that is intangible and

Table 3–6 For Routine/Preventative Care, Consumers Willing to Tradeoff MD Choice for Lower Costs

	Yes	No	Not Sure
Total	42%	51%	7%
By Type of Insurance			
Fee-for-service	31	63	6
Preferred Provider Org.	46	47	7
Health Maintenance Org.	49	46	6

Courtesy of Yankelovich Partners, Inc., Claremont, California.

experiential, like a banking relationship. Similarly in health care, it is easier to brand those parts of the system that are more easily defined.

Branding Hospitals

Hospitals exist as physical entities: they are bricks and mortar that consumers can see and touch, they have images and create brand equity for their owners and users. Consumers don't have to make too great a leap of faith to understand a brand of hospitals. For example, wherever there is a Brand X Hospital, there is a consistent look and feel to the experience. The logos and signs look alike. The Pharmacy and Outpatient Surgery departments are each located in the same place. Policies and procedures are similar, with little opportunity for management and staff to develop the attitude of *we do it differently here.*

At the same time, consumers have a certain set of expectations for Brand X hospitals. If Brand X promises that all of its hospitals have a 24-hour emergency department, changing that policy at one of its hospitals will clearly upset the consumer who, expecting to find the emergency room open, visits the Brand X hospital only to discover that it closed at 10 PM. From a consumer perspective, the brand lied. Now the consumer starts to question everything the brand has ever promised. Given a choice, the consumer will defect to the competition. The solution to this dilemma is consistency, and it is critical for brand success.

Branding Health Care Providers

Health care insurance providers can also create strong, meaningful brands. While not as tangible as hospitals, insurance providers are perceived by consumers as service companies. The challenge for insurers, however, is in understanding how their brand can be unique and different from the competition. Why would a consumer choose Brand A insurance instead of Brand B?

It could be a lower premium. However, being the low-priced leader is rarely a sustainable advantage and frequently leads to an unwinnable price war. The airline industry is a classic example of the dangers of price as a lead marketing strategy. It took the airlines—at least the ones that remained in business—over four years to financially recover from the deeply discounted fares and the frequent-flyer triple-miles promotions offered in the early 1990s.

If price is a secondary variable and serves the consumer poorly in helping to distinguish Brand A from Brand B, what else should serve as criteria? Beyond price, a brand must provide benefits, both functional and emotional, that will create value for the consumer. Functional benefits include responsive customer service and efficient claims handling, while emotional benefits include a feeling that the plan listens to you and values your business. These benefits should be distinctive and "owned" by the particular brand. Brands distinguish themselves from the competition with consumer-valued benefits. Benefits and their perceived value are the core of a brand's identity and what it represents.

There is an additional challenge when branding health care plans. Health insurance involves a two-part sell: health insurance providers must market to both employers and consumers, each of whom use a different set of criteria when making their purchase decision. Employers are primarily concerned with price and quality; consumers focus on physician choice and maintaining existing physician relationships. The brand must stand for the same essential promise across all target audiences.

Communication efforts such as advertising and marketing materials can emphasize different issues, depending on the receiver of the message. But the core image that the brand represents in every effort must be consistent across all audiences. Reconciling the potential incongruities of this marketplace reality is key to developing a successful health insurance brand.

For example, an insurance brand's key competitive strength could be its claims operation. In communicating the benefits of an efficient claims operation to the employer purchaser, the message focused on cost savings, both in terms of lower premiums and in terms of freeing up the employer's staff from having to interface with Claims to correct mistakes. On the other hand, the benefits to the employee consumer are different and focus on the system working the way it should and the consumer not having to worry about bills getting paid. Both target audiences receive the same message: Brand X's claims operation is superior, which reinforces how smart the customer is in choosing Brand X.

As demonstrated above, it is possible to develop meaningful brands for both hospitals and health care insurance providers. In fact, the marketplace has evolved to the point that without clear, distinguishing brands, many health care providers are disappearing because they can no longer compete. Countless communities have seen this happen with their local hospitals closing or becoming part of a larger network of hospitals. The mega-mergers among insurance companies are also an indication of the importance of brand and brand strength. The acquisition of Aetna by U.S. Healthcare resulted in giving the Aetna name primacy in its logo because of its greater brand recognition than U.S. Healthcare. When managed care plan PacifiCare acquired FHP, however, it eliminated the FHP name because of its poor brand image (dissatisfied members frequently referred to it as Fatal Health Plan).

Branding the Physician-Patient Relationship

While it is possible to brand hospitals and insurance plans, is it possible to create a meaningful brand within the most important component of health care: the patient-physician relationship? Can a physicians practice group be branded? What would the brand represent? What would the benefit be to the consumer, the patient? How would you ensure consistent delivery of service so that consumer expectations are met?

This is likely the most challenging health care arena in which to apply branding. Physicians themselves may resist branding efforts since one of the basic tenets of branding focuses on consistency. Physicians are likely to see this as restricting their ability to do what they think is best for their patient. From the consumer perspective, there are both pros and cons. On the positive side, knowing a doctor is part of Brand Z Physicians Group may help consumers make a more educated decision when choosing a physician. On the negative side, due to the individual nature of patient-physician relationships, if a consumer is dissatisfied, is it because of the doctor or because of the *brand*?

CONCLUSION

Brands are the natural outcome of a consumer-driven marketplace. They emerge as tools to simplify and help guide consumers' marketplace decisions. Today's consumers are looking for "right-hand brands" as they search for smart solutions to complicated lifestyle issues. They want accessible brands that address and solve tangible problems, that offer very specific answers to the complex how-to—endemic to each and every day.

As the health care marketplace is transformed into a consumer-driven world, brands of health care providers will play a more critical role. As consumers become more active participants in health care, they will demand that health care brands exist and deliver value. As health care brands emerge and become a marketplace reality, consumers will turn to those brands that best address their needs and will help them see their way clear of the maze of health care choices. The successes will be the brands that consumers trust to consistently provide relevant benefits and value.

Chapter 4

The Fundamentals of Identity, Image, and Brands

Neil A. Johnston

Some people refer to a company's logo as its "identity." Others say that a company's identity is the same as its "image." One more might say a corporate identity is conveyed through the company's "brand." Still others claim that "brand identity" and "brand image" are one and the same. Moreover, the term "branding" has, it seems, become almost synonymous with what was in the past referred to broadly as "marketing." In other words, in today's fast-changing, increasingly demanding business environment, there are a multitude of definitions and uses of these terms. It is no wonder managers are often confused when trying to make decisions on how to direct the critical business activities that depend on these concepts.

So what do we mean when we refer to "image, identity, and branding" in business? What is the difference between these terms? And most important, how can a corporation or other business enterprise really put these concepts to work so that they actually help make the business more successful?

With clear, consistent answers to these questions, it can be much easier for business executives to manage "identity"—and its corollary, "image"—to build and maintain profitable "brands."

START WITH FUNDAMENTALS

Most business executives would not think of Aristotle when first considering concepts such as identity, image, and branding. Yet, as with any problem that needs solving—and because of the often contradictory uses of the word "identity" in particular—it helps to turn to philosophical fundamentals when attempting to get to the truth of the matter. And Aristotle is a good place to start because he can help us define identity in its original, metaphysical sense, which in turn can help us understand it better in a modern-day business sense.

If he were alive and running a company today, Aristotle would surely be described as a no-nonsense, gotta-have-the-facts kind of businessman. He spent a great portion of his life searching for answers to questions that dealt with metaphysics—the study of existence—and objective reality, one of his goals being to determine how we as human beings perceive things, and another to discover what motivates us, particularly in our search for truth and reality.

Tom Morris, a modern-day business philosopher, agrees. He is author of the book *If Aristotle Ran General Motors: The New Soul of Business* (T.V. Morris, New York: Henry Holt & Company, 1997), and points out that "Aristotle had the key that unlocked the door to all kinds of powerful insights. Aristotle gives us the way to make the next step forward in our understanding of organizations and human motivation." Thus, Aristotle can help us, as business people, understand business realities and human nature so we can learn how to build higher levels of excellence on a foundation of truth, happiness, and satisfaction; so workers feel good about what they're doing in the long run and, thereby, can sustain the kind of excellence and financial success businesses hope to achieve.

With regard to the concept of "identity" in particular, Aristotle's pursuit of truth and reality is reflected in his philosophic formulation known as The Law of Identity (which is one of the three "principles of thought" that also include The Law of Noncontradiction and The Law of Excluded Middle). The Law of Identity is regarded as ontologically real—that is, it is something that describes the ultimate features of reality. It can be expressed simply as such: If A is true, then A is true. Or, a thing is what it is.

For a company (or product), like anything else, this means that Company X is Company X. It is what it is; its unique characteristics constitute its identity. Company X cannot be Company X and Company Y at the same time. Or, stated another way, it cannot be an entrepreneurial, risk-taking, lean-and-mean-type specialty company while at the same time being a bureaucratic, conservative, money-spending conglomerate. *A company's unique capabilities and characteristics constitute and define its true "identity"—what it is—in reality.*

Image Presupposes Identity

While identity then refers to reality, "image" has more to do with perception. Fundamentally, we must have identity before we can have image. A company's identity drives the image that observers will form based on how they "see" the company—how they respond to the company's look and behavior. Philosophically then, image applies to how we imagine things that we perceive—or, in other words, how our minds translate and understand reality. Our perception of an organization creates our image of that organization.

If this is the case, what about the often pronounced marketing maxim that "perception is reality"? It may at first sound sensible, but in actuality, it is not true. *The implication of "perception is reality" is that a customer's perception of a company, for example, is all that matters—that perception is what creates reality.*

Consider an example using an experience a customer might have at a leading hotel chain. If a customer calls to make a reservation and must wait ten rings before the phone is answered; if she arrives at the hotel and must wait in line for five minutes before being helped; if her messages are not delivered on time—these experiences will be perceived as service shortcomings and she may form a negative image of the hotel as a result. But her perceptions are not creating "reality." They are simply creating negative images of how she happened to see the hotel at that point in time. The reality may be that the hotel had a first place industry ranking in customer service and satisfaction, yet during the brief time that this particular customer came into contact with it, the hotel's building may have been experiencing telecommunications glitches, or management was training a new receptionist, or the hotel was just basically having an off day. The point is, a perception is just that: perception. And while a particular perception may cause an individual to form a specific idea of an organization, and they may think this perception equals reality, further experience may reveal a gap between perception and reality.

Indeed, one of the crucial challenges of identity and brand management is to try to close the gap between an organization's true identity and customers' image of the company—that is, to align the positive reality of an organization and its unique characteristics and capabilities with the perceptions of customers and other key audiences. In this way, audiences will become more aware of the company's offering, more familiar with how it behaves, and more favorable to supporting its business.

DEFINING A BRAND

Unlike the concepts of identity and image, the heritage of the word "brand" does not go back as far as Aristotle. Brand is exactly what one might guess: what we refer to today as a "brand" literally came from the idea of a "cattle brand." (See Figure 4–1.)

While they did not have quite the commercial worth of modern brands, cattle brands did come to represent specific values. Indeed, when one cowhand wanted to take the measure of another—possibly to determine what made him unique and different— he would ask, "What do you ride for?" And frequently, the answer would be, "I ride for the brand," meaning this cattle brand or that cattle brand. A brand meant ownership of the cattle bearing it by a particular cattle company, of course, but it also meant more. It meant consistency of quality. It meant to a cattle buyer a consistency of the quality of care and feeding of the cattle by the cattle company. This involved the day-to-day work of individual cowhands, in the saddle, hour after hour, keeping the herd in the good grazing areas, moving them to healthy watering holes, ensuring that the cattle weren't diseased or damaged before they got to market. It also meant protecting them from cattle thieves, called rustlers. "Riding for the brand" meant you rode to protect the interests of the com-

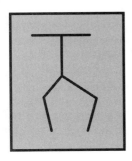

Tongs
Simon Green
Austin, Texas

Open A Triangle LB
A. Bahn
Austin, Texas

Circle Lazy S Circle
G. S. Jones
Austin, Texas

Figure 4–1 What We Refer to Today As a Brand Literally Came from the Idea of a Cattle "Brand." Courtesy of McKinney Engineering Library, The General Libraries, University of Texas, Austin Web Central, Austin, Texas.

pany. These were the "unique capabilities and characteristics" of those employed by the brand.

We have all heard of "rustling," involving either branding unbranded cattle with the rustler's own brand, or altering an honest brand to make it look like the rustler's own. The reason for either action is obvious—without the work, the effort and sweat, the rustlers wanted the profits. Sometimes, ranch owners would hire "stock detectives" to police the herds against rustlers. Nowadays, "rustlers" are called "infringers"—but they are still the same, trying to make an unearned profit by doctoring a brand—or trademark—to confuse purchasers as to where the goods or services came from, and as to their quality. And today, the stock detectives are, of course, the trademark attorneys, out to stop brand rustling, or trademark infringement.

But how do we define "brand" in today's world of Coca-Cola, Nike, McDonald's, American Express, and Viagra? From a business standpoint, one of the simplest definitions is this: *A brand is a promise.* It is not so much about the tangible thing, but the abstract idea of the thing. A brand is a pledge; an assurance of quality and consistency in a product or service. In fact, we often hear that "products are made in the factory, but brands are made in the mind." In other words, the product is what's real—it has an identity—and the brand is the image that is formed based on that identity. *The brand image is shaped in the consumer's mind as a result of the orchestrated communications created by the brand's owners and managers.*

Brands are what companies use to tell customers that the product in question will live up to certain expectations. So brands are really all about perceptions; about the feelings, ideas, and emotions people have toward a certain product or company; how a product's characteristics and qualities contribute to creating certain images in people's minds.

The Heritage of Corporate and Brand Identity Management

During its early inception, "identity and image" as practiced by most large U.S. corporations did not have as strong a basis in business strategy as it does today. Instead, it was for the most part a function of logos and letterheads, visual style and graphic coordination, as companies searched for ways to create their own corporate and product signatures. Eventually, a special niche of professional service firms emerged and applied the term "corporate identity management." During the 1950s and 1960s, the term came to encompass package design as well, and eventually the entire system by which a company used its name, logo, and trademarks.

In the 1970s and 1980s, corporate marketing and communications managers began to see the value in extending corporate identity activities across the entire company. This new management practice expanded significantly to encompass all aspects of a company's communications activities and came to be appreciated as one of the primary tools for shaping a corporation's image among all constituencies. Finally, today, identity management is correctly recognized as an integral communications component of the corporate strategic planning process.

In the broadest sense of the term, identity management is part of the process of managing the way a company looks and acts—the way it communicates—to shape public perceptions, aligning them with management's own view of its corporation, who it is in reality. When developed properly, a well-defined identity—one based on the unique capabilities of the company or product—lends integrity to and creates a credible context for the verbal, written, and visual messages that a business communicates to its constituencies (employees, customers, and shareholders) through such media as advertising and press releases, publications and annual reports—from logotypes, signage, and packaging to the architectural and environmental design of retail and other spaces.

Managing Identity: Three Key Business Applications

Successful companies recognize that the management of their identities is a mainstream business activity, a unique communications process for:

1. achieving competitive advantage
2. solving diverse business problems
3. leveraging change.

First and foremost, identity management is a competitive tool. It is the single most important means for telling the world "this is what is unique and different about us and this is how we create value for you." Indeed, to compete successfully for human, technological, and financial resources, and for the distribution networks and new technology needed to create value and competitive advantage, all businesses must find ways to differentiate themselves from all others. A strong, relevant, and credible corporate identity supports that primary objective.

Second, all kinds of companies have applied the discipline of identity management to solving major business problems. They include those whose market share is stagnant while their industry is booming; whose national or international expansion is thwarted because they are too strongly identified with a local or regional market; or those that cannot recruit talented senior managers because of misperceptions about the nature of their businesses. Some companies have trouble attracting the attention of the securities analysts who should be tracking their performance; others find their stock is unreasonably undervalued; or some have adopted, but not properly communicated, a new business strategy. In short, companies can turn to identity management to correct problems that are in a large part a result of an incorrect "image" of the organization.

Third, corporate identity is also an important strategic tool for managing change. Mergers, acquisitions, changing regulatory barriers, the Internet, and other influences have altered the competitive dynamics of entire industries in recent years. What is more, globalization has compelled corporations to compete for customers and capital against many more players in many different cultures and economies around the world.

So, clearly, identity is much more than a logo on a business card or a graphic on a company's vehicles and print materials. *Identity, properly managed, can help a company gain an advantage over competitors, can help solve business problems, and can assist in leveraging the changes that a company inevitably faces on a day-to-day basis.*

Brand Alignment

Even while identity management, as a business tool, has come a long way in the past two to three decades, too often corporate or brand identity is, unfortunately, still regarded as the surface visuals, the gloss and packaging. While these can certainly be effective and useful results of identity programs, they do not really represent the essence of the organization or product, only the tactics for creating its image in the marketplace. "Identity," as we have seen, is the true and unique characteristics and capabilities of the organization or product. It works to create an important image in the eyes of key audiences. Consequently, the most successful identity programs are not temporary fixes, flashy adaptations, or short-lived campaigns. Successful identity programs reflect the true entities they represent and address the unique communications challenges they face—challenges that are also a key part of an organization's business strategy.

Indeed, a company's business strategy and its identity strategy should work hand in hand. When they are "aligned," a company can more easily create communications that convey an accurate reflection of the organization and its unique capabilities—communications that are instantly recognizable, that conjure up strong images and associations of the company or product—that is, the brand—it represents.

This process of alignment, aptly called Brand Alignment™,* helps translate a company's business strategy into a communications strategy. It can tie everything—from the largest ad campaign, to the most common business document, to the smallest business card—together and give a company a decisive advantage in every market where it competes. Brand Alignment can infuse a unique tone and manner to all communications, conjuring strong images and associations, establishing a consistent, distinctive expression for a company's communications. Through Brand Alignment, every facet of a company's communications can build on its core business strategy and contribute to the definition of its unique character and value.

The Brand Alignment process is a strategic process that includes four essential phases: Discovery, Definition, Expression, and Action. When developing and managing an identity program, these are all critical steps that should be carried out by managers in order for the program to convey the true essence of the organization or product, if the program is to be about more than just surface graphics and visuals. In this way, the visual aspects of an identity program such as names and logos— what many people incorrectly refer to as "the identity"—can be developed based on strategic business realities rather than the often subjective "artistic" tastes of individual managers.

Working with brand identity specialists, managers can accomplish these four phases in an objective fashion and be ensured that the resulting identity program is a true reflection of the company's or product's business strategy.

To begin, the Discovery phase answers questions like: Who are we? What are our products? What is our market situation? How are we perceived by key audiences? This is accomplished by analyzing such factors as business fundamentals, market dynamics, current communications practices, and key audience perceptions. Only with this fundamental base can a company begin to define its true identity and brand promise.

With the answers to critical business questions, managers can move to the second Brand Alignment phase, Definition. Here, the goal is to begin defining the brand's unique promise, by addressing questions such as: What do we stand for? What value do we really have to offer? How do we want to be perceived by key

---

*Brand Alignment™ is a trademark of Enterprise IG, Inc.

audiences? This is achieved by developing and clearly articulating the business's or product's positioning, personality, and core messages.

With an articulation of the brand's promise, of how the brand should be positioned, management can begin developing visual and verbal manifestations of the brand.

This is the Expression phase, where the company answers crucial questions like: How should we bring our brand strategy to life? How should we look and act? This is accomplished by creating the appropriate brand architecture, product and business names, logos, graphic design, environmental design, and writing style.

With basic brand expressions established, the final phase, Action, answers the questions: How should we weave the brand into the fabric of the organization? What do we need to do to implement change? This is done by implementing the appropriate design systems, guidelines, launch and roll-out plans, training sessions, internal communications, and external communications to support the overall brand program. (See Figure 4–2.)

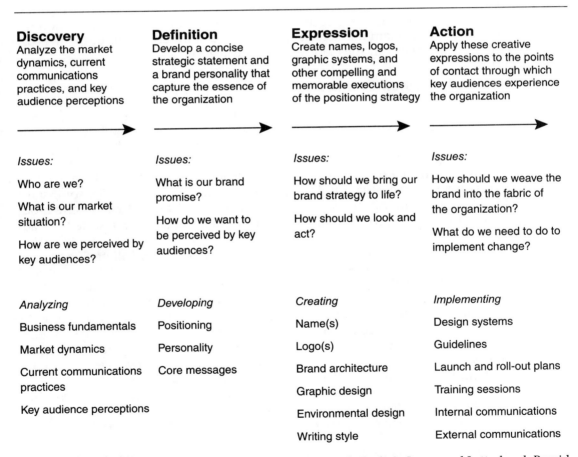

Discovery	**Definition**	**Expression**	**Action**
Analyze the market dynamics, current communications practices, and key audience perceptions	Develop a concise strategic statement and a brand personality that capture the essence of the organization	Create names, logos, graphic systems, and other compelling and memorable executions of the positioning strategy	Apply these creative expressions to the points of contact through which key audiences experience the organization

Issues:	*Issues:*	*Issues:*	*Issues:*
Who are we?	What is our brand promise?	How should we bring our brand strategy to life?	How should we weave the brand into the fabric of the organization?
What is our market situation?	How do we want to be perceived by key audiences?	How should we look and act?	What do we need to do to implement change?
How are we perceived by key audiences?			

Analyzing	*Developing*	*Creating*	*Implementing*
Business fundamentals	Positioning	Name(s)	Design systems
Market dynamics	Personality	Logo(s)	Guidelines
Current communications practices	Core messages	Brand architecture	Launch and roll-out plans
Key audience perceptions		Graphic design	Training sessions
		Environmental design	Internal communications
		Writing style	External communications

Figure 4–2 Brand Alignment™ Goes Beyond Surface Visuals Such As Logos and Letterhead, Providing the Fundamental Basis for Expressing a Company or Product's Unique Capabilities and Characteristics in Any and All Media

REAL-LIFE IDENTITY AND BRANDING CHALLENGES

So how should companies today address the critical issues that involve branding, identity, and image? What real-life business problems and opportunities are marketing and communications managers facing today? In the health care industry in particular, what do companies need to begin doing to differentiate their brands? How can company leaders orchestrate the components of brand and identity to gain a competitive advantage, to solve business problems, or to leverage change to their benefit? Some real-life identity and branding examples offer positive insight.

Gillette: How To Build a Global Master Brand

Although it is regarded more as a "Health and Beauty Aid" brand than a true "Health Care" brand, Gillette offers a universal brand lesson from which any company can benefit.

Four unsuccessful hostile takeover bids and a declining global market share could well spell disaster for many companies. But at Gillette during the early to mid-1980s, those competitive pressures spawned a rethinking of the company's business strategy and a successful re-emergence as a global leader. Gillette set out to become "raider-proof" and regain market share with a bold, ambitious commitment: to be the number one player in the blade and razor category, period.

The First Challenge: A New Product

Management's first assignment was to develop the identity and brand for a new product, the Gillette Sensor razor. Rather than introduce this revolutionary new shaving system as an individual product, management saw it as the starting point for building a global "masterbrand."

Combining the equity in Gillette's corporate identity with this truly innovative product was a win-win situation. Leveraging the Gillette name gave Sensor instant credibility and communicated the quality that comes with all other Gillette products. Furthermore, the product's innovative technology and design resulted in leading-edge image spillover across the entire company's blade and razor product line.

The brand identity was brought to life with a dynamic new Gillette logotype, a proprietary alphabet and new branding system for use on all of Gillette's blade and razor brands. But the design was only the foundation of Gillette's branding system.

Just as important is the change in the relationship between the Gillette masterbrand and individual product brands—especially on product packaging. In the past, product names were two to three times as dominant as the Gillette name. Consumers were buying individual product brands, not Gillette. The new masterbrand gave Gillette and individual products equal exposure. Now every consumer product impression is also a Gillette impression. (See Figure 4–3.)

This stronger and more consistent relationship of Gillette to its respective product brands resulted in greater product awareness, enhanced shelf impact, and the ability to introduce new product brands under the Gillette brand identity.

As the lead product under the Gillette masterbrand strategy, the Sensor went on to represent the first major launch of a new shaving product under the "Number One Player" business strategy. Because Gillette committed the necessary marketing,

Figure 4–3 The Gillette Masterbrand Logotype and a Proprietary Alphabet Helped To Express a Clean, Consistent Brand Identity for All Product Names, Anywhere in The World. Courtesy of Gillette, Boston, Massachusetts.

identity, and positioning resources, it was a global victory. The most successful razor in history, 21 million Sensors were produced in the first six months.

Once the Sensor program was in place, other Gillette brands, such as Atra, Trac II, Daisy, and Good News also adopted the masterbranding system. A totally new product line reflected the masterbrand and its distinctive appearance, communications clarity, and leadership tone. As new products such as Gillette Sensor for Women, Gillette SensorExcel, and Gillette SensorExcel for Women came to market, consumer acceptability was instant. Now for the first time, consumers anywhere in the world could see a clear Gillette identity and positioning across all product lines. (See Figure 4–4.)

The positive cumulative effect of Gillette's masterbranding across all product lines was instant. Through heightened awareness, its brands began to regain market dominance. Once again Gillette owned the sales environment. Gillette Sensor is the number-one selling razor in the world—a $1 billion brand. Razor and blade product sales increased 14 percent each year since the masterbranding's introduction. A fading brand name has been transformed to a vital growth brand, and financial markets noticed. In the months following the introduction, Gillette stock increased 33 percent. And both its stock value and market share continue to grow based upon its global marketing strategy. Here we see a business strategy that recognizes the importance of the concepts "identity and brand."

Pfizer: Using Identity To Clarify Real Business Capabilities

Pfizer had last reviewed the company's identity in 1969, when management implemented a superficial visual and verbal identity change—"Chas." was dropped from the corporate name. After more than 20 years, the company had changed a great deal, driving the need for more than just a name modification.

Acquisitions and new ventures, peripheral to Pfizer's pharmaceuticals core business, made it increasingly difficult to articulate the company's unifying business proposition. Its basic capabilities had changed, yet it had not done anything

Figure 4–4 New Gillette Brand Packaging Provided Greater Product Awareness, Enhanced Shelf Impact, and the Ability To Introduce New Products with a Consistent, Memorable Brand Identity. Courtesy of Gillette, Boston, Massachusetts.

significant to communicate the change. Names, logos, and graphic styles of acquired companies were being retained at a cost to perceived coherence and quality, and visual identification standards were in disarray.

Faced with these facts, management began to see an opportunity to leverage the change through identity management—through fine-tuning, refocusing, and reenergizing the corporation (Figure 4–5).

At the core, the company articulated a new corporate brand promise, a definition of the company's unique capabilities and characteristics. Simply put, this helped define Pfizer as a "research-driven health care company." Next, the company looked at its business-naming practices. Management adjusted the nomenclature of principal operating units to help explain and support the research theme. Animal Health Group became the new name for the Agricultural Division. Specialty Minerals Group replaced Materials Science Products, and within the Consumer Products Group, Leeming/Pacquin became known as the Consumer Health Care Division.

Corporate and product logos are often seen as the rallying point for a changed identity. To help signal change—indeed, an enduring commitment to change—at Pfizer, management modified the traditional blue Pfizer Oval, making it more assertive and progressive—"neotraditional" (see Figure 4–6). Finally, the company adopted a new visual identification system, including guidelines relating subsidiaries more consistently to the corporate parent.

For management, the payoff was renewed expression of the coherence and cohesiveness of the corporation, and its rededication to a culture of innovation. The

Figure 4–5 New Corporate Identity Standards Codified a Distinctive Graphic Look for All Pfizer Divisions, Contributing To a More Cohesive, Understandable Presentation of The Entire Organization. Courtesy of Pfizer, New York, New York.

Old Logo   New Logo

Figure 4–6 As the Visual Rallying Point of the Pfizer Corporate Identity Program, the Blue Pfizer Oval Needed To Be More Assertive and Progressive. Courtesy of Pfizer, New York, New York.

company had begun to align its business strategy with its brand strategy. As Chairman Edmund Pratt said in introducing the new corporate identity system: "Innovation defines us. It is the source of our success."

Sulzer Medica: Achieving Competitive Advantage with Identity

Sulzer Medica's real identity had been that of a $1 billion provider of cardiovascular and orthopedic medical devices. Its problem, however, was that key customers did not recognize the real breadth and resources the company offered, and how these compared with rivals'. Management turned to identity management in order to regain lost ground against competition.

Sulzer Medica, a part of Sulzer of Switzerland, a $5 billion conglomerate in a variety of industrial and engineering-related businesses, was built during the late 1980s and early 1990s through a series of acquisitions. The Sulzer Medica family of companies included Carbomedics, a heart and valve manufacturer; Intermedics, a leading pacemaker company; and Vascutek, a maker of bone grafts. For several years following the acquisition, each of the eight companies operated independently and went to market under its original name and identity. Given the desire of Sulzer Medica management to give individual company managers the freedom to operate autonomously, no attempt was made to bring the individual companies under a common identity system.

The assumptions underlying this approach began to change rapidly in the mid-1990s. The buyers of Sulzer Medica's products, major health care purchasing organizations, began to narrow the number of suppliers they were willing to deal with, favoring the larger, well-established medical device companies. Companies such as Carbomedics and Vascutek were having difficulty remaining on the preferred-supplier lists because of the fact they were perceived as small and potentially risky suppliers.

During the same time frame, Sulzer management wanted to raise additional capital for Sulzer Medica through an initial public offering (IPO) in the United States. Sulzer's corporate identity advisors recommended that investors would be more interested in a single, powerfully branded medical devices company than a collection of small, independent companies.

Working with the consultants, management developed a research-based rationale for moving to a single Sulzer Medica identity system. Gaining internal support for an identity change can often be one of the most important success factors. Consequently, the company first worked closely with the presidents of the individual business units to help make the transition from the existing identities to a single masterbrand.

On the outside, management and its identity consultant surveyed customers and prospects. Through in-depth interviews with many of its buyers, the company found that few customers recognized or understood that Sulzer Medica was in fact a large, well-established provider. *To change these perceptions, the company created a single masterbrand that reflected the size and strength of the enterprise.*

The consultants created an identity design system that could be used consistently across all individual business units, creating cost savings in the design of marketing material, advertising, and all other communications materials.

With its new unified identity system, Sulzer Medica achieved a competitive position it had been unable to attain with a fragmented, diffuse identity. It became recognized as a leader in the medical device business along with companies such as Medtronics, St. Jude Medical, and Boston Scientific. Shortly after the launch of the new identity system, Sulzer Medica also successfully completed its IPO and became a New York Stock Exhcange–listed company.

Monsanto: Aligning Brand Strategy with Business Strategy

Monsanto began as a chemical company nearly 100 years ago and has built a reputation of integrity, dependability, and financial soundness. In 1997, Monsanto management began implementing a new strategic plan that involved spinning off its chemical business and redefining the company as a global life sciences organization.

Although Monsanto has numerous subsidiaries in the life sciences, such as Searle, Ceregen, Protiva, and NutraSweet, the marketplace continued to associate Monsanto with chemicals. In other words, after divesting itself of the parts of the company that contributed to its "image" as a chemical company, its real "identity" as a life sciences company was still not being understood by key audiences. Monsanto had a business problem that fundamental identity management could help solve. *The challenge involved communicating to employees, regulators, customers, partners, and the investment community that although the stability and strength of the company had not changed, it now had a new reality and vision for the future.*

The Corporate Brand Name

While one of the strongest communications tools Monsanto had was its corporate brand, that was also one of its greatest obstacles to indicating a shift in the company's focus. Working with identity consultants, management weighed very carefully the decision to continue using the Monsanto name. Interviews with employees, customers, partners, and the investment community proved that while there was still an association with chemicals in the United States, this was not the case in the rest of the world: the brand equity in the Monsanto name was far too valuable to abandon.

The Corporate Logo and Visual Identity System

The most visible manifestation of the changes at Monsanto can be found in the new corporate logo. With the decision to continue using the Monsanto name came the mandate that the company develop a strong new corporate logo to carry the message of change forward. *The consultants developed a range of logo directions that leveraged the strengths of the corporate brand, while clearly communicating the life sciences focus. Monsanto's global involvement made research a critical part of the logo development and selection process.*

Monsanto conducts business in local communities globally from India to Africa, to North and South America, to Asia, and to all points in between. The organization could not afford to choose a logo that did not clearly communicate its new vision, or worse, that offended any of the communities in which it does business. The new "growing vine" logo, which consists of the Monsanto name, the vine symbol, and the tagline "Food • Health • Hope," expresses the company's strategic direction, business goals, and promise to citizens everywhere. The company also developed a complete visual identity system to govern the use of the vine logo and to provide guidance on how to create communications that are consistently and distinctively Monsanto. (See Figure 4–7.)

Branding Strategy

Prior to the spin-off of the chemicals business, Monsanto's subsidiaries operated completely independently from the parent company—there was no indication of a relationship with Monsanto. However, the new vision for the life sciences company required that all subsidiaries, while maintaining their independence, work together to support Monsanto's new singular brand promise. After developing a number of branding alternatives, management agreed that endorsing each subsidiary with the Monsanto logo would unify the organization under one common banner. This endorsement strategy also allowed subsidiary companies the opportunity to benefit from the relationship with Monsanto, while maintaining their independent identities. (See Figure 4–8.)

Identity Implementation

Launching a new identity program and rallying the support of crucial internal audiences is one of the most important aspects of identity management. To ensure a successful launch of its new identity program, Monsanto organized an identity implementation team, a group of professionals that worked to implement the new identity across all parts of the organization. The team's charge was to ensure that all Monsanto communications in both content and design reflect what the company stands for. Professionals from all parts of Monsanto including subsidiaries and international divisions, as well as agencies and vendors, were brought together to coordinate the simultaneous introduction of the new Monsanto identity worldwide. The identity implementation team conducted an audit of all Monsanto communications materials, coordinated the production and distribution of stationery items and forms worldwide, managed the production and installation of the sign system around the world, and conducted training of employees and vendors in elements of the new visual identity, among many other tasks.

Monsanto launched the new identity with an international media campaign. While integrating a diverse and decentralized organization under a common ban-

Monsanto

MONSANTO

Food · Health · Hope™

Old Logo   New Logo

Figure 4–7 Monsanto's Old Logo Contributed to Its Image of a "Carpet and Chemicals" Company. The new "growing vine" logo, which consists of the Monsanto name, the vine symbol, and the permanent tagline "Food•Health•Hope" expresses the company's change to a "life sciences" company as well as its promise to people all over the world. Courtesy of Monsanto, St. Louis, Missouri.

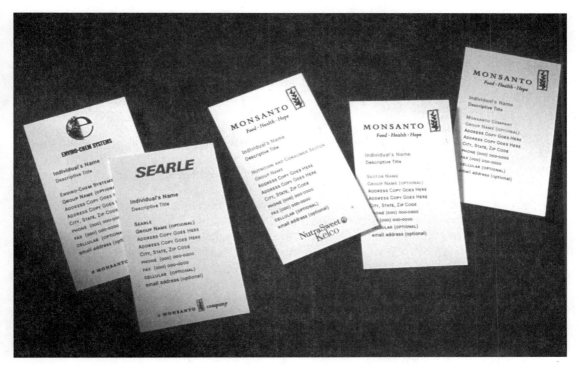

Figure 4–8 The Monsanto Brand Endorsement System Establishes Standard Templates for Relating the Corporate Brand to Divisional Brands. Courtesy of Monsanto, St. Louis, Missouri.

ner does not occur overnight, Monsanto has the tools and the momentum to continue aligning its new business strategy with its brand strategy. Monsanto is a global life sciences company working to develop new and better ways to feed and nourish people, improve the health of our surroundings as well as the personal health of our fellow citizens, and contribute to a future with abundant food, healthy living, and a planet that is safe and beautiful.

Developing a Consistent Identity Strategy for a World-Renowned Medical Institution

What does one of the world's leading medical institutions do when it has an identity problem? In spite of a pioneering place in health care research, education, and practice, a highly respected leading hospital had neither an identity system nor a communications plan worthy of its excellent character. Management recognized that the organization had a disjointed communications approach, which was making it difficult for the organization to differentiate itself from other, more aggressively marketed medical institutions.

Brand messages and communications were fragmented, leaving both internal and external perceptions of the hospital's unique characteristics and culture ambiguous. The marketing messages and graphic expressions of the organization's identity that were being created in the various hospitals, laboratories, schools, and offices were neither coherent nor standardized. Moreover, the different marketing communications managers did not fully understand the inherent brand value of the hospital's name and how it could be utilized effectively in the marketplace.

This is where effective identity management came into play. The hospital's marketing management recognized an opportunity to mold a singular, unified identity for the entire organization. ***Through a brand discovery and definition process, management codified the institution's principles and its primary value of "The needs of the patient come first."***

A focal point of the hospital's new identity system is a more unified use of its traditional graphic signature. Management recognized the value of the graphic and began using it as an integral, uniform part of all institutional communications, to both internal and external audiences.

As a part of the new identity initiative, the organization created and implemented a strong, representative brand identity system that could be applied at all levels and in each market and environment in which the organization does business. Across all of its hospitals, laboratories, schools, and offices around the country, this new, ***single identity approach*** has enabled the hospital to present itself in a more unified, more cost-efficient manner to the public. The organization now has greater control over all communications content and presentation. And most important, its integrity and professionalism are now represented at the most visible of levels, without dilution of the individual locations' respective areas of concentration and achievements.

THE LAWS OF BRAND REVITALIZATION

Whether an identity program was developed to solve a business problem, leverage change, or gain a competitive advantage, it will need continual updating. In fact, all brands—particularly corporate brands—will experience decline unless they are constantly revitalized. And the need for revitalization occurs for a variety of reasons: more competition, complacency, arrogance, etc.

We have seen that Aristotle originally provided us with the Law of Identity, which helps us begin to define identity, image, and brand in a business context. While not quite in the same philosophic or metaphysical realm, we can also consider the Laws of Brand Revitalization, which supply a framework for thinking about the problem of branding and asking questions we might not otherwise ask in relation to brands.

Like many of the branding examples given previously, brand revitalization is not just a matter of repackaging or redesigning logos, although these play a role. It is a matter of looking at how the company is going to present what the brand stands for today, and what it will stand for in the future. ***It is about determining a true point of difference in reality, based on a powerful, consistent individuality.***

Law of Value Creation

The value of a brand will outlive the products and services that represent it. In effect, the value proposition or "promise" behind the corporate brand transcends the products and services that represent the brand in the marketplace. We must realize that a successful brand proposition transcends products and services over time no matter what changes may occur in relation to those products.

Law of Substance

The brand is only as strong as its infrastructure. We often think of a brand as superficial, as only a name, logotype, or advertising. But that is not a brand at all. A brand is built on the strength of the business that supports it—the capabilities, experience, vision, culture, and operations that underpin the brand. ***To understand what your brand is all about, dig deep and understand its infrastructure.***

Law of Great Expectations

Great packaging cannot save poor brands, and good brands cannot survive bad packaging. It is not just about image. Essentially, what you see is not always what you get. You cannot cover up the reality of flawed brands, their promises, or their performance. Likewise, a bad visual presentation or bad design will always undermine an excellent brand.

Law of Relationships

Customer loyalty is directly proportional to customer empathy. In today's modern economy, we have gone from simple transactions to much more complex relationships with consumers as well as business-to-business customers. To respond effectively, you have to empathize with customers and understand what they think and feel in relation to your products and services. Managing identity and brands is not only about selling products and services; it is also about building relationships.

Law of Human Involvement

Brands succeed when people succeed. ***In a sense, your employees are brand ambassadors.*** Brands are defined and delivered through your employees. During brand development and the implementation of brand strategy, always look at how to engage employees in bringing that brand to life.

Law of Totality

The brand whole is always greater than the sum of its business parts. Today, we are faced with decentralization and the resulting empowerment of diverse business entities, which often leads to a tug of war between business units and the brand that basically ties those units together. No one unit or collection of units can ever outperform the brand in terms of its real or perceived economic value.

Law of Performance

The business is only as strong as the brand it is built upon. The message is that the brand is not built upon the business as much as the business is built on the brand, its value proposition, promise, and distinctiveness. Business investment should flow in ways that constantly enrich the brand.

CONCLUSION

Identity. Image. Brand. These concepts clearly have different meanings. Particularly in a business context, identity drives image, which drives brand. At the same time, identity and image are never separate issues, and image can actually support identity. If a company or product has a real image problem, for example, there is most likely a problem with identity, or the substance, as well. Fortunately, we can use image to help create substantive change. The rule to follow here is to allow a bit of lead time between image and substance because it takes longer to change the performance content of the brand than it takes to change things like advertising and other communications. While we can use image to lead change, we should always remember that it cannot really lead reality. In other words, we cannot out-drive our headlights. We need to be sure that the reality and promise of the brand is credible, and that if we are using image to create change, then we need to deliver on it in a short period—no longer than 18 to 24 months. Then, image can appear to lead reality as long as substance follows close behind.

In today's fast-changing, increasingly demanding business environment, we see an abundance of marketing concepts. *For those who strive to understand and meaningfully interpret their company's and product's identity, image, and brands, these concepts become assets.* They are marketing resources at the beck and call of managers involved in strategic and marketing planning. In the end, identity management can be viewed as a line function. It is a means of protecting customer franchises, sustaining customer loyalty, leveraging innovation and change, solving business problems—in essence, gaining a competitive advantage. For managers who want to make their businesses more successful, this fact and its implications are fundamental.

Chapter 5

The Cleveland Clinic: Protecting and Enhancing a Power Brand

Thomas Jefferson once said that the price of liberty is eternal vigilance. The same goes for the value of a brand. Whether it is an old and honored trademark, or a hot new start-up, you can't let your brand run wild in the marketplace. A brand is like Victorian maidenhood. It needs to be guarded and cultivated, and not allowed to appear inappropriately garbed or in low company. When the Cleveland Clinic Foundation recently found its brand threatened with dilution, it stuck to these precepts, and kept the virtue of its brand intact.

HISTORY OF THE CLEVELAND CLINIC FOUNDATION

The Cleveland Clinic Foundation is a leading American health care center, founded in 1921 by four veterans of World War I medical units. The founders gave the institution a unique directive: to pursue patient care in an environment that also included research and physician education. Beginning small, with a staff of 14 doctors, including several surgeons, a radiologist, a urologist, a few internists and a biophysicist, the Clinic has since grown into one of the largest hospitals and outpatient services in the country. As a not-for-profit group practice, the Clinic is led by a board of staff physicians, overseen by community trustees. Staff physicians receive a salary, and have no financial incentive to order unnecessary tests or procedures.

The founders of the Cleveland Clinic were inspired by what they experienced working in military hospitals during the First World War. There, they saw the advantages to patients of having doctors from a variety of specialties, working together to share their knowledge and solve complex medical problems. They saw that this arrangement not only benefited the patient, but it was also an ideal situation for the pursuit of research, and the training of physicians.

Although the Clinic began strictly as an outpatient service, its founders quickly realized that they needed a facility to hospitalize their more seriously ill patients. At first, patients were hospitalized in nearby private homes, renovated to meet medical needs. By 1924, the Clinic opened its first dedicated hospital building (Figure 5–1). Since then, the Clinic has expanded its hospital capacity many times, and its inpatient and outpatient services work together to offer a seamless continuum of patient care—from birth to the most complex surgeries.

From the beginning, the Clinic was distinguished for the quality of its specialty care, as well as its achievements in basic science and practical medical research. Innovations pioneered at the Cleveland Clinic have changed the face of medicine, surgery, and preventive care around the world. Cleveland Clinic physicians inaugu-

Figure 5–1 Built at a Cost of $400,000, the First Cleveland Clinic Building Opened in 1921 on the Southwest Corner of East 93rd Street and Euclid Avenue. Courtesy of the Cleveland Clinic Foundation, Cleveland, Ohio.

rated the modern era of interventional cardiology with the invention of coronary artery angiography. They transformed the surgical treatment of the heart by developing and refining the coronary artery bypass operation, and aortic valvuloplasty. The Clinic was first with kidney transplantation and kidney dialysis. Research firsts include the isolation of serotonin (the biological substance affected by antidepressants like Prozac) and the synthesis of angiotensin, which transformed the study of hypertension.

The culture at the Cleveland Clinic is driven by the collaboration of specialists. A patient who comes to the Clinic with a complex medical condition has access to doctors with expertise in everything from psychiatry to endocrinology, who can compare notes, and bring their combined expertise to bear on the patient's problems. Talented and ambitious physicians need the challenge of research, and the opportunity to pass their knowledge on to future generations of doctors. The Clinic gives them the chance to do both, through its extensive research and education programs.

Physician leadership is a tradition at the Cleveland Clinic, enshrined in its earliest charter. Specific elements of the organizational structure have been refined by decades of practice. Today, strategic decision making is centralized in the office of the chief operating officer, a physician, who is also chairman of the Board of Governors. A Board of Trustees from the community provides broad oversight of policy. A nonphysician chief operating officer oversees the administration of the Clinic's physical plant and most, nonmedical support functions. All in all, the Clinic has more than 10,000 employees, in 32 major departments of care, overseen by 11 divisions and centers.

More than 2 million patients from every state in the nation and 100 foreign countries have come to the Cleveland Clinic for care. The Cleveland Clinic is one of the ten best hospitals in America, according to *U.S. News & World Report's* prestigious annual rankings since 1990 (Figure 5–2). The magazine ranks the Clinic's Heart Center number one in America, and cites the Clinic's services in gastroenter-

BEST HOSPITALS

The Honor Roll

Every year, U.S. News recognizes hospitals that perform at a very high level across many specialties by listing them in the Honor Roll. To be included, a hospital must demonstrate unusual competence in at least six of 16 specialties. Only 13 hospitals made this elite list this year out of 188 different facilities that were ranked.

1. Johns Hopkins Hospital, Baltimore
(28 POINTS IN 14 SPECIALTIES)

2. Mayo Clinic, Rochester, Minn.
(24 POINTS IN 12 SPECIALTIES)

3. Massachusetts General Hospital, Boston
(23 POINTS IN 12 SPECIALTIES)

4. Cleveland Clinic
(21 POINTS IN 11 SPECIALTIES)

5. Duke University Medical Center, Durham, N.C.
(19 POINTS IN 11 SPECIALTIES)

6. UCLA Medical Center, Los Angeles
(18 POINTS IN 11 SPECIALTIES)

7. Barnes-Jewish Hospital, St. Louis
(15 POINTS IN 10 SPECIALTIES)

8. Brigham and Women's Hospital, Boston
(15 POINTS IN 9 SPECIALTIES)

9. University of Michigan Medical Center, Ann Arbor
(11 POINTS IN 8 SPECIALTIES)

10. Hospital of the University of Pennsylvania, Philadelphia
(10 POINTS IN 7 SPECIALTIES)

11. New York Presbyterian Hospital
(10 POINTS IN 6 SPECIALTIES)

12. University of Pittsburgh Medical Center–Presbyterian
(8 POINTS IN 7 SPECIALTIES)

13. University of Chicago Hospitals
(7 POINTS IN 6 SPECIALTIES)

Note: Listed hospitals scored two or more standard deviations (S.D.) above the mean on the U.S. News Index in at least six of 16 specialties. Order is based on total points. A hospital got two points if it ranked 3 or more S.D. above the mean and one point if it ranked from 2 to under 3 S.D. above the mean. In ties, the number of specialties determined the order.

THE RANKINGS BEGIN ON PAGE 75

Figure 5–2 Best Hospitals: The Honor Role. *Source:* Copyright, July 19, 1999, *U.S. News & World Report.*

ology, endocrinology, rheumatology, geriatrics, neurology, orthopaedics, and pulmonology among America's ten best in their categories.

As a not-for-profit institution, the Clinic has a humanitarian mission to the community it serves. It has no owners or stockholders. Profits above costs are used to finance the non-income-producing activities of research and education.

THE GROWTH OF THE BRAND

While the marketing of products and services such as automobiles and entertainment has become remarkably refined over the decades, health care marketing is still in its adolescence. Twenty-five years ago, the Cleveland Clinic's approach to marketing was not unlike that of most hospitals nationwide: it was directed toward a physician audience. Its function was to motivate local physicians in private practice to refer their sick patients to the Clinic for hospital and specialty care. At that time, most physicians considered any broader marketing practices as incongruent with the dignity of the profession and counter to the image of disinterested devotion to patient well-being.

What promotion there was at the Cleveland Clinic at that time consisted mainly of a glossy magazine, called *Cleveland Clinic*—a combination fund-raising brochure and media relations press release. Overall, the Clinic's marketing efforts were no more or less developed than those of any other hospital in the nation.

This situation changed markedly in the early 1980s. Long-range planners were beginning to see that health care providers were going to need to get into marketing with both feet, if they wanted to survive in the evolving business environment. Although the word "marketing" was never used, the Cleveland Clinic began a number of formal efforts at this time that in effect represented an embryonic marketing push.

The first step was the combination of the following areas: fund-raising, media relations, consumer and physician outreach and patient ombudsman, into one area (each function has since been spun off into its own department). The stated purpose remained the development of physician relationships for the purpose of driving referrals. But a number of fresh initiatives were undertaken. These included the development of an alumni relations program (for doctors who had been trained at the Cleveland Clinic and gone on to other hospitals), the Clinic's first staff directory, and *Consult,* a color magazine highlighting Clinic staff and their cases for a medical audience.

It was a process of doing and learning. As a scientific institution, the Clinic was quick to grasp the value of market research. Surveys and focus groups revealed much about consumer attitudes toward the institution. For instance, it was shown that a significant majority of local consumers considered the Cleveland Clinic to be by far the superior health care provider in the region. Paradoxically, this same perception was accompanied by the belief by a small cohort of consumers, that to get into the Cleveland Clinic, one had to be referred by a doctor, have a serious illness, or be an executive or celebrity. Access became an issue.

To counter this perception, the Clinic launched *Challenge Magazine* (Figure 5–3) to inform the community of its activities in a friendly, consumer-oriented format. Media tip-sheets were sent to local and national newspaper, radio, and TV outlets to encourage coverage of the Clinic's medical accomplishments and breakthroughs. "Clinic Consult," a newspaper column answering patient health queries, was

Figure 5–3 The Cleveland Clinic Foundation *Challenge Magazine.* Courtesy of the Cleveland Clinic Foundation, Cleveland, Ohio.

launched, along with a radio program covering health topics. A one-off special newspaper supplement was produced—breaking the ice for all print advertising to follow.

These efforts were among the factors that helped push the number of patient visits to the Clinic well upward in the 1980s. Yet it was only in 1986 that these efforts were formally designated "marketing." It was not until 1990 that the Clinic finally took the step of actually advertising its services. With this, came the recognition that one of the Clinic's most valuable properties was its own good name—the Cleveland Clinic brand.

Branding Challenges

On the business side, health care is coming more and more to resemble other retail services in America. Health care consumers look for a reliable brand name, just as they do with cars and soft drinks. In the early 1990s, the Clinic began taking steps to protect and grow the brand it had created and fed through 75 years of hard work and outstanding medical care. Market research showed that the name Cleveland Clinic was the gold standard for health care among local consumers. Such an asset was not a thing to be squandered on unplanned or haphazard marketing. The brand was a thing to be nurtured and protected to retain its value not only for the present generation, but also for many generations to come. If the price of maintaining a valuable brand is constant vigilance, one of the Clinic's most serious marketing tasks is the maintenance, protection, and carefully directed growth of its valuable brand.

The Cleveland Clinic's brand protection efforts are carried out in an environment replete with marketing challenges. The Clinic's outstanding academic programs turn out hundreds of highly qualified physician specialists every year. Many of these excellent doctors can and do go to work for competing medical institutions. The Clinic shares its marketplace with the University Hospitals Health System of Cleveland, which is associated with Case Western Reserve University. This well-regarded hospital is located less than a mile from the Clinic's main campus, and could be seen by consumers as an alternative to the Clinic for some services.

As a national referral center, the Clinic is in the same marketplace as hospitals like Johns Hopkins, the Mayo Clinic, and Duke University Medical Center (all of which rank with the Clinic at the top of the *U.S. News & World Report* annual hospital survey). On a specialty basis, the Clinic's nationally prominent departments of heart and cancer care share their market with specialty hospitals like the Texas Heart Institute and Memorial Sloan-Kettering Cancer Center.

Internationally, geography can be the determining factor behind patient choice. The Clinic competes with hospitals in Germany and England for Middle Eastern patients; Miami and Houston hospitals are attractively close for patients from South America; and Far Eastern and Pacific Rim patients may choose hospitals in Singapore. However, the Clinic's reputation and international marketing efforts are such that thousands of patients from around the world have overlooked potential geographical liabilities and given Clinic one of the largest international patient counts of any hospital in America.

The Clinic recognizes that overseas patients have special needs, and goes to great lengths to see that they are accommodated. Most overseas patients are processed through the Cleveland Clinic International Center, a central clearinghouse for all international services. The International Center can provide interpreters, make appointments, help patients navigate the Clinic campus and the city, and serve as general concierges to the Clinic's international clientele.

International patients are guided to the Clinic by a variety of means, some formal, some informal, and based upon personal relationships. Outreach efforts include Embassy contacts, lectures at international symposia, and networking with government agencies. Over the years, the Clinic has trained hundreds of physicians from overseas, many of whom will refer their seriously ill patients to the Clinic for high level care.

As a national referral center, the Cleveland Clinic is ambitious to serve patients around the country, and especially from its own seven-state region. Many patients from Southern Ohio, Pennsylvania, West Virginia, Indiana, Kentucky, New York, and Michigan do come to the Cleveland Clinic. Marketing to these states has included some experimental advertising in large cities, but mainly consists of building relationships with physicians in those states, through personal and educational contacts, to encourage referrals.

In the early 1990s, however, the Clinic began to concentrate on its own immediate neighborhood. It was becoming clear to all that the health care marketplace was changing. Managed care was growing, and employers and insurance companies were becoming the primary payers of America's health care costs. Hospitals who wanted employer and insurance contracts had to be able to provide the full range of health care services, from maternity, to the most complex surgeries. Location was also becoming more important, as employer and insurance payers demanded that those they covered have convenient access to their health care provider.

At this time, the Clinic unveiled its outer-ring strategy: a plan to gird the city with a network of satellite clinics, in strategic locations. Today, there are 12 of these Cleveland Clinic Family Health Centers, offering everything from primary care to ambulatory surgery. For patients in the outer suburbs, they provide the family doctors and pediatricians, and serve as a conduit for seriously ill patients to services on the Clinic's main campus.

Goals and Strategies of the Cleveland Clinic's Branding Program

Over the past few years, the Cleveland Clinic has begun to consciously cultivate and protect its brand. The Clinic's leadership has acquired a sophisticated awareness of brand value, and the responsibilities of brand stewardship. Now their goals include increasing awareness of the brand on a national and international level. They will attempt to extend the brand halo without losing brand equity.

Even as this new brand consciousness was taking shape, the Cleveland Clinic was entering into a series of business partnerships that would challenge the brand integrity as it had never been challenged before.

Over a two-year period, the Clinic merged with ten local community hospitals to form a new system: The Cleveland Clinic Health System. Each of these hospitals already had its own identity, and all were well regarded in their communities. Nonetheless, they all recognized that they could benefit by as close as possible an association with the Cleveland Clinic brand.

The Clinic's challenge was to determine how much of its own brand identity it could lend to these affiliated hospitals without diluting its equity.

Some of the issues included the use of the Cleveland Clinic name and logo on the affiliated hospital's signage and advertising. Decisive action was necessary to prevent widespread independent use of the brand by newly affiliated hospitals. Cleveland Clinic marketers went into overdrive, quickly establishing firm parameters around the use of the Clinic name and logo. Restrictions were placed on the size and placement of Clinic identification by the system hospitals, and approval was required for all uses of the name and logo (Figure 5–4).

Cooperation has been outstanding. The system hospitals understand that it is in their long-term benefit to help the Clinic protect its core brand. The behavior of hospital patients is no different than that of consumers in any marketing field. Consumers buy brands they trust. Consumers in Northeast Ohio trust the Cleveland Clinic. The Cleveland Clinic needs to cultivate and maintain that trust for many years to come, for its own sake, as well as the sake of its system hospitals. Dilution would be disastrous.

There is no question that health care is becoming a retail commodity. More and more patients are coming to the Clinic on their own initiative—not waiting for a doctor's referral. That behavior is motivated by trust. And the brand is the priceless embodiment of that trust.

THE CLEVELAND CLINIC HEALTH SYSTEM

Changes in the health care marketplace swept over Cleveland in the late 1990s like a windstorm off Lake Erie. Managed care was burgeoning, and national, for-profit hospital chains were getting ready to pounce upon and devour vulnerable and isolated health care centers. Affiliation became the key to survival. Hospitals began looking for partners.

With the formation of the Cleveland Clinic Health System, at least ten local hospitals had found a haven. The system was attractive to insurers, employers, and other payers for many reasons. These included the broad range of services the system could provide, and the geographic diversity of its access points. They no longer had to negotiate with a number of small entities for care, but could deal with a single source. From the Clinic's point of view, the arrangement guaranteed leverage in negotiating contracts with their managed care clients.

The ultimate goal is to integrate the system into a decentralized regional and community health care delivery system. Where possible, integration is to be achieved, and economies of scale pursued. However, each system hospital is encouraged to maintain its identity, corporate culture, and community profile.

As described above, this situation represented a unique branding challenge. The philosophy of the system is mutual benefit. This means that the Clinic will allow use of its brand halo where doing so will add luster to an affiliated hospital; but will not permit such use to an extent that it detaches the brand from the parent, and diminishes its accumulated value.

Whatever affiliations it may make, the Cleveland Clinic itself will remain a unique institution. Unlike the system hospitals, the Clinic is a group practice, where doctors are employees who earn a salary. Cleveland Clinic doctors are highly credentialed, selectively recruited, and subject to annual performance reviews. Doctors at the community hospitals are in the main self-employed or members of independent group practices. They partake of the region's general level of medical excel-

Figure 5–4 Cleveland Clinic Health System Hospitals Ad and Logo. Courtesy of the Cleveland Clinic Foundation, Cleveland, Ohio.

lence, but they are not subject to the same type of performance reviews as Clinic doctors.

There is a qualitative difference between the parent and system hospitals. In applying the Cleveland Clinic name to the system hospitals, there is the danger that patients will expect their care to be directed or overseen by Clinic physicians, at the same level of specialized expertise as in the parent hospital. They may also expect seamless access from one hospital to the next, and a uniform system of records. On the negative side, community hospital patients may fear that with its inclusion in a large system, their hospital may be less likely to treat them on a warm, personal basis.

The Clinic's brand managers need to finesse these delicate issues. As the system quickly fell into place, they made the necessary bold moves to protect their brand. Now they must move carefully and bolster the community hospitals' prestige, without misleading consumers as to the nature of community hospital care.

The stakes are high. Once a brand has been diminished, it can take a generation to restore.

The Branding Solution for the Cleveland Clinic Health System

It was a complex challenge. The Clinic needed to respond to the needs of consumers, integrate the affiliated health care organizations, and maintain the integrity of the Cleveland Clinic brand. It was also a unique opportunity.

The merger that created the Cleveland Clinic Health System did not combine equals. It combined a dominant power brand with reputable community brands. Clinic marketers discussed their options, and chose to extend its brand to its affiliates through an endorsement strategy. The rejected choices included monolithic or co-branding strategies. Their reasoning included the fact that the community hospitals already had fine local reputations, and brand equity in their own market areas. The sum of Cleveland Clinic brand equity plus the community hospitals' brand equity could conceivably add up to an exceptional net gain.

Extensive market research underlay the endorsement strategy. Consumers were asked specifically what they would expect from a Cleveland Clinic-branded health system. The results indicated that while they did not expect a Cleveland Clinic physician, they did expect the Clinic to oversee the quality of care provided by the affiliated hospitals. In addition, they expected to have at least facilitated or preferred access to the main campus if they needed to see a Clinic doctor. Lastly, they wanted seamless operations from organization to organization (e.g., ubiquitous medical charts).

Set against these findings, the endorsement strategy had a distinct value. Endorsement lends the credibility of the parent organization's name, without promising any specific services or level of care. It provides the system latitude, as it completes the crucial work of self-auditing and consolidation. To maintain this latitude, advertising for the system has been modest and limited to a few ads in local magazines (Figure 5–5).

The Tiered Approach

The story of the Cleveland Clinic over the past ten years might be titled "The Multiplying Hospital." Today, it is a presence in a complex array of venues. They include:

THE CLEVELAND CLINIC
FOUNDATION

INNERPULSE

Volume XXIV Number 2 Summer 1999   W O R L D   C L A S S   C A R E

Introducing...

Community
hospitals...

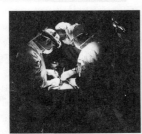

...community
care

Cleveland Clinic
Health System

NEW HORIZONS IN COMMUNITY CARE — *Cleveland Clinic Health System enables communities all across Northeast Ohio to have easy access to high quality care.*

O ver the past two years, a remarkable series of events has changed the face of health care in Greater Cleveland. To keep costs down, and to assure that Greater Clevelanders continue to have access to quality care, ten of the area's most outstanding community hospitals have joined forces to create a regional system of care called Cleveland Clinic Health System (CCHS).

The member hospitals of CCHS are among Northeast Ohio's most trusted names in medical care: Marymount Hospital, Hillcrest Hospital, Euclid Hospital, South Pointe Hospital, Huron Hospital, Fairview Hospital, Lutheran Hospital, Lakewood Hospital and Ashtabula County Medical Center.

Operating as community hospitals, and as part of a broad system, these hospitals comprise one of the most valuable health resources in the region. This unique combination of resources brings unique benefits to the communities served by these hospitals.

Operationally, CCHS is able to take advantage of tremendous economies of scale. That means that costly functions can be shared out among the member hospitals, and savings can be passed on to payers and consumers. It means that employers and insurers can contract with one system to provide the full range of health services, from birth to the most complex surgeries, in convenient locations all across the area.

In terms of health, it means that these neighborhood hospitals, long known for excellence and compassion, are now associated with the world-class resources and personnel of the Cleveland Clinic. This combination of neighborly care, in partnership with the outstanding clinical, research and educational abilities of the Cleveland Clinic, makes for a system whose potential is almost without limit. ⊕

Figure 5–5 The Cleveland Clinic Health System Hospitals Awareness Campaign. Courtesy of the Cleveland Clinic Foundation, Cleveland, Ohio.

- Cleveland Clinic Family Health Centers
- Cleveland Clinic Florida, Ft. Lauderdale and Naples
- Cleveland Clinic Health System Hospitals
- Management of unowned hospital departments
- Special Managed Care relationships
- Cleveland Health Network (intrahospital managed care network).

Commensurately, the Clinic's marketing has multiple targets, including physicians, consumers, managed care providers, employees, and affiliates.

In order to preserve order within this complex range of corporate personalities, the Clinic has established a system to classify entities using the Cleveland Clinic brand. It arranges the Clinic's entities into a hierarchy, based upon their essentialness to the core institution, the Cleveland Clinic Foundation. It gives each entity graded access to the brand, depending upon its place in the hierarchical ladder.

The Tier 1 entities represent the core brand. They are the irreducible essence of the Cleveland Clinic. All messages and materials coming from these areas relate to the Cleveland Clinic only. Here, the core brand is nourished, so as to be able to lend its strength to the entities below it. Marketing is directed out of Tier 1, and all Tier 1 communications emanate from here and are approved here.

Tier 2 consists of Cleveland Clinic-owned entities. The entities have brand equity of their own. But association with the Cleveland Clinic brand adds value to the existing equity. For example, Marymount Hospital retains the use of its own brand in promotional materials because it is extremely strong locally. They do not use the Cleveland Clinic logo in their ads and marketing materials. However, the words "Cleveland Clinic Health System" appear beneath their name in their logo, in prominent half size. (The words "Cleveland Clinic Foundation" never appear in these entities' materials.) All advertising is reviewed by Tier 1 leadership.

Tier 3 is individual Cleveland Clinic departments in non-owned hospitals. The primary focus of all messages is the Tier 3 entity itself, and the Cleveland Clinic relationship is explained for added value. For example, MetroHealth is a county-owned hospital, but Cleveland Clinic physicians travel there to perform surgeries. With Tier 3 messages, it is important that the relationship be clearly spelled out. There can be no confusion that the Tier 3 entity is part of the Cleveland Clinic Foundation or the Cleveland Clinic Health System. The Cleveland Clinic name, logo, and tagline may not be used in any integral part of Tier 3 advertising. All advertising must be approved by Tier 1 marketers.

Tier 4 consists of organizations to which the Cleveland Clinic belongs. The primary focus of all messages from this area is the Tier 4 entity itself, using the Cleveland Clinic name for added value or informational purposes. In this type of relationship, the Cleveland Clinic logo may actually be used, but only in a visual arrangement that includes the logos of other hospital members. All advertising must be approved by Tier 1 marketers.

Since it was established, the four-tiered approach described above has been instrumental in helping the Clinic meet its branding objectives. It supports the integrity of the Cleveland Clinic image, maintains the branding strengths of related entities, extends the halo of the brand to other entities and does not dilute anyone's existing brand equity. The Cleveland Clinic is a "megabrand," and as long as it is capably managed, internally and externally, branding goals may continue to be successfully met. However, the price of branding success is eternal vigilance. Core brand marketers must continue to monitor use of the brand in the lower tiers, and prevent its too-rapid extension or inappropriate use.

Within this multi-level branding system, tiers are marketed in an independent, but coordinated fashion. Advertising is decentralized, but coordinated at the approval level. The Cleveland Clinic must sign off on all ads by entities in any tier that mention the Cleveland Clinic name.

Collaborative Marketing

Twice a month, marketing managers from all the Cleveland Clinic affiliated hospitals meet to discuss ways to market cooperatively while maintaining the value of their individual brands. For example, the group recently decided to create a marketing program around the community health problem of youth smoking. The result was "Word of Mouth," a curriculum-based anti-smoking program offered under the auspices of the system of as a whole, in schools throughout the city.

Community health issues have presented numerous opportunities to market cooperatively throughout the system. Group approaches like this help build brand equity and reduce competition among the individual organizations. They do good, foster camaraderie, and help erase lingering competitiveness among personnel from different hospitals.

A unique advantage of the "Word of Mouth" program from a branding standpoint is that it targets the school age audience. It plants brand awareness in a group that will be coming of age around the time that the Cleveland Clinic Health System will have reached its full integrative power. These young people and the system will have, as it were, grown up together, with all the comfort and familiarity that implies. By the time they are old enough to make their own health care choices, the Cleveland Clinic Health System will be an old friend.

Brand equity is a long-term investment, not to be squandered on goals and programs whose effect will offer only a temporary advantage. Having a strategic branding plan means creating a consistent format for existing hospitals and future acquisitions.

A BRAND WITH NATIONAL REACH

Most of the examples of the Cleveland Clinic's branding efforts thus have dealt with local and regional promotion. However, the Cleveland Clinic may justly be called a national brand, and maintaining that status is crucial to its halo effect on affiliated organizations. A number of national brand initiatives have been launched. The Clinic has affiliated with an international publishing company to produce patient-oriented newsletters for heart disease and men's health (Figure 5–6). Cleveland Clinic physicians serve on the editorial boards of these newsletters, and Cleveland Clinic writers and editors provide the content. The publishing company is responsible for printing, national distribution, and direct-mail promotion of subscriptions. As branding tools, these newsletters carry the Cleveland Clinic name into thousands of homes of educated consumers with an interest in current health topics. It shows one of many alternatives to advertising as a means of elevating a brand.

Figure 5–6 Men's Health and Heart Health Newsletters. Courtesy of the Cleveland Clinic Foundation, Cleveland, Ohio.

QUALITY CONTROL TODAY AND IN THE FUTURE

The Clinic maintains quality control over the use of its brand by establishing strict parameters for its use. As earlier noted, all advertising by any entity that uses the Cleveland Clinic brand in any form must be authorized and approved by the Clinic's marketing administrators. This ensures that the brand will appear only in appropriate environments, and in accurate relation to the advertisers' organization. Proper advertising placement within a given publication is also monitored.

Yellow pages advertising is critical for health care, and Clinic marketers are currently developing a template for yellow pages advertising that will give a united look to all the system hospitals' listings. They've also established shared media schedules, so that each hospital knows where and when another is advertising, avoiding overlap, duplicated effort, or clashing messages. Another effort involves developing brand architecture guidelines for everything from lab coats to hospital signage.

Internationally, trends indicate that health care providers in other countries want to be associated with American power brands like the Cleveland Clinic. In response to this, the Clinic has launched several brand-extending pilot projects in foreign countries. These are being carefully monitored for brand integrity. Further expansion is contemplated, with infant programs in Egypt and India showing a great deal of promise. The future could see major growth in this area.

Lessons Learned

What has the Cleveland Clinic leadership learned from this episode? First, they've come to understand that brand maintenance requires a high level of sensitivity on all sides. ***That means those who want to share the brand as well as those who want to use it conservatively.***

They've also learned:

- You need to move slowly when extending your brand. Once your brand is tarnished, it can be difficult to restore its luster.
- Branding is a long-term commitment. As one of an organization's most valuable assets, a brand must be stewarded not only for this generation, but also beyond.
- Top management must be won over to the branding strategy. In some organizations, this may require a major internal dialogue between marketers and administration. But without support from the top, the strategy cannot succeed.
- Marketing personnel must establish guidelines for making objective decisions about where and when to use the brand. Ad hoc decisionmaking can diminish long-term brand equity. In an era of savvy consumers, messages must be carefully conceived and closely managed.

As the Clinic grows in size and number of affiliates, its branding program grows more complex. New branding challenges surface daily. Since leadership is committed to the established branding policies, challenges are no threat; and the branding system is evolving in an orderly fashion. The Clinic is in brand management for the long term.

The founders of the Cleveland Clinic established a unique institution, dedicated for all time to patient care, research, and education. Over the decades, the Clinic's leadership has taken steps to protect that mission, for the good of patients in their own time, and in decades to come. Protecting their brand from misuse is part of the stewardship of that mission. Enhancing the brand, building its strength and potency, is their gift to the future.

Chapter 6

Branding an Academic Medical Center: A Case History

Joel G. Lee

AN APOCRYPHAL TALE

In the early 1990s, the marketing staff at Vanderbilt Medical Center held a series of focus groups to see how the institution, its staff, and, in particular, its physicians were perceived in the market. The moderator led participants through a series of questions designed to tease out people's perceptions and feelings about the doctors who practiced there. Some of the questions asked participants to paint a picture of a Vanderbilt doctor, by describing the clothes, car, and dog the doctor would own.

The results have been etched in the mythology of the institution. The "archetypical" Vanderbilt doctor was described as a 60-year-old gray-haired man, dressed in expensive clothes. He drove an expensive car (a Jaguar), too fast, to his expensive home in Belle Meade, Nashville's most prestigious neighborhood. As for the breed of dog, participants speculated little, imagining instead that the doctor had probably run over the poor pet in his driveway.

While this story may be only partly true, it is instructive because it was believable—both to the staff within the institution and to the people outside it. Despite Vanderbilt's international reputation and repeated listings as one of America's best hospitals in *U.S. News & World Report*, by the mid-1990s Vanderbilt was in a dead heat for fourth place among consumers in its hometown. Costs were perceived to be above market, with many health plans trying to exclude Vanderbilt from provider panels for all but the most critical services. While Vanderbilt's competitors were gaining ground, its own crown was slipping.

Situation Analysis

The 1990s were a watershed for many participants in the health care delivery sector. Like most other academic medical centers, Vanderbilt was ill-prepared for the sweeping changes that were about to take place in American medicine.

Managed care took hold across much of the country, aggressively controlling costs by reducing access—and payments—to hospitals. The mounting costs of the federal Medicaid program—fueled by its unfunded mandates for service—gave rise to managed care programs for the poor and uninsured in many states. Tennessee led the nation when it unveiled TennCare, its managed care Medicaid alternative, in 1994, thereby ushering in Clinton-like health care reform *and* managed care to the state, all in one fell swoop.

Hospitals from coast to coast suffered another painful blow when the federal government began to tighten payment to providers in the Medicare program—first by the nationwide effort to curb billing and coding "excesses" and then by the across-the-board cuts imbedded in 1997's Balanced Budget Amendment.

This triple whammy—aggressive cost management by commercial payers, the imposition of managed care under TennCare, and provider payment cuts in Medicare—threatened to undermine the margins of health care providers throughout Tennessee. Viewed through the prism of the incredibly fragmented and competitive Nashville market—where the acknowledged leader had little more than a 16 percent market share—the future looked dim.

For Vanderbilt, the situation was critical. As one of 125 academic medical centers in the country, it had a three-part mission: to train the next generation of doctors and nurses, to discover new approaches to human health, and to offer clinical care. At all academic medical centers, the cost of training, at both the graduate and undergraduate level, has always outstripped tuition and government stipends. To supplement training costs, academic medical centers traditionally relied upon cash-flow subsidies from other undertakings, most notably clinical care. Yet, the margins for providing clinical care were rapidly eroding under pressure from both government and private payers.

Simultaneously, medical research experienced a growth spurt. Buoyed by Congress and the President's hope to double funding for the National Institutes of Health (NIH), federal research grants grew by 79 percent between 1990 and 1999. But the cost of the next generation of biomedical discovery proved to be quite high. For research institutions like Vanderbilt, the cost to build programs in genomics and functional genomics, in cell biology, in molecular biology, and in signal transduction required massive new investments in infrastructure—research space and analytical tools—and in intellect. And as time went by, it became apparent that NIH funding had not grown as quickly as many had hoped.

Vanderbilt faced a dilemma: how to continue to support its important missions of teaching and research, with a required annual subsidy exceeding $20 million, in the face of dwindling margins from patient care. Against this challenging backdrop, Vanderbilt needed to build its clinical service component or risk the health and vitality of its other missions. In order to sustain the Medical Center's growing appetite for teaching and research, Vanderbilt's clinical volume, clinical revenue, and margin from clinical activity must grow.

The Historical Perspective

Steeped in 125 years of academic tradition and imbued with Southern gentility, Vanderbilt historically shunned marketing, the result of its already established reputation for excellence as well as an institutional mind-set that viewed marketing cautiously, if not disdainfully (Figure 6–1). Vanderbilt's realm was the rarified air of tertiary and quartenary medical care, with a marked preference for teaching and research. The hospital's culture was, and is, physician-led and physician-driven; and physicians, as a rule, do not advertise.

The institutional bias against marketing was strengthened by a seminal, if short-lived, experience. In 1987, the Medical Center flirted briefly with advertising by promoting its obstetrical service. While the campaign did what it was supposed to do, the demand for services outpaced Vanderbilt's capacity to deliver them.

Figure 6–1 1925 Vanderbilt University School of Medicine, from the Historical Collections, Eskind Biomedical Library, Vanderbilt University Medical Center. Courtesy of Vanderbilt University Medical Center, Nashville, Tennessee.

Rather than satisfying consumers, Vanderbilt alienated them. The campaign was quickly terminated.

With undisputed leadership in trauma, transplantation, neonatal intensive care, and pediatrics, Vanderbilt rested upon its considerable reputational laurels. But by 1996, it began to feel the effect of changing times. Consumer surveys showed that Baptist Hospital was Nashville's hands-down favorite, with a preference share of 16.8 percent. Closely behind at 12.2 percent was St. Thomas, a Daughters of Charity hospital known for its cardiac program. Bringing up the rear was Vanderbilt, and the fledgling network of Columbia HCA hospitals, with preference ratings of 7.8 percent and 7.5 percent, respectively.

The results were both surprising and sobering. Despite its international reputation, Vanderbilt was losing preference on its home turf to community hospitals. Preference shifts almost always signal future market share shifts, and Vanderbilt's market share was already less than eight percent. Local competitors were accumulating strong bottom lines, fanning program expansion into services and specialties once solely the province of Vanderbilt and its faculty physicians.

Under the leadership of Dr. John Sergent, Chief Medical Officer for the Vanderbilt Medical Group, Dr. Jim Wilson, head of Vanderbilt's primary care practice, and Ron Hill, then-head of strategic planning and marketing, a plan was devised to actively market the physician group practice. Their daunting objective: rebuild consumer demand for Vanderbilt's services and establish a consumer preference that will be strong enough to command premium prices from commercial payers.

The Plan

Vanderbilt had some catching up to do. For more than 20 years, front-runner Baptist Hospital had advertised heavily in the market, employing a particularly aggressive campaign over the last decade that emphasized its familiarity, its caring—and its "hospital-to-the-stars" reputation, cementing ties to fans of country music as well. St. Thomas had pursued a successful community outreach campaign and physician affiliation strategy that brought its cardiology service to the community. Columbia HCA had acquired seven community hospitals to add to its downtown flagship, the Centennial Medical Center, and was beginning to build a reputation for convenience, with locations throughout the metropolitan area. Only Vanderbilt had relied chiefly upon coverage from the print and broadcast media to position itself.

In September 1996, Vanderbilt turned to Lewis Communications for help in promoting its physicians to the community. The Birmingham, Alabama–based firm immersed itself in the Medical Center, analyzing Vanderbilt's substantial existing quantitative research on both patient satisfaction and attitude/awareness. Lewis supplemented Vanderbilt's research by holding focus groups and interviewing approximately 30 Medical Center employees, including physicians and administrative and operations personnel.

The focus groups uncovered a real difference in perception between people who had used Vanderbilt and those who had not. Consumers who had previous experience with the Medical Center were much more positive about the institution than those who had never crossed its threshold. Strong biases and misunderstandings about academic medical centers were also rife among those who had never been to Vanderbilt. Fears about being a research guinea pig or a specimen for young doctors in training were frequently mentioned (Exhibit 6–1).

Because the Vanderbilt brand name was so strong, the negatives that surfaced about the Medical Center would adversely color any positive promotion of Vanderbilt's physician group. What began as a campaign to drive patients to Vanderbilt physicians quickly metamorphosed into a branding campaign for the entire Medical Center.

Following the research and analysis, Lewis developed a comprehensive strategic plan for a multi-year image campaign to raise awareness of the Medical Center, to soften its image and to associate Vanderbilt with quality of care. Research findings and conclusions were presented to key decision makers at every level, to ensure corporate buy-in of survey results and their interpretation. Only after internal consensus did

---

Exhibit 6–1   Misperceptions about Vanderbilt

- "Patients are guinea pigs"
- "You never know who your doctor is"
- "Too many medical students"
- "These doctors are in medicine for their own career, not for patient care"
- "I'm not sick enough to go there"
- "Lots of smart doctors, but difficult to negotiate, not personal"
- "They don't have real doctors, only students"
- "It's the hospital of last resort—you go there to try to save your life when all else fails"

Lewis begin to develop a creative approach, designed to change the way people felt about the institution and to change the words used to describe it. An umbrella marketing theme, "V*and*erbilt: Hearts *and* Minds," capitalized upon the positives of the Vanderbilt brand—a brand well-known for expertise, quality, and training, but short on warmth and caring—and injected a powerful emotional element.

Form Follows Substance

As the 1987 advertising experience had shown, for the brand to be believable, its promise must be deliverable. Vanderbilt's new claim of being a nicer, friendlier place needed to be rooted in reality.

Fortunately, the Medical Center had already identified problems that adversely affected perceptions by consumers and managed care organizations. Adhering to tried-and-true marketing principles, Vanderbilt began to address problems in its *Product, Price*, and *Place*, before undertaking *Promotion*.

In September 1995, the Medical Center introduced a multi-year, institution-wide campaign to examine and improve operations and culture. Pricing had always been an issue, and perceptions that the institution was more expensive than competitors had not always been wrong. Earlier in the decade, Vanderbilt's charges had exceeded the market norm by as much as 25 percent, but a series of cost-containment strategies and other belt-tightening measures made Vanderbilt's fees competitive by 1995.

Vanderbilt's undeniably first-rate product was nevertheless delicately balanced on a three-legged stool of patient care, research, and teaching. If it was to attract the steady stream of patients necessary to support its other two legs, more Vanderbilt physicians needed to join the ranks of primary care physicians, managed care's gatekeepers. Beginning in the early 1990s, the Medical Center began ramping up its primary care capacity, tripling its full-time equivalency of primary care physicians, and also concentrating on such other avenues to tertiary care as internal medicine and obstetrics/gynecology.

Lastly, the interaction of Vanderbilt staff and its public was a particular concern, because of its great influence over consumer perceptions of the place. Previous financial pressures on the Medical Center had resulted in job restructuring, with fewer personnel performing more tasks. The toll had begun to show, especially in front-line positions.

Vanderbilt took corrective action. Jobs were restructured, again, so that receptionists and other staff members dealing with the public were not saddled with conflicting responsibilities. Internal training programs were upgraded to focus on customer satisfaction and hospitality. Not confined to front-line employees, Vanderbilt physicians, residents, and medical students were also schooled in the importance of public perceptions.

By the spring of 1997, with the brand promise shored up, the first full-fledged advertising campaign in the history of Vanderbilt Medical Center was prepared for take-off.

Pre-Launch

Before going public, however, Vanderbilt recognized that employee buy-in would be critical to the campaign's success. Coming on the heels of a $50 million cost reduction plan, the new and expensive advertising program could have produced hostility or, at best, indifference among Medical Center personnel. Nothing would have scuttled the campaign more effectively.

The campaign's objective was not only to remind the marketplace of Vanderbilt's high quality, but also to humanize the imposing institution by portraying the character of its physicians, nurses, and staff. Vanderbilt crafted an internal launch strategy, designed to energize employees and turn staff members into ambassadors. Internal posters with the same feel as the consumer campaign featured a modification of the overall theme—**Vanderbilt: You *and* Me**. Tag lines were designed to raise employee awareness of the important role each played: *I will take responsibility for finding a solution to any problem or complaint that a patient or family member may have; I will give our patients and their needs my highest priority; We treat patients and each other as we wish to be treated* (Figure 6–2).

A week before the public launch, the inaugural television spot was unveiled in-house to an enthusiastic response, and aired 24 hours a day. A series of internal presentations helped ensure that all employees had the opportunity to hear, first-hand, why Vanderbilt was embarking upon this campaign, and its importance to Vanderbilt's future. An elegant, oversized internal brochure—mirroring the theme, feeling, and images of the ad campaign—was mailed to all physicians and employees, reinforcing the message that employees are the people who "put a face" on Vanderbilt each and every day (Figure 6–3).

The strategy worked. Despite the fact that the Medical Center postponed salary increases the year before, employees embraced the two-year advertising campaign, with an annual expense of $4.5 million, wondering why Vanderbilt had not "gone public" earlier. The campaign's messages resonated with, and modeled behavior for, the staff. It appealed to and reinforced their sense of pride in working for Vanderbilt.

The campaign helped usher in a powerful cultural change in the Medical Center staff, and has since been incorporated into all new employee orientations.

The Campaign

To create a new mind-set about the institution as a whole, Lewis proposed beginning with an image campaign. The campaign was designed not only to remind the marketplace of Vanderbilt's high quality, but also to humanize the institution by portraying the character of its physicians, nurses, and staff. Promoting individual services or product lines would follow in subsequent campaigns.

Vanderbilt's lack of market presence for so many years required an intensive, orchestrated effort that would saturate local television, radio, and print markets. The formal campaign kicked off on Monday, April 7, 1996 with an unheard-of 90-second spot, roadblocked on all three regional networks for the evening news. Through evocative images, music, and words, the commercial began to paint a picture of Vanderbilt as a center of medical excellence and as a warm, caring, compassionate place (Figure 6–4). The inaugural spot ran for the first two weeks of the campaign.

Four 60-second spots followed in equal rotation, pulling sub-themes from the first. Each ad—*"Thoughts and Feelings," "Perception and Reality," "Questions and Answers,"* and *"Time and Attention"*—focused on adjusting perceptions. To help consumers understand the value of the many doctors a Vanderbilt patient sees,

Figure 6–2 Sample of an Internal Poster for Vanderbilt You and Me Campaign. Courtesy of Vanderbilt University Medical Center, Nashville, Tennessee.

Figure 6–3 Employee-Physician Brochure. Courtesy of Vanderbilt University Medical Center, Nashville, Tennessee.

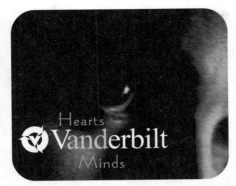

While you're busy going about the business of thinking about your life, you can rest assured that the brightest minds in medicine are busy thinking about it too.

Figure 6–4 TV Ad Campaign Showing Vanderbilt As a Caring Institution. Courtesy of Vanderbilt University Medical Center, Nashville, Tennessee.

---

one ad paraphrased the old adage that many minds are better than one. Another ad touted Vanderbilt's primary care services, reminding viewers that Vanderbilt provided the most comprehensive, sophisticated, and seamless panoply of services with the tag line *"If you know you might end up here for the most complex health concerns, why don't you just start here?"* The remainder of the campaign featured three 30-second spots cut from the 60-second spots.

Print ads supported broadcast, and homed in on special audiences. A series of full-color spreads in such mainstream consumer magazines as *Nashville Life* and the regional edition of *Southern Living* showed the professional and the personal sides of an individual Vanderbilt employee (Figure 6–5). Actual letters from grateful patients were turned into page-dominant ads for *The Tennessean.*

To reach the managed care and business audience, Vanderbilt profiled its key physicians, ending with the question: *"Is she in your health plan?"* Ads ran in local business publications *(Nashville Business Journal, Business Nashville)*, the business section of *The Tennessean,* and the Nashville editions of *Time, Newsweek,* and *U.S. News & World Report* (Figure 6–6).

Within a short eight months, the needle began to move.

Media Relations

The reinforcement of messages that is possible through the interplay of paid media (advertising) and unpaid or earned media (news/editorial coverage) is powerful. Harnessing that synergy can be a complex and subtle undertaking but one that can increase exponentially the impact of an advertising campaign. Recognizing that promotion encompassed both paid and unpaid messages, Vanderbilt Medical Center began to expand its media relations program around the same time that it contemplated an advertising campaign.

The growth of the media relations program was due, in part, to the media's own increasing level of interest and investment in health information. Driven in large

Figure 6–5 Example of a Magazine Ad. Courtesy of Vanderbilt University Medical Center, Nashville, Tennessee.

Former UROLOGY CHIEF RESIDENT *at* VANDERBILT MEDICAL CENTER.

Received the H. WILLIAM SCOTT JR. PRIZE *in* SURGERY.

Directs the area's only COMPREHENSIVE CENTER *to offer* BIOFEEDBACK *and* BEHAVIORAL TRAINING *for* FEMALE INCONTINENCE.

FIRST UROLOGIST *in* MIDDLE TENNESSEE FOCUSING EXCLUSIVELY *on* FEMALE UROLOGY.

Is she in your HEALTH PLAN?

DR. JENNY FRANKE

Jenny Franke was the state's first female urologist. She is one of the many people at Vanderbilt who is accomplishing things every day that improve the lives of women throughout our region. In fact, when it comes to women's services, Vanderbilt has subspecialists, diagnostic procedures and treatment options that cannot be found anywhere else. Like the nation's first center to conduct gene therapy for breast cancer. So the next time you wonder who's in your health plan, call 936-6011 and find out more about Jenny Franke and the over 600 other doctors in the Vanderbilt Medical Group.

Hearts and Minds ♥ Vanderbilt Health Services

Figure 6–6 Ad Profiling Key Physicians. Courtesy of Vanderbilt University Medical Center, Nashville, Tennessee.

measure by studies that show an expanding consumer interest in health care, the media have been spending more and more of news and features budgets on health over the past decade. The result is that the media—and their advertisers—have created more opportunities for health news, especially coverage of advances in medicine.

From an organization content to react to media interest, Vanderbilt became an active participant in trying to shape media attention. Since 1996, the Medical Center's news and public affairs staff has expanded by 10 percent. Focusing principally on breakthroughs in medicine and research, Vanderbilt's media placements increased by 12 percent in 1997, by 18 percent in 1998, and by 20 percent in 1999. Even more significant were increases in national media placement.

This increase in media coverage helped pave the way for the advertising campaign's ultimate success. Because the cognitive elements of the Medical Center were being advanced so effectively through news media coverage, the advertising campaign was free to focus on the emotive, humanizing aspects of Vanderbilt's message.

The Results

To establish a benchmark, Vanderbilt conducted a pre-advertising consumer tracking study in late 1996, and repeated it in 1997 and again in 1998 as the campaign was under way. Conducted by the polling firm PRC, phone surveys took in a sample of 1,900 consumers from 57 counties. Identity of the survey's sponsor was withheld until questions were completed.

The findings were remarkable. In two years, the percentage of consumers preferring Vanderbilt increased by 48.7 percent. Those naming Vanderbilt as their regional referral center or alternative hospital (as opposed to local hospital) increased nearly as much (48 percent). Vanderbilt moved from a close race for fourth place to come in as number two in hospital preference, while all other competitors lost ground (Figure 6–7).

The gains took place not only in perception but in actual behavior. Vanderbilt Medical Center increased its market share for primary care, for emergency and trauma, for outpatient and for inpatient care.

PRC had never seen such significant preference and market share shifts in its 12 years of conducting health care studies. While many of its clients show progress in three or four areas, they may lose ground in others. Only about 5 percent of the hospitals PRC has surveyed ever achieved such solid gains across the board.

Other studies measured such attributes as warmth, demonstrated by *physician care, treating patients with compassion, and friendly/helpful employees.* The perceived quality of physician and nurses shot up an astounding 114 percent and 111 percent, respectively. Vanderbilt's consumer rating as "excellent" on general impressions increased by 31 percent (Figures 6–8, 6–9, and 6–10).

Even though *"Hearts and Minds"* was an institutional image campaign, specific medical specialties also benefited from the halo effect. Vanderbilt gained significant ground in oncology (↑98 percent) (Figure 6–11), cardiology (↑94 percent), emergency (↑132 percent), birth services (↑105 percent), and orthopedics (↑101 percent)—all at the expense of a major competitor.

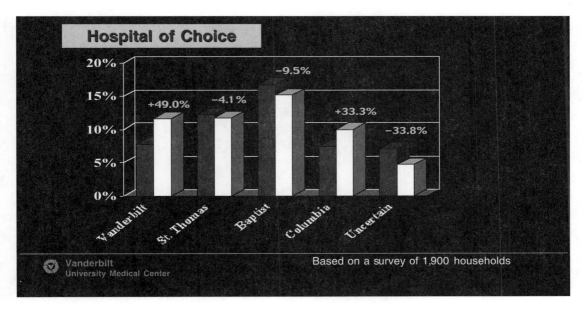

Figure 6–7 Consumer Hospital Preference Comparative Rates 1996 vs. 1998. Courtesy of Vanderbilt University Medical Center, Nashville, Tennessee.

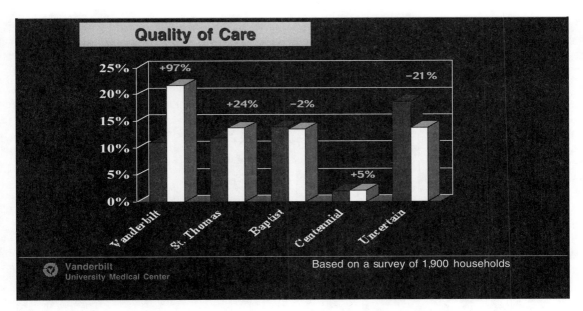

Figure 6–8 Consumer Hospital Preference Comparative Rates 1996 vs. 1998. Courtesy of Vanderbilt University Medical Center, Nashville, Tennessee.

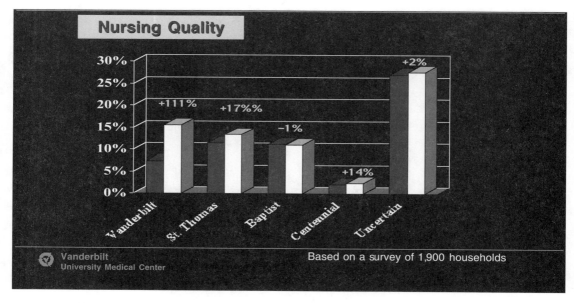

Figure 6–9 Consumer Hospital Preference Comparative Rates 1996 vs. 1998. Courtesy of Vanderbilt University Medical Center, Nashville, Tennessee.

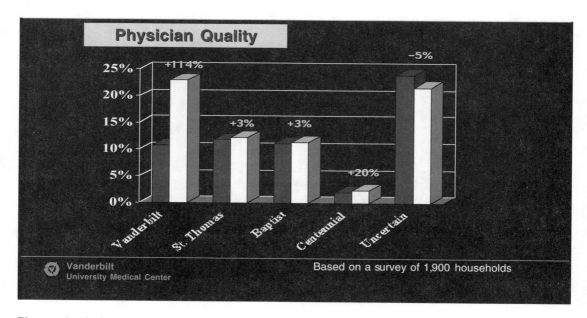

Figure 6–10 Consumer Hospital Preference Comparative Rates 1996 vs. 1998. Courtesy of Vanderbilt University Medical Center, Nashville, Tennessee.

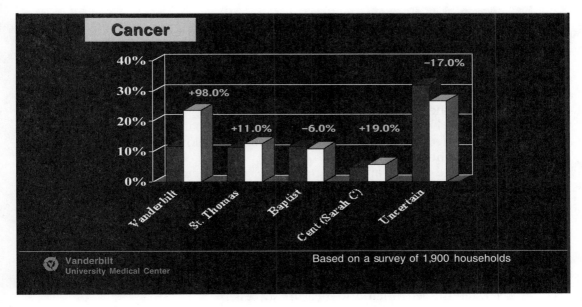

Figure 6–11 Consumer Hospital Preference Comparative Rates 1996 vs. 1998. Courtesy of Vanderbilt University Medical Center, Nashville, Tennessee.

Next Steps

Based upon the success of the institutional branding campaign, Vanderbilt Medical Center recommitted to the value of advertising. By 1998 the Medical Center was ready to move to the next stage, and began to roll out product-specific advertising starting with children's services and heart services.

The messages and feel of the product campaign reinforced the branded attributes set by the image campaign: ***competence and quality, compassion and caring***. But the product-line campaigns included a call to action.

The Children's Services campaign had achieved two goals: to solidify its already strong market position, and to prime the pump for a $50 million capital campaign for a new Children's Hospital. The heart campaign was designed to reverse the widely-held opinion that a competitor was the top heart hospital in Nashville. Timed to coincide with an emerging affiliation with the premier cardiology practice in town, Vanderbilt's campaign targeted new patients. Tied together by common imagery, pacing, musical tone, and graphics, all three product campaigns trace their roots to the branding campaign.

CONCLUSION

The image campaign successfully raised awareness and improved the public image of Vanderbilt Medical Center, converting negative perceptions into positive ones and raising market share across the board. In the two years since its advertising campaign began, Vanderbilt experienced a steady growth rate of 8 percent to 10 percent per year, as competitors declined. After years of benignly ignoring the inherent value of its brand, Vanderbilt had entered the marketing arena with a bang.

Lessons Learned

- Know your institutional capacity: if you're going to create expectations, make sure you can deliver them.
- Research, research, research. You must constantly measure and understand the market's perception of your institution, and be prepared to correct it when the perception's off-base.
- A well thought-out strategic institutional campaign and message can exert a halo effect upon all other aspects of the institution, including specific department and programs.
- Base the creative approach upon facts and research findings.
- Involve physicians in the process from the beginning. Physician buy-in can help muster CEO buy-in.
- Create messages that appeal to consumers, and take care to convince internal stakeholders of the importance of that patient-centered discipline.
- Don't let your "family"—employees and staff—find out about your campaign when the public does. Use inside-out communications.
- Ads can have a profound impact upon employee morale, increasing pride.
- Establish benchmarks to measure success.
- Stay the course. Marketing is a function of doing business and should be a sustained effort, not a faucet to be turned on and off.
- For maximum effectiveness and "bang-for-the-buck," try to incorporate paid and unpaid media. Through the right mix of marketing vehicles, you can reinforce your messages significantly and boost results.
- Make sure the message is consistent for all audiences: patients, physicians, insurers, and potential donors.

Chapter 7

Leveraging Scientific Discoveries To Further Brand Recognition

Elaine Freeman, Joann Rodgers, and Carol Bloomberg

"Our mission is our margin."

INTRODUCTION

Those seeking to establish, then leverage a service or product "brand name" first need a clear view of what they want that name to *mean*. Like the House of Rothschild's *grand cru* vintners or the makers of Mercedes Benz S class sedans, the leaders of Johns Hopkins Medicine decided literally from Day One that "excellence"—in our case in the form of scientific discovery and the rapid application of research to patient care—would form the foundation upon which Hopkins would build its reputation and its revenues.

Thus, when the doors of The Johns Hopkins Hospital opened in 1889, the first trustees and administrators of the hospital and university already had recruited the best clinician-scientists to head departments; then committed to admitting only college graduates with a thorough grounding in science to The Johns Hopkins University School of Medicine (discarding the traditional practice of admitting any high school grad who could pay the fees); crafted their mission statement to dedicate the institution to the "advancement of knowledge" for the "relief of suffering"; predicted the unheard-of control of infectious disease and a life span of 70; and fostered such confidence in the quality of their "product" that they boldly and publicly promoted it, achieving full-page illustrated articles in the press.

Ever since, this dedication to bringing results from the lab bench to the bedside has been the substance behind the Hopkins brand name in medicine, the key not only to Johns Hopkins Medicine's scientific reputation, but also to its clinical and commercial success. While leaders of some medical centers quip "No margin, no mission," the leaders of Hopkins Medicine insist "Our mission *is* our margin." Whatever the vision of each new generation of Hopkins leaders, whatever their plans to meet dynamic change, they burnish and protect the original mission.

Today, like a grand old wine or a classic automobile, the Johns Hopkins Medicine brand name has become synonymous with excellence in its field. And in turn, the key component of that excellence—discovery—has become the hallmark of our public relations enterprise. We use the "halo" of discovery to illuminate and enhance all of Hopkins' interests. The more attention we bring to a procedure or a field of expertise, the more people with related conditions seek care and counsel, increasing opportunities for further advancement of knowledge in these fields and

103

more research dollars. Those newspaper clippings from more than a century ago demonstrate the founders' understanding of the value of good public relations *and* their keen awareness of the need for something substantive to promote in the first place. Today's clippings underscore their wisdom, as do Gallup Polls and nine consecutive years' rankings by *U.S. News & World Report* that name us one of the top two big brand names in medicine.

The packaging, of course, must change with the times, but we understand that the quality of the product is what brings the buyer back again and again. Thus, our approach is to put our old wine in new bottles, leveraging discovery and innovation as the "default" mode of our promotions. As examples detailed in this chapter demonstrate, our strategy is to reinforce whenever possible the strong links between innovation and care, between the lab and the clinic, drawing on and refining the century-old vision and foundation of the Hopkins brand name.

A CASE HISTORY: THE FAMOUS "BLUE BABY" SURGERY

The story of this development in surgery is a template for how Hopkins has used the tools of public relations and media relations to leverage its reputation—and enhance the flow of patients. The story has it *all* from the Hopkins public relations standpoint: a unique clinical insight used to relieve a complex and previously untreatable disorder; a diverse team of people—including a brilliant surgeon, a stubborn, heroic woman, and the grandson of a slave—whose personal and professional skills drove them to devote years to finding a solution, first in the lab and then in the operating room; good historical timing; and compelling patient stories.

Here's the story in brief: Despite a hearing defect and severe dyslexia and dyscalculia, Helen Taussig was so brilliant that she was near the top of her Hopkins medical school class. As a pioneer in the field of pediatric cardiology, she often relied on the subtle differences in the feel of heartbeats caused by congenital abnormalities. In this way, before diagnostic imaging, she recognized that the abnormal flow of blood in one heart defect was the key to correcting another. She perceived that the typical "blue baby," short of breath and blue on exertion, had decreased blood flow to the lungs. At a time when no one dared operate on the heart, Taussig convinced surgeon in chief Alfred Blalock and his technician, Vivien Thomas, the grandson of a slave, that they could compensate for the inadequate flow of blood by altering the course and function of a major artery coming out of the heart. Connecting it to the artery going into the lungs gave the blood a second chance to pick up essential oxygen (Figure 7–1).

Taussig later recalled for reporters the moment when the success of the operation became dramatically visible. She described the patient as "an utterly miserable, small 6-year-old boy who was no longer able to walk." His skin was intensely blue, his lips deep purple. After the final stitches were tied and the clamps released, the anesthesiologist joyfully called out, "The boy's a lovely color now!"

That moment marked one of the truly great medical accomplishments of this century. The blue-baby operation broke a barrier. The treatment for one congenital heart condition made it obvious that precise diagnosis could lead to treatment of other abnormalities. This, in turn, led to greater use of cardiac catheterization and extended the reach of heart surgeons and cardiologists.

The story of the first successful operation has become legendary, and Blalock and Taussig helped to spread the legend. Several weeks after he demonstrated the surgery in London, Blalock described the procedure to a surgical conference, then

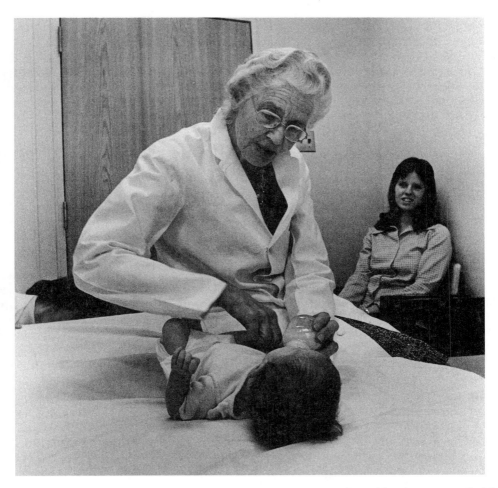

Figure 7–1 Helen Taussig, M.D., with a Young Patient. *Source:* © Tadder Associates, Baltimore, Maryland.

sat down. The lights dimmed for a few moments, then spotlighted Blalock with a beautiful, rosy-cheeked young girl on his lap—the very "blue baby" whose surgery he had just described. Photographers were there to document the moment.

Fueled by such international exposure as well as by the media coverage it engendered, parents streamed to Hopkins from around the world to bring their frail children for this unique procedure. In addition, the great heart surgeons, pediatric cardiologists, and cardiac physiologists of the second half of the 20th century received their training at Hopkins at this exciting moment. The new era of cardiology and cardiac surgery began here and spread throughout the world.

This story illustrates the value of featuring faculty in public relations efforts and underscores the importance of building on faculty willingness to participate in the rapid dissemination of new knowledge to clinicians and the public worldwide.

It further demonstrates the long shelf life of a good science-based story, particularly those with good patient components. For more than five decades, Hopkins public relations efforts have continued to build on the story, with updates on the surgery and the genetics of cardiac birth defects. The renown of this surgery and the key people involved also were used to advantage in such diverse issues as women's and minority rights.

A key lesson of this story is that effective leveraging of scientific discovery is no accident. Beyond the published research and clinical work were dramatic personalities and patient stories that required excavating and exploitation in the best sense of the word. The Blue Baby story has been the subject even in recent years of a planned television special and award-winning magazine articles—and, as we write, there are battles going on over who will be first to produce it as a made-for-TV movie. This story, like Johns Hopkins Medicine, is a model of its kind.

A MODERN EXAMPLE: FROM SURGERY TO STAMPS

Prostate cancer is the second most common cancer in men. Every year, in the United States alone, about 100,000 men are diagnosed with this condition. Patrick Walsh, director of the Brady Urologic Institute at Johns Hopkins, was distressed that, time after time, patients came to him after the cancer had spread beyond the prostate, too late for a surgical cure. He realized that men often delayed seeking medical help because they feared impotence and incontinence, which usually, but not always, accompanied surgical removal of the prostate gland. Why not always? Walsh realized there must be an explanation and was determined to discover why a few men were spared the demoralizing side effects.

Working with a Dutch anatomist, Walsh conducted the first detailed study of the nerves leading to the male reproductive organs. First, he identified the bundle of nerves that must be spared if a man were to retain sexual function after prostate removal—and then developed the operative procedure for removing the entire gland without slicing the crucial nerves.

In the spring of 1984, the first of thousands of men would undergo the new procedure. Overall, nearly three-quarters have retained potency and more than 95 percent are continent. And, perhaps most important of all, only about 1 percent have had a local recurrence of their cancer.

Today, the research and treatment center Walsh heads is extending its nerve-sparing surgical approaches to bladder cancer with dramatic results in survival and function.

In the Hopkins tradition, Walsh did not attempt to keep the new operation exclusive to Hopkins. Instead, he trains surgeons from around the world to spread the new treatment as swiftly as possible.

Because of the demographics—men often at the height of their success—promotion of Walsh's work has brought not only huge numbers of patients, but also "grateful patients" with donations and the ability to carry our message and our interests to high places.

For example, when Hopkins was seeking a U.S. postage stamp to mark the Centennial of Johns Hopkins Medicine, Pat Walsh and his patients were key. *Every member* of the Congressional subcommittee on the postal service signed a letter to the Postmaster General in favor of such a stamp. And influential business tycoons who had the Postmaster General's ear used their access on our behalf. The result was a stamp issued as part of the Centennial opening ceremonies, complete with sale of first day covers, mugs, and aprons—all with our founder's dour likeness! (Figure 7–2).

The large number of patients also has fueled and facilitated the search for the genetic roots of prostate cancer, a story we continue to tell.

Figure 7–2 Stamp Marking Centennial of Johns Hopkins Medicine. Courtesy of Johns Hopkins Medicine, Baltimore, Maryland.

The circular benefit to Hopkins, to patients, and to research that comes from media exposure is also apparent with pancreatic cancer. When the current chief of surgery developed a new procedure for pancreatic cancer with better outcomes at lower cost, we brought this to the attention of the media at a National Press Club briefing (because of the business angle)—and issued follow-up releases with each new study he published. As a result of this and related studies, the Institute of Medicine now has recommended that complex surgeries be conducted at high volume centers—in essence creating regional centers of excellence. Other outside experts have gone further and claimed that it would be unethical to send patients with these conditions anywhere other than centers such as Hopkins.

Similar case histories could be described for colon cancer. Media attention to discoveries brings in a high volume of patients who, in turn, lead to insights about the more subtle genetic underpinnings of the condition, diagnostic tests, new treatments, even prevention—and more media attention.

HOW WE DO IT: OLD WINE, NEW BOTTLES

At a time of intense competition and diminishing resources, Johns Hopkins still relies primarily on "earned" or "free" media, with the addition of niche publications and of marketing communications campaigns to enhance patient flow and revenue for specific "product lines" in our local region. While there are several models for conducting media relations and overall public relations in this context, the Hopkins model, as noted, field-tested and refined for years, owes its success to public relations practices and principles that leverage discoveries and innovation.

Historically, these practices have met with extraordinary success among such traditional media targets as the science and medical press, editorial page editors, opinion leaders, women's and general interest magazines, and broadcast and cable television stations. On average, more than 10,000 substantive press calls are logged annually by Hopkins Medicine's public affairs staff, and pick-up of more than 100 research news releases produced each year brings a blizzard of clips. Rarely a week goes by without the presence on campus of a network news producer and crew. Our brand visibility among these media targets remains high as long as service to them continues, and they, in turn, convey our brand to the broader public.

The brand name challenge of the 1990s and beyond, however, has been to reach beyond traditional media "fans" to increase visibility among not-so-traditional audiences, whose tastes for *grand vin* quality are nonexistent or just forming. Increasingly, these audiences get their information in less traditional and more diverse ways. Among them: business and technology writers and publications, reporters online, and overseas journalists. Through them we reach corporate health and communications partners, managed care organizations (MCOs), physician networks, and overseas patients.

Our approach to the challenge? To fill new bottles—the World Wide Web, for example—with vintage Hopkins. And, while we were at it, to pour some new wine—most notably high-profile news and information for the non-traditional business and entrepreneurial side of Johns Hopkins Medicine—into bottles old and new.

In public relations and communications terms, we set out strategically and imaginatively to recycle and repurpose information that best serves our brand, rather than to reinvent or segment our brand. Instead of striving to be "New Coke," we opted to be Classic Coke, promoted more distinctively and creatively.

Caution: this approach won't work everywhere. Other institutions, particularly those without the strong, credible brand loyalty Hopkins enjoys, might do better to pretest, then experiment with "all new" looks and services. But where there is evidence of excellence and brand loyalty, a solid option is to build creatively on a field-tested base.

Some rules govern this approach.

First, consistency of quality in content and service. For example, Hopkins has been careful to promote such things as the "business" of medicine with the same intellectual rigor and *dedication to news value* as it promotes clinical care, education, and research. The Office of Communications and Public Affairs integrates, when *logical and possible*, strategic marketing initiatives into media and public relations, but vigorously resists the temptation to go for fads or quick "fixes" like credibility-destroying infomercials or gimmicky media campaigns that might "do harm" by undermining the painstakingly achieved, long-term relationships—built on mutual trust—with the media, our faculty and staff, and the public. It's essential for those who would establish and leverage a brand name in health care to adapt the Hippocratic Oath's pronouncement to "first do no harm" to that image and brand, to entertain no promotional activity that would trade away or sully values and dignity.

Second, care must be taken to match techniques and tools to what target audiences actually use now, while implementing newer tools when the timing is right. For instance, when Hopkins nearly a decade ago decided to use radio news outlets as a massive, nationwide media relations vehicle, we learned that most stations were not yet online, and many had no access to satellite transmission. Thus, the decision was made at that time to offer daily feeds, five days a week, via telephone line as well as electronic bulletin boards and even via mailed tapes for a few stations. As stations across the United States and worldwide quickly moved to all-digital formats, Hopkins expanded to satellite and World Wide Web delivery. As described later in more detail, we also knew stations would reject the radio spots if we used them to call attention directly to Hopkins clinical services, so this, too, was carefully avoided.

Similarly, trend spotting told us when the time was right for Hopkins to move more aggressively to produce national consumer newsletters and Web pages, segmented Experts Guides for media, electronic news delivery services for journalists, PC-based contact management software, increased coordination of some media relations with strategic planning and marketing initiatives, and increased "wholesaling" of our discoveries and experts to selected mass media with a thirst for big name brand tie-ins.

Third, in the interest of maintaining credibility with news organizations, appropriate "fire walls" between news operations, marketing, and revenue-generating consumer health enterprises must be kept if this model is to work. This is not always simple. For example, the consumer health information group at Hopkins often is asked by business partners in a Web site branded with Hopkins' name to provide "exclusive" access to faculty discoveries in advance of distribution to mass media, or to deny news organizations that also have Web sites access to certain sources at Hopkins. This would hold the news and information operation hostage, however. So such requests routinely are denied, and there are "carve outs" in contracts with business partners to shield the public relations aspects of our institution and allow unfettered distribution of news to all media and electronic outlets.

Another example: infomercials. Some Hopkins faculty members are the targets of increasingly imaginative drug company marketers who offer to produce and place in major regional and national media outlets high quality educational videos that amount to product endorsements. To date, Hopkins has elected to reject such infomercial use, in part because of the potential damage to our media relations program and credibility.

As we worked to parlay the Hopkins reputation for excellence more broadly and in new ways, we came up against the reality that journalism and news organizations are changing dramatically. Competition among daily newspapers in a single market, for example, which once could be exploited to generate coverage, has nearly disappeared in major markets. Local television stations are more willing than ever to "sell" news time and news anchors to the highest bidder in a blizzard of veiled infomercials; news organizations have limited travel budgets for reporters to attend national meetings or travel to institutions to cover stories in person; networks are losing market share to cable organizations; and the fragmentation of the print and electronic media makes it increasingly difficult to generate earned media in a planned, strategic way.

At Hopkins, therefore, we search for other ways to reach journalists consistently and keep our name and services at the top of their "source" pile. We have partnered, for example, with the Foundation for American Communications to produce media guides for academics and business executives and get Hopkins faculty on FACS seminars for journalists across the United States. With the institution's heavy support, we have held volunteer leadership positions with the National Association of Science Writers and the Council for the Advancement of Science Writing, positions that generated co-sponsorship for science writers' seminars at the university and visibility in press rooms at national science and medical meetings. These posts also assured Hopkins public information officers a voice in setting guidelines for release of published research on the Internet and gave us a seat at the table during discussions with high-ranking journalists about journalistic ethics and the role of public relations services.

Each summer for more than two decades, a Hopkins public relations (PR) executive—whose time is paid for by Hopkins—has helped organize a major seminar for journalists devoted to heavy-duty genetic science at The Jackson Laboratory in Maine. The press week is part of a two-week course for scientists and physicians. Contacts made and nurtured during these meetings—and over lobster dinners and blueberry muffins—have brought consistent and growing visibility to Hopkins scientists among the elite cadre of reporters who cover genetics.

Nowhere has the mandate to tailor the Hopkins public relations enterprise to new audiences been more evident than in the array of periodicals carrying the Johns Hopkins Medicine insignia. Both our flagship alumni magazine and an extensive group of tabloids and newsletters have subtly adjusted their voices to a growing health care system, a wider network of referring physicians, a new group of international contacts, and an increasingly significant involvement with managed care. We created one new publication, *International Physician Update*, by repurposing and repackaging stories from our domestic *Physician Update*, and developed a totally new publication, *Managed Care Partners*, for MCO executives, as well as a growing network of physicians forced to think about costs because of capitation.

Results of Hopkins' "earned media" and other consumer health and public relations programs are gratifying, and although results often are difficult to quantify, the projects have triggered hundreds of physician and patient referrals for disorders ranging from minimally invasive heart surgery, epilepsy, and chronic fatigue syndrome to colon, breast, and brain cancer. They also have kept the Hopkins brand name in the public discourse to serve as a nurturing environment for fund-raising, technology transfer and corporate partnerships, faculty and student recruitment, lobbying, community relations, and advertising campaigns for clinical services. Details of some of our recent "wine and bottles" projects are discussed in the following section.

The Business of Medicine Program

When Johns Hopkins Medicine had to adapt to new economic realities imposed by managed care and other market and regulatory forces, the need for new revenue streams put technology transfer and corporate partnerships alongside traditional goals. Among the consequences was the need to position Johns Hopkins Medicine as a national, regional, and local leader in the business of health, just as it is known as a premier player in research, teaching, and patient care. Leveraging the discovery brand, Hopkins needed to be perceived as a worthy and efficient business partner and, at the same time, as an institution that rigorously guarded and protected its commitment to put patient care, research, and teaching first, or above bottom line considerations. Its various business initiatives and priorities required strategic media support.

Capitalizing on the institution's high credibility with the mass media and with specialty journalists and publications, we set up a parallel universe of credible sources of news with the press that covers the business of health care, technology transfer, partnerships and alliances, new business ventures, consumer health, reengineering, critical paths, and so on.

In sum, we set out to build a media relations program directly serving business and technology writers in much the same way we have long served science, medical, and feature writers. We also expanded the service to cover international business, Business of Medicine degree-granting programs in the School of Medicine, and business ethics. The challenge was to develop widespread interest in a new Hopkins enterprise on the part of media more attuned to Hopkins' research and medical discoveries. This required, above all, sensitivity to the sometimes open hostility on the part of some reporters toward the idea of academic medical centers profiting from their intellectual properties, engaging in new business ventures, and taking on the accoutrements of Wall Streeters. As they moved through the minefields of competitive negotiations, Hopkins' administrative leaders, who had historically taken a low profile with the press on business and related issues, often were reluctant to work with the media or actively court their attention.

Therefore, we initially focused media outreach on stories that used peer-reviewed information to demonstrate the relationship between cost and clinical outcomes, rather than on mere announcements of deals or stories about how efficient we were becoming. By emphasizing the economic *and* medical benefits of our business dealings, by staying close to the research/discovery tradition, we were able to meet the demands for solid business news, while not overtly antagonizing our traditional constituents who expected Hopkins not to "sell out" to commercial pressures. A strategic plan was developed to guide business of medicine media relations activities.

Materials produced to enhance our service included:

- ***A Journalist's Resource for Business of Medicine Reporting: Guide to Experts and Glossary on the Business of Medicine,*** a publication distributed to more than 100 reporters who cover the economics of health care and the business of medicine;
- A fact sheet of Hopkins business arrangements, affiliations, and contracts, mailed to selected press members;
- A tip sheet service for business of medicine items of interest to selected business publications.

We also expanded relationships with hospital industry and health policy journalists, and, as noted, organized a Washington, D.C., press conference to present research that demonstrated the value of having complex surgery performed at a major academic medical center.

Most significant, perhaps, we worked hard to put reporters in touch with Hopkins faculty we identified as "business savvy and friendly." Again, our strategy was to position Hopkins' leaders as people who were first and foremost devoted to teaching, research, and patient care—who would marry business acumen only to rigorous "scholarship" and clinical or research outcomes. We avoided, for the most part, putting forward "Wall Street whizzes" who might be perceived as limousine lovers instead of compassionate, but efficient, medical/business entrepreneurs.

Stories that developed around this strategy were of great importance, because their collective results reinforced the superiority of health care delivered at Hopkins while disproving the widespread perception that Hopkins health care was consistently more expensive. And whenever possible, we couched our messages about moneymaking ventures in language that showed why academic medical centers (centers with teaching hospitals and schools of medicine) needed unrestricted revenue to enhance medical education and the discovery of new knowledge.

As our reputation for having an honorable and successful business enterprise grew, we increasingly were able to promote stories that were strictly business to selected reporters. In this parallel universe we also invested our efforts heavily in opportunistic media relations, providing prompt service to business writers on deadline and exploiting opportunities as they arose to advance Hopkins' business of medicine issues. One venture was to work with Bloomberg Financial Networks to have our highly successful Health NewsFeed radio program distributed on Bloomberg terminals to the nation's business leaders. In another, when *U.S. News & World Report* released its "Best Hospital" rankings for 1998, we worked with the magazine to feature our kidney transplant team on the cover of the issue. (Our living donor kidney transplant center was designated by leadership as a business priority.) By establishing long-term credibility as fact providers, not fluff merchants and flacks, and by being ready to help the press cover stories that reporters already were prepared to cover, we were able to inform their coverage and tailor stories that reflected our internal initiatives.

Thus, when *The Baltimore Sun* editorial page editor asked us to put together a half-day program for an Association of Editorial Writers meeting in Baltimore, we focused on business of medicine activities and prepared a proposal for the association's executive board. That invitation, by the way, grew out of an earlier program done for the American Society of Newspapers Editors on behalf of the *Sun* editorial page editor, who then suggested us for the new project.

Clearly, the model calls for the business of medicine program or any "new bottle" project to be a long-term service game, not a hit-and-run effort. To get the issues-and-themes-oriented coverage we prize, the kind that puts Hopkins forward as a leader and its staff as statesmen of medicine, we must put reporters and their outlets on a learning curve *with* us, not outside of us or on an ad hoc basis.

Since the inception of the business of medicine media relations campaign, positive media coverage of Hopkins' business enterprises has risen dramatically, especially in our region. Media inquiries and coverage have quadrupled since the inception of the program. Equally significant has been the successful positioning of Hopkins' leadership as commentators for the press on national, regional, or international business of medicine issues. Just as we provide media training for researchers and clinicians in preparation for a major news event, we formally and informally encourage our business leaders to prepare for media encounters. By offering media training, insisting on appropriate financial interest disclosures in our press materials, and carefully briefing spokespersons prior to interviews, we built a cadre of highly effective business of medicine experts for the press to call upon.

We are careful, however, to remind leadership that media relations and public relations cannot be substitutes for advertising, marketing, or lobbying, but can complement and enhance those efforts. The following discussion includes two examples.

During Johns Hopkins Medicine's initial struggles to convince MCOs to contract with Hopkins, marketing communications launched a carefully targeted advertising campaign. Directed at corporate benefits officers and CEOs, the campaign used humor to encourage them to offer their employees only HMOs that included Johns Hopkins as a full participating provider. Placed on business pages, the intent of the ads also was to help bring to the table any HMOs missing from our list. We backed up the campaign with direct mail in the guise of personalized letters and with a new publication, ***Managed Care Partners.***

In 1998, when a critical piece of legislation designed to force insurers to pay for the costs of lifesaving clinical trials was at a make-it-or-break-it status in the State Legislature, Hopkins not only searched for stories that would put a personal face on the complex issues involved, but it also shared much of the information and materials it had with the other academic medical center in Baltimore. And it let others, such as insurers and the legislators involved, take most of the credit. Any other strategy would have seemed too self-serving, since Hopkins does the lion's share of clinical trials in the region. But it also ensured a wider credibility and unified position with the public and the media. By sharing the resources of the "brand," we helped support the legislation, which became a model bill nationwide.

Few things result in loss of credibility faster than exclusionary behavior. A hallmark of public relations at Hopkins, particularly with the press and with opinion leaders, is to reflect the essential hallmark of the academy: knowledge gathering and knowledge *sharing* on behalf of the public. When the media come calling, PR staffers at Hopkins will send them to experts at other institutions where appropriate, conveying the message that we stay informed about subjects of interest to the press and are committed to serving audiences, not just ourselves.

Health NewsFeed Service

Radio in the television and personal computer age is easy to overlook, but the search for new, cost-effective vehicles led us to consider new uses of older vehicles as well. Health NewsFeed (HNF), a *free,* daily, national and international radio news service, was first launched a decade ago and now reaches 1,300-plus stations in the United States, the Far East, and Europe. The fully digital medical audio news and text service is produced in the Office of Communications and Public Affairs by a former CBS radio correspondent and producer with more than 15 years of journalism experience. Health NewsFeed features 60-second radio news reports on medicine, each including interviews with Hopkins experts. It also offers "sound bites" of Hopkins news makers for use by radio stations that wish to produce their own health news programming. Health NewsFeed covers the broad spectrum of medicine, health, and medical research. Topics are chosen for their scientific importance but, equally important, for their relevance to the lay public. Every Health NewsFeed strives to answer the question: "What does this mean to me, the listener?"

Health NewsFeed illustrates beautifully the wisdom of our public relations model's "fire walls." While some institutions would be tempted to use such tools as a one-minute radio spot in drive time to market or promote competitive clinical services, we knew that such programming would not be acceptable to radio news directors locally, much less nationally. "Buy an ad," they would say, and they'd be right. The goal was to keep Hopkins' expertise for research discoveries heard in every time zone every weekday of every year. Rather than directly promoting a Hopkins physician or service, we use Hopkins' reputation and expertise to create a "halo" around news of medicine from anywhere.

As a consequence, the program features physicians, scientists, and experts in all medical disciplines talking about their work, their discoveries, and the scientific advances that will make the world a healthier place. Our interests range from geriatrics to pediatrics and all points in between. The short format is ideal for stations to drop into drive-time news. Ironically, some stations around the country sell ads in their local markets around the feature.

Health NewsFeed is distributed by satellite and an innovative toll-free phone network that provides CD-quality sound over ordinary telephone lines. The programs are fed by satellite each Friday at 11:00 AM. Numerous networks, including CBS, Bloomberg, USA, and Voice of America, refeed HNF via their own satellites. Since programmers are not tied to a specific feed time, they can retrieve the feeds when they want them, and air them when their audiences need them most. In cost per impression, it's the best public relations value in our portfolio.

The Internet

Like most organizations keeping pace with communications technologies, Hopkins recognized the need to deliver its information via World Wide Web sites and other electronic communications modes to reach internal and external audiences ranging from reporters to consumers.

As content providers and image makers, the public relations professionals decided to influence as much as possible the content and style of communications in these venues. Although responsibility for the Hopkins World Wide Web presence is widely fragmented, the public relations office has been able to mold and guide the content of the "front page."

Among the innovations:

- a Web site for journalists that includes a searchable database of all news releases dating back six years plus a list of all public affairs officers and their beats for quick access
- an electronic version of a highly popular 300-page *Experts Guide* source book, cross-indexed with all divisions of the university.

For our internal audience, we've developed an electronic clipping service that uses tailored search engines to pull news of Johns Hopkins Medicine and its faculty from thousands of news outlets, then groups and distributes them in a daily, free subscription service for faculty and staff that also includes information about upcoming television and radio programming featuring Hopkins.

In conjunction with the university news service, we also offer working journalists embargoed versions of all news releases via a proprietary listserv operation, increasingly with digital, downloadable images and related Web site hot links. Hopkins also participates in numerous electronic services for journalists provided by scientific and commercial groups, including EurekAlert (operated by the American Association for the Advancement of Science), Quadnet, Sci-Med News, and others. These services provide quarterly and sometimes monthly reports of downloads and queries from journalists, used as one way to track usage and guide future press and PR efforts.

As described below, Hopkins Medicine's most prominent Web presence thus far has come about at no cost to the institution—as a result of the brand name.

THE STRENGTH OF THE BRAND NAME: THE SNOWBALL EFFECT

Periodically over the past 15 years, Gallup Polls confirmed for us that Hopkins had become one of the two most trusted names in medicine. When asked specifically to rank valued sources of health information, the public places Hopkins ahead of the National Institutes of Health, Harvard, or Mass General. Another question in the survey asked: "If you or a family member needed hospital care for a serious illness or serious medical problem, how likely would you be to consider traveling to Baltimore in order to use Johns Hopkins Hospital?" An amazingly high one in three Americans say *they would be* likely to consider traveling to Baltimore to use Hopkins Hospital, with 17 percent "very likely" to do so.

Even before *U.S. News & World Report* ranked Johns Hopkins as the "Best Hospital in America" for nine consecutive years (Figure 7–3), communications entrepreneurs offered opportunities that reinforced this reputation and further spread the Hopkins name. Many of these opportunities brought income to Johns Hopkins in direct payments and/or royalties for communications projects of the type that were revenue drains to other institutions. Several of these projects are described below.

Health after 50

A decade ago, when consumer newsletters were proliferating at a rapid rate, we recognized the desirability of putting the Hopkins brand on one that would bring to Hopkins not only revenue but also direct visibility in homes nationwide.

Unlike other institutions, however, Hopkins resisted the temptation to become direct mail "publishers" in the traditional sense of the word because of the high capital costs and overall ignorance of the business. We recognized that what was needed were strategic partners who shared Hopkins' sense of brand and values, who had national direct mail marketing muscle, and who could envision collateral products and a newsletter of the quality that Hopkins required.

The Johns Hopkins Medical Letter: Health after 50, published with our partner, Rebus, Inc., emerged from this approach and from substantial research showing that

1. Americans over 50 were most likely to purchase health letters
2. Hopkins' brand name and reputation were most recognizable among Americans over 50 (who also use most of the health care services available)
3. There was a lopsided dependence by this population on print, as opposed to other vehicles of mass media.

Ten years later, *Health after 50* has 500,000 paid subscribers and has spun off numerous books and monographs that have earned more than $2 million in royalty for the university. All are promoted via direct mail by our publishing partner, giving Johns Hopkins Medicine millions of dollars in free promotion in addition to royalty earned by the products. Equally important, the newsletter's success catalyzed institutional interest in a fast-growing consumer health information industry. With other publishing partners, Hopkins now produces health encyclopedias and a continuity book series sold in supermarkets, and has a strong presence on the Internet.

Congratulations!

We're number one again.

By providing the best care to
Johns Hopkins patients,
You've made us "Best of the Best"

1991-1999

Figure 7–3 Poster Congratulating Staff for Making Hopkins "Best of the Best" Again. Courtesy of Johns Hopkins Medicine, Baltimore, Maryland.

InteliHealth

Winner of this year's Webby for Internet health sites, *InteliHealth* is a joint venture of Johns Hopkins and Aetna U.S. Healthcare. Branded on the Web as "Home to Johns Hopkins Health Information," InteliHealth also provides the health component of such sites as CBS.com and the *Washington Post*'s Web site, and is an anchor tenant on the America Online (AOL) health site.

Medcast

Johns Hopkins was invited to be an original contributor, with a channel of its own, on this cybercast venture providing information for physicians. Medcast was recently acquired by Healtheon/Web M.D.

Wholesaling

Network television has offered a particularly attractive way to leverage the Hopkins brand name, reinforcing the brand on an ongoing basis. Hopkins has refused to pay for packages sold by local stations promising regular time on news broadcasts in exchange for a long-term advertising commitment. Faced with such a blurring of the line between advertising and news—determined to avoid it, yet equally determined to keep the Hopkins name before the public and to disseminate messages that are not just product-line marketing—Hopkins public affairs practitioners developed a remarkable solution. In cooperation with two of the most popular medical shows on television, "ER" and "Chicago Hope" (the School of Public Health with "ER" and Hopkins Medicine with "Chicago Hope"), we developed news segments with a health message relevant to each episode. The segments were produced in cooperation with the networks' Baltimore stations, but aired on local news programs on all of the network-owned and -operated stations in major markets, because the networks were able to obtain national sponsorship for the segments, in large part because of our brand name. These were labor-intense projects that earned Johns Hopkins prime time media exposure every week throughout the nation.

THE DISCOVERY BRAND'S IMPACT ON MARKETING EFFORTS

Hopkins' scientific discovery brand has attracted patients from across the nation and around the world, but offers a marketing challenge in our local region. While we increasingly draw from outside our immediate area, 85 percent of our patients reside within Maryland and the border counties of neighboring states. HMO dominance and other insurance restrictions limiting physician and hospital choice to defined networks ensure this situation is likely to continue. We then need to understand how this image impacts Hopkins' ability to attract and retain patients in our own backyard.

Years of primary market research, including a recent brand research effort, confirm that the public strongly identifies Hopkins with research and scientific discovery. Consistently, focus group respondents describe us as having highly qualified physicians with access to the latest techniques and technology. The public feels secure and has hope in knowing they will receive the most advanced treatment possible here. A widespread civic pride in having Hopkins as part of the Baltimore community surfaced, too. These perceptions are overwhelmingly positive and provide Hopkins with an enviable market position.

But this august position can have its negative side. Some reasons we've heard from consumers and physicians for avoiding Hopkins follow:

I'm Not Sick Enough—The emphasis on groundbreaking research in serious diseases leads people to believe that Hopkins is appropriate only for matters of "life and death." Time after time, we listened to people say that a referral to Hopkins meant they were close to death.

I'll Be a Guinea Pig—The scientific discovery emphasis fosters a belief that all Hopkins patients are research subjects. A pervasive oral tradition in the surrounding community warns children not to walk alone near the hospital lest they be snatched for experiments.

I'm Not Important Enough—Hopkins' number one ranking and the press coverage of our well-known patients leads people to think that you have to be a celebrity and/or rich or know someone important to be able to see a Hopkins doctor.

I'm Just an LMD (Local Medical Doctor)—Private physicians often don't refer to Hopkins because they feel that our physicians are arrogant due to their reputation. Community doctors believe that the Hopkins faculty look down on them, not bothering to communicate about the referred patient's progress, nor to return patients when treatment is complete.

From a marketing viewpoint, how can we mitigate some of these negatives without compromising the strong advantage the scientific discovery offers? ***Three efforts are under way to address this concern:***

1. ***Hopkins from the Start***—When people finally seek care at Hopkins, it can be too late. If our physicians saw them earlier in their disease process, these patients might have had a better outcome. We need to motivate people to see us first when initially diagnosed with a serious illness. Advertisements have featured this theme in a subtle fashion. Hopkins cannot be overly blatant in soliciting patients from its own referring physicians, or in questioning their care.

2. ***You Can Come to Hopkins***—To overcome the perception that Hopkins caters only to the rich and famous, we've published an interactive voice response system directory of all Hopkins services. Distributed throughout Baltimore, the directory invites people to call us directly to learn about and access our services.

3. ***We Do Respect Referring Physicians***—An Office of Referring Physician Services has been created to improve communications and increase contact with referring physicians. A well-respected physician with both Hopkins and community ties is now responsible for helping Hopkins physicians work better with their private practice counterparts.

On the whole, the scientific discovery brand has created more positive than negative contributions in attracting and retaining patients.

CONCLUSION

Futurists and other analysts in the health care marketing field report that, increasingly, the race for survival and success will go to those institutions that provide consistent quality of research and patient care. From a branding perspective, then, building on these themes, and emphasizing that our service is the equal of our science, is a no brainer. But it is a process that requires a high degree of persistence, resistance to a marketing model for all communications or to change for change's sake, and systematic and sophisticated attention to the world's news media and its dynamics.

At Hopkins, there is substantial support for the public relations and communications strategy detailed in this chapter, perhaps best described by novelist Tom Clancy in his colorful characterization of the difference between Japanese and American style baseball. In the United States, Clancy explained, the emphasis both by fans and players is to hit home runs. That approach gives a few players and a few teams enormous visibility and marketing clout. Mark McGwire is the hero. In Japan, by contrast, the strategy is to build up scores and teams and loyal fans by encouraging players to hit singles and doubles all day long every day. *Our goal is to keep the Hopkins reputation for excellence as part of the news that reaches every corner of the United States and many places beyond every day.*

While certainly not eschewing or ignoring opportunities for the big play—when it counts and when it's really vital to the interests of Hopkins—Hopkins leaders understand that, as with scientific discovery itself, public relations success comes out of a commitment to substance, quality, and integrity. That's the brand Hopkins science built and the only one worth promoting.

Lessons Learned

- Make sure your brand has real substance behind it.
- When you've built a strong brand identity, don't sit back; constantly reinforce it.
- Exercise caution in altering the brand, but don't hesitate to alter tactics for promoting it; you may only need to change the mechanisms for promotion, especially if there is evidence of brand loyalty.
- Once you have identified a product or service that enhances the brand, constantly reinforce that link to the brand.
- Identify early on what tactics may damage the brand and build stringent guidelines to resist the risks.
- Create a broad-based group of communications, public relations, and marketing resource people to evaluate requests to brand products and services.

Chapter 8

Protecting Brand Equities Post-Merger

Tony Swartz Lloyd

THE CHALLENGE

The challenges in merging any two large, nationally acclaimed academic medical centers are formidable. Add to this the mandate to establish a new brand identity for the merged organization in what is a highly competitive, unpredictable, and rapidly changing marketplace, and the challenge intensifies. Our task was to create such a health care brand. We were asked to do so while capitalizing on the considerable equities of the identities of two major Harvard-affiliated teaching hospitals. The difficulty would lie in creating an entirely new brand for a health care system that included these two hospitals and four others, while sustaining the loyalty of the various communities who had supported these distinct centers of patient care for decades.

When Boston's Beth Israel and Deaconess hospitals merged in the fall of 1996, health care branding was a new phenomenon (Figure 8–1). As with all mergers, ours was a uniquely personal journey. With few case studies to guide us, the branding strategy for what is now Beth Israel Deaconess Medical Center was, and continues to be, evolutionary. *It is the complex process one might expect, particularly given the challenge of merging two major teaching affiliates of Harvard Medical School, with distinct cultures, traditions, and facilities, and then developing one symbol—one look—to represent them both.*

Each hospital brought to the merger a rich history and strong community presence: Beth Israel was rooted in the Jewish community and the Deaconess had an enduring relationship with much of "old" Boston. The BI, as it was affectionately known, was a pioneer of primary care nursing and the Deaconess an innovator in solid-organ transplantation. Together, they had a combined history of nearly 200 years. Sustaining the equity in the brands of these two great centers of patient care, research, and community service is at the heart of our efforts today. So is acknowledging Harvard's crucial role in fulfilling our shared academic mission.

Why Merge?

The merger was in response to unprecedented, dramatic changes in health care and a trend toward consolidation. The marketplace propelled us: declining federal reimbursements, the shift from inpatient to outpatient care, the move away

---

Note: I am indebted to Carla Roudabush for her editorial contributions.

Beth Israel Hospital
Boston

Deaconess
Hospital

A member of Pathway Health Network

Figure 8–1 Logos of Beth Israel and Deaconess Hospital before the Merger. The Beth Israel logo invoked an image of the Medical Caduceus (Staff of Healing). The Deaconess symbol evoked the warmth and care for patients with a profile of a deaconess. Courtesy of Beth Israel Deaconess Medical Center, Boston, Massachusetts.

from fee-for-service to managed care, and the need to cut costs. In the midst of this uncertain environment, we began bringing together more than 7,500 staff and employees and a combined population of some 350,000 patients. Plans called for the new medical center to be organized around national centers of clinical excellence, building on the strengths of both institutions in such areas as AIDS, cancer, diabetes/vascular surgery, obstetrics and gynecology, women's health, cardiology and cardiac surgery, gastroenterology, neurology, and musculoskeletal diseases.

Our common goal was survival of our missions. Our common ally, our shared values. We also had a common mantra: combining the two institutions would create a stronger one. Ultimately, the symbol of our union needed to honor the predecessor hospitals, galvanize the troops, and reassure patients. We needed a graphic identity with shoulders broad enough to reinforce the brand and promote loyalty to it.

Two Mergers in One

Fueled by a volatile health care market and a burst of health care alliances, Beth Israel Deaconess Medical Center emerged on October 1, 1996. On the same day, the parent organizations of Beth Israel, Mount Auburn, and Deaconess hospitals also merged, forming *CareGroup*. This second merger brought together six nonprofit hospitals and their affiliated health networks, and produced one of New England's largest integrated health care delivery systems. The new network had 1,139 beds and estimated revenue of $1 billion.

Creating *CareGroup* was an answer to the simultaneous introduction of several other giant regional health care systems. The affiliation of Boston's Brigham and Women's and Massachusetts General hospitals to form Partners Healthcare System; Boston City Hospital and Boston University Medical Center to form Boston Medical

Center; and New England Medical Center and the national for-profit health care network, LifeSpan, intensified the competition in a city—home to seven major teaching hospitals—that is aptly characterized as a Medical Mecca. CareGroup was essential to the success of the newly merged BI-Deaconess.

GETTING TOGETHER

Early on, senior leadership at Beth Israel and Deaconess agreed that the merger should be in full: with BI-Deaconess operating with one board of trustees, one board of overseers, one administration, one management, and one set of chiefs for its clinical services and research departments. While this meant making quick decisions about key positions, it also set the tone for the merger overall.

In the early spring of 1996, with a lead time of little more than five months, merger preparations began on parallel tracks for BI-Deaconess and CareGroup. Well before the definitive merger agreements were signed, a 25-member communications task force, with representation from every level of the medical center, began the arduous task of mapping a communications and marketing strategy to support the new brand.

The corporate communications departments from Beth Israel and Deaconess had to grasp quickly the realities involved and, as a team, develop plans for internal education, patient information, two new identity systems, and two public announcements.

We began with an intensive internal communications campaign that would bridge the pre- and post-merger information needs of employees and staff. In short order, our efforts to address employees' anxieties and questions about the merger evolved into a new image for the combined medical center, but not without several missteps and a host of challenges, obstacles, and unanticipated reactions to the branding process.

Internally, there was a hunger for information that we could not immediately satisfy. It was an enormous challenge to ease the merger anxieties of two large clinical and administrative staffs and emphasize why the merger made sense. Employees were asking "Why merge?" and "What will this mean to me?" With few specifics, we had to quell quickly the rumor mill while building a case for the merger and laying the groundwork for the brand we would soon promote.

Our plan was to use broad communication tactics whenever and wherever possible to answer questions about the merger, announce new leadership and direction for the merged organization, and introduce and explain the brand. This included group meetings, both formal and informal; memos; regular weekly and monthly employee and medical staff publications; messages from the president; and hospital intranets.

Our internal communications campaign involved several components, all of which emphasized the purpose and benefits of the merger and introduced the identity. They included an employee guide, printed in English, Spanish, and French Creole; audio-visual presentations and a video for senior administration, employees, and medical staff; and a new monthly employee publication. The first issue of this new, combined employee newsletter featured articles and photographs of the new leadership, and a question-and-answer session on issues important to employees and medical staff. *A spirit of togetherness was further fostered through employee events and giveaways that included mugs, tee shirts, and balloons featuring the new logo.*

Making the Merger Real

A communications audit helped us evaluate the internal newsletters, interoffice memos, and e-mails of each hospital and the way employees and staff routinely learned about important news. A 15-member subcommittee of the original task force resolved to address employees' concerns, promote better communication between the merging organizations, and encourage the merger's acceptance.

In these meetings we experienced, for the first time up close and personal, the intense loyalty individuals had toward the hospital for which they had worked. This realization informed the ongoing exploration of an identity for Beth Israel Deaconess Medical Center. A lot was at stake. Sending the right signals about the significance of this merger would incline staff, employees, and donors to accept the medical center and its new symbol and to subsequently promote the new brand to patients and visitors.

To deliver news leading up to the big event, we introduced Getting Together, *a weekly bulletin whose name reflected the merger process itself.* It offered the latest news about the merger's purpose, new senior management, and FAQs (frequently asked questions) about human resource matters such as benefits and vacations.

With fixed deadlines looming, and moments of levity scarce, we embraced any attempt at humor. Laughter helped us shed (if only for a moment) the unavoidable tension of our circumstances and brought the group closer together. We had a good chuckle over our first choice for the bulletin's name, *Together,* after someone suggested that naming the newsletter after a popular dating service was probably not suitable for a world-class academic medical center. Nor was it as honest a reflection of the earliest stages of the merger as our ultimate selection, *Getting Together* (Figure 8–2).

The masthead name and design emphasized the exchange of ideas necessary to resolve merger-related issues. The masthead design for *Getting Together* and the newsletter itself were never intended to be more than they were: a communications tool for bridging the pre-merger and merger phases. A shaded circle joined the last and first letters of the name, symbolizing unity and foreshadowing the brand to come. Placed side by side, both hospital logos appeared beneath the masthead. Our group was learning quickly the importance of compromise and finding sanctuary in our shared mission and values.

Shared Values

A passionate concern for the health and well-being of patients and a commitment to discovery and innovation characterized Beth Israel and the Deaconess. Although expressed differently in the way we talked about and visualized ourselves, the importance of warm, personalized patient-centered care was central to us both. "Where science and kindliness unite" was the Deaconess tag-line, while Beth Israel emphasized the triumvirate of patient care, teaching, and research, and was sometimes jokingly referred to as Harvard with a Heart.

East and West: Signposts To Guide Us

It was imperative to convey the sense of unity our values evoked. We needed to stop calling ourselves the former Beth Israel or former Deaconess. We needed a natural moniker that did not suggest primacy of one hospital over the other.

Getting Together

A periodic communication to help keep us all informed.   **Issue No. 4, Thursday 22 August 1996.**

Frequently

Asked

Questions

*The following **F**requently **A**sked **Q**uestions are about benefits and other matters affecting employees at Beth Israel and at Deaconess related to the merger into Beth Israel Deaconess Medical Center. The responses have been prepared by members of the two departments of Human Resources.*

Q. *What will change on October 1 in the way of pay, benefits, and working conditions?*

A. When the merger agreement is signed on or about October 1, employees can expect to see few immediate changes in terms of their pay, benefits, and working conditions.

Like everything else in the bringing together of the two hospitals, developing an employee pay and benefits structure is a complex process. We are committed to treating these issues with the full consideration and sensitivity that they deserve, and we will keep employees informed of our progress. Merging is more of a process than an event, and in effect we have already embarked on the process as we learn more about each other and strive to evolve reasonable and understandable policies and procedures.

Q. *Will I keep my years of service when the merger takes effect?*

A. Yes, your years of service with the Beth Israel or Deaconess hospitals will be maintained.

Q. *Will I be covered by a different benefit program as of October 1?*

A. No, initially Beth Israel and the Deaconess will maintain the benefit programs that are in place. These include flexible benefits, paid time-off programs, pension plans, etc. It will take time and a thoughtful evaluation to create a single benefit program for all employees of BIDMC.

Q. *When will we know what changes will be made in our benefits program?*

A. Our goal is to continue to offer a competitive benefits program. We recognize that even though the BI and Deaconess programs are very similar, we will have to make some changes to create an attractive program for all employees. We plan to announce flexible benefit plan changes by the fall of 1997, in time for the January 1, 1998 flexible benefits re-enrollment. Employees will be informed of the timetable for decisions to be made on other benefit programs, such as paid time off and pension, as they evolve. It is unlikely any program changes will be initiated before next fall.

Figure 8–2 An Example of the Weekly News Bulletin *Getting Together.* Courtesy of Beth Israel Deaconess Medical Center, Boston, Massachusetts.

Internally, we made the distinction by referring to one campus or another, natural enough for a Harvard affiliate in a college town. The hospitals, located diagonally across from each other on Brookline Avenue, are within a short walking distance of each other. With plans for the integration of clinical, research, and administrative functions getting under way, we searched for a simple means of directing people to their destination.

Looking at a map, we realized the two hospitals fell, like points on a compass, as either north and south or east and west. We chose the east-west designation, thinking it free of any subtext, such as that suggested by the Civil War's north-south divide. Beth Israel became the east campus, Deaconess the west.

A compass graphic, dubbed the campus compass (Figure 8–3), boldly displayed the names of each campus. It appeared in information packets for employees and patients, and on note pads, posters, and buttons for distribution a few weeks before the merger and on announcement day. An employee handbook emphasized the medical center's mission and commitment to patient care. Handed out the week of the merger, the pamphlet introduced the new corporate logo.

Symbols and Their Importance: A New Identity

Symbols are an important visible part of branding. We worked diligently to develop a symbol that would carry elements of both hospitals and be recognizable and familiar to the communities they served. For more than 19 years, the Beth Israel caduceus was synonymous with compassionate patient-centered care. Similarly, the Deaconess with her ever-burning candle had come to represent kindliness in medical science. We knew we had to retain elements of the former logos and yet create a new symbol.

Over a period of several weeks, the task force met regularly to review and discuss the design directions. Some subcommittee members imagined the Olympic flame or a flaming screw when looking at early iterations of the logo; another thought it seemed phallic. Although everyone had strong and sometimes idiosyncratic opinions, we were clearly walking on eggshells during what became negotiations to emerge satisfactorily with a symbol that would be considered proprietary by both institutions. Even the colors of the new mark were carefully selected to avoid reminiscence of one logo over another. The object was to produce a symbol that everyone would salute once in use.

To help ease the tension, a member of the staff designed a mock logo for Beth Israel Deaconess featuring the deaconess, replacing her candle with a lighted menorah. During a meeting of about 300 managers of the two merging organizations, we showed an overhead slide of the fake symbol (Figure 8–4). After the initial astonishment wore off, the group response was as hoped for. It was the first time anyone had heard the combined leadership in unrestrained laughter.

The final, approved logo retained the caduceus of medical care and the flame of new knowledge (Figure 8–5). The mark appeared inside what we call the circle of community care, further strengthening the symbol's impact. It was produced in purple.

Given the green light for the Beth Israel Deaconess identity, we went on to create a stationery system that would underscore the relationship between the medical center and Harvard Medical School. It is impossible to overstate the importance of this affiliation. In the early 1920s the relationship was sought to ensure a

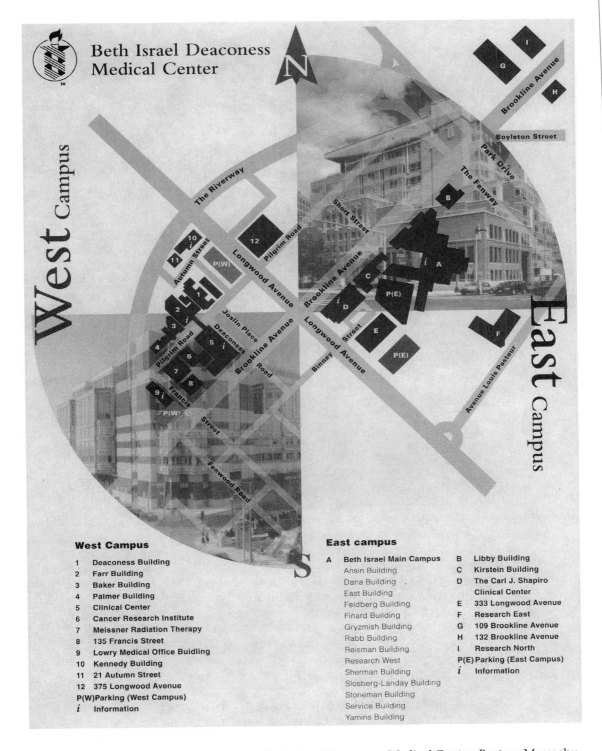

Beth Israel Deaconess Medical Center

West Campus

East Campus

West Campus

1 Deaconess Building
2 Farr Building
3 Baker Building
4 Palmer Building
5 Clinical Center
6 Cancer Research Institute
7 Meissner Radiation Therapy
8 135 Francis Street
9 Lowry Medical Office Buidling
10 Kennedy Building
11 21 Autumn Street
12 375 Longwood Avenue
P(W) Parking (West Campus)
i Information

East campus

A Beth Israel Main Campus
   Ansin Building
   Dana Building
   East Building
   Feldberg Building
   Finard Building
   Gryzmish Building
   Rabb Building
   Reisman Building
   Research West
   Sherman Building
   Slosberg-Landay Building
   Stoneman Building
   Service Building
   Yamins Building

B Libby Building
C Kirstein Building
D The Carl J. Shapiro Clinical Center
E 333 Longwood Avenue
F Research East
G 109 Brookline Avenue
H 132 Brookline Avenue
I Research North
P(E) Parking (East Campus)
i Information

Figure 8–3 Campus Compass. Courtesy of Beth Israel Deaconess Medical Center, Boston, Massachusetts.

Figure 8–4 Illustration of Lady with a Menorah. Courtesy of Beth Israel Deaconess Medical Center, Boston, Massachusetts.

teaching and research role for the then-young Beth Israel Hospital. Similarly, the Deaconess has a Harvard Medical School affiliation. All members of the joint medical center staff hold faculty appointments at the medical school.

However, the brand for Beth Israel Deaconess needed to evoke Harvard's dual missions of teaching and research without obscuring the medical center's central mission: the delivery of humane patient care.

Meeting this goal with a single stationery system was problematic, in part because too many symbols would convey mixed messages that could confuse patients, the principal intended audience. In addition, the eagerness of several senior high-profile physicians to help design the stationery system resulted in 51 individual versions and gave new meaning to the phrase "too many cooks in the kitchen." An eight-page graphic standards manual set forth the rationale behind maintaining the integrity of the new identity, as well as the rules by which to do so.

Introducing Beth Israel Deaconess

The introduction of the newly merged Beth Israel Deaconess Medical Center to patients, referring physicians, visitors, payers, the media, and the public was part of a well-orchestrated marketing/communications strategy. Letters to the various constituencies announced the merger and placed it in context, depending on the target audience. A substantial media buy for merger announcement ads in the local media was made. Yellow Pages advertising carried the new logo and iden-

Beth Israel Deaconess Medical Center
SM

Figure 8–5 Logo of the Beth Israel Deaconess Medical Center. Courtesy of Beth Israel Deaconess Medical Center, Boston, Massachusetts.

tified the two campuses by their individual telephone exchanges. Buttons and map pads were widely disseminated to staff and affiliated physician offices to ensure that patients would not get lost on the way to their medical appointments (Figure 8–6).

A press kit was prepared to announce and explain the merger and outline its benefits to the various constituencies. National, regional, and local media were invited to a press conference announcing the merger, identifying the leadership, and unveiling the new brand. Senior administrators and business and political leaders were available for interviews. We were looking to the media to report accurately on the merger, its meaning to patients, and its impact on the regional health care scene. Reporters and editors were responsive, giving the union of the two Harvard teaching hospitals appropriate play on their pages and newscasts. The tone and tenor of this coverage mirrored our own internal reporting of the merger, which served to underscore the positive message being communicated.

CareGroup

We approached naming the parent company the way we had other aspects of the merger: get as many people as possible to dedicate themselves to solving the problem and have them meet frequently to brainstorm. Over a period of several weeks we developed a running list of 167 potential names.

Arranged in alpha order, they were sent by e-mail to members of the naming committee. Early leaders included AppleTree, Acacia, and HealthGroup. We needed one word to express the group nature of the parent organization and describe what it did. A trustee of the parent company came up with the idea of *CareGroup* and it quickly became the committee's favorite.

In the months before the merger, CareGroup's role as the premier brand was not clearly defined. Because we knew the logo might be temporary, a simple typo-

Beth Israel Deaconess Medical Center

J. Antony Swartz Lloyd
Senior Vice President
Corporate Communications

330 Brookline Avenue
Boston, Massachusetts 02215 USA
Internet:
tlloyd@bidmc.harvard.edu

617 667-4431
Fax 617 667-4488

Figure 8–6 Letterhead with New/Interim Beth Israel and Deaconess Style. Courtesy of Beth Israel Deaconess Medical Center, Boston, Massachusetts.

graphic treatment for the CareGroup identity was selected (Figure 8–7). Created in Bembo, the logo and logotype appear in large and small caps, in indigo. The logotype is punctuated by a stylized AR, reminiscent of the apothecaries or neighborhood drugstores of a bygone medical era. *The typography purposefully emphasized the word "care."*

The communications/marketing tools used to talk about the new parent organization with both internal and external audiences were similar to those used in announcing the merger of Beth Israel Deaconess. Internally, the CareGroup brand was announced in the new employee newsletter. Additionally, a special and ongoing section called "Inside CareGroup" was introduced, becoming a regular feature of the Beth Israel Deaconess publication. *CareGroup Connections*, a new publication for CareGroup-member hospitals, was unveiled to keep them up-to-date on important matters involving the health care system and its mission. *Hospital-wide memos, e-mails, and audio-visual presentations to managers and vice presidents also were part of the communications campaign.*

Externally, a press conference was held, featuring the principals of the merged hospitals and an ardent supporter of health care reform, Senator Edward Kennedy of Massachusetts.

The news was carried by local, regional, and national print and electronic media. A story in the Boston *Globe* about CareGroup also featured the new graphic identity, which was prominently displayed in print advertisements that broke the same week.

Signed, Sealed, and Delivered

When the sun came up the morning of October 1, 1996, signs posted at key entry points to the east and west campuses and bright indigo banners hung from medical center buildings along Brookline Avenue proclaimed the merger to create Beth Israel Deaconess Medical Center, a fact noted by the local media (Figure 8–8).

Staff and employees celebrated the BI-Deaconess merger on the lawn of Harvard Medical School. Enticed by the promise of free ice cream, and moving to the beat of the medical center's own band, Managed Care, an estimated 3,000 employees gathered to celebrate. More than 1,200 employees joined a breakfast reception held at the west campus, and a cookie break on the east campus drew another 1,500 employees.

Reports in the Boston *Globe*, Boston *Herald*, and local network affiliates of ABC, CBS, and NBC television positioned the merger in a positive light, reinforcing the good news about the new organization to which employees and staff now belonged.

375 LONGWOOD AVENUE
BOSTON, MASSACHUSETTS 02215 USA

617 975-5000

Figure 8–7 Initial CareGroup Logo. Courtesy of Beth Israel Deaconess Medical Center, Boston, Massachusetts.

Figure 8–8 Banner Celebrating Merger. Courtesy of Beth Israel Deaconess Medical Center, Boston, Massachusetts.

Our News, a consolidated employee newsletter to be published monthly, was unveiled the week of the merger. The inaugural edition offered the first, formal visual introduction to the new organization's leadership, featuring bold photographs and stories and a question-and-answer format.

MERGER DYNAMICS

Creating a brand post-merger cannot be separated from the actual act of merging. It is a dynamic process that can quickly get out of control. In many respects, a merger is like a snowball that starts at the top of a hill and gets larger as it heads downward. The larger it is, the less time people have to react to it, internalize its true nature, and move on. Statistics show that in the first year of a merger, the average employee spends one to two hours out of every day talking about the merger. For a merger to become fully ingrained in an organization's culture takes another five to seven years.

Cultural differences plagued the BI-Deaconess merger from the start. Seemingly little things, such as the setting for joint conferences, would make one or the other parties uncomfortable. Our initial town meetings—big affairs involving hundreds of managers—were held on the west campus, because it had the only facility large enough. The meetings were strained and awkward, in part because BI staff was accustomed to more intimate gatherings.

When two organizations enter a new relationship, it is marked by a pattern of conflict and resolution. While the public initially experiences the building of a new brand as a series of events (merger announcement, unveiling of logo, advertisements, banners, news stories, etc.), in actuality it more closely resembles a long-term partnership involving courtship and marriage, in which the two parties move through predictable stages—preparation, announcement, transition, and integration.

A year after the merger announcement, the medical center consolidated emergency services, a dramatic step that set the stage for full integration of all clinical departments. An initial plan for integration, presented to the board of trustees in the fall of 1997, was aggressive in terms of goals and time frames. It provided for the maximum use of space and the minimum amount of capital outlay.

At the heart of the plan was the clustering of acute-care services around a single, state-of-the-art emergency department (ED). Since more than 60 percent of all admissions originate in the ED, it made sense to organize the consolidation this way. This first phase of the plan was expected to save $2 million and develop new admission practices to help avoid unnecessary use of an overused resource. In the past two years, the pace of integration has quickened, with the consolidation of several services.

From the beginning, the leadership at Beth Israel Deaconess knew that the medical center's long-term success depended on its ability to integrate clinical services physically. It was apparent that the success of these efforts would foster trust in the new brand. Less obvious, perhaps, was the need for staff and employees of one hospital to bond with individuals from the other. This was and is particularly critical for many doctors and nurses whose sense of belonging and entitlement could not be easily separated from the institution where their careers had been made.

Building CareGroup

Based on visual identity, a brand is the way an organization expresses itself and what it stands for. It should be as close as possible to reality. If a brand is not an accurate representation of the real thing, it loses meaning and can no longer be trusted—an unkept promise. Because a brand's symbol conveys organizational essence, the identity for CareGroup evolved over time, as leaders discovered how best to distinguish the health care network in a way that would be meaningful to patients, families, and communities.

Since CareGroup is recognized as one of the largest health care systems in the Northeast, it has become more important than ever for the network's hospital affiliates to convey membership in this unique delivery system. The network serves more than half a million patients, has a medical staff of 1,145, and employs more than 5,000 people.

Development and implementation of the branding strategy for CareGroup are a principal component of CareGroup's strategic planning efforts. For months, members of network-wide communications and marketing councils worked with senior management at CareGroup and BI-Deaconess to develop a new graphic identity program (logo and logotype) that would strengthen CareGroup's burgeoning identity as a family of care providers.

Nationally recognized consultants with a proven track record in branding strategy were hired to direct and manage our efforts.

A sustainable brand for CareGroup was created in several ways:

- developing an internal consensus about what the brand stands for
- developing the architecture and infrastructure to support the brand
- developing the appropriate visual identity for the brand
- developing guidelines for implementation of the brand.

More than 70 individuals from within CareGroup were interviewed about their impressions of CareGroup to help us develop a brand that would reflect the DNA of the organization.

In early presentations of logo directions, staff and consumers cited the examples as too abstract. One focus group participant said he saw three people impaled on a stake, hardly the image a health care organization wants associated with its services. Ultimately, the design consultants responsible for the graphic identity presented us with four design directions and we selected the last option.

At the time of the merger announcement, Mitchell T. Rabkin, MD, then-CEO of CareGroup, discussed with the Boston *Herald* the centrifugal focus that the merger would bring to health care. Dr. Rabkin, who had managed change many times during his 30 years as president of the former BI, emphasized that CareGroup, unlike its competitors, would draw upon its affiliated health centers to keep care in the community where it belongs. When Dr. Rabkin's successor was named after an intensive six-month search, new CEO James Reinertsen, also a physician and administrator, reiterated the importance of not losing sight of relieving suffering, the essence of what CareGroup does. ***This philosophy of care was central to the choice of a final logo for CareGroup.***

When CareGroup unveiled its new look to members and patients in the fall of 1998, we felt we were finally delivering a strong and consistent message about who we are and what we do (Figure 8–9). The image builds on the heritage, values, and distinctiveness of the member hospitals, while reinforcing the idea of the network as a family of providers. The heart of the new graphic identity, the joining of two hands, symbolizes a commitment to caring that is patient-focused and personal, yet integrated with an array of providers.

The new identity program offers a systemwide look for all institutional logos, letterhead, and signage. CareGroup members currently use different typefaces, colors, and logos. The graphic identity will build awareness of CareGroup and create a sense of unity among member hospitals.

The Post-Merger Branding Strategy Positions CareGroup

In the Boston and regional health care arena, it was clear that several integrated systems of care were emerging as the dominant forces: CareGroup, Partners HealthCare System, Boston Medical Center, New England Medical Center, and the national for-profit health care network, LifeSpan. Our post-merger marketing and branding strategy was to align CareGroup with these major health care systems, so that we, too, would be seen as a leading player, while at the same time distinguishing ourselves from them.

We aligned our brand with these leaders by deliberately selecting the generic "health care system" as a way to describe us, fully aware that this name was in use by Partners.

Caring at the Leading Edge ℠

BETH ISRAEL DEACONESS
MEDICAL CENTER
A member of CAREGROUP

Figure 8–9 CareGroup Health System Logo and New Beth Isreal Deaconess Logo. Courtesy of CareGroup, Boston, Massachusetts, and Beth Israel Deaconess Medical Center, Boston, Massachusetts.

However, we chose the name CareGroup because it emphasized the warmer side of health care, in direct juxtaposition to the Partners name, which from our point of view spoke more to the organization and delivery of care than to the inherent humanistic nature of patient care itself. We wanted and needed to capitalize on the warm, personal experience with which both Beth Israel and Deaconess had long been associated.

How will we measure the success of our branding efforts for CareGroup and Beth Israel Deaconess Medical Center? Following the merger, we conducted focus groups to gauge top-of-mind awareness among consumers about the newly formed medical center. The research suggested that consumers accepted the union of these two premier hospitals and retained some information about their respective health care legacies. More recently, inpatient data are being collected by the marketing department to determine whether the branding efforts have helped increase market share in certain key clinical areas.

Changes in leadership and senior management at CareGroup helped pave the way for the kind of historical amnesia necessary to stimulate change. Mergers require patience, and brands need time to take hold. Beyond increases in top-of-the-mind awareness, market share, or managed care discharges, the success of our branding strategy will be decided not by whether reality can live up to the brand, but whether the brand can live up to reality.

Lessons Learned

Benchmarking the Branding Experience

Many valuable lessons can be taken away from our branding experience, post-merger. For even if hindsight is not 20-20, it is certainly nearer to perfection than the best-laid plans executed in the heat of battle—i.e., during the merger process itself.

- You cannot over-communicate, either with internal or external audiences. Whatever you do will not be enough, so communicate all the time, in every venue. Keep the message the same, but vary its form, tone, and the method of delivery. Frequent and inventive communication will increase the likelihood that the message will be received.
- Once you have identified the leadership of the merged organization, urge this group to be up-front and out front. The new team should take every opportunity, both formal and informal, to discuss the purpose, intentions, and benefits of the merger with audiences inside and outside the organization.
- Enlist the support of the leadership and the understanding of the organization, and accept the limitations involved in your role as a communicator, without the authority to change the organization in an operational sense or to create policy.
- Establish the medium over which you have control and seek to make this one communication vehicle the hot source for information, whether it is e-mail, traditional interoffice memos, internal news postings, etc.
- Establish the brand identity and its goals as a first priority. Be clear about timing. Create schedules and deadlines and be inflexible about changing them.

Chapter 9

Scripps' Branding Story: A Step-by-Step Account

Deborah C. Routt

THE HISTORY

Ellen Browning Scripps (Figure 9–1) founded Scripps Hospital and Metabolic Clinic (Figure 9–2). More than 100 years ago, Mother Mary Michael Cummings (Figure 9–3) founded what would become Scripps Mercy Hospital (Figure 9–4). Together the two women started a journey that would make great strides in San Diego's health care field.

Who knew then that Scripps would grow into a community-based health care delivery network with a vision of serving 1.25 million people through more than 2,600 affiliated physicians? Regarded today as San Diego's premier not-for-profit health care provider, Scripps (both Scripps Health and its physician integrating partner Scripps Physicians) is at the forefront of health care delivery, pioneering a new "patient first" focus and advocating the channeling of a greater share of the health care dollar directly to patient care. Scripps is committed to restoring health care decisions to patients and their caregivers as well as to continuous improvement in the health and well-being of patients and the community.

In the last decade, Scripps growth was due to several mergers or acquisitions that turned one hospital into a system of six, culminating in the 1995 affiliation with one of its oldest peer organizations, Mercy Hospital (Figure 9–5). With the added acquisition of numerous outpatient facilities, two convalescent hospitals, a home health care agency, and assorted support services, it is easy to see how Scripps landed in the middle of an identity crisis (Figure 9–6). In addition to Scripps' disparate looks, this surname is used by dozens of nonhealth care-related businesses in San Diego County due to the generosity of one its first families, that of Ellen Browning Scripps.

Recognizing that the unintegrated and widely used name would ultimately weaken Scripps' image, Scripps pursued a logo change, but then put it on hold to focus on other pressing issues presented by the recent mergers. It wasn't until 1997 that Scripps made its comprehensive branding project a priority, dubbing the journey a "strategic transformation"—an overall plan to prepare Scripps to do business in the future of health care. *Scripps was transforming from a hospital-centered organization to a totally integrated health care system.*

THE CHALLENGE

Scripps has always had top-of-mind name recognition in the local communities where it has facilities. *The goal of the branding process was to achieve countywide recognition and identification of the entire Scripps system* (Figure 9–7).

Figure 9–1 Ellen Browning Scripps, Founder of Scripps Hospital and Scripps Metabolic Clinic. She was one of San Diego's most famous—and certainly one of its most generous—resident philanthropists. Courtesy of Scripps, San Diego, California.

Considering Scripps' many acquisitions and mergers over the years, the decision to rebrand was a natural one. Not only did Scripps need to redefine itself to the public; it also needed to consolidate internally. The new logo both symbolized a new organization and signaled the reality of the transformation Scripps was about to make. It let the Scripps family of medical, nursing, and administrative staffs know that this was not just business as usual—this was the evolution to a new health care organization.

One of the biggest challenges presented by rebranding was getting buy-in from the Scripps family-at-large. Senior leadership would drive the transformation, but it was still necessary to educate the rest of the clinical and administrative staff about the long-term benefits of this investment. In many areas of the organization, the

Figure 9–2 Founded in 1924 in La Jolla, the 44-Bed Scripps Hospital and Scripps Metabolic Clinic. It would grow into a community-based health care delivery system that would eventually touch the lives of millions of San Diegans. Courtesy of Scripps, San Diego, California.

Figure 9–3 Mother Mary Michael Cummings Founded Mercy Hospital as Part of the Catholic Sisters of Mercy Religious Mission To Help and Heal the Sick. Courtesy of Scripps, San Diego, California.

Figure 9–4 Founded in 1890 As the Area's First Hospital, Mercy Hospital Was Centrally Located in San Diego's Uptown Community of Hillcrest. Courtesy of Scripps, San Diego, California.

transformation was perceived as a drain on limited resources instead of an investment in the future. While Scripps was employing strategies to build internal consensus by continuing to hone systems, processes, and procedures that would leverage its brand equity, old logos and brochures still kept turning up. Scripps realized it would take commitment to a systemwide transformation process to train every member of the Scripps family to become "brand managers"—a team that understands, buys into, and champions the entire rebranding effort.

While being a not-for-profit organization may seem like a challenge—even an obstacle—in a rebranding effort, it actually enhanced Scripps' clarity and focus throughout the process, since its mission mandates its direction. As a not-for-profit health care provider, Scripps is committed to being a community-based, values-driven organization that maintains and improves the health of the community it serves. Through efficient use of resources and state-of-the-art information systems, Scripps provides high quality care across the entire continuum of care. A countywide network of physicians and facilities provides accessible, consistent care that meets the expectations of the community.

To this end, the entire transformation process was dubbed "Project Scripps"—a six-year journey that included these strategic goals:

- Maximize the percentage of premium dollar available for direct patient care
- Develop a countywide physician network

A

B

Figure 9–5 A, Mercy Hospital's 1995 Merger with Scripps Health Was the Catalyst for Scripps' Rebranding Transformation To Better Represent Its Newly Integrated Facilities and Services. **B,** Today Scripps Memorial Hospital La Jolla Is Part of an Integrated Health Care Delivery System. It includes six acute-care hospitals, two skilled nursing facilities, a home health care agency, numerous outpatient facilities, comprehensive support services, and over 2,600 affiliated physicians and 7,600 employees. Courtesy of Scripps, San Diego, California.

- Develop appropriate infrastructure, facilities, systems, and information technology capabilities to provide population-based medicine
- Care for 1.25-million people

Achievement of these goals takes more than rebranding—it calls for vision.

THE VISION

We always talked about being in health care, but we were really involved in sick care. If Scripps' goal is to take responsibility for managing the total health care of a population, our objective should be to help keep people as healthy as possible. You can't do that in a hospital setting—you need programs and services that address the whole gamut of lifestyle issues.

Sister Mary Jo Anderson, Senior Vice President, Mission and Values

At the commencement of the rebranding project, Scripps was dealing with serious health care and organization issues: keeping up with changing technology; evolving medical practices; accommodating the growth of the San Diego community; managing an organization that had decentralized and was concentrating on individual facilities versus systemwide contracting.

Though Scripps' initial goal was to determine how to better present a uniform image, during the process it became clear that this was about more than the external image. ***The organization realized it needed to look internally at values, customer service philosophy, and community presence.***

Therefore, the entire branding process was developed to address all these concerns. Though the most tangible outcome of the process may be the new name and logo, Scripps' commitment to delivering on its new identity goes much deeper.

With the allocation of $250 million in capital over a six-year period, Scripps will be able to develop the information systems, redesign and improve ambulatory and hospital facilities, and conduct the transformation necessary to accomplish its vision. Financial analysis of this enterprise shows that by utilizing innovative health plan partnerships, attaining the goal of caring for 1.25 million individuals, utilizing 2,600 physicians and approximately 1,300 hospital beds, both Scripps and its physicians can be financially successful. Specifically, it is projected that by the year 2002, the enterprise will realize revenues of close to $2 billion, with a net operating income of 5 percent for both Scripps and its physicians.

THE PROCESS

Health care is a very human service—physical, emotional, spiritual. People respond to health care identities and symbols that are comforting, warm, diverse and inclusive.

Jerry Kuyper, Senior Partner, Lippincott & Margulies

Branding is always a complex process, but especially so in the health care field. Not only is it an industry dealing with tremendous change, but the delivery of health care is much more difficult to control than a widget packaged on an assembly line. Couple that with the presence of many key audiences, from patients to physicians to health plans, and the plot thickens.

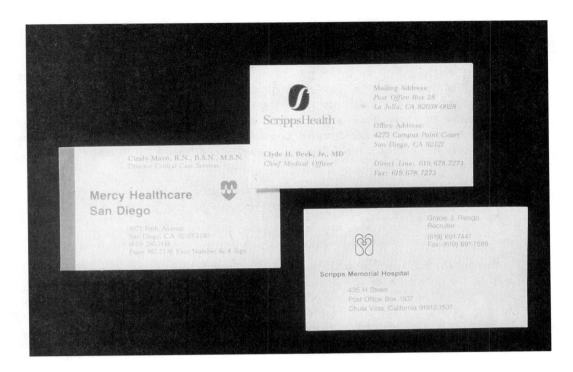

Figure 9–6 Previously Scripps Had Several Distinct Logos throughout Its Six Hospitals. In addition, each facility had its own individual color scheme, collateral design, naming system, stationery, signage, and more. This lack of uniformity created confusion among Scripps patients, as well as with staff. Courtesy of Scripps, San Diego, California.

To undertake the challenge of rebranding, Scripps partnered with Lippincott & Margulies (L&M), an internationally recognized branding consultant, to create a new image commensurate with Scripps' presence in the marketplace. L&M pioneered the discipline of corporate and brand identity and image management consulting. L&M has left a legacy of impressions on the world's public with programs that are recognized as classic examples of enduring brand identities.

Working together with a committee of representatives from management, physicians, and boards, L&M embarked on a two-step process to develop a communications plan that would present a consistent image for Scripps, including options for a new logo.

> The blueprint L&M constructed for Scripps was much like a song sheet given to members of the choir to ensure that everyone is not just singing the same song— they're harmonizing.

Kathy Feakins, Senior Partner, Lippincott & Margulies

During the rebranding process, L&M discovered that Scripps was changing its direction—a new view of the patient-doctor-hospital relationship was emerging. Scripps' vision for its future is what L&M used to lead the rebranding effort. Positioning and image attributes were developed, from which a communications platform was born. The result was the creation of message profiles ready for practical application.

First Steps

Lippincott & Margulies initiated the branding process with a corporate/brand image assessment, taking inventory of Scripps' current status by undertaking a comprehensive research and strategic background review, and conducting interviews and a communications audit. A branding committee, with representation from physicians, employees, senior management, and the Scripps Board of Trustees, identified target audiences, key messages, brand attributes, and a positioning statement.

Working in tandem, Scripps' Communication & Marketing department immersed itself in researching its audiences. L&M did an audience analysis that led to the categorizing and prioritizing of key constituencies, then developed communications objectives.

Branding is more than a logo—it's an experience. *From the initial interviews, inventory, and research, L&M developed a communications plan that served as a tool for guiding Scripps through the phases of rebranding. Specifically, it included several components:*

- Prioritize **audiences** and develop respective communications objectives
- Articulate **message platforms** for communication with key audiences
- Define a **positioning statement** that reflects Scripps' services and differentiates it from its competitors
- Structure a **brand strategy** that specifies the relationships between Scripps services
- Define desired **image attributes** that create a compelling personality for the brand

    • Recommend appropriate **media vehicles** for achieving communications objectives

Audiences

Priority audiences were identified and communications objectives were developed (Table 9–1).

Messages

Key messages were delineated by asking questions about Scripps' future direction, culture, style, and strengths, and then assessing the facts.

- Where is Scripps going?
- How does Scripps uniquely go about its business?
- What are Scripps' competitive advantages?
- What are Scripps' fundamentals?

Scripps determined there were several points that needed to be consistently reflected in its messages.

- Dedicated to patient-focused health care
- Mission-focused
- Collaborative
- Established excellence and continuous learning
- Community-oriented, not-for-profit
- Substantial and enduring

Table 9–1 Priority Audiences and Objectives

Audience	Objective
Patients, Employers, Coalitions, Insurers/Payers, Brokers/Consultants, Community Organizations	Increase the understanding of Scripps, including its mission, breadth and depth of services, and leadership position in the marketplace. Communicate its goal to make more of the health care premium dollar available for direct patient care.
Scripps Employees, Partner Employees, Scripps Physicians, Medical Staff, Internal Boards, Volunteers/ Auxiliaries	Increase understanding of the goals and mission of Scripps and participation in its unique culture. Build a sense of unity and pride that motivates existing employees and partners while increasing the likelihood of building new relationships.
Local News Media, Business/Civic Community/Leaders	Advocate the Project Scripps agenda, Scripps' community-based, not-for-profit commitment and its locally governed operations.
Local Legislators	Maintain a positive social, regulatory and political environment to facilitate the ease of operations.
Individual Donors, Financial Planners	Increase the ability to obtain philanthropic support.

Courtesy of Scripps, San Diego, California

Positioning Statement

The positioning statement sets the direction for communication about the organization. While the statement itself is not intended as advertising copy and would not be used outside the organization, the concepts set forth in the statement—leadership, quality, pioneering, and restoring health care decisions to the patients and caregivers—would drive promotions and advertising.

Scripps, San Diego's leading not-for-profit health care system, has provided quality health care service to the community for over 100 years. Regarded as San Diego's premier health care provider, Scripps is at the forefront of health care reform, pioneering a new patient-first health care delivery model that channels a greater share of the health care premium to patient care. Scripps is committed to restoring health care decisions to patients and their caregivers and to the continuous improvements in the health and well-being of patients and the community at large.

Image Attributes

Image attributes were created to further shape a personality for Scripps:

- *Collaborative.* A team of professionals who work together and partner with physicians to reach their common goal of patient-focused care. Empowered individuals who share their ideas, expertise, and resources to benefit those around them.
- *Renowned Excellence.* An established organization with a deep tradition of excellence that permeates all facets of clinical service, management, operations, programs, and processes. A leader that sets the standard for others and seeks improvement to raise its benchmark.
- *Visionary.* An organization with a clear purpose. A group with intelligence, foresight, and compassion that plans for the future while fulfilling its mission with passion today.
- *Trusted Neighbor.* Someone who can be counted on to protect the best interests of those close by, especially those who are less fortunate. Someone who is involved in the community and speaks out on behalf of others.
- *Change Agent.* A leader with progressive ideas and the courage to take action. A pragmatic idealist who sees the "big picture" and understands what needs to be done to realize its vision. A "doer" who makes a difference in both the lives of individuals and the health care industry as a whole.
- *Community Partner.* An organization with roots in the community that partners with like-minded providers with an aim toward improving the quality and accessibility of care for its constituencies.

Media Observations

For starters, L&M showed Scripps that its marketing mix was quite different from the industry average. For example, Scripps was dedicating 41 percent of its marketing budget to television while the industry average was 9 percent. Likewise, Scripps was spending only 5.2 percent on newspaper advertising while the industry average was 46 percent. Scripps' Yellow Pages expenditures were 50 percent higher than the industry average. As part of the rebranding effort, L&M detailed how the

Figure 9–7 Scripps' Revitalized Image Includes a Contemporary Logo, Vibrant Color Scheme, and Consistent Designs throughout Its Collateral Material. Courtesy of Scripps, San Diego, California.

various kinds of media and marketing vehicles could be better leveraged to target Scripps audiences. L&M also highlighted target versus mass media strategies consistent with Scripps' intention to develop a deeper, more meaningful relationship with its constituencies.

THE PRACTICE

The rebranding effort was just one piece of Scripps' five-year strategic transformation. *The communications plan positioned Scripps to achieve several milestones early on in the process.*

- Scripps attained a significant level of *internal buy-in* thanks to a series of events and ongoing communications to keep constituents informed.
- *Graphic identity standards* were published and new signs and collateral were introduced at Scripps facilities.
- *Scripps Physicians*, the pivotal strategic integrating partnership with physicians, was formed.
- Other *strategic health care partnerships* were formed via collaborations between health plans, community-based health care organizations, and Scripps physicians. In particular, new contracts emphasizing "patient centered care" have been negotiated with health plans.
- A new *care design* featured the introduction of seven Systems of Excellence.
- Funding was secured for the six-year strategic *information systems upgrade*.
- Baselines were set in *patient and customer satisfaction* from which future measurements will mark Scripps' progress.
- *Service pilot programs* were implemented to train "brand managers" throughout the entire Scripps system to manage Scripps' new brand image and patient expectations for service excellence.

Embracing the Change Internally

The first step in any rebranding effort should be to get the staff to really embrace the change internally—especially when there are multiple organizations involved. It is vital to ensure that the deliverers of the brand will deliver on its promise.

From the start, representatives from all branches of the Scripps family were rallied to contribute their ideas and experiences throughout the process. For example, employees were asked to assess Scripps' performance relative to its value statements. Subsequently, a values task force was formed to oversee the consistency between the mission and value statements and the branding practices. Action plans were developed to make course corrections.

Scripps recognized that there might be some resistance to this organizational transformation from the various smaller facilities that merged with the system. Scripps addressed this by celebrating old and new logos in many ways, with the intent of giving the transformation the significance it deserved. Poster-sized copies of the mission and value statements were framed and hung in all Scripps facilities (Exhibit 9–1). Ceremonies were held in various locations that symbolized the passing of smaller entities and the rebirth of a stronger and better family of health care services. Tee shirts with the new logo and redesigned service award pins were given to all employees (Figure 9–8).

Exhibit 9–1 Embracing the Change Internally in Order To Present a Unified Image to the Community Is the First Step in the Success of Any Rebranding Effort. To reinforce the "new" organization's commitment to its original vision, among the staff and patients, poster-size copies of Scripps mission value statements are framed and hung throughout each of its facilities.

Our Mission

Scripps seeks to make a measurable, positive difference in the health of the individuals in the communities we serve.

We will continue to devote our resources to quality, cost-effective, socially responsible programs that deliver all levels of acute and convalescent care, promote wellness, and improve the quality of life for those with chronic illness.

We strive to collaborate with others in programs that improve the health of our community.

Our Values

We provide the highest quality of service. Scripps is committed to putting the patient first and quality is our passion. In the new world of health care, we want to anticipate the causes of illness and encourage healthy behavior for all who rely on us for service. We teach and encourage patients to participate in their care and to make well-informed decisions. We will be their advocate when they are most vulnerable. We measure our success by our patients' satisfaction, their return to health and well-being, and our compassionate care for dying patients, their families and friends.

We demonstrate complete respect for the rights of every individual. Scripps honors the dignity of all persons, and we show this by our actions toward one another and those we serve. We embrace the diversity that allows us to draw on the talents of one another. We respect and honor the cultural, ethnic and religious beliefs and practices of our patients in a manner consistent with the highest standard of care. All this is done in a compassionate setting. Our goal is to create a healing environment in partnership with all care-givers who are committed to serving our patients.

We care for our patients every day in a responsible and efficient manner. Scripps serves as a major community health care resource for San Diego County and, as such, we are accountable for the human, financial and ecological resources entrusted to our care as we promote healing and wholeness. We begin from a base of excellence and collaborate with co-workers, physicians, patients, and other providers to find new and creative ways to improve the delivery of health care services. All members of our community will have access to timely, affordable and appropriate care.

Courtesy of Scripps, San Diego, California.

Figure 9–8 Scripps Recognized the Importance of Making the Rebranding Process an Inclusive Effort and So Hosted Logo Launch Parties in the Spring of 1998 for All Staff Physicians and Volunteers. Courtesy of Scripps, San Diego, California.

After the new logo was introduced to the Scripps family, it was unveiled publicly at all six hospitals during a one-day, countywide community event. Each venue hosted enormous community health fairs, inviting local residents to not only see the Scripps brand in action, but also learn about Scripps' investments in technology, facilities, and charitable care.

While the most difficult part of the process was helping the Scripps family to value the investment of resources (time, money, staff) in this transformation, the most rewarding part of the process was seeing people's pride in becoming a part of this important collaboration—the new team. It was a very powerful chapter in Scripps' history.

Graphic Identity Standards

"Health care organizations have traditionally been conservative, but health care is changing and we wanted a brand identity that shows we're changing with it."

Deborah Routt, Vice President, Marketing and Branding

In the early stages of Scripps strategic transformation, the new logo was the "calling card" for what was to come. The L&M design team worked with Scripps' six image attributes to inspire the logo design. Eight initial designs were presented, each with varied look and appeal. Some were conservative, expressing heritage and excellence. Others were humanistic and spirited. The range of ideas stimulated an interesting discussion, to say the least. Scripps chose the design that evolved into what is being used today because it matched their needs best (Figure 9–9).

The Symbol

The three figures in Scripps' new logo represent the vision of a renewed collaboration and partnership between patient, physician, and hospital. It conveys a sense of unity, support, caring, and community. Initial designs were refined as questions such as Are the figures male or female? How old are they? What race? were asked. The simplicity of the final Scripps symbol resolves those queries. L&M recommended a design that was easily understood, not too abstract, and describable in words that resonate with the audience.

The Logotype

The "Scripps" logotype is based in Times New Roman, and Scripps uses the Times New Roman and Universe type families in its collateral material. Both have a wide range of variations that provide a rich typographic palette. L&M selected a classic typeface that is timeless, not trendy. Two versions of the logo exist, with the logotype on the right of the image (the preferred version) and another with the logotype underneath. This provides flexibility in the way the logo is used.

The Colors

Color is a powerful means of visual identification, yet two-color logos are almost a standard. With today's technology and printing, however, companies are discovering three colors are not much more expensive and are a strong means for differentiation. That's why Scripps is using the blue, green, and orange combination—a far cry from the previous corporate blue and gray. *The goal was to use three colors that are quite different and vibrant. Although colors cannot be "owned,"*

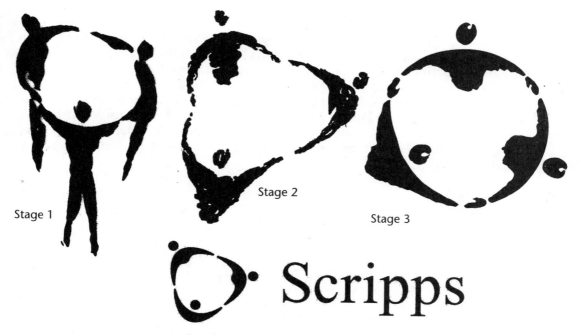

Stage 1

Stage 2

Stage 3

Fourth and final stage of logo development.

Figure 9–9 Scripps New Logo Was To Be the "Calling Card" of Its Rebranding Effort, So Ample Time Was Dedicated to Its Creation. After an evolutionary process, the final logo represents a sense of unity, support, caring, and community—hallmarks of Scripps' renewed collaboration and partnership between patient, physician, and hospital. Courtesy of Scripps, San Diego, California.

---

the color combination will become strongly associated with Scripps, according to L&M.

> *About 60 to 70 percent of businesses present themselves as blue, including companies like IBM, General Motors and AT&T. The second most common color is red, like Pacific Bell and Exxon, for example.*

Jerry Kuyper, Senior Partner, Lippincott & Margulies

Imagery

L&M also presented many photographic suggestions that featured engaging shots of people, which express the more humanistic face of the company.

Changing the logo for a company the size of Scripps is not an overnight job. Since Scripps is a nonprofit organization, the company made a commitment to use the old materials and incorporate the new imagery when the old stock was depleted. Immediate changes were seen in signage, stationery and name badges, but the journey continues.

Along with aesthetic appeal, use of the Scripps design has been delineated in a comprehensive graphic standards guidebook. These standards establish proper use in every conceivable format variation: size, black and white, color, logo on various color backgrounds, two-color and black and gray options, and even in positive and negative treatments. Other unique considerations include three-dimensional versions, animated applications, and versatility in electronic environments. The guide even addresses incorrect uses. Graphic standards are available to all employees, physicians, and staff on the Scripps intranet.

One of the fundamental goals of the guidelines is to protect the organization's greatest asset—the Scripps name. Scripps used to promote itself by allowing its many partners to wield the name as they pleased. Promotion is now recentralized in the corporate office and the name can be used only by express authorization.

Formation of Scripps Physicians

Doctors are the "distributors" of health care. Scripps depends on doctors to refer patients to Scripps services. However, until the formal organization of Scripps Physicians in 1998, Scripps patients, doctors, and hospitals were subject to the whims of how health plans wanted to support each element of the patient-care equation. The alignment of the patient-doctor-hospital relationship is not to promote "cookie-cutter" medicine, but instead to create a system of health care that is patient-driven. Scripps and its physicians are committed to creating proactive care delivery systems by devising the best models of care that perpetuate the best outcomes in the most cost-effective way. *A formidable team, Scripps Health and Scripps Physicians are in lockstep—strategically aligning with only those health plans that share Scripps' mission, contribute to its transformation, and support its Systems of Excellence.*

Strategic Partnerships

Scripps recognized that it couldn't achieve its goal to deliver care to 1.25 million people by itself. Thus, forming the right partnerships, especially with health plans, is one of Scripps' highest priorities. However, as a result of the rebranding effort, Scripps has become more selective in choosing its partners. In order to maintain the image Scripps has worked so hard to rebrand, partnerships are considered based on whether they have the same standards of clinical and service excellence. Scripps now proactively seeks out partners across the field, not just in direct providers but support services such as labs and equipment suppliers. At the front of the search for good partners is Scripps' aggressive relationship-building with health plans that care about Scripps' strategic transformation and its patient-focused mission.

System Design

New relationships between physicians, hospitals, and health plans are necessary to create systems of care that serve the best interests of patients and the community. The new partnership between Scripps and Scripps Physicians will effect real change in how health care is organized, financed, and provided in San Diego. Scripps is critically examining how to reduce variation in care by creating Systems of Excellence in seven care areas: primary care, women's and children's, critical care and cardiology, orthopedics/neurology/rehabilitation, oncology, hospital based, and behavioral health. The strategic planning effort of "System Design" was the first effort at joint planning between Scripps and its physicians. As a result of the planning process, a series of recommendations were made regarding what services should be provided where, how the system should be organized to deliver these services, and the economic framework within which these recommendations will be implemented over the next five years.

Information Systems Upgrade

As a result of the transformation, Scripps embarked on a Strategic Information Systems overhaul. *As mentioned earlier in the chapter, Scripps' new strategy is to diverge from mass marketing in favor of developing a deeper relationship with the community—asking permission to talk with them, telling them about the medical staff they want to meet, offering them choices about information they can receive.* To succeed in this endeavor, it was necessary to develop and maintain an information system that keeps track of both prospective and current patients and customers. With the allocation of $250 million over the next five years, Scripps will be able to develop the information system necessary to accomplish the vision. Not only will the new system help target prospective patients throughout the county, but it will also advance Scripps' ability to better service patients. At the point of initial contact, the patient's data will be captured and forevermore electronically available to any appropriate medical department within the organization so that the patient's medical history is readily accessible and care can begin immediately.

Customer Service

Scripps touched 206,000 unique households in San Diego last year, but until recently there were limited data on the demographic and psychographic composition of those households. The rebranding process demanded that Scripps take action to rectify the lack of information. Scripps has built a proprietary customer information file for relationship marketing management, surveyed and set baselines in seven care areas, capturing customer satisfaction data systemwide in order to improve customer service. One of Marketing's key roles is to measure customer satisfaction organizationwide and provide systems to physicians and hospital staff to solicit and act on customer feedback. Marketing documents the information and quantifies the "brand promise" gap. At first, there was resistance to systemizing customer satisfaction programs, which were initially based on models not conducive to health care. Off-the-shelf "guest relations" programs don't take into account a "product" that is usually not *wanted* by the customer but is *needed. Scripps realized that to be successful it must pioneer its own systems that would resonate with the health care industry and marketplace.*

Service Pilot Programs

Underpinning Scripps' customer satisfaction program is the ability to teach its family how to deliver a consistent brand experience. Now that the brand has been reinvented, it is vitally important to ensure it is both *perceived* and *received* consistently and positively. To assist with this effort, Scripps has initiated systemwide training of front-line staff to create corporate advantage by helping organizations to becoming customer centered. Over the next five years, Scripps staff will be certified to train present and future employees to provide a reliable, consistent, excellent experience. Working on designing the best care and delivery practice throughout the system is no small undertaking—especially when there are 10,000 staff to ultimately train. Nevertheless, its importance cannot be understated. No matter where someone is in the system, he or she contributes in some way to the unique experience Scripps has promised to the patient. Empowering employees to deliver on the brand promise is paramount in strategic transformation.

Reality Check

While no one provider has successfully achieved dominant brand preference in San Diego, preliminary external customer research suggests that Scripps has the lead. The challenge remains in reinforcing the preference of San Diegans for Scripps and converting those with no stated preference to proactively choose the Scripps brand for health care.

Lessons Learned

While Scripps is still in the thick of the strategic transformation, several lessons have already been learned from the rebranding process.

- *There can never be too much attention given to how the effort will affect the organization internally.* A key element of managing the process internally should be to maximize "buy-in" from the start. Keeping everyone over-informed, with an emphasis on making sure announcements are not only made but are embraced internally, should happen before any information is communicated externally.
- *When it comes to rebranding, "think very big."* It may be tempting to target various parts of an organization, but in reality it is a systemwide endeavor, the whole scope of which needs to be critically analyzed from the start.
- *Timing is everything.* Building a brand is a journey, not an overnight tactical development. Everyone from senior management to the front line—even the volunteers—needs to commit to forging the brand, a process that is a multi-year journey.
- *Integrate and educate physicians and their staff.* As integration proceeds at hospitals with physicians, a proactive educational communications effort is required to bring the physician front and back office staff into the "fold," as they are so very much part of the entire systemwide brand process.

The Children's Hospital of Philadelphia: Creating Image and Identity for a Specialty Hospital

Shirley Bonnem

INTRODUCTION

Institutions must have strategic plans today, if they are to flourish, or indeed survive. It has taken almost 200 years to reach this point. At the beginning of the 18th century, hospitals were established as places for the final days of critically ill patients. Eventually, they became institutions where the health of patients was restored or improved, places where the lives of critically ill people were saved. Post–World War II, hospitals with grants for research and fresh infusions of funding for new buildings to make up for time lost by the war wrote "mission statements" so that people would understand the role of each hospital within its community.

THE PAST QUARTER-CENTURY

In recent years, hospitals have become even more specific in defining their roles as they have acquired planning and marketing expertise. The Children's Hospital of Philadelphia, the nation's first, pioneered in using marketing techniques, mainly research, as early as 1970. The public relations department bore responsibility for carrying out the marketing function directed by the then chief operating officer. Planners and marketers with MBAs were relatively rare. They came into the health care field by the early 1980s. Mid-decade, a trend in self-referrals by parents was observed at the Children's Hospital, certainly a change from the physician referrals that had almost predominated up to that time. A separate department was organized because of this difference. A planner came on board to work with a newly established Long-Range Planning Committee comprising members of the Board of Trustees, physicians, and management. The changing environment was assessed, developments in the health care marketplace were evaluated, and an internal audit was conducted. The results brought about strategic initiatives that are analyzed annually, with modifications made as needed.

Initiatives

The initiatives are:

1. Development of networks
2. Organization of a physician-hospital group to provide a coordinated approach to managed care

3. Enhancement of the hospital's infrastructure and systems
4. Growth of clinical programs in response to the demand
5. Improvement of services to patients, families, and referring physicians
6. Promotion of research in cellular biology, molecular genetics, neuro-sciences, metabolism/spectroscopy, and infectious disease
7. Medical education
8. Community service

Concurrent with the strategic initiatives that were articulated by the Long-Range Planning Committee was the development of the Children's Hospital role in pediatric health and identity that is clearly defined and accepted by the institution's various publics. In order to understand the present and move in the right direction in the future, it is necessary to be aware of the past and the evolvement of the present corporate culture. It is equally necessary to have a strong marketing communications program in place to communicate the plan.

A BRIEF HISTORY

The Children's Hospital of Philadelphia was the nation's first hospital dedicated solely to sick children. Founded in 1855, the hospital had earned an international reputation within the scientific community for its research. Over time, Children's Hospital's physicians have developed about 50 advances in pediatric medicine to improve the health of children worldwide. The specialty of pediatrics was started by the Children's Hospital; it had begun its medical training program not long after it opened. It formalized its teaching relationship with the University of Pennsylvania School of Medicine in 1919, but has remained autonomous administratively, medically, and financially. Children's Hospital has strong teaching programs in nursing and social work, as well.

By the time Children's Hospital was eight years old, the three doctors who established the hospital together with another attending physician called for communicating about it. When the Annual Report of 1863 was published, it contained a paragraph that said, "The principal obstacle to the development of the in-door [inpatient] department undoubtedly consists in the difficulty of giving proper publicity to the hospital, not only among the better classes who support it, but also among those it is designed to benefit...." The report was signed by T. Hewson Bache, MD, Francis W. Lewis, MD, R.A.F. Penrose, MD, and Hilborn West, MD.

In the decades that followed, the hospital became well known in the city. It outgrew its first building and by 1867 had moved to a much larger facility. In 1916, the hospital moved into a new building once more. It remained there until members of the Board of Managers realized in the mid-1950s that the hospital building had finally outlived its usefulness. Over the years they had coped with the problem by making repairs where possible and adding space through the purchase of brownstone houses that not only surrounded the hospital, but extended to the next block. Two possibilities were explored: expanding and modernizing the buildings, which were located in a deteriorating part of South Philadelphia, or building a new hospital in another part of the region. A move seemed to be the most pragmatic solution.

The late Alexander B. Wheeler, who had spent 25 years in advertising and public relations before joining Children's Hospital, was Director of Planning and Development. As part of the planning process before embarking on a fund-raising campaign for the new facility, Mr. Wheeler organized a series of conferences with national authorities in the field of child health as speakers. Major goals were to enable those who would be involved with the drive to keep abreast of the ultimate in children's health care services and to make sure that the new Children's Hospital would offer even more comprehensive care than it did at that time. Subjects ranged from the latest clinical therapies to research. As a result of the conferences, Board members and physicians became aware that additions and changes would have to be made to their original plans.

For example: since 1925, Children's Hospital had referred patients with mental health problems to the Philadelphia Child Guidance Clinic, an ambulatory psychiatric service with its own Board of Managers, administrators, professional and ancillary staff, and finances. An independent agency, it was located close to the hospital on ground contributed by Children's Hospital. In order to be a "comprehensive pediatric medical center," Children's Hospital would have to have a psychiatric component under its roof. In preference to starting its own mental health service, the Children's Hospital Board invited the Child Guidance Clinic's Board of Managers to join in a move to the new building by raising its own funding. The Child Guidance Clinic accepted the invitation.

In 1964, Mr. Wheeler and his fund-raising consultants from John Price Jones, New York (later becoming Brakely John Price Jones) began to plan necessary fund-raising materials. In the process, they discovered that one element was missing; it was considered important by everyone who was involved. There was no symbol or logo that represented the hospital, nothing that would give Children's Hospital immediate identification. The need for such a mark was particularly evident to Mr. Wheeler, who had spent so many years in a field focused on logo development as a major part of overall communication programs.

LOGO DEVELOPMENT

If the hospital had a symbol at all it was a picture of a bás relief showing a little girl holding a silver cup in her hands. The caption read, "Dear God, let me hold up my silver cup for them to drink." Former U.S. Surgeon General C. Everett Koop, who had spent his entire surgical career at Children's Hospital before going to Washington, remembers imploring the hospital's Board of Managers to stop using the picture, which had first appeared in the hospital's 1924 annual report (Figure 10–1). He felt that the message was entirely inappropriate for the times.

According to David R. Oakley, Mr. Wheeler's assistant at that time, Mr. Wheeler contacted Raymond I. Ballinger, a highly respected Philadelphia graphic designer. Mr. Ballinger spent months developing a logo that could be recognized with absolute clarity whether reproduced in the size of a child's fingernail or drawn by an airplane in the sky. Several members of the hospital's Board of Managers were part of the committee that was established to shepherd the project through the approval process.

Mr. Ballinger came up with a simple logo using "ch" in lowercase letters. The "c" and the "h" were to be reproduced in an understated two shades of gray, one quite dark and the other light enough to provide contrast on an original document, but dark enough to reproduce the logo in its entirety on a copier. Inside the letter "c" was the profile of a little girl, one that resembled one of four statues on the front gates of the hospital (Figure 10–2).

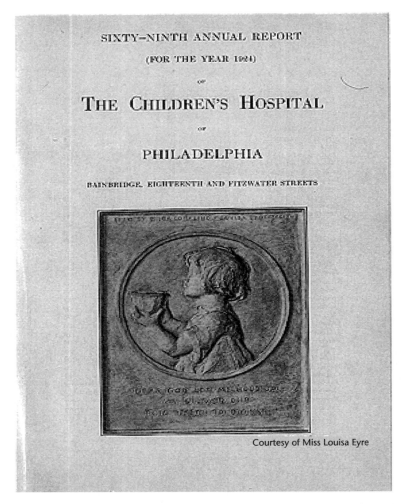

Courtesy of Miss Louisa Eyre

Figure 10–1 Early Symbol used by The Children's Hospital of Philadelphia. Courtesy of The Children's Hospital of Philadelphia, Philadelphia, Pennsylvania.

Beatrice Fenton, a famous Philadelphia sculptor, had created the statues in 1931 using as models a boy and a girl chosen from among dozens attending a picnic. Every patient, sibling, parent, physician, intern, resident, and employee associated the life-size statues with Children's Hospital. Much of the public did, as well. Ms. Fenton made two statues of each child. In recent years, the little girl in the logo has been dubbed "Mary CHOP" (Children's Hospital of Philadelphia).

The late Richard D. Wood, chairman of the Hospital's Board, was so enthusiastic about the logo that he wanted to have a hospital flag. He helped design the flag that flies to this day in the hospital's auditorium and outside with the American flag (Figure 10–3).

Mr. Ballinger produced the logo, a design for stationery, and a book of instructions that illustrated the format for all letters. Because of the layout and placement of the logo, Children's Hospital's letters were distinctive enough to be different from the dozens of solicitation letters a recipient might see every day. The logo and the name and address of the hospital were rather large, extending more than two inches across the top of the page and, with the addition of the Board's officers, almost six inches down the left side.

During the first few years of the logo's existence, the secretaries read the instructions and knew what the format of a letter ought to be. However, as the secretaries were replaced and when the hospital finally moved, many of the secretaries failed to read the manual. They started their correspondence almost halfway down the sheet of paper. As a result, a letter that would fill an ordinary 8-1/2 x 11–inch piece of stationery took two sheets of paper. The format was changed to a horizontal layout in the late 1970s, enabling the secretaries to type an entire letter on one sheet of paper (Figure 10–4).

The logo presented by Mr. Ballinger was flexible and could be modified with ease. During the spring of 1965, the little girl's profile in the "c" was exchanged for a picture of a daisy that filled the entire letter. A variation of the logo is still used by the hospital's Auxiliary. The flower is a symbol of Daisy Day®, the annual street corner exchange of money for paper daisies. The drives in the 1960s were conducted by 3,000 volunteers who solicited funds in Philadelphia and its surrounding counties. Daisy Day spread into New Jersey and Delaware not long thereafter. Within a decade, the Daisy Day army had reached 4,000. However, in recent years there have been fewer volunteers because women have entered the work force. Much of the drive is based on a mail campaign today; however, there are still volunteers on street corners and in shopping malls exchanging daisies for money as they have for many years.

The Children's Hospital–Daisy Day logo was seen everywhere during the week that preceded the four-day event. Bank windows, specialty shops, department stores, banks—all contained displays featuring paper daisies and their own merchandise, or displays featuring specific hospital services and the cans with wraparound Daisy logos printed on them. The drive was imitated by a hospital nearby and a hospital in one of the seashore resorts located 90 miles from Philadelphia. As

Figure 10–2 Logo, The Children's Hospital of Philadelphia™. Raymond I. Ballinger, Designer, 1964. Courtesy of The Children's Hospital of Philadelphia, Philadelphia, Pennsylvania.

THE INTERNATIONAL
YEAR OF THE CHILD

COMMEMORATIVE STAMP

THE CHILDREN'S HOSPITAL OF PHILADELPHIA
FOUNDED 1855

FEBRUARY 15, 1979

Figure 10–3 American Flag and Flag of The Children's Hospital of Philadelphia. Courtesy of The Children's Hospital of Philadelphia, Philadelphia, Pennsylvania.

Figure 10–4 Stationery Design Using Logo and Officers, Board of Managers (A). Stationery Design with Logo but without List of Names (B). Courtesy of Janet M. Andereck, former Director of Development, The Children's Hospital of Philadelphia, Philadelphia, Pennsylvania.

soon as the incident occurred, the Hospital registered the Daisy logo and the words Daisy Days (Figure 10–5). According to the Hospital's attorney, this marked the first time a charitable fund-raiser service mark had been registered.

In 1973 Her Serene Highness Princess Grace of Monaco was honorary chair for Daisy Day. Staplers, a Philadelphia fabric house, voluntarily designed fabric in cotton and in a silk-like polyester printed with the Children's Hospital Daisy logo. They offered the fabric for sale in their shop and sent Princess Grace a bolt of cloth as a gift. Several months later a wire service picture of Her Serene Highness walking her small son to school in Monaco appeared in the *Philadelphia Inquirer*. She was wearing a dress made out of the Stapler fabric. It wasn't possible to see the daisy motif, but the Children's Hospital logo in an overall print was clearly recognizable. Response from the hospital's Auxiliary was positive and enthusiastic.

The material was used in Philadelphia the following year when the hospital moved to its new building. Enough had been purchased to make up 200 scarves, which were then given to the volunteer tour guides of the nine-floor facility. The scarves could be worn in a variety of ways. The guides were identifiable because the "ch" logo was noticeable from afar.

In the meantime, Mr. Wheeler and his volunteer band of fund-raisers were preparing to launch the drive for a new hospital. Since Children's Hospital and the Child Guidance Clinic were working together, it was decided to use two logos for the campaign so that donors would understand that two entities were raising money for one building. The Child Guidance Clinic logo was placed next to the one for the hospital. It had a "g" in a similar typeface. However, a stylized sun with lines indicating different directions was drawn inside the "c" as a graphic depiction of psychiatry's goal, which was to help people choose a direction, one that would be

THE CHILDREN'S HOSPITAL FOUNDATION

THREE CHILDREN'S CENTER
34TH STREET AND CIVIC CENTER BOULEVARD, PHILADELPHIA, PA. 19104
387-6078

THE AUXILIARY

Figure 10–5 Daisy Day Logo. Courtesy of The Children's Hospital of Philadelphia, Philadelphia, Pennsylvania.

happier (Figure 10–6). The two logos were used on all printed material throughout the fund-raising effort, groundbreaking, dedication, and move.

The double logo was dropped in 1974 when the present building opened and the old facilities closed. The Child Guidance Clinic had its own area and a separate entrance. Two years ago, because of the changes in payment for mental health services, Child Guidance requested a merger with Children's Hospital, an event made

Figure 10–6 Logos Used at Groundbreaking Ceremony (A) and to Mark All Activities Associated with the Fund Raising, Construction, Dedication, and Move to the New Facility (B). Courtesy of The Children's Hospital and Child Guidance Center, Philadelphia, Pennsylvania.

less traumatic by the longtime working relationship between the two institutions. The Child Guidance Clinic is now Children's Hospital's Department of Psychiatry.

The development of Children's Hospital's logo was evidently a success. A number of children's hospitals across the country developed logos using the lowercase "ch" letters in various ways. Some used the space provided by the letter "c" filled with something characteristic of a particular children's hospital; others placed a drawing at the top of the "h." Philadelphia's Children's Hospital used its logo on a man's silk tie, embedded in Lucite paperweights, on coffee mugs, and on tee shirts. The logo appears in red marble five feet in diameter on the main floor of its Richard D. Wood Pediatric Ambulatory Care Center. Surgeons and surgical nurses have the logo on their "greens" and patients have it on their pajamas. Also, it has been on notepaper that utilized an embossed version of the logo instead of a printed one. Since it was introduced, the "ch" has been printed on every piece of literature that has emanated from the hospital.

In the mid-1980s a survey was conducted for the Delaware Valley Hospital Council by Joe Inguanzo, Ph.D., President of Professional Research Consultants, Inc. of Omaha, Nebraska. The professional hospital association was interested in the public's attitude toward hospitals. Each Council member was offered the opportunity to piggyback onto the major survey by providing a limited number of its own questions. Answers would be confidential and available only to the hospital making the inquiry. The Children's Hospital of Philadelphia participated in the project.

When respondents were asked to name a hospital in answer to a question regarding pediatric care, the first answer given in more than 95 percent of responses was The Children's Hospital of Philadelphia. Name recognition was therefore almost universal for that particular "brand" of pediatric care. That information was factored into the long-range plan contemplated at that time by Children's Hospital.

In 1987, Children's Hospital reached out by establishing through a joint venture a pediatric service at Abington Memorial Hospital, located in Philadelphia's northern suburbs. Both institutions were confident that the partnership would be successful for two reasons. First, the name and quality of Children's Hospital were so visible, and Children's Hospital was to be responsible for the medical component of the service. Abington was to handle nursing and administrative duties. It was a highly regarded community teaching hospital. Second, placing a Children's Hospital satellite in the suburbs responded to the expanded growth of women in the work force and their inability to take great blocks of time to bring their children to Children's Hospital, which was at the opposite end of the city.

Traditionally, the referring physician had been the indirect consumer of Children's Hospital's services. Until the 1980s, parents would bring their children to the hospital upon recommendation of their pediatrician. (The exceptions were those in the surrounding neighborhood of the hospital, who used the emergency department for sporadic care.) The hospital, which had one of the earliest marketing programs among the not-for-profits, dating back to 1970, directed its efforts to the physician community. The Public Relations Department operated the marketing program. The staff conducted its research among 3,900 physicians in Southeastern Pennsylvania, New Jersey, and Delaware. The hospital responded to the physicians by modifying its services to meet the doctors' needs and by introducing new services. These responses were buttressed by communication with parents so that they would be comfortable with their doctors' referrals and would know about the hospital and its work.

TRENDS

However, another trend was taking shape. A 1985 article written by Dr. Inguanzo and Mark Harju, published in *Hospitals* magazine (January), stated that American women were making 67 percent of the health care decisions. Children's Hospital's medical staff had noticed that self-referrals were increasing rapidly. Those changes were further complicated by the growth of HMOs as the industry penetrated the Greater Philadelphia region. As the 1990s approached, strategic planning called for a different way to provide pediatric service. A new trend now concerns self-referrals via the Internet.

According to Michael E. Porter, the C. Roland Christensen Professor of Business Administration at the Harvard Business School in Boston, "operational effectiveness and strategy are both essential to superior performance. . . ." In his article, "What Is Strategy?" published in the *Harvard Business Review*, November–December 1996, Dr. Porter wrote, "Strategic positions can be based on customers' needs, customers' accessibility or the variety of a company's products or services." Within the past decade, the hospital had strengthened its operations to better serve its patients and keep pace with the way patient care was reimbursed. It had modified its products and services. Its association with Abington Hospital is an example.

In the late 1980s, President and Chief Executive Officer Edmond F. Notebaert had declared that a new strategy was needed to create a network of relationships with other pediatricians and institutions, the best hospitals with the best care in areas they served. By working with the hospital's Board of Trustees (formerly Managers) and its Long-Range Planning Committee, the medical staff, and management, the hospital was able to implement its new strategy and make major changes.

Within a decade, The Children's Hospital of Philadelphia had established joint ventures with five regional hospitals. The Hospital now owns and operates 8 specialty clinics, 4 primary care centers, and 28 private practice groups of pediatricians located as far away as 60 miles east of the hospital on the New Jersey coast and 40 miles south in the Wilmington, Delaware area.

ANCILLARY LOGO DEVELOPMENT

According to Jeffrey A. Rivest, Children's Hospital's Executive Vice President and Chief Operating Officer, *the branding philosophy the hospital pursued was based on validating the high recognition factor of the name and its association with high-quality pediatric care and innovative research.* This was accomplished through professionally conducted opinion surveys, market research, and analysis. As the hospital branched out, it diversified and developed its own pediatric health care system, one that was very different from the traditionally defined pediatric hospital. In today's terms, Children's Hospital provided "seamless pediatric health care," beginning with fetal surgery in high-risk pregnancies and going up to age 19. Only two or three hospitals in the United States offer fetal surgery as a service.

Mr. Rivest said the challenge was how to show this change to Children's Hospital's audiences. At the same time, it was necessary for people to know that they were going to receive the quality and expertise that had always been associated with the Children's Hospital name, although health care was being provided to them in a different location and form.

Much thought, debate, and market research brought about the conclusion that a presence, an Ambulatory logo, was needed. Because the services were not in the hospital setting, the logo would have to be different from the hospital's traditional mark; the new logo would have to give an instant message to everyone. However, the logo would include the CHOP mark, in a smaller, separate version. *The purpose was to let various publics know that the patient was receiving the quality, tradition, reputation, and service associated with the Children's Hospital name, but in a different setting.*

Trent C. Smith is Children's Hospital's Senior Vice President, Ambulatory Services and Network Development. His work in Pennsylvania, New Jersey, and Delaware reinforced the need for ancillary trademarks. The potential for confusion was all the more possible now that there were four related entities: the hospital itself, community hospitals, physician practices, and the centers. A trademark already in use at the hospital seemed logical for the clinics, which were housed in large buildings with signs outside that could be read from the street. The hospital had used tumblers, designed by Environmental Graphics, as sign indicators on an enclosed bridge going from its Richard D. Wood Ambulatory Care Center to the Main Hospital. The tumblers hung from the ceiling and marked the way for adults as well as children (Figure 10–7). They were colorful, playful-looking, and friendly in their appearance. Thus, the tumblers became the main Ambulatory logo. *The "ch" logo was on all printed material along with the tumblers. It was used in signs as well. The message: the new modalities were* not *the hospital, but they were associated with* the *hospital.*

The tumblers were incorporated into every possible place within the Ambulatory clinics. They can be seen on lamps and on counter decorations at the eye level of a small child. External signs have the tumblers along with a smaller version of the hospital's logo nearby. Tumblers have appeared in other places within the hospital so that if a child has used the local clinic before becoming an inpatient, he or she understands the two are connected. Feedback from focus groups has been enthusiastic. Everyone likes the whimsical tumblers. People who work in the hospital have said that the tumblers make them smile.

As new private practice groups or long-established ones joined The Children's Hospital of Philadelphia, it became obvious almost immediately that there had to be a way to connect each group to the hospital. Hospital management and pediatricians in the community practices realized as far back as the acquisition of the first practice that a name was needed. Everyone was aware, too, that the hospital's name had to be secondary, or those going to the doctors' offices would be confused. Neither hospital officials nor doctors in the practices wanted to miss having the hospital's imprimatur associated with the newly established Children's Hospital groups. Mr. Smith reported that no external agency was used for this project.

An informal committee was put together that included members of the hospital's marketing staff and some of the pediatricians from the first practice to be opened. Many names came up that utilized the word *kids*. The committee finally selected *Kids First*, which had a double meaning. The Children's Hospital of Philadelphia was the first hospital for sick children in the United States. Also, the phrase indicated that children were the first priority of the group of pediatricians. A graphic artist was invited to create the *Kids First* logo, which in its final form had the number 1 between the two words *Kids First* and a tumbler shown in the number. The words *a pediatric and adolescent practice* were put beneath the *Kids First*

A

B

Figure 10–7 Tumbler Logo. Courtesy of The Children's Hospital of Philadelphia, Philadelphia, Pennsylvania.

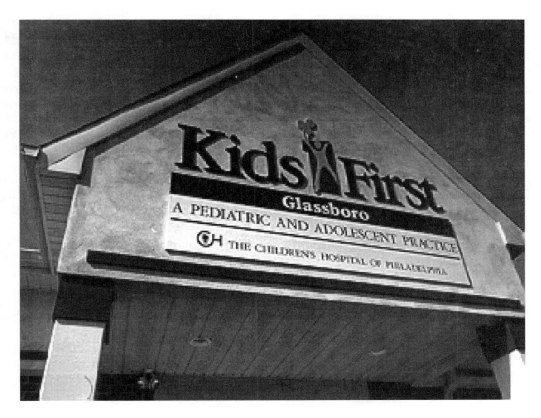

Figure 10–8 Kids First Logo. Courtesy of The Children's Hospital of Philadelphia, Philadelphia, Pennsylvania.

phrase to make sure that no one mistook the name for a child care center or private school. Placed near the *Kids First* logo is the "ch" logo and the words "The Children's Hospital of Philadelphia" (Figure 10–8).

Mr. Smith reported that as he signed up physicians, he offered them the option of using the *Kids First* logo; it was not mandatory. All 75 doctors among the 26 groups chose to use the *Kids First* name. With such acceptance in the medical community, it was decided that all practices established thereafter would use the *Kids First* name and logo. Pediatricians have informed Mr. Smith that the name has become a positive symbol of quality and recognition among patients' parents.

Many doctors who have private practices in the community mentioned positive feedback among their patients' parents because of their association with Children's Hospital. A number of inquiries have been made by groups of physicians who have not been acquired by Children's Hospital, but wanted to use *Kids First* as the name of their practices. They erroneously believed they could use it because it was a franchise. An application to trademark the name is pending.

The five-year-old organization of the primary care and specialty centers combined with the establishment of the *Kids First* practices, which are still expanding, has resulted in almost doubling the number of ambulatory care visits under the aegis of Children's Hospital. In fiscal year 1996, Children's Hospital reported 229,667 visits; in 1998, the number went to 443,024. In fiscal year 1999, the visits exceeded 600,000.

Its growing link with other hospitals was one aspect of the Children's Hospital system that did not yet have a brand name. This was more daunting than the other branding experiences because five long-established institutions were involved with Children's Hospital in joint ventures. Each institutional agreement had individual characteristics. Each had its own culture, its own logo, its own personality. A committee with two representatives from each hospital was organized. They requested proposals from several advertising/public relations companies. The Weightman Group, a venerable Philadelphia advertising agency, was selected. Their account executives met with representatives of each hospital to explore possibilities. Children's Hospital's Michael Sher, the Planning Associate, coordinated the project. Consensus-building among the hospitals was a fairly long evolutionary process. Weightman proposed *The CHOP Connection* as the name because it was applicable to all of the hospitals and because of the almost universal recognition factor when the Children's Hospital name was mentioned.

CHOP, the acronym for Children's Hospital of Philadelphia, was rejected by Children's representatives and its executives. The hospital had never used the sobriquet officially. The CHOP name had been created more than 50 years ago by Charles C. Chapple, M.D., a pediatrician at Children's Hospital who in 1938 invented what is known as the Isolette-Incubator®, used around the world. Not long thereafter, Dr. Chapple entered a hospital contest to name its new coffee and gift shop. He came up with the idea *CHOP SHOP*, which was adopted with alacrity. *CHOP* has been the hospital's nickname ever since. Weightman insisted that everyone knew the hospital by that name and that The CHOP Connection would be identified very easily with Children's Hospital. They commented that it was a known acronym and no one would have trouble recognizing the name. Children's Hospital people remained unconvinced.

Weightman conducted four focus groups with people from different geographic areas in the region. They expressed similar feelings about health care in general for children. Their responses about having Children's Hospital services in the area were positive. The executives and other Children's Hospital representatives were comfortable when they learned that everyone in the focus groups knew the CHOP acronym; they recognized the name immediately.

All of the hospitals represented in the group liked the idea of having *The CHOP Connection* as the overall title. The hospitals' reaction combined with Weightman's finding enabled Children's Hospital's leaders to support the idea. The hospital does not use *CHOP* in its literature or in any printed information because the word fails to describe in any way what it is supposed to represent. A series of advertisements was created by Weightman using *The CHOP Connection* and placed in the local newspapers in each hospital's market and the *Philadelphia Inquirer* (Figure 10–9). The familiar tumblers were on each ad; the "ch" logo was omitted for obvious reasons.

Advertising emanating from Children's Hospital has been modest. Except for a series of four television ads—each with a kernel of health care education and each focusing on a pediatric subspecialty, made and used for three months in 1987—the

Figure 10–9 CHOP Connection Logo. Courtesy of The Children's Hospital of Philadelphia, Philadelphia, Pennsylvania.

hospital had not advertised its services since. With the development of its off-campus services, Children's Hospital began a series of ads that featured its major on-site surgical services and its off-site clinics and Kids First practices. They appeared in the *Philadelphia Inquirer*, *Philadelphia Magazine*, and the suburban papers of areas in which the services were located. In each, the tumblers appeared as major elements of the tagline and the "ch" logo appeared in smaller print (Figure 10–10).

The Children's Hospital of Philadelphia logos are an integral part of the entire marketing communications plan. The project's success can be documented using several measurements. There has been increasing use of the services, the addition of two fully equipped operating rooms to one specialty center two years ago, the building of a larger clinic with the potential for additional rooms for surgery or other services, the requests from physician groups to join the *Kids First* practices, and the growing number of patients using Children's Hospital's services (Figure 10–11).

Lessons Learned

Throughout the years, Children's Hospital has refined the use of its logo and identity and the process has illuminated the following truths about the perceptions of the hospital's audiences:

- All audiences identify very strongly with the logo, and
- No matter what, everyone still calls the hospital "CHOP."
- In addition, the results of the market research and years of experience have reinforced the need for the hospital to communicate, consistently and effectively, with its three major audiences: physicians, parents, and children and several other audiences, as well. These audiences determine the perceptions of the Children's Hospital of Philadelphia. The hospital plans to continue to measure the success of its entire marketing communications plan, with particular emphasis on its logos. The logos are the face of the organization, and the hospital is committed to upholding and protecting it.

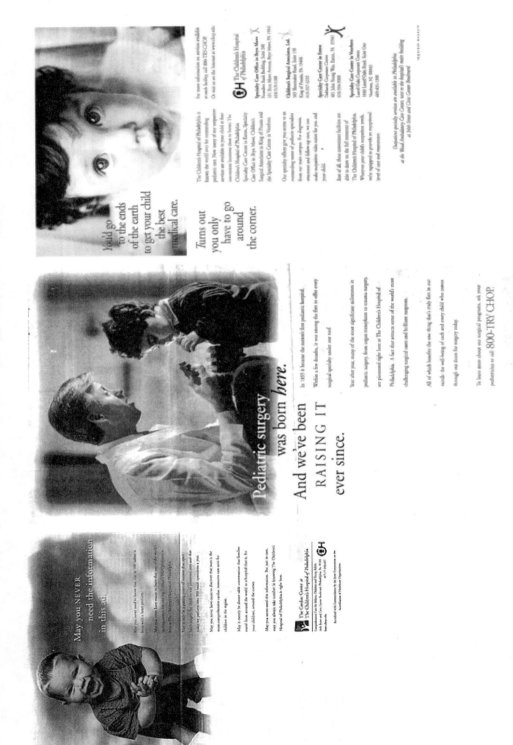

Figure 10–10 Examples of Ads for Cardiac Center and Fetal Surgery. Courtesy of The Children's Hospital of Philadelphia, Philadelphia, Pennsylvania.

Figure 10–11 Example of Kids First Ad. Courtesy of The Children's Hospital of Philadelphia, Philadelphia, Pennsylvania.

REFERENCES

Inguanzo, Joe M., Ph.D., and Mark Harju. 1985. Creating a market niche. *Hospitals* (January): 62–67.
Porter, Michael E. 1996. What Is Strategy? *Harvard Business Review* (November–December): 61–67.

SOURCES

Janet M. Andereck
Former Director of Development
The Children's Hospital of Philadelphia

Julia Ebner
Account Executive
The Weightman Group
Philadelphia, PA

Edmond F. Notebaert
President and Chief Executive Officer
The Children's Hospital of Philadelphia

David R. Oakley
Former Assistant Director of Planning and Development
The Children's Hospital of Philadelphia

Brian Pomeroy
Web Programmer, Information Systems
The Children's Hospital of Philadelphia

Jeffrey A. Rivest
Executive Vice President and Chief Operating Officer
The Children's Hospital of Philadelphia

Michael Sher
Former Project Manager
The Children's Hospital of Philadelphia

Trent C. Smith
Senior Vice President
Ambulatory and Network Development
The Children's Hospital of Philadelphia

Chapter 11

Women and Heart Disease: Building a Service Line Brand

Lisa M. Wyatt and Donna L. Arbogast

THE CHALLENGE

In early 1996, many people in the nation's capital weren't sure what the Washington Hospital Center was or where it was located. That was rather alarming considering the word "hospital" is in its name. Others who had heard of the hospital thought of this 4-million-square-foot facility as a poor person's hospital in a bad part of town—not the best image for a 40-year-old hospital with the fifth busiest heart program by volume in the United States. Clearly the hospital had an image problem that its 40 years in operation had yet to rectify.

But the public's perception of this institution could not be further from the truth. Washington Hospital Center is the largest hospital in the Washington metropolitan area of 5 million people. The hospital's heart program has among the highest heart program volumes in the United States, and its MedSTAR shock-trauma and burn programs are ranked among the best in the country. As a major specialty tertiary hospital, the Hospital Center is known clinically as the place to go for the tough stuff, the highly complex cases that are too risky to handle at smaller community hospitals.

Yet the general public knew little of the hospital's greatness. That deficit needed to be corrected quickly. The District of Columbia is massively over-bedded with only two hospitals operating profitably. The Hospital Center was one of the lucky two. Changing the hospital's image and increasing its positive top-of-mind awareness were essential to long-term survival and to keeping the private physicians happy.

Positioning Washington Hospital Center as the area's premier heart program was the best and fastest way to attract attention and elevate public opinion. To build the super "heart brand," we needed a communications platform that would capture public interest, break through the enormous Washington, DC, information clutter, and allow the Hospital Center to shine in a very competitive environment. Being visible in the nation's capital is tougher than in other cities.

Finding the "hole" in the market is a challenging assignment, as any marketer can attest. We hired Hill & Knowlton to conduct a thorough analysis of our current heart program and identify opportunities to fill "holes" that existed in the marketplace.

Previous consumer awareness research indicated that Washington-area residents knew Washington Hospital Center primarily for its heart program, but they were largely unaware of the depth of its resources—the program's international reputation, specialized expertise, and cutting-edge technology. In interviews with Hospital Center cardiologists and cardiac surgeons, Hill & Knowlton heard from the physicians that the hospital's heart program was the region's best-kept secret and deserved greater recognition locally as a nationally ranked facility.

These interviews also revealed a particular interest among our physicians in the issues surrounding women and heart disease. Many of our cardiologists—both male and female—expressed concern that women were not getting the information they needed about their risk. Hill & Knowlton began to research this issue outside of the Hospital Center and determined that while women with heart disease was a significant clinical issue—it is the number one cause of death among American women—no single institution or organization had claimed ownership of the issue or sustained an educational campaign. A few had tried, but they had fizzled after lackluster launches. Hill & Knowlton also found that consumers needed to be educated on how to select a physician or institution for heart services.

To position Washington Hospital Center as a leading authority in cardiovascular disease, we decided to seize ownership of this area of heart health and become the authority on the subject. A three-year campaign on women and heart disease was selected as the best vehicle to propel the hospital's image forward.

It was an opportunity on multiple fronts.

1. Research indicted that the public, particularly women, was unaware that heart disease is the number one killer of women. The majority of the public believed that breast cancer was a bigger threat to women than heart disease. How very wrong they were.
2. The news media had given heart disease in women scant coverage compared to other hot health topics, such as breast cancer or infertility. It clearly had news potential.
3. Heart disease in women is completely misunderstood by both consumers and physicians. The symptoms of heart disease in women are very different from those in men, and our cardiologists had found that some primary care doctors did not recognize these important differences.
4. The topic was a natural for the hospital from a clinical and staffing perspective. The Hospital Center has a large staff of 13 female cardiologists and surgeons who are knowledgeable about the latest research and nuances of women with this disease.
5. By reaching out to females, we'd be targeting the group that makes 70 percent of all health care decisions—women.

Given these factors, we believed that we had found that compelling, elusive, unexplored "hole" in the market that would serve as the foundation for a major awareness- and image-building campaign. We decided to fill that hole in a big way.

Doing Our Homework

The first thing we did was research, research, research. We explored the clinical aspects of women with heart disease, identifying interesting new facts to use in press materials. We also conducted an exhaustive Nexus search to determine what the press had already written on the topic. It was pretty open territory.

We discovered that heart disease is the leading cause of death among women, killing more women than men. In the United States alone, 479,000 women die each year from cardiovascular disease compared with 447,000 men. Women are six times more likely to die from heart disease than from breast cancer. This was a complete contradiction of public opinion. A national Gallup survey of women sponsored by the American Heart Association (AHA) in 1995 found that four out of five women did not recognize heart disease as their leading cause of death. While this survey did receive some mention in the press, it was low-key and limited primarily to a wire service report. In general, people considered heart disease a man's health problem, and the news media fixated on breast cancer and women, giving the impression that its fatality rates were much higher than the actual numbers. At the same time, the media totally underrepresented the greatest killer of all.

In actuality, one in nine women between 45 and 64 years of age has some form of cardiovascular disease, and this increases to one in three women over age 65. The death rate for coronary heart disease is more than 33 percent higher for African-American women than for white women. Perhaps most interesting was the difference in the symptoms of heart disease between men and women. Rather than the gripping chest pain that men experience, women's warning signs are subtler. Women experience angina, which they describe as a fullness or discomfort in the chest; isolated discomfort in the jaw; pain in the left or right arm or stomach; shortness of breath; or chronic fatigue. While these symptoms are red flags for women, most women and their doctors were unaware of these differences, and women often delay seeking treatment for these vague, but significant, warning signs of heart disease.

While these statistics were alarming, they were not widely reported in the media and were still unknown to the vast majority of women.

Mapping Out a Strategy

By this time, we'd found the hole and the facts to fill in the gap. Now we needed an overall strategy to take it public and maintain momentum for three years—all within an affordable budget. We chose an integrated marketing communications model that combined a public information approach with a strong commercial message.

Our goals for the campaign were threefold:

1. to generate greater awareness among women and physicians about women and heart disease
2. to build on this awareness, linking the topic to Washington Hospital Center and establishing the hospital as a regional and national leader in heart care and a national expert on women with heart disease; and
3. to increase heart referrals to our physicians.

CREATING THE "LOOK"

First, we needed to establish a theme or slogan. After reviewing a number of options, we chose "Listen to Your Heart: Women at Risk," which we often shortened to "Listen to Your Heart." Next, we needed to package it in an eye-catching, bold, and inviting way. We envisioned a visually dramatic piece that would make people notice it, read it, and save it. Working with the funky-style design firm, Bremmer & Goris, we evolved a graphic design in bold yellow and purple with a hip-looking heart that would become very recognizable and lend itself well to promotional items (Figure 11–1).

Partnerships: Media, Public Affairs and Corporate

Second, to ensure that we would make as broad an impact as possible, we began to take our "show on the road" to interest potential partners in our campaign. By partnering with powerful allies in the media, public affairs, and corporate arenas, we felt that we would enhance the campaign's credibility, effectiveness, and reach. To begin, we targeted Washington's NBC-owned-and-operated TV station,

Figure 11–1 Graphic Design Developed for Campaign. Courtesy of Washington Hospital Center, Washington, DC.

NBC4. With the highest-rated Washington, DC, newscast and the most popular news anchor, Doreen Gentzler, NBC4 was our top choice. Doreen, who also covered the health beat, was considered the most believable anchorwoman in town. Her mother had suffered a heart attack, and we believed that Doreen would be supportive of the campaign premise. We were correct. Over a six-month period, we courted NBC4 through a series of letters, meetings, and presentations.

Finally, they agreed to be our broadcast partner and, most important for us, to allow Doreen to be the talent in the public service advertisements that they were to create for the campaign—the first time that a news anchor was ever allowed to participate directly in such an initiative. As part of our partnership agreement, they would create and produce five TV ads promoting the issue. In exchange, we would allow them to promote the campaign as an exclusive and have first crack at any news aspects the campaign generated. We also agreed to participate as a major sponsor in their Health & Fitness Expo, an annual event that draws 65,000 to the Washington Convention Center.

Next, we sought a public affairs partner with a legislative or regulatory interest in the subject. Through our research, we discovered that powerful Congresswoman Maxine Waters (D-CA, 35th District) had recently sponsored legislation to increase funding for women and heart disease research. Congresswoman Waters' bill (H.R. 3001) was entitled "Women's Cardiovascular Diseases Research and Prevention Act" (Figure 11–2). Introduced in March 1996, it addressed the number one killer of American women—cardiovascular diseases—which includes heart disease, stroke, and high blood pressure. Twenty-seven members of Congress joined her as co-sponsors.

Her press materials stated important facts: "Cardiovascular disease has claimed the lives of more females than ALL forms of cancer combined. Yet research funding for heart disease in women is scarce." The bill would authorize $140 million to the National Heart, Lung, and Blood Institute within the National Institutes of Health to expand and intensify research, prevention, and educational outreach programs for heart disease, stroke, and other cardiovascular diseases in women.

For us, partnering with Congresswoman Waters would be a real coup, and would help to round out the program. We sent her a letter requesting a meeting, and were thrilled when she responded positively. The results of the meeting were beneficial for both sides. Congresswoman Waters was interested in our program and agreed to be a guest speaker at the upcoming event that we were planning to launch the campaign. In exchange, we would support her bill and solicit petitions of public support. We would also make our physicians available to give testimony at public hearings, and we agreed to host public events on the Hill, such as health screenings and breakfast briefings. The congresswoman also encouraged us to work closely with the Washington regional office of the AHA. A series of meetings was held with AHA and a strong relationship was established. Over the next two years we would jointly sponsor several programs.

The final leg of the stool was to identify a corporate sponsor. We sent a number of letters to specifically targeted corporations with an interest in women, health, or heart issues, including pharmaceutical companies, retail chains, and fitness organizations. Parke-Davis Pharmaceuticals responded positively. They agreed to contribute $50,000 toward the launch event, and we would print their logo on our consumer and press materials and provide them prominent exposure at the kick-off.

Figure 11–2 Congresswoman Waters' Bill, "Women's Cardiovascular Diseases Research and Prevention Act." *Source:* Copyright © Charles Votaw Photography.

Packaging the "Call to Action" and Developing the Measurement System

We recognized that, to support the many aspects of the campaign, we would need a substantive package of printed materials. Most importantly, we needed to offer something to women via the TV ads that NBC4 would produce. In meetings with our physicians, we developed plans for a ***Women's Heart Health Kit*** that would prove to be a highly coveted and award-winning package.

In planning the kit, we had to balance the need to convey important information to women with the need to be cost-effective, both in printing and mailing. We also wanted the kit to use the eye-catching graphic design as effectively as possible. Bremmer & Goris, with a specialty in packaging, developed a bright-yellow, die-cut folded "envelope" that held five printed pieces and opened up to reveal a bold purple heart. The package was held together with a metallic-gold heart stamp (Figure 11–3).

The final kit included: a 20-page informational booklet that comprehensively covered heart disease statistics, prevention, diagnosis, and treatment; a heart risk assessment quiz specifically designed for women; a bookmark listing the ABCs of women's heart disease symptoms; coupons for *Prevention* magazine, a women's health club, and heart-related books; and heart-healthy recipe cards.

The Women's Heart Health Kit was distributed through the hospital's physician referral line, called DOCtors Line. This referral system was key to measuring the impact of our campaign. It is set up to allow us to track callers through our system. Every time someone calls to request a kit, they are entered into the database. If they ever use the Hospital Center as an inpatient or outpatient, we can identify which service they used, who their referring physician was, and the dollars generated. Our primary methods of publicizing the kits were the TV ads on NBC4, press releases, and one radio flight during Valentine's Day.

Creating the TV Promotion

Working with award-winning producer Robin Fader, we created five public service ads that featured Doreen Gentzler and focused on different aspects of women and heart disease and our campaign. Each 30-second spot was unique. In the most moving ad, Doreen talked about her own mother's heart attack and encouraged women to "get the facts before it's too late." Others established the fact that women are at risk, identified the differences between men's and women's heart disease symptoms, described the Women's Heart Health Kit in detail, and showed the faces of heart disease by featuring real women who survived heart attacks. Each ad ended

---

Women's Seven Warnings Signs of Heart Disease

Angina—chest pain that creates a discomfort or fullness in the chest. Women may also have isolated pain in the jaw, arm, or abdomen.

Breathlessness—shortness of breath or waking up breathless at night.

Chronic fatigue—this may be a symptom of heart disease when it is overwhelming and out of character.

Dizziness—blackouts that occur on a regular basis may be a sign of arrhythmia.

Edema (swelling)—when your heart is not working properly, your body may retain water, causing swelling, particularly in the lower legs and ankles.

Fluttering or Rapid Heartbeats—your heart may pound for a short time or for several hours and may be accompanied by difficulty in breathing and pain.

Gastric Upset (nausea)—this may be a symptom of heart disease when it occurs unrelated to your diet.

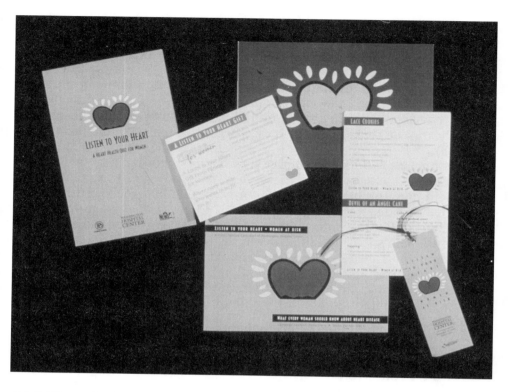

Figure 11–3 Women's Heart Health Kit. Courtesy of Washington Hospital Center, Washington, D.C.

by encouraging women to call Washington Hospital Center for the free kit. The phone number was announced and shown on the screen.

The News Hook: Breaking through the Clutter

With all of the building blocks in place, we now needed a grabber—that strong news hook that would make this story come alive for the news media and for women. We were planning to launch the campaign at an event in November 1996, and we wanted press coverage—a tough task in any market but a real challenge in Washington, DC. From our research, we knew that the press had given lukewarm coverage to the results of the 1995 AHA survey of women that had identified their lack of awareness. Another survey like that would not be our answer. We believed that the news hook was in the lack of awareness among physicians.

Toward that end, we commissioned a Gallup survey of primary care doctors to determine whether or not they knew that heart disease was a risk for women, could identify the differences between men's and women's symptoms of heart disease, and recognized the different levels of effectiveness in diagnostic techniques. Our physician advisory board established for this campaign was consulted before we proceeded with this approach. It was certainly a risk. If we found that primary care doctors were lacking in their knowledge about this issue and then announced it at a press conference, we risked offending an important referral source for our specialists and us. Fortunately, our physicians were very supportive and encouraged us to move ahead. We decided that if the results proved to be what we expected—that there is a lack of awareness—we would present the information in a positive, "let's work together to solve this problem" manner. After all, reaching physicians with important information about women and heart disease was a critical part of the equation for this campaign.

The survey findings were extremely significant, and we focused on one key area—the issue of symptoms being different between men and women. Nearly two-thirds of the 256 primary care physicians surveyed nationally inaccurately reported "no difference" in the symptoms, warning signs, and diagnosis of heart disease in women as compared to men. This fact alone gave us the lead for our press release, and grabbed the attention of nearly all of the major news organizations.

Other Survey Findings. While angina (chest pain) is a major indicator of heart disease in both women and men, other symptoms in women, such as shortness of breath and chronic fatigue, are very common and should not be ignored. Although two out of three physicians surveyed identified shortness of breath as a warning sign of heart disease in women, chronic fatigue was listed by fewer than one out of five respondents and only 10 percent mentioned nausea, dizziness, or swelling of the ankles—other important symptoms.

Despite the number of women affected, physicians surveyed said they are not as knowledgeable about heart disease in women as in men. Only 39 percent responded that they had extensive medical training in diagnosing heart disease in women, compared to 69 percent who had extensive training in diagnosing the same disease in men.

Sixty-eight percent said there is no difference in diagnostic tests for men and women, when in actuality heart disease can be diagnosed more effectively and accurately in women using a nuclear stress test or stress echocardiogram, rather than a simple treadmill electrocardiogram (ECG), commonly called a stress test.

Half of those surveyed listed health problems other than heart disease as the greatest health risks facing women over 50; 18 percent listed breast cancer and 10 percent said osteoporosis. Yet twice as many women die of cardiovascular disease each year than die of all forms of cancer combined.

With these results, we moved full-steam-ahead with plans for our press conference and launch event held on November 20, 1996.

THE LAUNCH: HOW TO GO PUBLIC AND MAINTAIN MOMENTUM

After six months of development, we were ready to launch our three-year campaign from a prominent platform designed to gain maximum visibility that could be sustained over time. We designed an elaborate event that featured a press conference, a panel discussion hosted by NBC4 news anchor Doreen Gentzler and featuring many prominent physician and media experts in the field, and a luncheon keynote address by best-selling author Gail Sheehy, author of *Passages* and *New Passages*. Congresswoman Waters agreed to speak at the lunch as well, but was detained at the last minute by an important vote on the House floor.

Several hundred of Washington's health, community, business, civic, and association leaders were invited to attend the event. The press was also invited to the full day's activities, but we held the press conference early to allow them to get their news and leave, if necessary. The compelling data from the Gallup survey attracted far more press coverage then we ever imagined.

The findings were so incredible that it was the lead story on *ABC World News Tonight*, and aired the next morning on *Good Morning America* and *The Today Show*. In addition to the national coverage, which also included a number of radio, broadcast, and print wire services, we blitzed the local market. As anticipated, we raised the ire of the American Academy of Family Practitioners (AAFP), which immediately took issue with our survey of primary care doctors and demanded a retraction. But Gallup's research and methodology were airtight, and we responded to AAFP by offering them a chance to work with us on our educational efforts. They declined. Except for that one negative, the response to our survey, the campaign, and the launch event was overwhelmingly enthusiastic and positive.

The panel discussion generated a lot of excitement among those in attendance. It was designed to be a low-tech, easy-to-understand discussion of the issue of heart disease and its implications for future policy decisions. Many heavy hitters in the field of coronary heart disease and in the media participated. Dr. Nanette Wenger, long recognized nationally as a spokesperson on women and heart disease, came from Emory University in Atlanta to join the panel. And from the policy side, our heaviest hitter was Dr. Susan Blumenthal, the deputy assistant secretary for women's health and assistant surgeon general in the U.S. Department of Health and Human Services. Dr. Patricia Davidson, a cardiologist who serves on the board of the AHA and is a faculty member of Howard University Medical School and the University of Maryland Medical School, was also among the group. Our representative was Dr. Wm. James Howard, then president-elect of the AHA's local chapter and the senior vice president and medical director of Washington Hospital Center. Renowned heart surgeon Dr. Paul Corso also participated, along with Dr. Debra Judelson, an internist and cardiologist with the Cardiovascular Medical Group in southern California and the president of the American Medical Women's Association. Rounding out the panel was Dr. Elizabeth Ross, a cardiologist, author of *Healing the Female Heart* and past chairperson of the AHA's committee on women and heart disease.

In addition to NBC4 news anchor Doreen Gentzler, who served as the panel moderator, other media panelists included Laurie Abraham, the health editor of *Mirabella* magazine, and well-known health writer Sally Squires, of *The Washington Post*. The panelists briefly presented their specific points of view, whether on research, diagnosis, or media responsibility, and Doreen then led a lively discussion, culminating in a summary that identified the campaign's communications agenda for the next three years.

Luncheon Speaker Hits a Chord with the Crowd

If anyone can make getting old seem desirable, it's best-selling author Gail Sheehy. She provided the right combination of Hollywood glitz—needed to turn out a crowd in competitive Washington—and the content expertise that the venue demanded. She spoke passionately about heart disease in the context of aging overall, and helped lend credence to the campaign's premise. A Library of Congress survey lists her book *Passages* as one of the 10 books that has most influenced people's lives. Her speech enraptured the crowd. She also signed copies of her book following the luncheon. It was the perfect mix of style and substance and it added sizzle to the day's activities.

Launch Results: The Phones Rang Off the Hook

Two days before the launch, Doreen Gentzler produced a six-minute news segment for the 6 P.M. newscast that took women step-by-step through the heart risk assessment quiz. Expecting a few calls, we staffed the doctors' referral line with two people after hours (normal closing time is 5 P.M.). That segment alone generated over 400 phone calls for our heart kits, and we realized then that we had struck a nerve.

The day of the launch, the ads featuring Doreen began airing on NBC4 and, supported by the news coverage of the physician survey, our phones rang more than they had for any other promotion in the hospital's history. Not only did women request kits, they asked for referrals to our specialists and scheduled appointments immediately. We had to hire several temporary operators to assist with the onslaught. We were on our way.

THE NEXT STEPS: KEEPING THE GROUNDSWELL MOVING

The kick-off event, the ads, the consumer kit—all were just the beginning. In the third month, we decided to take a different approach, introducing humor into the campaign. We bought a two-week radio flight right before Valentine's Day. The 30-second spot featured a guy trying to impress his girl by giving her a special gift. He gets excited describing the gift, and in the background her heart beats faster and faster. He tells her it's something she'll really enjoy.... "like tickets to the hockey game" (her heartbeat gets slower) or how about (heartbeat speeds up) "locker room passes for after the game" (heartbeat slows up again). Finally, it ends with the announcer saying, "Why don't you give her a gift that will save her life.... a free Women and Heart Disease kit." Again, we were astounded at the response. We received more than 500 calls in two weeks—more than any other radio spot had ever produced.

Overall, each new component was designed to reinforce the campaign and the key messages. Each tactic reinforced another. It was integrated and powerfully effective. Another tactic was our community newsletter, *CenterScope.* We dedicated an entire issue to the campaign, doubling the distribution to 250,000. Again, we were flooded with calls, more than the publication had produced in its 10-year history. Another approach was the use of real patient stories, told by vibrant women who had experienced heart disease. The press readily used the stories and they brought to life all the facts and figures that we were promoting.

Physician Education

Throughout the next two years, we used every resource available to us to reach both women and physicians with our key messages. In March 1997, a physician education program was held for primary care physicians, family practitioners, and obstetricians/gynecologists focusing on the diagnosis and management of heart disease in women. A senior writer with *Washingtonian* magazine attended the program and used the clinical information as a basis for a comprehensive feature that ran in July of that year. Her article focused on a woman whose complex heart case required the attention of two of Washington Hospital Center's most prominent female physicians—a cardiologist and cardiac surgeon.

In addition, we prepared a summary article based on our physicians' presentations at that seminar, and mailed it with sample consumer materials to 5,000 physicians in the mid-Atlantic region, targeting key referral areas for our heart program. Included in that mailing was a business reply card that doctors could use to request free additional copies of the consumer materials—a new brochure, the quiz, a bookmark, and a poster. The response has been a steady stream of requests since the mailing, and we plan to produce another similar package following an upcoming seminar that we are sponsoring with the support of the American Heart Association and Bristol-Myers Squibb.

Community Outreach

Every month since the launch event our female cardiologists and surgeons have been involved in community outreach programs ranging from health fairs on Capitol Hill and at local malls to speaking engagements at women's health clubs and senior centers. One of our physicians also participated in a women and heart disease "chat" through American Online. Our major community outreach event was held in Heart Month (February 1998) in partnership with the American Heart Association. A half-day educational seminar on a Saturday was publicized using a direct mail brochure and spot print advertising. Washington Hospital Center's auditorium can seat 300 people, and until this program, that space had always been adequate. For the women and heart disease seminar, however, we had over 450 registrants, and we had to schedule a second program to accommodate those who couldn't get in to see the first.

Media Strategy

Our goal throughout the campaign has been to focus on high-impact, strategic activities and relationships that generate phone calls and referrals. Toward that end, our media efforts have targeted the women's magazines and several local publications that reach key audiences. We have had articles in almost all of the major magazines, including *Mirabella, Harper's Bazaar, Woman's Day, American Health for Women*, and *Self*. And in January 1998, one of our leading physicians, Dr. Elizabeth Ross, was featured prominently in an article in *USA Weekend*. We were also fortunate that *The Journal*, which publishes daily papers in all of the counties surrounding Washington, DC, agreed to allow us to write regular columns on heart disease bylined by our physicians. While not all have been specifically about women and heart disease, they have allowed us to reinforce our campaign's messages and feature our female cardiologists prominently.

Relationship Building

In late 1997, one of our most important cardiology groups established a Women's Cardiac Health Initiative headed by a young, very energetic female physician. We have supported her efforts to educate physicians, and at the same time we have been able to reach out to other organizations as well. In January 1998, for example, she sponsored a day-long symposium for physicians that, for the first time, examined female-specific data from various national heart-related studies.

The evening before her program, we sponsored a dinner for her speakers and representatives from the American Heart Association, the Society for the Advancement of Women's Health Research, and Congresswoman Maxine Waters' office, among others, to bring together prominent people in the field.

Through these kinds of programs, we have been able to ensure that Washington Hospital Center is positioned as a leader on the issue of women and heart disease. Our ongoing connection with the American Heart Association, for example, has played an important role in our physician education efforts. When the local chapter received a $50,000 grant to sponsor an educational program for doctors, the AHA contacted Washington Hospital Center immediately because we can offer the continuing medical education credits so important to the physicians. This seminar was held at the National Museum of Women in the Arts and attracted over 200 doctors from the mid-Atlantic area.

Marketing

Looking to branch out, we have begun to offer our program to other non-competing hospitals, with the stipulation that our logo will continue to appear on all materials. One hospital in a nearby county, already a strong heart referral source for Washington Hospital Center, has reprinted some of the campaign materials with both their logo and ours featured on the cover. For them, the association with the Hospital Center's heart program provides credibility and prestige. For us, it broadens the reach of our name, logo, and heart brand. We will begin working with another regional hospital very soon.

WRAPPING UP: GOING OUT WITH A BANG

We are now planning the campaign wrap-up, which will again include a survey and a high-visibility forum held in downtown Washington. We will survey women nationwide to determine two things: whether or not we have increased their level of awareness of their heart disease risk, and whether or not they know their cholesterol level. While our campaign focused on basic awareness, not specific risk factors, we would like to take the next step and address behavioral issues in our wrap-up initiative. Cholesterol is an important issue related to heart disease risk, and again, women lag behind men in addressing this area of their health. The final ad for the campaign produced by NBC4 will focus on how important it is for women to know their cholesterol level and to do something about it if it is high.

As with other components of the campaign, the wrap-up will follow an integrated approach. While our main focus will be high-impact news coverage, we will reach out to a targeted audience of influentials in key arenas through the panel discussion and luncheon, and we will use existing vehicles (our CenterScope community newsletter, NBC4 ads, speakers bureau, and our *Journal Newspaper* column) to reinforce the final campaign messages.

THE FINAL WORD: RESULTS

To date the campaign has received 11 awards, including the highly coveted "Silver Anvil." It also received the "Best of the Best Award" given to the Women's Heart Health Kit by the Washington Regional Chapter of the International Association of Business Communicators (IABC). The National Capital Area Chapter of the Public Relations Society of America also recognized the kit with its Thoth Award of Excellence. And IABC recognized our campaign launch, as did Healthcare Marketing Report, which also gave a Gold Award to the campaign logo.

Most importantly for Washington Hospital Center, we have received over $3 million worth of media coverage (as measured using data provided by Burrelle's), we have had nearly 15,000 requests for Women's Heart Health Kits, and through these calls, we generated over $2.4 million worth of business for the hospital in the first 16 months of the campaign (the time period for which this financial information was available). Public opinion scores increased dramatically after the campaign. Washington Hospital Center went from a 15 percent to 23 percent score as being the "best hospital for heart problems" and from a 15 percent to 22 percent score as being the "best hospital for open heart surgery." Forty-six percent of local women recognize the differences in women's symptoms from men's, while only 27 percent recognize differences nationally. It is ranked as the top hospital in the region for heart care and cardiac surgical procedures.

Lessons Learned

Undertaking a major campaign has taught the public affairs department of the hospital some valuable lessons. The most critical lessons were learned in the planning stages, as we mapped out our strategies and tactics. The following lessons are the most essential to planning and executing a sound campaign:

- *Do your homework.* Research conducted to explore your audience, subject matter, and the marketplace is key to the development of a strong campaign.
- *Cultivate influential partnerships.* Targeting prominent partners in the community can lend credibility to your campaign and your institution as a whole.
- *Develop a quantitative measurement system.* A system of measurement will ensure that you and the management of your institution can gauge the success of your program quantitatively.

Through an integrated, high-impact strategy, the public affairs department has moved the awareness needle and had a significant, measurable impact on Washington Hospital Center's bottom line.

Chapter 12

The Evolution of a Health Care Brand

Martin B. Rosen

INTRODUCTION

The Aetna U.S. Healthcare® brand is a relatively young creature, born as recently as 1996 in the acquisition of U.S. Healthcare by Aetna Inc. Despite health benefits operations and traditions reaching back nearly 150 years, the "new" company was faced with building a fresh identity, one that would clearly differentiate the new entity while at the same time defining a leadership role in the complex and still evolving managed care marketplace.

Indeed, the Aetna U.S. Healthcare brand had to do more than merely represent an array of products and services. It had to become a strategic platform embodying the company's mission and aspirations, even as the company continued to grow. It had to bring together employees—from widely disparate markets and under constant criticism while doing a job they believe in—and inspire them with a collective mission and sense of self-worth. And the brand had to turn a new face toward the public at large, one that reflected a vision of the managed care company as an information source.

In the best of conditions, this reconstruction would be a difficult task. As it happened, the 1990s saw a dramatic increase in criticism of managed care from many sectors. As the most visible industry leader, Aetna U.S. Healthcare became a prime target for activists and politicians alike. This is not the proper venue to rehash the arguments and counter-arguments of the so-called "managed care debate."

What will be done here is to outline the way in which brand development can serve a variety of mission-critical business functions by facilitating the development of relationships. As an instrument for multimarket and postmerger integration, the brand is used to draw formerly competitive businesses together. Internally, the brand has served as a focal point for an employee community whose alignment and inspiration are crucial for the company's success.

And, most significantly, the brand is a mechanism to communicate messages of depth and substance to a variety of stakeholders—consumers, business customers, physicians, shareholders, public officials, and the media. Through these relationships, we hope to be defining a new path for the managed care industry.

WHO WE ARE

Aetna U.S. Healthcare is the health care and related benefits business unit of Aetna, Inc., a 147-year-old Fortune 100 global company. While Aetna has long been an industry leader and innovator—and in fact celebrated its 100th anniversary in selling health benefits in 1999—the Aetna U.S. Healthcare entity was formed in 1996 with Aetna's acquisition of U.S. Healthcare. U.S. Healthcare was a regional health maintenance organization (HMO) with a well-established reputation for effective provider contracting, high quality customer service, and excellent market penetration in New York, New Jersey, and Pennsylvania. Currently, Aetna U.S. Healthcare provides health care and related benefits to 30 million people throughout the United States and contracts with approximately 400,000 health care providers to deliver high quality services to them. Revenues in 1998 were $13.4 billion. Aetna and its collective subsidiaries (Aetna U.S. Healthcare, Aetna Financial Services, and Aetna International) is publicly traded on the New York Stock Exchange. The health benefits business includes two subsidiary companies: InteliHealth®, Aetna U.S. Healthcare's online health information affiliate, and U.S. Quality Algorithms™ (USQA), a data management company with the largest health care benefits database in the country.

Over the years our business has evolved into offering a complete spectrum of products and services, ranging from traditional indemnity benefits to a complete line of managed care programs as well as a host of group and specialty related products. We have HMOs in 33 states and preferred provider organizations (PPOs) in 48 states and Puerto Rico. We continue to offer indemnity medical benefits in all 50 states.

In addition to our health care products and services (which also include dental, pharmacy management, and vision care benefits), we offer our customers group life, disability, and long-term care benefits. In total, we have a comprehensive portfolio of products with a wide variety of plan designs in each to meet the needs of our employer customers and their employees.

THE DEVELOPMENT OF THE AETNA U.S. HEALTHCARE BRAND

The development of the Aetna U.S. Healthcare brand is a study of bringing together two very different companies in the context of significant acquisition activity and regulatory oversight. Aetna had a long history and tradition as a major publicly traded insurance company, with significant emphasis on corporate giving and public sponsorship. U.S. Healthcare had achieved significant market penetration and leadership through innovative advertising, sales, and consumer-driven marketing and service. Aetna U.S. Healthcare's brand is the result of the successful integration of two different cultures and styles. Today, we are one company with a singular focus and our branding activities serve to support our vision and strategy.

The Environmental Backdrop

The branding activity discussed below took place in the throes of some of the most pointed "managed care bashing" that the industry had seen in years, often focused very specifically on Aetna U.S. Healthcare as representative of the industry. Such challenges are felt especially keenly in a shareholder environment and have the potential to significantly undermine employee morale.

General Goals and Objectives for Branding

We intend that our various constituent groups perceive Aetna U.S. Healthcare to be the premier health care benefits company in the country, not just because of its unique size and product array, but because of the dedication and capability of the people who compose the organization. Our products and services are without parallel in the industry, and we have historically dedicated ourselves to delivering the highest-quality customer service.

Our focus is on quality and access to care. Our tag line, *"Raising the Quality of Healthcare® in America,"* clearly defines our goal. As discussed below, our vision and its supporting values set an uncompromising standard for excellence and dedication at all levels of the organization. But it's taken us a long time to get to where we are today. We continue to evolve in a very challenging time. Establishing a brand is, of necessity, a somewhat fluid process. Nonetheless, we know where we want to be as a company and what we have to do to get there. It is now incumbent upon us to educate the public about our goals, how we can accomplish them, and how our doing so can accrue to the benefit of both our members and shareholders. We want to firmly establish our brand in all corners of the marketplace.

The Physical Embodiment of the Brand

A company's logo is the physical embodiment of its brand. When seen by consumers or by any of our key constituents, it should convey the brand promise that we stand behind. As you will see below, this was a significant consideration in the development of the Aetna U.S. Healthcare logo following the merger in 1996. This logo for the health care division of a large multinational company directly ties to the brand of the parent company. At the same time, it recognizes the value and strength of its newly acquired entity.

The Aetna U.S. Healthcare identity is intimately tied to the brand of our parent company. Aetna itself launched a new advertising campaign in 1998 that united its three major lines of business (health care, financial services, and international benefit programs). This *"For What Matters Most"* campaign told consumers that Aetna recognized the overriding importance in their lives of their health and financial security, and was prepared to support them in both areas. The brand strength built on the solid foundation of integrity and reliability that has distinguished Aetna during nearly 150 years of hard work and dedication to its customers makes that tag line ring true for them.

Aetna U.S. Healthcare also introduced in 1998 a new tag line: *"Raising the Quality of Healthcare® in America."* We wanted people to understand that our commitment to quality was unmatched in our industry. We were determined to distinguish ourselves from our competitors by highlighting that commitment and by making full accreditation of the National Committee for Quality Assurance (NCQA) a cornerstone of our platform.

Tag lines should be used carefully. They are not complete mission statements in and of themselves. Instead, they succinctly highlight the company's most immediate goals. "Raising the Quality of Healthcare® in America" projects our confidence in our ability to anticipate and to meet our customers' highest priority needs, and it is directly linked to the overall branding message of our parent. At the same time, it allows us to highlight discrete characteristics of our products, services, and business strategies that will enable us to accomplish that goal (stability and integrity; simplicity and breadth of services; and commitment to quality).

Logos are not readily changed, principally because you want a well-established and readily recognizable image to present to the public. Tag lines, however, can be used in a variety of ways without losing their impact. In fact, they can be a unifying force among various brand representations (Figure 12–1).

HISTORY: THE BEGINNING OF THE BRAND

Aetna U.S. Healthcare has experienced a period of extraordinary growth through merger and acquisition during the past several years. Aetna Inc., our parent company, committed itself to making employee benefits its primary line of business in an era when other insurers were deciding that this business offered too low a return for the risks it involved. Aetna divested its property and casualty lines of business in 1995 and focused on employee benefits both domestically and internationally. The employer is their principal customer, with employees often being second-tier buyers through coverage selection or plan participation.

Aetna has been in the insurance business for nearly 150 years and in the health benefits business since 1899. During the company's long history, it forged valuable relationships with some of the country's most prestigious companies, consistently focusing on serving the needs of those customers in innovative and fiscally responsible ways. As a publicly traded company, Aetna is likewise committed to providing a good return on investment for its shareholders.

In July 1996, in order to bring an influx of managed care expertise into the organization and capitalize on the extraordinary success of a younger, regionally based, public HMO company, U.S. Healthcare, Aetna acquired the company. Founded in 1976, U.S. Healthcare had been one of the fastest growing and most profitable HMO companies in the country, with a membership of approximately 2.9 million.

A new company was effectively created, merging systems, provider networks, and structures from both entities. There was little precedent, at least in the health care industry, for the magnitude and scope of this merger. Senior management focused on the very basics of running the combined operations with an emphasis on building

Raising the quality of healthcare® in America.

Figure 12–1 Aetna U.S. Healthcare Logo and Tag Line. Courtesy of Aetna U.S. Healthcare, Blue Bell, Pennsylvania.

systems to support customer needs. Following a year and a half of considerable change and adjustment, the new consolidated brand emerged as a powerful entity.

Much like most mergers, the marriage between these two organizations was a challenging one. Management styles, history, business strategy, and corporate cultures lived in sharp contrast and had to be modified on both sides to create a new, stronger entity. And both shareholders and the public at large needed to perceive and accept the value-added nature of the alliance in a positive way to grow market share and maintain financial stability. Branding the new entity was to become a key to its success.

The Early Stages

Prior to their merger, both organizations had been known for their commitment to customer service. U.S. Healthcare was further recognized for its ability to negotiate very competitive provider contracts that helped to control costs and for a unique data management and warehousing initiative that began to emerge in the late 1980s. Aetna Health Plans was the group benefits arm of a well-established national brand. In bringing the two together, management hoped to forge a new brand that would continue to command respect within the industry and among customers while projecting a new image of the future of health care benefits—managed care.

Creating a visual image was only the beginning. A significant challenge arose with regard to maintaining the high level of customer service for which both companies had been well-known, while bringing the two systems and cultures together. Company executives spent the greater part of the year and a half following the merger creating a unified organization while ensuring that customer needs were being met. Considerable effort was expended to streamline and integrate systems from two companies and to build an infrastructure capable of supporting one of the nation's largest health care companies.

Another Opportunity Arises

In early 1998, not long after the dust had begun to settle following the Aetna and U.S. Healthcare merger, Aetna made another significant acquisition. NYLCare^{SM} Health Plans, the managed care subsidiary of New York Life Insurance Company, was another strong regional player with nearly two million members, many of whom were concentrated in key markets for Aetna U.S. Healthcare. With this second acquisition completed in July 1998—nearly two years to the day from the Aetna/U.S. Healthcare merger—the company saw its membership pushed into the top three plans in several key markets (i.e., Texas and the greater Washington, DC metropolitan area, including suburban Maryland and Virginia).

As NYLCare was, in its own right, a strong regional player, we needed to be careful not to undermine our acquired equity by changing the brand too abruptly. There was also concern that if this merger wasn't very carefully managed, it could resurrect the specter of reduced-quality service and low customer satisfaction that Aetna U.S. Healthcare had tried so hard, and successfully, to overcome. In the smaller NYLCare markets of New York, New Jersey, Seattle, Chicago, and Maine, the transition occurred fairly quickly, with most business converted to Aetna U.S. Healthcare products and systems in less than a year. With careful planning and execution in those areas, the change of brand name from NYLCare to Aetna U.S. Healthcare was pretty uneventful.

Interestingly, there were both regulatory and business considerations regarding the timing and process by which we changed our market presence. Regulators in Washington, for example, were concerned that consumers not become confused by the merger. They wanted a name change that would make the relationship between the two companies clear but would also indicate to consumers that they were not leaving one company for another. "Aetna U.S. Healthcare, the new name for NYLCare Health Plans of the Northwest" was used during open enrollment for the state-sponsored Basic Health Plan so that NYLCare members would understand that if they stayed with their NYLCare plan of benefits, they would become part of the Aetna U.S. Healthcare book of business.

In Maine, where NYLCare had an HMO license and Aetna U.S. Healthcare did not, we filed for a legal name change that became effective shortly after the start of calendar year 1999. Until that point, the NYLCare Health Plans of Maine name continued to be used.

In Dallas, Houston, and the Washington, DC metropolitan area, however, the NYLCare name had been better established, and it was decided that the brand transition should be slower and more deliberate. A transition logo was used until about mid-1999, with the goal of maintaining the NYLCare brand equity while we went about linking the two organizations in the minds of our constituents (Figure 12–2).

Prudential HealthCare

In December 1998, six months after the NYLCare acquisition closed, Aetna announced its intent to acquire Prudential HealthCare, the managed care business of the Prudential Insurance Company of America. Prudential had publicly made well known throughout the industry its plans to divest itself of the health benefits business so that it could concentrate on its other businesses and expand internationally. Other offers had been entertained, but Prudential agreed that Aetna offered the best opportunity to continue to provide the level of service, breadth of products, and quality of care to which its customers had become accustomed.

Having recently undergone the NYLCare transition, we were sensitive to the regulatory concerns about abruptly changing plan names. In addition, this situation required the cooperation of Prudential, Inc., which owned all trademarks related to the health care business. Working together with Prudential, Inc., we de-

Figure 12–2 Transition Logo. Courtesy of Aetna U.S. Healthcare, Blue Bell, Pennsylvania.

vised a transition logo that, while still prominently displaying the Prudential name, clearly indicated the new relationship to Aetna U.S. Healthcare. We also negotiated a fairly aggressive timetable by which to phase out all uses of the Prudential HealthCare name and brand.

In many ways the Prudential HealthCare culture was similar to Aetna's, both having evolved out of old, well-respected insurance businesses and organizational structures. Consequently, it was expected that the cultural transformation would be less intense, making it somewhat easier for employees to stay focused on serving our customers during the integration period. That could make it easier for our customers to make the transition as well.

BUILDING THE BRAND FROM THE INSIDE OUT

The Integration Kick-Off

The historic Aetna and U.S. Healthcare merger provided a good number of lessons upon which to build future acquisitions. For both NYLCare and Prudential HealthCare, we began building our brand from the inside out. The importance of our own employees as ambassadors for the company, representative of what we stand for in the way they performed their everyday jobs, could not be overestimated.

Very shortly after closing both transactions, we conducted "town meetings" in all acquired locations with all new staff. This was done to share the background of the organization and to welcome them. We also emphasized the importance of continuing our focus on customer service even during the challenging period of integration, explained in general terms how that integration would proceed, and communicated a comprehensive report of benefits and employment information to better enable them to make personal decisions regarding their future careers.

These town meetings were designed to give people the opportunity to meet their peers informally and share information and experience in a nonthreatening way. Pennants were posted to promote the meetings; giveaways helped to create some excitement and gave our new employees some physical evidence that the acquisition had taken place, even though there might be few visible changes otherwise for some time. As discussed further below, it became critical for us to communicate regularly with employees throughout the transition period to help keep them focused on our business priorities and informed about their emerging personal options as the two companies came together.

Reaching Out

Communication to our external constituents was also important. We communicated with our key constituents about both proposed acquisitions immediately after they were formally announced in the media. Our emphasis was on their strategic significance to both our company and our constituents—employer customers, producers (agents, brokers, consultants), health care providers, legislators, and others who were integral to the services and products we brought to market—and stressed the importance of working collectively toward the good of the end users, our members (Figure 12–3).

A Multimedia Effort

Our outreach efforts utilized a variety of media that enabled us to have the greatest impact on each audience. This included standing and customized newsletters, our internal and external websites, letters, phone calls, video, and manage-

FOCUS ON   SEPTEMBER 1999 • VOLUME 2

Aetna US Healthcare ***Producers***

HIGHLIGHTING PRODUCTS AND OPPORTUNITIES FOR SELLING PROFESSIONALS

Aetna Completes Acquisition of Prudential HealthCare

Aetna announced that it has completed its acquisition of Prudential HealthCare for approximately $1 billion, making Aetna the country's largest provider of health benefits, with more than 21 million members, and adding to its position as the nation's leading managed care company, with more than 18 million managed care members. The company also will be a leading provider of dental benefits, with approximately 16 million members.

"We are pleased that we have completed the acquisition of Prudential HealthCare, which we expect to be accretive to earnings in 1999," said Richard L. Huber, chairman and CEO of Aetna. "We now will be able to provide our members with a wider choice of physicians and extend to Prudential HealthCare members the benefits of our industry-leading disease management and preventive programs designed to help keep them healthy."

"We now will begin implementing our integration plan, which is designed to emphasize continuity for employers, members and physicians, while preserving and, in some instances, improving service levels," said Michael J. Cardillo, president of Aetna U.S. Healthcare®. "As previously announced, we will retain the Prudential HealthCare national service centers in Cranbury, NJ; Jacksonville, FL; Sugarland, TX; and Los Angeles, CA, as well as dental service centers in Albany, NY; Jacksonville, FL; and Simi Valley, CA."

Cardillo noted that during the integration period, the company will introduce a new transition logo — "Prudential HealthCare, a member company of Aetna U.S. Healthcare."

Aetna is a leading provider of health and retirement benefit plans and financial services, with three core businesses — Aetna U.S. Healthcare, Aetna Retirement Services and Aetna International. The company provides more than 40 million people worldwide with quality products, services and information that help them manage what matters most — their health and financial well-being. □

Make a Note

The Aetna U.S. Healthcare Commissions Department phone numbers are as follows:

- Blue Bell, PA   1-800-622-3435
- Middletown, CT   1-888-327-7360
- NYLCare   1-800-695-1374
  (customer service)

IN THIS ISSUE

2
USAccess™ Plan Offers Members Choice and Flexibility

3
A No-Cost Way to Enhance Your Customers' Benefits Plans

4
Aetna U.S. Healthcare Launches New Product for Uninsured Working Americans

5
Aetna U.S. Healthcare and Federal HIPAA — Key Reminders

6
Aetna U.S. Healthcare Sales Map

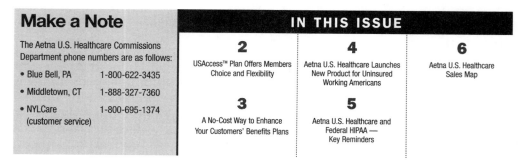

Figure 12–3 Sample of Member Communication. Courtesy of Aetna U.S. Healthcare, Blue Bell, Pennsylvania.

ment/employee meetings (Figure 12–4). Integration messages consistent with our overall business goals and objectives were reinforced in all communications.

Consistency of Messages

Throughout the very busy three-year merger and acquisition period, every effort was made to provide consistent messages to our key constituents. In all instances, our focus remained *on service, quality, choice, and access* as the foundation of our business and our commitment to our employees and our customers. This effort continues every day as we forge a strong, flexible brand image that will enable us to grow and change as an organization without disrupting the perception people have of us in the marketplace.

UNDERSTANDING CONSTITUENT PERSPECTIVES

It has always been important to understand the varying perspectives of our key constituencies in order to work effectively with them. And, of course, it is necessary to weigh the needs and preferences of one against another to guide many of the business decisions we make. What do these groups want and expect from us? How

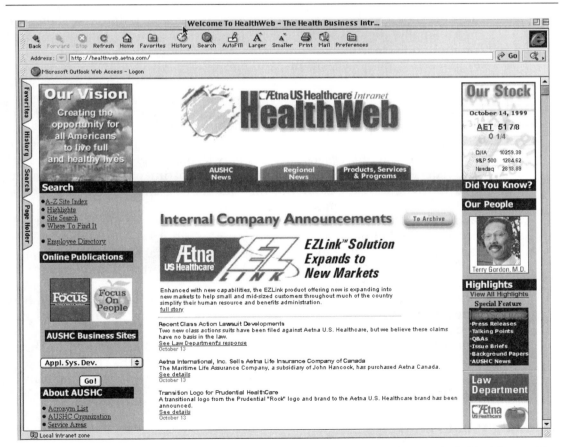

Figure 12–4 Aetna U.S. Healthcare Intranet Home Page. Courtesy of Aetna U.S. Healthcare, Blue Bell, Pennsylvania.

can we make our relationships mutually rewarding? How can we communicate with them in ways that will permit an exchange of ideas?

First and foremost, as noted, our messages must be consistent. People outside the organization needed to understand where we stood on the issues, how we wanted to work with them, and how, together, we could better serve our mutual customers—our members, their patients, employees, or constituents. While there are some unique twists on the concerns of each group, there is also considerable overlap, particularly in terms of their interest in quality, choice, and access.

Highlights of the concerns of each constituent group follow:

- *Plan Sponsors*—The principal concerns of employers are with regard to network, price, quality, and service. They generally want to offer their employees the best benefit value for the money with minimal or no disruption to their own administration.
- *Providers*—Physicians are concerned with our ability to direct patients to them, the fees we negotiate with them and the timeliness with which they are paid, and the simplicity of processing for reimbursement and patient referrals.
- *Members*—In general, members want to know that their physicians are in our network, or that they will have an adequate choice among providers if they are not. They want access to necessary care and treatment in times of medical need. Finally, they also want simple processes with limited paperwork and prompt and responsive customer service.
- *Producers*—The brokers, agents, and consultants who work with us want to know that we will make a full spectrum of products and services available at competitive prices, that our networks will be extensive, that our service will be so good that they will not need to field client complaints, and that the commissions we pay them will be competitive.
- *Legislators and Regulators*—The managed care industry has been the focal point of much recent legislation and many legislative proposals, at both state and federal levels. The "protection" of their constituents is critically important to them, as is the assurance that quality care and broad access will be part of any package of products and services we market.
- *Media*—The media will focus on what makes news. Typically, bad news sells better than good news. With that caution in mind, we were determined to develop a rapport with reporters and to make ourselves available as a resource to them to help ensure that we would have an opportunity to comment on stories that concerned us.
- *Our Employees*—Our employees need to know that we and our members value the work that they do. They also need the company's support to be able to do that work effectively.
- *Our Shareholders*—Because we are a publicly traded company, our shareholders expect a consistent record of earnings and growth. They also expect that the company has a well-designed strategy to remain at the forefront of our industry.

Branding Proof Points

While our initial efforts at branding focused on communicating a consistent message to our various constituents, the essence of our brand promise is to deliver products and services that reinforce the brand personality. Traditionally, health care companies used branding to create an image. More recently, however, branding has taken on its own functionality and been integrated into the overall value proposition presented to the customer.

It is not a coincidence that a number of initiatives that bring our brand to life—our proof points—have been introduced in recent months and years. In fact, they have grown out of our commitment to our customers and to fulfilling our brand promise. Those initiatives have been promoted both internally and externally to firmly and positively position our brand in the minds of our key audiences. In many cases, our company developed programs that were firsts for our industry. By being proactive and getting to the marketplace early with innovative initiatives, we established an important brand presence. A number of examples follow:

- *Affordable HealthChoices from Aetna U.S. Healthcare™*

  Introduced in 1999, Affordable HealthChoices was the platform from which we launched a nationwide effort to raise awareness of and seek private sector solutions to the problem of the working uninsured (Figure 12–5). This issue is about access to health care and how health insurance can help provide that access. Aetna U.S. Healthcare has been a thought leader in the industry for quite some time, representing its own views alongside those of its industry peers and customers. The working uninsured represent a significant and rapidly growing problem that can undermine the growth of the American economy over the long run. We were determined to begin driving private sector leadership on this important public policy issue.

  In addition to our product launch, we are working with other organizations to help sponsor regional and national forums at which the issue of America's uninsured will be brought to light and solutions can be proposed. It is our hope that by engaging the private sector more actively in the examination of the issue, we will be able to identify and generate support for several initiatives that will help to solve the problem.

- *External Review Program*

  In early 1999, the company took the proactive step of being the first managed care company to voluntarily offer an external review program to all of its managed care members throughout the nation. The external review program will give members, for whom coverage has been denied on the basis of medical necessity or the experimental nature of the treatment proposed, the right to appeal that denial to an objective third party outside of the company. The program enables members and their providers to submit additional information that they believe will sway the determination of coverage in favor of the member to a third party, with the company agreeing to abide by the expert's determination.

- *Provider Contracts*

  Ensuring strong relationships with physicians and other health care providers has been a top priority for the company. In recognition of the need to be responsive to physician and consumer needs, our managed care physician contracts were rewritten in 1998 to more clearly state several provisions. In addition, we very specifically noted that our participating providers were encouraged to share all treatment options with their patients, our members, regardless of whether the treatment might be covered by the plan and regardless of the type of reimbursement we had in place for the provider. By taking

43 million Americans*
don't have health coverage even in an emergency.

That is an emergency in itself.

Even more alarming is eight out of ten of these uninsured Americans live in working

families. The truth is, simply because someone holds a job, has a family or owns a

home, that doesn't necessarily mean they have health insurance. For one reason or

another, millions of Americans go without what many of us would consider a necessity.

The peace of mind of insurance coverage.

Many have trouble making ends meet, so insurance simply isn't a priority

when faced with all the other day-to-day expenses of a family.

At Aetna U.S. Healthcare,* this is a concern. We believe every working American

should be able to afford health coverage for their families. That's why we're proud to

introduce Affordable HealthChoices from Aetna U.S. Healthcare.™ It's health coverage**

designed to help ease the heavy weight of uncertainty that many working Americans

have reluctantly learned to live with.

We understand this is only a first step. To advance the search for a true solution,

Aetna U.S. Healthcare is inviting America's business and legislative leaders to join

in a public dialogue on this issue. To create an environment where every American

can discover the peace of mind that comes with health coverage.

If you are an employer interested in affordable coverage for your employees, or if you

simply want to learn more about Affordable HealthChoices from Aetna U.S. Healthcare

and whether it is available in your state, please call toll free 1-877-451-6815.

RAISING THE QUALITY OF
HEALTHCARE® IN AMERICA

www.aetnaushc.com

Figure 12–5 Sample Ad for Affordable Health Choices. Courtesy of Aetna U.S. Healthcare, Blue Bell, Pennsylvania.

this extra step, we were able to communicate our desire to work cooperatively with our physicians and to simplify and enhance access to appropriate health care providers for our members.

- *InteliHealth®*

    InteliHealth was founded by Aetna U.S. Healthcare in 1996, in a joint venture with Johns Hopkins University and Health System, to build an online consumer health care website. The company recognized early on the inherent value in providing health care information to consumers through the Internet. The InteliHealth site contains millions of pages of information about health care conditions and treatment in a consumer-friendly style. Winner of the 1999 Webby Award as the best consumer health care site, InteliHealth (Figure 12–6) now enjoys a large consumer following. It is an excellent example of the way that we have been able to bring technology and information together for the benefit of our members and for consumers in general.

- *U.S. Quality Algorithms™ (USQA)*

    USQA is a subsidiary of Aetna U.S. Healthcare dedicated to the application of data and information management to the enhancement of quality and improvement of managed care processes. Their work has been instrumental in a number of our disease management programs, helping to identify members at risk of illness or of avoidable deterioration of their condition. USQA routinely provides participating physicians with information about their patients, which can be used to improve health care outcomes.

- *Academic Medicine and Managed Care Forum*

    Recognizing the importance of building alliances with the medical community, Aetna U.S. Healthcare founded the Academic Medicine and Managed Care Forum in 1996 as a vehicle to support managed care outcomes research projects. The Forum is dedicated to issuing grants to academic medical centers that conduct research related to improving access and quality, creating clinical guidelines and otherwise enhancing the value of managed care to its members. Today, 45 of the nation's leading academic medical centers are members of the Forum and have received more than $20 million in research grants. To broaden its membership, the company has also invited several pharmaceutical companies to participate in the Forum.

- *National Medical Excellence Program®*

    In order to ensure that members with complex medical conditions have the best possible chance to get high quality care from the most experienced and effective providers, we have identified the nation's premier facilities in critical care areas based on a comprehensive set of criteria, and negotiated

Figure 12–6 InteliHealth Logo. Courtesy of Aetna U.S. Healthcare, Blue Bell, Pennsylvania.

fees with them. This structured network of critical care providers (e.g., organ transplants, burn treatment, cardiac care) around the country has been contracted by Aetna U.S. Healthcare to provide specific services to our members and their families. When a member presents with a need that is best addressed by these special providers, we make medical transport and family/companion travel arrangements to the applicable Mational Medical Excellence Program participant.

As noted, proof points bring our brand to life. They are the actual products and services designed to deliver our brand promise to our customers. Each of the above examples is evidence of our focus on offering customers what will be most meaningful to them rather than what is necessarily simplest or most efficient for the company. Certainly group insurance is not the only industry that has evolved to a more consumer-oriented perspective in recent years—the banking industry has blazed an enviable trail in that regard—but the types of unconventional insurance and related products and services we now offer clearly speak more directly and effectively to our commitment to customer access and quality in all areas of health care and benefits administration than ever before.

Internal Communications

All our efforts to build a consistent message with our various external constituents and to introduce products that reinforce our value proposition could unravel if our employees are not focused on the vision and strategy of Aetna U.S. Healthcare. As part of our branding activities, we are continually conveying our brand promise to our employees and enlisting them to support efforts to reach out to our customers in a way that is consistent with our brand promise.

As noted above in the overview of our integration activities, employees are potentially the best ambassadors for our organization. That potential can be realized only when we share with them our priorities, give them the tools to help achieve our objectives, and reward them for helping us to succeed. And, as noted earlier, the politically charged environment in which we often operate can impose additional stresses on the normal workday. One of our challenges, then, was to reinforce the value that we and our members place on the extraordinary work done every day by Aetna U.S. Healthcare employees.

Building the Brand Internally

Our employees are usually our first line of contact with our members. Customer service and patient management staff in particular deal each day with the needs of members and their families, often during very troubling or emotionally charged periods. While the personal reward and satisfaction can be considerable, seeing people through such situations and working through our internal processes to do so can be stressful as well. In light of the external pressures imposed by media reports often triggered by unfortunate anecdotes that overlook the day-to-day value we bring to people's lives, it becomes increasingly important to build pride and boost morale among employees.

Focus, *the Employee Newspaper*

Effectively communicating to our own employees the great work that they and their peers were doing became a top priority in this environment. While we had a company newspaper already in place, its tenor had historically been businesslike and reportorial. The facts were there, but the excitement and commitment of our employees were not. We needed to build enthusiasm and pride in the work being done so that employees would be better able to be ambassadors for the company, with their friends, their neighbors, and the customers they served.

In the last quarter of 1998, *Focus* was reborn in a *USA Today*-type format (Figures 12–7 and 12–8). We highlighted key statistics, covered every business area, brought people to the fore in our stories, and increased the number of stories we could cover by making them more concise and impactful. Our goal was to encourage employees to read all the stories, not just the ones with which they identified, so that they would become more familiar with all aspects of our business.

One thing we did with the redesign was to build our apple logo prominently into the *Focus* masthead. The apple's significance goes beyond just the good health image apples have traditionally enjoyed ("an apple a day...") to encompass all that we do to maintain the health of our members.

Focus on People: *Bringing Our People to the Fore*

Even with its new look and an increase in the number of stories covered, *Focus* remained a newspaper—with the news at its center. While it hinted at the critical roles played by our employees, it did not capture the personal profile that brought our business to life.

In the fall of 1998, we introduced *Focus on People,* a quarterly magazine that put staff at the heart of the story (Figure 12–9). It asked:

- Who came up with the idea?
- Who figured out how to implement it?
- Whose contact with the member helped them through a difficult period?
- How did teamwork make the difference in meeting a critical deadline?
- Most important, what were the faces of managed care and how could relating to those faces help to change the perception of our business?

Focus on People delivers our most critical messages to our most critical assets. Today, employees and their managers are clamoring to have their stories told in each issue, proudly touting the work that they or their peers have done. We include a section on the compliments and thank you letters that staff receive from members. This is more than a feel-good publication. It is designed to help build a core value system to help bind our company into an integrated and cohesive entity.

HealthWeb Helps To Create Ambassadors

Today's electronic environment has increased the demand for timely information. Since the formation of Aetna U.S. Healthcare, dependence on our company intranet, known as HealthWeb, has grown tremendously, notably with regard to business applications. However, we also need to prepare employees to respond to late-breaking news.

When media coverage turns negative, they can expect to be contacted by members, providers, plan sponsors, brokers—even their own friends or family—who will want to know how we can or will respond. This year we started to post our responses on our website as a resource for employees in these situations. *A comprehensive portfolio of materials is posted to the site within 24 hours of breaking news. It includes:*

Vol. 4, No. 2 — **March/April 1999**

Focus
The Pulse of Aetna U.S. Healthcare®

Coming Next Issue!
Recognizing the role Aetna U.S. Healthcare nurses play

In Brief

InteliHealth® Is Best: InteliHealth, Aetna U.S. Healthcare's online health information affiliate, won a 1999 Webby Award, the Internet equivalent of an Oscar. The award, presented during a live, online ceremony in San Francisco March 18, recognizes InteliHealth (which beat out five other nominees, including the Mayo Clinic) as a leader in providing health information on the Internet.

Heart Honor for Huber: Aetna Chairman Dick Huber received the "Heart of New York Award" from the American Heart Association (AHA) on Feb. 9 for the contributions he and Aetna have made in the fight against cardiovascular disease. More than $7 million has been committed to the AHA through Aetna U.S. Healthcare and the Aetna Foundation. The award was presented at the AHA's annual gala in New York City, which raised $800,000 for research and education.

Bus Donated: A 15-passenger bus with handicapped accessibility has been donated to the Robert Dewitt Shelter in North Philadelphia by Aetna U.S. Healthcare's Mid-Atlantic Region office. The bus will be used to transport the shelter's 54 residents for medical care and family visits, and for transporting food. Robert Dewitt Shelter is a community-based residential care facility that houses homeless and mentally impaired clients.

Pictured are Dr. Donald Park, founder of the shelter and Dr. Jay Krakovitz, Mid-Atlantic Region Medical Director.

A Net Gain: A new intranet site has been added to HealthWeb. A quarterly Legislative Roundup, produced by the Law Department, provides information concerning recent state and federal legislative and regulatory developments applicable to the managed care industry. It can be accessed at http://healthweb.aetna.com/apps/legis-lative_roundup/about.html

Quality recognition times four

Demonstrating a strong commitment to quality health care across the country, Aetna U.S. Healthcare recently earned three-year, full accreditation for three different health plans and full accreditation for another health plan from the National Committee for Quality Assurance (NCQA), an independent, not-for-profit organization that evaluates managed care organizations.

NCQA has issued three-year accreditation to Aetna U.S. Healthcare's HMOs in Florida, Arizona and the Washington, D.C. area, and Aetna U.S. Healthcare's Connecticut HMO also received full accreditation. Three-year, full accreditation is the highest level of recognition awarded by the NCQA. Accreditation by the organization is a nationally recognized standard.

"We're very proud to have earned the NCQA's highest stamp of approval in these three locations," says Abbie Leibowitz, Chief Medical Officer. "This acknowledges the commitment we have made to work with our physicians and hospitals to help our members live healthier, more productive lives."

NCQA reviews health plans against approximately 60 specific quality standards. The accreditation process includes rigorous on-site and off-site evaluations, comprehensive interviews, access to quality committee minutes and review of clinical and service data.

U.S. Papcheck®

Annual reminders and educational materials for female members age 18+.

1.8* million packets sent.

*1998 national figures.

14428-4/99

Vision lights the way!

Our Vision
Creating the opportunity for all Americans to live full and healthy lives.

Cover Story

By Christine Erb

Aetna U.S. Healthcare's new vision (left) and the supporting core values (below) debuted March 30, helping the organization tap its true potential and create a dynamic work environment.

Success in the new millennium will require three things: a clear vision of what our company is working to accomplish; thoughtful values to guide us as we work toward that vision; and the dedication of each and every employee to both. Aetna U.S. Healthcare took the first step toward achieving future success March 30 when it introduced the company's vision and core values to employees nationwide.

In the first years following the monumental merger that created it, Aetna U.S. Healthcare focused its energies on immediate tasks — integrating a strong workforce, creating a broad spectrum of products, building a nationwide provider network, bringing customers into a single company and managing incredible growth.

Now, on its third anniversary, with these tasks accomplished, Aetna U.S. Healthcare's senior leadership has introduced the vision — Creating the opportunity for all Americans to live full and healthy lives — and the nine core values that support it (see box) to help set our course into the next century. Earlier this year, these leaders had gathered to

consider the direction in which the company is headed, what it will take to get there and, most important, why we are headed in that direction.

"We wanted to paint a compelling picture of why we're doing what we're doing," says President Mike Cardillo.

The vision and values are much more than mere words, he explains. They are the driving force behind everything employees do, from outreach programs we undertake, the products we create, the emphasis we place on customer satisfaction, the way we value each other as colleagues, to the business decisions we make every day.

"We wanted this vision to capture what is unique about American culture," says Tim Nolan, head of the Field Organization. "It is about maximizing potential ... for our employees, for our members, and for all people in America."

"Our vision is a simple statement that captures the excitement, dedication, optimism and commitment of Aetna U.S. Healthcare," says Tracy South, head of Human Resources. "The vision statement focuses on what we want to achieve at Aetna U.S. Healthcare. The

values statements focus on how we want to achieve that vision."

The values should guide the ways in which we interact with our customers, our partners and each other, and how we plan for the future. Employees are invited to think about the values, adopt them and spend time talking with their managers, supervisors and colleagues about how to make these values truly live at Aetna U.S. Healthcare.

Communicating the vision and values is just the first step in providing the workforce with the tools, skills and knowledge required to unleash their potential. In April, as part of the next step, employees will begin to participate in an innovative, interactive learning activity to increase their business and financial literacy. In addition, quarterly broadcasts will update the workforce on the company's progress toward its vision, to explain strategy and to celebrate success.

"I want to invite all employees to join us on this journey to redefine health care in America," says Cardillo. "As your leaders, we can only conduct. You are the ones who are out there every day making this happen."

Values

Customer Focus

A Pledge to Quality

Aetna U.S. Healthcare People

Integrity

Strong Provider Relationships

Passion for Excellence

Performance-Driven

Innovation and Creativity

Embrace Technology

Customer service off to soaring start

By John Dube

Thanks to early planning and impressive teamwork by Aetna U.S. Healthcare Customer Service employees across the regions and home office, members were enrolled on time and their ID cards mailed by the date promised to a greater extent than ever during the 1998 fall open enrollment period — setting the stage for great customer service in 1999.

Across all regions, there were fewer calls attempted from members and customers in January because there was less need for them to call. When members did call, a greater percentage got answers, and they got them more quickly than last year — helping Aetna U.S. Healthcare deliver on its promise to build a reputation for superior service.

"This year, the call volume and customer comments tell us the fall open enrollment went great," says Doreen Goodnough, head of Member/Provider Service. "We reduced the need for members to call, and that means members were happier and so were our employees."

Open enrollment results were impressive across the board. The turnaround time for new customer installations with a Jan. 1, 1999, effective date (5,733 cases) was 4.4 days, well under the target for the busiest time of year. This process includes set-up of customer benefits and accounts structures so that bills

and ID cards can be generated. In addition, open enrollment included 16,000 renewal cases effective Jan. 1.

Customer Service issued 4.3 million ID cards for all products with a Jan. 1 effective date — 98 percent of which were mailed by Jan. 1. Those not issued by Jan. 1 were the result of missing information from the customer.

"The reason we were able to accomplish our goals is that we started intensive planning for open enrollment in July," says Michael Moore, head of Measures and Quality for Core Employer Services. "Everyone associated with open enrollment pitched in and made it happen."

The result was not only timeliness, but quality as well. Ninety-eight percent of all cases were installed accurately, from mistake-free ID cards to billing. Over 1,100 people, both home office and field, were involved in open enrollments.

"Our customers shouldn't be impacted by the fact that it's our busiest time of year, and they weren't," says Larry Harrington, Head of Core Customer Service. "Everyone really stepped up to the plate to help Aetna U.S. Healthcare establish a reputation for providing superior customer service."

> "This year, the call volume and customer comments tell us the fall open enrollment went great ..."
> — Doreen Goodnough

Aetna U.S. Healthcare President Mike Cardillo brings the Aetna Board of Directors up to date on e.Health from Aetna U.S. Healthcare™ initiatives during a recent board meeting at the Aetna Customer Center in Middletown, CT.

The board learned more about the organization's use of e.Health from Aetna U.S. Healthcare programs, such as EZLink™ and EZenroll,™ and the new Aetna Customer Center, which provides a high-tech environment for sales or service staff to meet with customers.

Figure 12–7 Sample of *Focus*, The Employee Newspaper. Courtesy of Aetna U.S. Healthcare, Blue Bell, Pennsylvania.

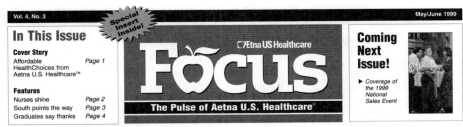

Vol. 4, No. 3   May/June 1999

Special Insert Inside!

In This Issue

Cover Story

Affordable HealthChoices from Aetna U.S. Healthcare™	Page 1

Features

Nurses shine	Page 2
South points the way	Page 3
Graduates say thanks	Page 4

Ætna US Healthcare

Focus

The Pulse of Aetna U.S. Healthcare

Coming Next Issue!

▶ Coverage of the 1999 National Sales Event

In Brief

Professorship at Johns Hopkins: Dr. Garry Cutting was introduced May 13 as the first recipient of the Aetna U.S. Healthcare professorship in medical genetics at The Johns Hopkins University School of Medicine. Dr. Abbie Leibowitz, Aetna U.S. Healthcare's Chief Medical Officer, said, "We are delighted to endow a research position that will help future generations maintain good health." Aetna U.S. Healthcare pledged $1.5 million in 1996 to endow the professorship.

Two Plans Accredited: Aetna U.S. Healthcare (Ohio) has received three-year, full accreditation from the National Committee for Quality Assurance (NCQA) while NYLCare Health Plans of Maine, an Aetna U.S. Healthcare company, has been awarded New Health Plan Accreditation from NCQA. NYLCare is the third health plan in the country to receive new plan accreditation.

Building Diversity Awareness: May was National Asian/Pacific American Heritage Month, and Aetna U.S. Healthcare's San Francisco office noted the occasion by hosting an exhibit of paintings by Peter Woo, a noted Catonese artist.

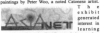

The exhibit generated interest in learning more about the Asian/Pacific populations as they relate to Aetna's recognition of emerging markets. The office also hosted a reception with city officials who wanted to honor the network and Aetna U.S. Healthcare's commitment to diversity.

Best in the West: In the Health Care Association of Southern California's 1998 Satisfaction with Health Plans Survey, Aetna U.S. Healthcare received the top rating among 13 health plans operating in Southern California. The survey of hospitals and large medical groups rated health plans against such measures as timeliness of eligibility and benefits, complete and accurate patient eligibility reports and timeliness of claims payments.

Credentialing earns certification

Aetna U.S. Healthcare has again demonstrated its commitment to quality by achieving certification for 10 out of 10 credentials verification services for our Credentials Verification Unit (CVU) for a two-year period. This accomplishment will streamline the NCQA review process for all of our local health plans.

This first-time certification for Aetna U.S. Healthcare acknowledges the quality of all 10 of our credentialing elements, which are employed to verify all Aetna U.S. Healthcare physicians' credentials. Certification means each of our local health plans will no longer have to oversee the CVU's structure and provider credentials verification performance.

According to Samuel W. Warburton, M.D., Core Medical Director for Quality Management, "Our CVU is now independently recognized as a quality organization. This certification again validates our efforts to provide members access to quality practitioner networks."

Efforts to create a nationally consistent credentialing process began in 1995. The Enterprise Provider Credentialing System, a proprietary credentials verification system, was implemented in 1996, helping Aetna U.S. Healthcare demonstrate its leadership in providing access to quality health care nationally.

The National Committee for Quality Assurance is an independent, nonprofit organization that certifies credentials verification organizations and accredits managed care organizations.

Customer Service

In 1998, Aetna U.S. Healthcare customer service professionals answered over 63 million phone calls and resolved over 150 million claims.

14428-6/99

We're taking the lead

Affordable HealthChoices *from Aetna U.S. Healthcare*

Cover Story

▼ *Affordable HealthChoices from Aetna U.S. Healthcare, a new health plan designed to provide an affordable health coverage alternative for the uninsured, grabbed the national spotlight when it was launched in May. U.S. Senator Bill Frist, below right, praised the Aetna U.S. Healthcare initiative, while Aetna U.S. Healthcare President Mike Cardillo provided an overview of the program's intent.*

Demonstrating its national leadership position in health care, Aetna U.S. Healthcare helped the national debate over access to health care take a giant leap forward by launching an innovative new plan that will help reduce the number of uninsured workers in America.

Joined by prominent U.S. Senators and members of Congress at a press conference in Washington, D.C., Aetna U.S. Healthcare President Mike Cardillo and Aetna Chairman Dick Huber on May 5 unveiled Affordable HealthChoices from Aetna U.S. Healthcare — a low-cost health insurance program specifically designed for small employers and their employees to help make health care coverage available and affordable to more Americans than ever.

"As the nation's leading health benefits company, Aetna U.S. Healthcare has a responsibility to take the lead in drawing various interests together to focus the attention of all Americans on the issue of the uninsured and serve as a platform for substantive change," said Aetna U.S. Healthcare President Mike Cardillo. "Assisting the working uninsured is at the very core of our vision —

"Creating the opportunity for all Americans to live full and healthy lives.'"

As part of this major initiative, the Aetna Foundation is providing $100,000 to fund a national conference and regional forums to help move the dialogue forward. This unique opportunity will enable business leaders, nonprofit organizations, medical representatives, elected officials and workers' advocates to come together to explore solutions to the problem.

Aetna U.S. Healthcare also is initiating an ambitious national television and print advertising campaign to help explain the serious economic issue of the uninsured.

At the National Press Club in Washington, D.C., a number of political leaders joined Aetna U.S. Healthcare in its call for a constructive national dialogue on this issue. Present were U.S. Senators John Breaux (D-LA) and Bill Frist (R-TN), and Representatives Bill Thomas (R-CA), Nancy Johnson (R-CT) and John Larson (D-CT).

"We need to find ways to put patients before politics, and initiatives like Aetna's are a good first step," said Senator Frist,

chairman of the Subcommittee on Public Health of the Senate Committee on Health, Education, Labor and Pensions and a board-certified surgeon.

"It's encouraging to see an insurance industry leader like Aetna accepting the role of corporate citizen and stepping up to a very difficult issue," said Representative Johnson.

Aetna U.S. Healthcare recognizes there is a clear need for serious dialogue — the ranks of uninsured Americans have grown by 36 percent in the past 10 years to more than 43 million today. Most are members of working families who would be helped enormously by low-cost options. Affordable HealthChoices from Aetna U.S. Healthcare is an inexpensive hospital indemnity policy intended for employers who wish to give their employees a basic coverage option.

"Affordable HealthChoices takes the sensible approach of providing basic coverage at a price that many small businesses can afford, but it is only the first step in a complex process," said Aetna Chairman Dick Huber. "That's why we're inviting business leaders and Congress to seek support for a more comprehensive answer."

The Ranks of Uninsured Americans

43 Mil. — 1999

32 Mil. — 1989

Leadership University charts course

In order to stay competitive in today's fast-paced economy, everyone needs to step back from the pressures of day-to-day work, refocus and look ahead to the organization's future initiatives.

That's just what 250 of Aetna U.S. Healthcare's senior leaders did when they came together in mid-May for the second annual "Leadership University" held in Scottsdale, AZ. During an intense four days, senior managers from across the health organization had the opportunity to discuss business priorities and overall strategies.

At last year's Leadership University, the company's leaders were introduced to the principles of high-performing organizations. This year's event built on that theme, with a focus on creating an environment in which employees want to perform at high levels. One important new initiative that received a lot of

attention during a series of intense breakout activity sessions was a new all-employee measurement tool called The Balanced Scorecard. Participants were asked to provide detailed input to the new scorecard, which is tentatively set to be rolled out throughout the organization in early 2001, replacing the current performance development review (PDR) form.

According to Human Resources Head Tracy South, The Balanced Scorecard is a performance tool that "measures what matters." The Balanced Scorecard, explained South, is currently being used successfully by numerous Fortune 500 companies including Mobil Oil. Once thoroughly refined and adapted to meet the unique needs of the health organization, the scorecard will provide employees with a line of sight from their day-to-day work to customer value.

The university maintained a fast pace throughout the three days as participants heard from senior management on critical issues.

President Mike Cardillo set the pace when he announced a pop technology quiz 15 minutes into the University's first general session. "This exam is designed to determine how well we all understand the awesome growth of electronic capability in the last 15 years," said Cardillo. "Our future is electronic capability."

With its full agenda, the Leadership University was one way of helping the organization look to the future so that Aetna U.S. Healthcare's leaders are prepared to support the workforce for the constant challenges we will continue to face as we create the opportunity for all Americans to live full and healthy lives.

◀ *Aetna Chairman Dick Huber shows students at Crockett Technical High School in Detroit how to use their new computers to find consumer health and medical information on the IntelliHealth® website. In April, Aetna U.S. Healthcare donated six new computers and accessories to help connect the school's labs, classrooms and libraries to the Internet.*

Figure 12–8 Another Sample of *Focus*, the Employee Newspaper. Courtesy of Aetna U.S. Healthcare, Blue Bell, Pennsylvania.

Figure 12–9 Quarterly Magazine, *Focus on People*. Courtesy of Aetna U.S. Healthcare, Blue Bell, Pennsylvania.

- a summary of the story in question and our position on it
- letters to all constituent groups
- talking points and telephone scripts
- questions and answers for use with the media

Broadcast e-mails are also proactively sent to all employees, hot-linked to the website content for more details. This rapid response system has been well received by employees. It has also increased the confidence they have that the company is going to equip them to deal with the challenges that arise every day.

Weekly Wrap-Up

The recently introduced *Weekly Wrap-Up* calls employee attention to the many developments or related news stories that occurred during the most recent week. Engrossed in the day-to-day demands of their jobs, it is likely that employees will miss some of what's gone on, particularly in other areas of the business. As a "push" technology, *Wrap-Up* brings the highlights together in one easy-to-read electronic communication that goes out on Friday afternoons (Figure 12–10).

The goal of these communications goes beyond building employee morale and recognition and keeping our people informed about relevant business matters. Internal communications is an effective tool for reinforcing the culture and values of Aetna U.S. Healthcare. Our internal communications are an integral part of our internal brand development process.

VISION AND VALUES

The brand is an important link between our mission or vision and our critical success factors or daily activities. We use our brand as an overall statement of the company's vision and values (Figure 12–11), reflecting what we stand for as a company and how we will delight our customers. In the same way that customers see our logo as the physical embodiment of the brand, the overall positioning of the brand translates words into actions. There is a cause-and-effect relationship between the company's vision and the various strategies employed to bring that vision to life.

In January 1999, the Aetna U.S. Healthcare senior management team, after a lengthy process of discussion and dialogue, developed a vision statement and supporting values that were broadcast to all employees in March. That vision statement captures what we believe will result from our collective efforts.

Figure 12–10 Internal *Weekly Wrap-Up*. Courtesy of Aetna U.S. Healthcare, Blue Bell, Pennsylvania.

Our Vision: *To create the opportunity for all Americans to live full and healthy lives.*

Our values help to frame this vision in terms of the commitments that we as a company and as individuals must make to see it fulfilled. Behind this statement came several "value assertions," proof points for the internal brand, and markers for

AETNA U.S. HEALTHCARE

Figure 12–11 Brand Showing Vision and Values. Courtesy of Aetna U.S. Healthcare, Blue Bell, Pennsylvania.

the employees to follow in common. These values included a pledge for health care quality and a commitment to building provider relationships; they explained how and why the company is innovative, performance-driven, and customer-focused. The value assertions also included a statement about the company's operational commitment to technology—a key component in turning the interior brand outward, which will be addressed later.

Our Values:

- *Aetna U.S. Healthcare People.* We recognize that our people create our success. We are committed to maximizing the power of the human spirit at Aetna U.S. Healthcare. We do this by valuing a diversity of people and ideas, by encouraging teamwork and cooperation, by providing ongoing opportunities for learning and growth, and by letting individuals define the boundaries of their career possibilities.
- *Customer Focus.* We seek to form long-term, mutually beneficial relationships with our customers where we create value by anticipating and exceeding customer expectations.
- *Pledge to Quality.* We pledge to raise the quality of health care in America. The needs and health of members are our priority. We will not compromise on medical excellence and we are committed to driving quality in a cost-effective manner.
- *Strong Provider Relationships.* We are committed to creating strong, effective, and lasting relationships with providers based on mutual respect and a shared commitment to high-quality, cost-effective health care for our members. Through the use of innovative technology and medical information, we are committed to supporting physicians in their desire to maximize the health of their patients.
- *Innovation and Creativity.* We challenge one another to look beyond the limits of today to create products, services, and solutions yet to be imagined.
- *Passion for Excellence.* We have an unrelenting drive to achieve excellence in our products, services, and approach to our work. We celebrate progress and reward commitment in our effort to continuously improve the products and service we deliver.
- *Integrity.* We demand honesty, decency, trust, and compliance in our relationships with customers, partners, and each other. We are committed to doing the right thing and matching our actions to the commitments we make.
- *Embrace Technology.* We are committed to making the innovative use of technology our competitive differential. We actively seek state-of-the-art solutions to business problems and embrace the effective use of technology throughout the organization.
- *Performance-Driven.* We approach our work with energy, intensity, and a focus on results. We hate bureaucracy and have a bias for action. We set aggressive goals for ourselves and each other and take individual accountability for achievement.

Learning Maps

Internal branding at Aetna U.S. Healthcare requires that employees understand the nature of the business we are in, not just from the perspective of their specific functions, but more broadly in terms of how outsiders view the industry—and our company as its premier representative.

In 1999, we introduced a series of "learning maps" (Figure 12–12) that are at the core of a companywide employee training program. The maps are used in group learning sessions during which employees walk through the history of managed care and the financial structure of the business (how revenue is generated and used to cover expenses).

Building the Brand Externally

In the public sphere, a strong corporate brand needs more than reputation management. In 1998, Aetna U.S. Healthcare began to take steps toward asserting a clear, *proactive* identity to the general consumer marketplace. Firm foundations had been laid in effective integration of new markets and employees, greatly assisted by a multilayered internal communications apparatus. Then, senior management believed, the time was right to reach out and, in the process, lay the groundwork for a redefinition of the value of managed care.

Key to this effort would be an integrated marketing communications approach, one that leveraged the synergies and resources of a number of disciplines and practices—media relations, advertising, and special events, as well as employee communications—all aimed at ensuring consistent delivery of positive messages to a broad spectrum of audiences.

An integrated communications strategy has the potential to generate the offensive strength needed to counterbalance negative opinions of the company. We believed that, by clearly exhibiting our considerable assets—in particular those rooted in our commitment to using technology to improve the quality of care—we might work toward a positive balance in the "trust bank" of public opinion. Moreover, integrated messages are the necessary fabric of a cohesive brand identity.

The underlying goal of our brand positioning is to increase customer satisfaction. Because Aetna U.S. Healthcare both integrates and packages health care services, our customer base includes a broad spectrum of constituents such as individual members, employers, and health care providers, each with different needs, attitudes, and wants. We believe that to satisfy and delight all of our customers, our brand must convey a consistent message to a variety of different audiences.

Our external constituents include a huge market of current and potential customers. The term *customer* is used in the broadest sense, to include plan sponsors (employers), providers (physicians, hospitals, ancillary health care service professionals), producers (the brokers and agents who compose a key distribution channel for our products and services), members, VIPs (politicians, regulators, associations, media), and shareholders. Because their perspectives on us as a company are often linked to their experiences with us, it is critical that we understand what they value and work to deliver our messages to them in the most effective way possible.

After considerable research and experience, we have formulated the following branding elements that we want to convey in the marketplace:

- *simplicity*
- *access*
- *choice*
- *quality*
- *information*

Figure 12–12 Learning Maps for Employee Training. Courtesy of Aetna U.S. Healthcare, Blue Bell, Pennsylvania.

As is the case with any branding initiative, we need to "walk the talk" with regard to these characteristics if we are going to be persuasive. The best-conceived advertising campaign will fall on deaf ears if our reputation in the market is not consistent with what we are telling people. That means that it must be simple for providers and members alike to interact with us. Our paperwork must be minimal and efficient. Calls must be promptly and accurately responded to. Our networks must be big enough that members will truly have a choice among providers, and we must be easy to reach and offer a wide variety of products that facilitate a wide range of customer flexibility. Quality must be our number one priority, evidenced by programs and services that meet our members' health care needs with high-quality providers and processes.

Finally, as we enter the 21st century, we want our brand to convey the importance we place on getting consumers the information they need when they need it, and in the most efficient way possible so that they can make appropriate choices for themselves and their families. We also understand that the health care marketplace is increasingly focused on the consumer. A study by Yankelovich reports that more than three-quarters of all U.S. adults believe that people should take primary responsibility for their own health, without relying so much on doctors. We want the Aetna U.S. Healthcare brand to signify choice, access, helpful information, and simplicity, and for the consumer to be *empowered* by this. Our goal here is for Aetna U.S. Healthcare to be identified as a progressive company that goes beyond its impressive array of products and services to provide a wide range of information that really can help people lead full and healthy lives.

Of course, the antimanaged care backdrop looms large in our external branding activity as well. In recent years, our industry has found itself in a defensive position. In 1998, the President of Aetna U.S. Healthcare and the Chairman of Aetna both determined that we would take a more aggressive stand, reaching out to key constituents and critics in a way that brought visibility to the positive side of our business and helped to cushion any negative coverage that might arise during the year. That seemingly simple yet ultimately profound change of direction resulted in the implementation of a major strategy shift and a unique set of tactics.

In the Media

One of our first steps was to introduce *soft outreach* with trade and business media. We took some basic managed care activities—prevention and health management—that are uniquely well handled by Aetna U.S. Healthcare and prepared media alerts to let them know about our capabilities. We offered them our medical experts as resources for these and related stories. Our goal was to raise awareness of the positive programs and services that managed care offers as well as to position ourselves as a resource to the media. Both goals would help to present our company and our industry in a more positive light with the media and, through the stories they reported, with the public at large.

A few examples of the outreach include:

- *Poison control*—how to avoid poison-related accidents in the home and how to respond if they occur. We also created a link to our website that enables visitors to download and print these tips for their reference and use.
- *Childhood immunizations*—Aetna U.S. Healthcare regularly sends reminders to parents of young children to ensure that they receive the appropriately scheduled immunizations.

- *Stress management*—some of the signs of stress and how to help reduce them, including a particular emphasis on the workplace.

In addition to the consumer-oriented stories, we have begun to cultivate trade reporters in two critical areas, technology and women's health. The Aetna Foundation donated $7 million over three years to the American Heart Association to help raise awareness that, despite the fact that heart disease is the leading killer of women, many steps can be taken to reduce risk. Our Women's Health Program addresses heart disease as well as a number of other health issues, including menopause and early cancer detection through Pap checks and mammograms. Also, our L'il Appleseeds® maternity management program helps to manage and improve the outcome of high-risk pregnancies.

Perhaps our biggest story, however, is in the area of health data information and how it can be used to manage care. Our USQA affiliate supports the largest health care database in the country, providing analyses to physicians that help them meet the health care needs of their patients, our members. Again, we have been able to position Aetna U.S. Healthcare spokespeople as resources to the media. They now reach out to us for input on stories they are writing in addition to those that we helped generate through our outreach to them. An added advantage of this burgeoning relationship is that it may give us the opportunity to present our position on what would otherwise be a negative story from our perspective. We are hoping to reinforce our brand via an improved relationship with the people who help to form public opinion.

On the Web—Aetna U.S. Healthcare in Action

The Aetna U.S. Healthcare website had historically been directed toward members and to providing them with online capabilities such as DocFind,® an electronic directory to our managed care providers, and EZenroll,® which enables members to enroll for our various managed care products and select their primary care physicians online. In addition we have included marketing information about our products and markets.

More recently, as the competitive environment has become more challenging and the demand for electronic communications has grown, we have added a feature to our website entitled "Aetna U.S. Healthcare in Action" (Figure 12–13). Highlighted on the home page, this section provides direct links to breaking stories and our responses to them or to new product or service highlights designed to anticipate and meet the needs of our members and other key audiences.

Public Affairs Program

Conceived in 1999, our Public Affairs Program builds on the work the company has historically done to more actively and specifically engage our employees as spokespeople for the company. We know that putting a face on managed care will help to reinforce our brand proposition in a number of ways. Among the most important is that it becomes more difficult for the public to disparage a system that is neither remote nor disinterested but that, in fact, comprises their friends and neighbors, the health care providers they are inclined to consider heroic in other environments, and, in general, people like themselves who are dedicated to doing their own jobs well.

Welcome to
Aetna U.S. Healthcare®

Aetna U.S. Healthcare is a leading provider of managed health care benefits, indemnity health care benefits, dental, pharmacy, vision and group insurance coverage.

For **Members & Consumers**

For **Employers**

For **Providers**

DocFind®
PROVIDER DIRECTORY

EZenroll
online enrollment

InteliHealth®
The Trusted Source™
for Health Information

Click below for two million pages of information for healthier living...

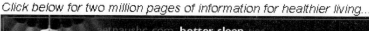

aetnaushc.com **better sleep** tips

InteliHealth **Ætna** US Healthcare

Aetna US Healthcare®
In Action | News & Views | In Your State | Your Health | About Us

Outage Notice: please note that DocFind® will be unavailable on Sunday, 11/7/99, due to maintenance.

Aetna U.S. Healthcare® Launches New Ad Campaign to Empower Consumers Through Use of Information on Internet

CareData Results Are In!
Aetna U.S. Healthcare® Members Rated our New Jersey HMO #1 in Overall Member Satisfaction!

Aetna U.S. Healthcare® Expands EZLink™ Capabilities and Broadens Market

"health.e.nation™" from Aetna U.S. Healthcare® Mobile Exhibit Launched in New York City.
In one of its most innovative and exciting initiatives ever, Aetna U.S. Healthcare unveiled its state-of-the-art, multi-media *"health.e.nation"* mobile exhibit Sept. 28 in New York City.

Figure 12–13 Aetna U.S. Healthcare Internet Web Page. Courtesy of Aetna U.S. Healthcare, Blue Bell, Pennsylvania.

We have begun the program by training medical directors and senior executives. All are being trained to speak with the media, diffuse confrontations, and make the points that are important to us within the framework of a story. Once these spokespeople have been trained, we will focus the efforts of our media and public relations staffs on identifying speaking opportunities for them so that they are not exclusively involved in defensive situations. We anticipate drilling down through management in all areas of the company to train employees to make effective presentations in group and one-on-one situations, and we will trumpet their successes throughout the organization.

IMPLEMENTING A MANAGED CARE BRAND FOR THE 21ST CENTURY

e.Health from Aetna U.S. Healthcare™

As we begin the new millennium, Aetna U.S. Healthcare's identity is being refined through a brand initiative called *e.Health from Aetna U.S. Healthcare™:* a concept that today forms the nexus of the company's integrated information, health care, and technology operations.

Currently, *e.Health* is a term used to distinguish a constellation of Aetna U.S. Healthcare products, services, and attributes linked through a common dependence on information technology. *e.Health* encompasses products for members, providers, and payers, including DocFind,® an online service that allows members to easily locate participating network providers and other services; E-Pay, a system that enables the company to rapidly process provider's claims and referrals; and EZLink, an integrated human resources management system that combines health and related employee benefits with payroll services in a single, web-based platform.

e.Health also helps position some core competencies that have remained in the background in the midst of the managed care debate. Foremost among these is USQA, Aetna U.S. Healthcare's research affiliate that uses the world's largest health care database to improve disease management programs. Also included is InteliHealth, Aetna U.S. Healthcare's online health information affiliate (Figure 12–14).

Beyond all this, however, *e.Health* has the potential to signify Aetna U.S. Healthcare's identity as a company dedicated to improving the quality of health care in America through the aggregation, analysis, and distribution of health care information to members, providers, and consumers. In this context, the company is branded as a knowledge source on issues that "matter most," and as a mediator of quality practices throughout the industry. By foregrounding business trends such as e-commerce, knowledge management, and information marketing, *e.Health* could play a role in adjusting popular opinion toward a consideration of managed health care as a responsive, quality-driven service industry.

Further, we believe that a brand initiative like *e.Health* can be a platform for articulating the company's mission and aspirations by motivating internal audi-

Figure 12–14   e.Health from Aetna U.S. Healthcare Logo. Courtesy of Aetna U.S. Healthcare, Blue Bell, Pennsylvania.

ences while displaying a unified, cohesive image to the company's many stakeholder groups. For instance:

- *For Members.* Not only does *e.Health* offer products that facilitate remote and continuous interaction with members, it also represents the company's commitment to using its knowledge base and the most advanced technology to manage the delivery of quality health care.
- *For Employers and Plan Sponsors. e.Health* can be used to show employers that Aetna is an advanced business-to-business partner, contributing to their profitability and employee satisfaction through network inclusion and technology solutions.
- *For Providers.* Providers will be shown that the company is both modern and modernizing—that is, a company that will make the business of health care quality-focused. *e.Health* will also make their job easier by delivering timely information to improve care.
- *For Investors and the Financial Community.* Shareholder value is increasingly dependent upon intangibles such as knowledge production and brand equity.
- *For Consumers.* Information can be used to build a *consumer community*— and thus a line of support and defense around a brand.

Supportive Advertising

Mass media advertising is used to communicate the consumer advantages of *e.Health*, which gives consumers access to valuable health care information and the ability to do much of their health business on line. Recently, in an innovative print campaign, simple but cleverly arranged photos of a computer mouse were used to illustrate that we conveniently make available information about childbirth, stress reduction, dental care, pediatric health, cholesterol, and other health topics (Figure 12–15).

And in our new national television advertising campaign, narratives of everyday life are punctuated by high-tech devices, to underline the need for health care information and to associate that need with Aetna U.S. Healthcare/*e.Health* branding. For example:

It's a bright sunny day as the Little Leaguer at the plate focuses intently on the pitch coming toward him. As he swings and laces a hit toward the outfield, his coach goes berserk shouting instructions to the base runner at second.

Suddenly, the action stops and a computer menu appears on the television screen. An unseen mouse scrolls down and clicks on "high blood pressure."

The action resumes as the base runner goes into a slide only to find his way blocked short of home plate as he makes contact with the catcher. The action freezes again, and this time the mouse clicks on "pediatricians" from the menu.

Again action resumes and television viewers now see the umpire unbelievably call the runner safe. The menu appears again, and this time the mouse clicks on "hallucination."

Finally, a key message: "e.Health from Aetna U.S. Healthcare™, information for healthier living."

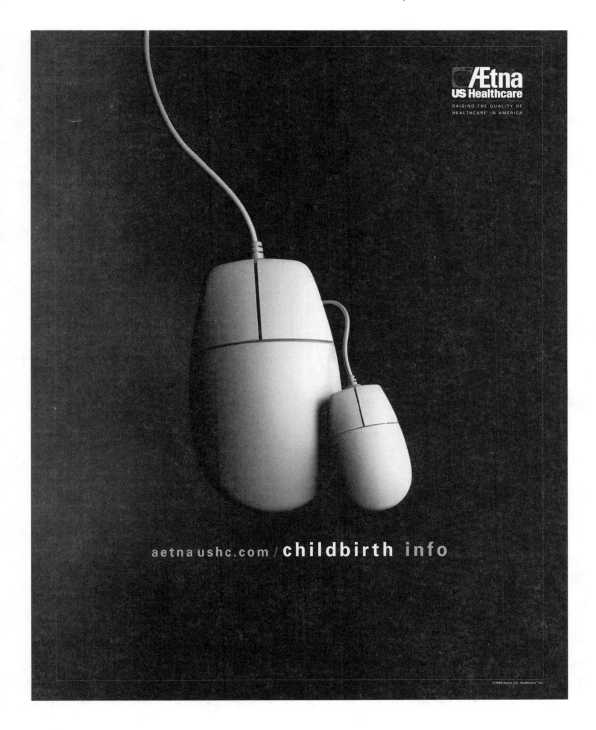

Figure 12–15 Sample Print Advertisement. Courtesy of Aetna U.S. Healthcare, Blue Bell, Pennsylvania.

health.e.nation

The centerpiece of the *e.Health* brand initiative—and, we believe, a landmark in managed care marketing—is the *health.e.nation* Mobile Exhibition (Figures 12–16 and 12–17). Aetna U.S. Healthcare is bringing to towns around the country an 800-square-foot interactive "experience," targeting community and opinion leaders, employers, providers, and health care consumers. The exhibit will make appearances in "town squares" and at major events in all of our major markets.

The mobile exhibit will include a theater experience and several interactive stations that will not only help deliver important information but will do so in a meaningful and memorable way. Most important, as we bring the exhibit from city to city, we will call upon our own employees to host and organize the exhibit and surrounding events with a goal of maximizing the number and categories of visitors who come through the exhibit.

Inside, each interactive component of the exhibit defines and illustrates the experience of the health care consumer in terms of both current Aetna U.S. Healthcare services and projections into the future of health care. Thus, for example, a component on information access and consumer wellness features an interactive display based on InteliHealth and descriptions of Aetna's Member Health Management capabilities, while at the same time looking ahead to further enhance-

Figure 12–16 *health.e.nation* Mobile Exhibition. Courtesy of Aetna U.S. Healthcare, Blue Bell, Pennsylvania.

Figure 12–17 *health.e.nation* Exhibit. Courtesy of Aetna U.S. Healthcare, Blue Bell, Pennsylvania.

ments in health communications through high technology. A section on medical treatment highlights ways information technology has changed the relationship between doctors and patients, while looking ahead to the future of real-time telemedicine.

In addition, we will have the opportunity in each market to invite VIPs for a private showing of the exhibit and discussion of any of a variety of issues or developments that we think are of particular note or concern to our key audiences. Media-trained management staff will be well-positioned to participate in the three- to five-day events in each location. And, a team of local employees will work together to identify and invite the constituent groups to whom they want to deliver specific messages, to generate advance publicity for the exhibit and maximize the number of visitors, and to host the exhibit and answer questions about Aetna U.S. Healthcare and the purpose of *health.e.nation*, etc. As they become actively engaged in supporting this initiative, finding ways in which it will be of particular value to their market, their customers or themselves, employees will find themselves developing an ownership interest in the exhibit itself.

We will be seeking a variety of ways to generate visibility for the tour and to more broadly communicate some of its messages to an audience beyond the tens of thousands of visitors we expect to reach directly. For this purpose, we expect to use a *health.e.nation* website that will provide information on tour locations, upcoming schedule, content, video footage of the events from city to city, etc. Direct mail pieces promoting the tour but also containing some of the "proof points" we want to raise to our detractors will also be prepared for local market use. Perhaps the biggest impact we might have, however, is in our face-to-face meetings with VIPs in each community we visit. While some people (plan sponsors, providers) are already predisposed to liking us, this will be an opportunity to meet with others in a relaxed, entertaining, but also educational venue for the purpose of exchanging ideas and looking ahead to the future of health care and managed care.

The goal is to create a physical presence for the brand unlike any in the health care industry, and to use that presence as a platform for delivering a cogent argument in support of the overall brand strategy. The argument is expressed in terms of a progression of specific message points:

1. Through information technology, Americans have become empowered health care consumers.
2. Managed care facilitates the empowerment of the health care consumer.
3. In the future, health care consumers, providers, health plans, and hospitals will interact more effectively using technology.
4. Aetna U.S. Healthcare is at the technology forefront of the health care industry.

Like the brand it is used to represent, the primary role of the *health.e.nation* mobile exhibition is to serve as a mechanism for building relationships—with our customers, with our investors, and with the communities where we do business. In each market, influentials from civic leadership and the corporate community are invited for private viewings of the exhibit, as well as for discussions on important issues or developments having to do with managed care and the company's presence in the community.

At each location, local management is trained to participate in the events, which take place during three-to-five day periods. Teams of local employees are used to identify and invite key audiences, to host the exhibit during consumer visits, and to generate advance publicity. Even though the tour is coordinated from national corporate headquarters, employees find ways for *health.e.nation* to be of particular value to their market, and they have themselves developed a sense of ownership in the project. They have become true brand ambassadors.

In a sense, then, *health.e.nation* can be seen as a true embodiment of Aetna U.S. Healthcare's corporate brand. It integrates markets and business units with a common event and a common message platform. It brings together employees in various markets through an identifiable and *positive* national brand. And it makes tangible the identity of Aetna U.S. Healthcare as a progressive company that goes beyond its impressive array of products and services to provide a wide range of information that really can help people lead full and healthy lives.

CONCLUSION

There is a tremendous amount of activity under way at Aetna U.S. Healthcare that is directed to reinforcing and establishing our brand credibility in the minds of our constituents. Many things about a brand evolve over time, from its basic proposition to its visual representation to the successful implementation of key branding proof points as the company becomes more proficient at "walking the talk." Key to that brand's success, however, will be consistency of message and reinforcement across all constituents, including the company's own employees.

Health care and managed care are enmeshed in some truly challenging times. Close scrutiny by the media makes even more difficult the task of communicating critical messages to key audiences without losing or watering down those messages. Using a variety of media and taking a comprehensive approach to branding are essential to Aetna U.S. Healthcare as we work at improving public perception and building loyalty to and trust in our own brand.

Our brand translates the vision of Aetna U.S. Healthcare into the strategies and activities that will delight our broad array of constituents. We have taken significant steps over the past year to build our brand internally and to build equity with our customers, partners, and shareholders. There is a cause-and-effect relationship between our vision and actions, and the brand serves as a critical two-way linkage between our vision as a company and how we will satisfy our customers. Creating this linkage through our brand-building activities has been our focus to date. As we move forward and start to build additional equity in our brand, we will need to place greater emphasis on managing our brand by measuring our success in the marketplace through various customer metrics. This will be our challenge in the future.

Lessons Learned

- We have learned that an integrated communications strategy has the potential to generate the strength needed to counterbalance negative opinions of the company. We understood that by clearly exhibiting our considerable assets—in particular those rooted in our commitment to using technology to improve the quality of care—we might work toward a positive balance in the "trust bank" of public opinion. Moreover, integrated messages are the necessary fabric of a cohesive brand identity.
- We also found that messaging itself could be quite complex when dealing with a company such as Aetna U.S. Healthcare. For any corporate brand, consideration must be made to the needs and concerns of all stakeholders—that is, any group or individual with interests that intersect those of the company. We had already seen how various stakeholder groups—members, employees, employers, providers, VIPs, and shareholders—all had to be considered during brand integration. Working proactively, consideration was also given to employers and plan sponsors, the company's direct business customers. And, of course, the media had to be considered, in this instance to be used as a conduit to other audiences rather than as an opponent.
- We began to reach out beyond corporate stakeholders to a much broader constituency in the consumer marketplace. While Aetna U.S. Healthcare deals mostly with corporate customers and plan sponsors, we came to understand that our image—how the corporate identity is perceived—affects millions of Americans.
- Advertising, Internet, and direct marketing have to be woven together to fit this consumer-centric strategy. A new approach to media relations was put in place as well. We began reaching beyond health care business reporters—many of whom have entrenched positions in the managed care debate—to

print, broadcast, and online media with focuses other than health care and with a bias toward providing interesting and useful information to consumers. These included lifestyle, health/fitness/wellness, women's issues, and technology media.

Our bottom line was that integrating communications and messages to all of our internal and external constituent groups would become the best way for us to establish and reinforce our brand promise to them.

Chapter 13

The American Cancer Society: Creating and Managing an Institutional Brand for a Voluntary Health Organization

Cynthia Currence and Steven D. Dickinson

The American Cancer Society (ACS), established more than 85 years ago, is now the nation's largest voluntary health organization. Its activities are in direct support of a singular but complex mission—to eliminate cancer as a major health problem through research, public education, advocacy, and service. The organization's current name was adopted in the mid-1940s. The modern logo was developed and implemented organization-wide in the early 1980s. Today, the American Cancer Society name, by virtue of its high public recognition and strong association with a universally identified public health issue, has become a strong nonprofit brand— even before the Society recognized it as such. ***The ACS has more recently begun systematic activities designed to nurture and develop the power of this brand recognition, in order to enhance accomplishment of its mission.***

WHY ENHANCE THIS NONPROFIT BRAND?

Recognizing the marketing power of the American Cancer Society's name and logo, and capitalizing on its potential for differentiating the organization amidst a sea of other charities, is vitally important for both the productivity and the protection of the American Cancer Society.

It is estimated that there are more than 800 organizations with the word "cancer" in their names now listed with the Internal Revenue Service. Most of these cancer organizations are legitimate and productive. Some are not. In any case, a public organization's first responsibility to its constituents and to its mission is to remain viable—hence the need to differentiate its special attributes to the public to ensure its continued support. Moreover, an entity such as the American Cancer Society need a means of assuring members of the public as to the authenticity of the organization, to prevent less scrupulous organizations from trading on its name recognition and intercepting donations intended for the good works of the ACS.

The ACS brand is also now frequently sought by for-profit companies for partnerships that have the potential for supporting their business goals, while at the same time creating significant benefits for the Society. Nationwide, marketing-based partnerships with corporations are a relatively new line of activity for the ACS. While they hold great potential for enhancing the organization's ability to accomplish its mission, they also must be managed intelligently, with a new and sophisticated approach to brand management, in order to avoid any implication of conflict of interest, damage to credibility, or implied product endorsement. Consequently, the volunteer and staff leadership of the American Cancer Society have dedicated themselves to better understanding the strength and value of the American Cancer Society name and how to protect it.

ACS BRAND ATTRIBUTES

The strength of this nonprofit brand lies in the urgency of the cause, the number of people affected by cancer, broad and favorable name recognition, strong public trust, and a track record of positively influencing consumer and public health behavior that has saved hundreds of thousands of lives. According to a 1998 Gallup study, cancer is the number one health concern of Americans. Epidemiological studies show that one in every four Americans will contract cancer at some point in their lives. The disease will touch the life of virtually every American. The 1998 Gallup study also indicates that the American Cancer Society enjoys a 96 percent aided name recognition among the American public and is a more trusted source of cancer information than even the respondents' personal physician.

The American Cancer Society has an impressive track record in its ability to positively influence consumer health-related behaviors. Medical professionals attribute the acceptance of the Pap smear as a routine feature of every woman's health exam to the American Cancer Society's grass roots mobilization in the 1940s. Similarly, dramatic reductions in adult smoking, the acceptance of mammography, and quality standards for mammography facilities are all largely attributed to the efforts of the American Cancer Society. With scientific evidence showing that fully two-thirds of cancers in humans are related to individual behavioral choices, the organization's demonstrated ability to influence consumer behavior is not only a core capability, it may well be its key brand equity point.

Other American Cancer Society brand strengths include the size of its donor base (18 million), the quality of its scientific research (28 Nobel Prize winners funded), and the community-based structure of the organization, which enables it to reach 100 percent of the general population.

THE DEVELOPMENT OF A BRAND MANAGEMENT FUNCTION

The American Cancer Society has a strong appreciation for the value of its name and exercises several important brand management practices to protect it. To further institutionalize the cultivation of this important corporate property, the organization is in the process of developing a formal brand management structure, strategy, and process. The process begins with research designed to further understand the attributes of the ACS brand. What makes the brand strong? How must we protect, maintain, and grow brand strength? The organization is putting significant energy into this process, since the Society's leadership firmly believes that strong name and reputation contribute immeasurably to the organization's ability to influence cancer risk behavior and generate the funds necessary to fulfill the promise of eliminating cancer and alleviating suffering.

To further the process, the organization has formulated branding and communications strategies that will be integral to maintaining the equity of the ACS brand:

- Understand the fundamental elements of ACS brand strength.
- Communicate the importance of brand management to internal audiences

and build support for methods of maintaining and growing the value of the brand.

- Build relationships with key external constituents (versus a mass marketing approach).
- Negotiate strategic win/win relationships with a limited number of appropriate corporate partners.
- Differentiate ACS from other organizations in the cancer niche.
- Monitor the power of the fundamental elements of ACS brand strength.
- Maintain a proactive system of crisis and reputation management.

Building on the development of overarching strategies for protecting and furthering the brand, the American Cancer Society developed a system for categorical brand management, including (1) market research and counsel relating to the health of the brand to staff and volunteer leadership; (2) specific internal program planning models that foster consistency in the organization's external communications and visual identity; and (3) tracking processes to monitor the major strengths of the brand.

Tactical elements that support the brand management system include:

- Graphics Standard Manual
- Marketing Planning Guidebook
- Corporate relations criteria
- Crisis management team
- Spokesperson training
- Turnkey promotional manuals for key promotional properties

Ongoing brand-tracking efforts include:

- Regular image studies and competitive analyses
- Behavioral change outcomes resulting from programs and corporate alliances

Partnerships and Tactics That Support the ACS Mission and Establish the Brand

The American Cancer Society's three-tiered mission of offering advocacy and education services, providing patient services, and furthering cancer research is reflected in the organization's recent public outreach programs. In the spring of 1996, the American Cancer Society unveiled a partnership with the Florida Department of Citrus (the Florida State association of orange juice growers and producers). This program is now an ongoing nationwide education campaign calling attention to the ACS message on the role good nutrition plays in preventing cancer. The campaign is staged in grocery stores across the country, supported by national and local advertising and promotion.

Through this campaign, ACS has communications power never before available to the organization for informing the public about its nutritional guidelines. In addition to funding the cost of the campaign, the Florida Department of Citrus makes an annual unrestricted grant to the American Cancer Society for its overall programs in research, education, and patient service. The ACS logo appears in advertising, in point of purchase displays, and on some store brand packaging of Florida orange juice.

Figure 13–1 Example of the Florida Citrus Campaign Brochure. Courtesy of the American Cancer Society, Atlanta, Georgia.

ACS has an established mission to inform the public about the role good nutrition plays in preventing cancer. In all programming relating to this subject, the partnership is careful never to suggest that one food has special cancer-fighting properties over another. The message is that a balanced diet with a variety of foods, featuring those high in fiber and low in fat as well as lots of fruits and vegetables, has been shown to reduce cancer risk. In the campaign with the Florida orange growers, ACS is given the opportunity to communicate this message to the public. Orange juice is positioned as one way to introduce fruit to this balanced diet.

The advertising and promotional campaigns funded by the Florida Department of Citrus have given ACS a new means for leveraging its brand to reach millions of consumers with its nutrition guidelines (Figure 13–1). The link between diet and cancer has heretofore not been well understood by the general public, despite the fact that perhaps a third of all cancer deaths are diet related. This increase in awareness will have long-term impact on the number of lives that can be saved from needless cancer.

The ACS also has a long-term partnership with a consumer pharmaceutical company marketing nicotine replacement products that aid smokers in quitting the habit. This partnership also creates a nationwide education and awareness program—on the subject of smoking cessation. Included in this partnership is the corporation's support of the Great American Smokeout, ACS's long-running program urging Americans to go smoke-free.

ACS has documented outstanding increases in participation of its tobacco control public education efforts since the commencement of the partnership. In the very first period in which ACS's corporate partner sponsored the Great American Smokeout, ACS reached 122 million adults, including 30 million smokers, with partnership-funded ads. That year, 26 percent of all smokers in the United States tried to quit or reduce their smoking—an increase from only 18 percent the year before. This increase is solely attributable to the partnership, since Smokeout participation has been declining in the last several years (Figure 13–2).

The American Cancer Society has noted that if everything that is already known about cancer prevention and treatment was applied universally, we could reduce the current rate of cancer death by perhaps two-thirds. The power of the American Cancer Society brand has energized partnerships with corporations into mutually beneficial relationships that accomplish business objectives for the corporate partner, while offering the ACS an exciting new line of activities that have created an entirely new platform from which to communicate to the public and save lives from cancer.

Leveraging Volunteers To Build the Brand

The American Cancer Society recognizes that one of its greatest resources for growing its brand are the more than one million volunteers who work at the grassroots level in support of the ACS mission. These are the people who hang posters on grammar school walls educating students about why they shouldn't smoke. They speak to high school girls about the importance of breast self-exams. And they help raise money to further the research efforts that ACS conducts.

The volunteers who take time out of their personal lives to work on behalf of the ACS mission grow the brand through the heartfelt work they do to benefit the health of their community and that of the general population. This type of branding is priceless and practically immeasurable because it results from passionate and caring individuals who work tirelessly because they believe in the cause, not because they get paid.

Figure 13–2 Example of the Smoke-Out Poster. Courtesy of the American Cancer Society, Atlanta, Georgia.

Investing in Scientific Research

The American Cancer Society sets itself apart from the many other cancer organizations through its major contributions to scientific research. A case in point is the identification of the gene that causes breast cancer—one of the most important cancer research discoveries of the decade. The American Cancer Society funded this research. As in this instance, each time a major advancement is made that is funded by ACS, the brand receives visibility through the media and the publication of the research findings.

Challenges to Effective Brand Management

The American Cancer Society, like many similar organizations with large and diverse constituencies, faces numerous internal and external challenges to effective brand management.

Major Internal Challenges to Effective Brand Management

1. *Complex Organizational Structure and Decentralized Decision Making.* The ACS has recently simplified its structure by reducing the size of the Board of Directors from over 250 members to 43 and reducing the number of regional offices from 57 to 17. It has also developed a process for clarifying roles between volunteers and staff and between national and regional operations. Even with these efforts to simplify the structure and focus decision making, the organization is still complicated. Strategic decisions cannot be imposed on the organization nationwide by some dictatorial centralized hierarchy. The organization is characterized by a great deal of local autonomy and consensus-style decision making. Organizations with this kind of complex decision making must guard against critical delays in actions needed to protect or grow the brand.

2. *Organizational Understanding of Brand Management Concepts and Practices.* The American Cancer Society leadership is notably strong in many respects, including the medical sciences, scientific research, legal counsel, solicitation strategies, and financial operations. Branding and brand management concepts represent relatively new territory for American Cancer Society volunteer and staff leadership, and these concepts are not broadly understood. Key milestones in proper brand management are on the horizon for the American Cancer Society, including the establishment of a formal structure and process for brand management.

Organizations must develop consistent and broad agreements among all internal constituencies about: (1) what the brand stands for; (2) what constitutes the brand's strength; (3) which strategies are best to maintain these strengths; (4) goals for public image and perception; and (5) evaluation strategies to measure success. Brand management must enjoy a high management priority and be properly funded so as to conduct appropriate trend tracking, competitive analysis, monitoring and measurement of key brand strengths, evaluation measures, and the initiation of personnel incentives related to compliance with brand management guidelines and policies.

3. *Integration of Marketing and Communications Activities across the Organization.* Although organizations may have a common logo, graphics standards, and an umbrella message designed to be woven into all external communications, there should be a formal and enforced integration of the activities of all business areas with the marketing and communications strategies of the organization. Business units within the organization should not have the autonomy to create images and messages that are relevant solely to their own specific objectives. Instead, they should employ those common themes, images, and strategies that enhance the overall organizational brand.

4. Multiple Internal and External Constituents with Varying Needs and Agendas. The American Cancer Society is fortunate to have over a million volunteers and approximately 4,000 staff serving all communities in the United States. Although it receives little government funding, the organization strives to complement the work of federal and local health agencies. It also works with the numerous other cancer organizations, coalitions, and cancer centers to further the fight against cancer. These various individuals and organizations do not all approach the cancer cause in the same way nor do they all agree on the priority points of focus. While there is great opportunity offered by the synergy of coalitions, care should be taken to retain the ownership of attributes specific to the organization.

5. Defining Consumer Value. When a consumer goes into a store and puts down cash for a pair of jeans, he or she has a specific point of reference from which brand value is assigned—they are satisfied with the product they've purchased or they are not. Their perception of the brand is driven by the transaction. For nonprofit organizations like voluntary health organizations, brand perception is not necessarily tied to a specific transaction. A person's decision to donate to the American Cancer Society is not necessarily connected to a service they might have received, but to a collection of often intangible, unconnected impressions about the organization's mission, efficiency, and personality. The most powerful points of value that people receive from the American Cancer Society are intangible. The thing people want most from the American Cancer Society is progress toward a cure and reason to hope that cancer won't touch their lives. They also expect the best, unbiased information about the disease. Finally, they expect "help" if they or their families are touched by cancer. Most of these ACS "products" are difficult to quantify. However, the ACS provides a number of products and services to cancer patients that create lasting impressions, like the gift pack, moral support, and rehabilitation instructions that the ACS delivers to mastectomy and other breast cancer surgery patients. Patients respond with remarkable gratitude, and such gestures often result in a lasting bond between the patient and the organization. In any case, creating brand value in the eyes of consumers is far more complex than for forprofit corporations.

6. Accountability. Although the image and reputation of the organization are very important to all volunteers and staff, and contributing to a strong reputation is a organizational goal that should be shared by everyone, ultimate responsibility for cultivating and protecting the ACS brand rests with a single, identifiable, and accountable person or department. As with the ACS, that department is usually marketing or corporate communications. This should not be perceived as a "control" issue. By establishing accountability, however, the entire organization can benefit from a centralized and well-resourced capability for conducting research and translating data into guidelines that are shared and consistent.

7. Differentiation is Difficult. Independent market research studies indicate that the public identifies the American Cancer Society as the leader in various activities related to the cancer cause. This is because the organization's name is so much better known than others are and consumer trust in the Society is so high.

However, people generally cannot list those programs and services the organization delivers, nor can they describe those attributes or offerings that make ACS outstanding in relationship to any other organization in the cancer arena. This is a competitively vulnerable position. Organizations in this situation need to leverage the strengths of their public recognition and trust and create means for focusing public attention on a few important but specific organizational points of uniqueness. Failure to do so can give rise to a situation where donations and support are mistakenly directed to another organization, simply because the name sounded like The American Cancer Society. Thus, the ACS goes to great lengths to ensure that it is represented correctly on all projects, programs, and collateral materials, in addition to protecting its overall image by selecting its associations and partnerships carefully.

8. Relationship-Building. The American Cancer Society is shifting from a one-size-fits-all mass marketing approach to the universe of potential constituents in favor of one in which public appeals are tailored to specific audiences. The belief is that if the organization can build personalized relationships with individuals as they come in contact with the organization, it can do the most to build commitment to the brand. However, these efforts require investment and planning across every facet of the organization. This strategy is borne out in the ACS's many campaigns targeted to young audiences. The messages are constructed with the audience in mind and the medium is chosen to resonate with a specific age group. Young people who have been exposed to posters and brochures throughout their school years then have a personal, long-term relationship with the organization, which is a solid foundation for the ACS's future dealings with them as consumers.

Major External Challenges to Effective Brand Management

1. Fast Pace of Change. We operate in a rapidly changing social, economic, technological, charitable, and medical environment. All of these changes bring unique challenges, threats, and opportunities for the organization. The ACS has increased the degree of speed with which it can track, interpret, and act on these changes, because this directly affects its ability to maintain strength, viability, and relevancy.

2. Increase in Competition. The number of nonprofit organizations has been growing steadily over the past decade and there has been nothing less than an explosion in the number of not-for-profit organizations in the cancer niche. There are over 800 groups registered with the Internal Revenue Service as 501(c)(3) organizations with the word "cancer" in their names. Although about half of these cancer niche entrants are very small, several are significant in size and savvy in marketing. With the level of competition increasing so much, the need for differentiation is critical.

The American Cancer Society conducts a biannual image-tracking study to measure the public perceptions of the urgency of the cancer cause and the public's recognition and trust of the organization's name. Epidemiology and market research studies are used to track behavior changes related to ACS activities in cancer risk reduction and early detection. Competitive analyses are conducted to compare the social effect of American Cancer Society programs with the achievements of other organizations in the field. All of these intelligence-gathering activities are consolidated and interpreted by a panel of seasoned professionals to identify urgent implications and issues on which the American Cancer Society should act.

Lessons Learned

The American Cancer Society has initiated the first in an ongoing attempt to monitor the health of its brand. It has recruited a number of external experts to respond to various brand-related questions for the purpose of formulating additional recommendations for the organization to consider regarding the ongoing process of maturing brand management strategies and practices.

In the course of the American Cancer Society's first venture into the world of branding, the organization has learned some valuable lessons about the complexity of the branding and communications processes:

- Structurally and culturally complex organizations cannot impose strategic decisions through a centralized hierarchy. They must be characterized by a great deal of consensus development honoring local autonomy.
- If branding is new to the leadership of an organization, proponents of brand management must invest appropriate amounts of time in education so that these concepts are well understood and appreciated before they are forwarded through the organization.
- Integration of marketing and communications activities across the organization is key to successful brand management.
- Nonprofit organizations cannot borrow directly from brand management theory designed for the profit sector. Nonprofit brand perception is not generally tied to a specific type of transaction, as it may be for the profit sector. It is built on a collection of often intangible and unconnected impressions about the organization's mission, efficiency, and personality. Such perceptions are not as easily quantifiable, but today's sophisticated measurement instruments are able to capture a significant portion of those impressions.
- Organizations must be able to keep up with the speed of change in the social, economic, technological, charitable, and medical environments. The ability to track, interpret, and act on these changes directly affects an organization's ability to maintain strength, viability, and relevancy.
- Volunteers can be a key component of brand growth and extension for nonprofit organizations.
- Brand management is pivotal to a nonprofit organization's ability to compete for share of mind and dollar.

Overall, the branding experience for the American Cancer Society has been a necessary and positive one. The organization is committed to the continuation of this essential process, and the marketing and communications departments look forward to the ongoing challenges associated with protecting and enhancing this valuable brand.

Chapter 14

Lessons Learned and the Future of Branding in Health Care

Gil Bashe, Nancy J. Hicks, and Amy Ziegenfuss

From Ben Franklin's foundation of what would become Pennsylvania Hospital to the introduction of the term *managed care* in the late 1980s, health services in the United States have undergone a steady, if sometimes dramatic, evolution. Throughout this rich history, each of the elements necessary for an age of health care branding has existed on its own. However, with the beginning of the new millenium, these elements have finally come together to present health care marketers and institutions with an amazing opportunity—to not only create successful brands, but also go beyond to the formulation of the most influential of assets: the megabrand.

Among the many components that have contributed to the birth of the branding age are the formation of the National Committee for Quality Assurance, the ability of pharmaceutical companies to advertise their products, the availability of studies' outcome data, and the development of a Patient's Bill of Rights. Together, these have contributed to the creation of an age in which both information and personal choice are more available to consumers than ever before. Previously, health care consumers were forced to rely on the instructions of doctors, with little or no understanding of the process through which treatment decisions were made. Doctors were trusted family friends whose advice was followed virtually without question. These days, though, the belt-tightening of managed care has translated into the age of the educated consumer. For example, patients now can compare notes with doctors and other health care experts the world over via the massive expanse of the Internet. No referrals are needed to consult these electronic physicians, and consumers have gained a new sense of empowerment—an emotion in strict opposition to the feelings of helplessness engendered by the perception of HMOs and other managed care organizations as medical juggernauts unconcerned with patients and focused, instead, on making money.

This era of educated consumerism, however dangerous if mismanaged, is also a tremendous opportunity for health care organizations, as successful brands are not possible without both choice and an engaged marketplace. Health care branding, when executed effectively, has the opportunity to work against negative perceptions and create the most powerful of bonds with consumers. Vanderbilt addressed negative perceptions of its doctors with a highly successful campaign that appealed to consumers' emotions by showing key physicians in a more personal and caring light. Patients yearn for doctors with whom they can develop a real rapport, and the process of branding can address these feelings by sending the message that "we are in this together."

With this book, we have addressed what we feel are the key aspects of health care branding. No one chapter in this book can completely illustrate this process, but, when combined, the case studies demonstrate the awesome potential of a successful brand. Each study represents unique aspects and examples of brand creation and management, and the institutions profiled are absolutely among the best-in-class where health care branding is concerned. Because of the fluid nature of branding, these examples cannot, in and among themselves, provide the key to unlock the full power of health care branding. Careful review of these case studies will give stakeholders the invaluable opportunity to learn from the best practices of other institutions, but it is up to the individual organization to take this information and add something extra—some unique piece of itself that will distinguish it in an increasingly competitive marketplace. The brand leaders will be the ones who go the extra step and are able to translate their brands into the ultimate value chain—emotional investment.

To create emotional investment on the part of consumers, an organization must be in touch with the outside world and speak to it from a place of knowledge and awareness. Nordstrom has achieved such a bond, and the company enjoys tremendous customer loyalty as a result. When General Motors created the Saturn line of cars, it brought the Nordstrom model to the car industry. Research showed that consumers, while happy with the overall quality of cars produced, were disgruntled with the process of car buying. GM's response was to do away with this process by saying "Here is a quality product, and here is the price." Consumers formed an emotional connection because the company extended an attitude of understanding by communicating the idea that "we hear you and are making an effort to make you happy." What made Saturn even more successful is that GM did not stop there. Through the creation of follow-up efforts, Saturn created a long-lasting engagement with consumers designed to get Saturn buyers to both recommend the product to others and purchase another Saturn in the future. Saturn employees were trained to make customers feel special—as if the purchase of the car made them part of a family. Employees cheer when customers arrive to pick up their cars; Saturn drivers and their families are invited to barbecues and other social gatherings and are invited to tour Saturn facilities. The company has established itself as a brand that represents quality, ease, and caring and has achieved an emotional connection among employees and consumers alike.

The most lucrative brands go beyond the qualitative and quantitative aspects of the institution. A brand must engender a feeling of positive regard through the creation of a system of empowerment. A holistic view of branding seeks to address the entire system, thereby making health care an emotionally engaging experience for all involved; from doctor to patient to corporate staff, buy-in must be comprehensive and enduring. Be forward-thinking; devise ways to get consumers to not only be happy with treatment, but also return should future problems arise.

Fear is a compelling emotion and can encourage or discourage action, and even the most informed patients tend to approach the thought of medical treatment with trepidation, especially in an age in which many consumers have an "us vs. them" attitude toward health care organizations. Washington Hospital Center (WHC) reversed negative conceptions about the level of care it provides by launching a campaign centered around its successful cardiac program. The public awareness campaign not only educated women on the risks of heart disease, but also helped to establish WHC as a market leader in cardiac health. Effective branding creates friendlier institutions, and this message of caring can help defuse the fear and uncertainty common among health care consumers. Health care institutions stand at the threshold of an age of change in which the invocation of effective branding practices can help consumers develop the courage to engage in the health care system, the result of which will be a healthier society. Therein lies the potential power of branding.

Long before the establishment of a lasting bond between institution and consumer, however, comes the birth of the brand itself. The 10-item checklist (Exhibit 14–1) reviews the key components of an effective brand. Keep in mind that this is not a simple "to-do" list—the tasks outlined cannot simply be ticked off, then forgotten. Branding is an ongoing process, and these steps must be revisited regularly if the organization and its brand are to achieve continuing success.

For the first time in history, health care marketers and institutions are presented with the inspiring opportunity to create a true and lasting emotional connection among health care organizations, consumers, and employees. It is our hope that this book will be used as a tool for brand building. Successful brands carry with them the potential to establish a powerful link between institution and consumer, and such links will prove invaluable as organizations continue to compete in an increasingly aggressive marketplace. In addition to creating stronger companies, the most effective brands will translate into friendlier institutions, which will, in turn, empower and inspire consumers to take an active role in their health management.

The chapters herein provide but a mere sample of the awesome potential of successful brands. It is up to you, as individual institutions, to go one step farther—to create positive and caring organizations that deliver quality care time and time again, and thereby establish that all-important emotional connection with employees and consumers. It is in this way that all of us—including hospitals, marketing and communications specialists, pharmaceutical manufacturers, and managed care organizations—will play a role in the establishment of a better future for health care and a healthier society for us all.

Good luck.

Exhibit 14–1 Defining Your Health Brand—10-Item Checklist

Are you going to enhance your brand's reputation and identity in the marketplace or launch a major brand-building campaign? If so, we invite you to use this Defining Your Health Brand—10-Item Checklist. One of the great assets of megabrands is their ability to do it right again and again. Branding consistently is key to earning customer trust. You have our blessing to copy this list and use it in your day-to-day efforts.

1. *Knowledge. Know the perceived and actual needs of your internal and external customers.* Keeping current on demographics and health trends allows brands to remain relevant in a changing environment. Research groups such as IMS Health, Migilari & Kaplan, and Yankelovich Partners offer a variety of different tools you can use. Consider conducting an annual benchmark survey of your target audiences. Comparing data from year to year will help you stay on top of changes and engage opportunity. Strategic insight hails from knowledge. Afterward, the big, brand-building ideas will flow.

2. *Chart your brand's value and the weight of its message along the lines of audience interaction.* A few years ago, physicians were the primary audience of hospitals and pharmaceutical companies. All the power resided in the hands of the prescriber. Next, the payer became powerful with the rise of managed care. Then the 1990s ushered in the consumer as an important part of the communications chain. Now, with the Patient's Bill of Rights, physicians have a renewed opportunity to advocate for patients and for better health care. If the patient buys in and the physician disagrees, the brand has lost the opportunity to mobilize customers. A fragmented marketplace is starting to realign—disease creates new communities, alliances, and relationships—and brands are at the core of that trend.

3. *Insight.* Insight drives your "big idea." It's the spark of clarity, the vision of possibility that allows you to invest in the brand and address audience needs. Insight is the strategic driver supporting the tactical plan. As the expression goes, "When you don't know where you want to go, any road will take you there." *Knowing your issue and market and having a firm grasp of customers and message flow are the first two steps to gaining insight.*

4. *Idea.* General Motors developed Saturn in response to knowledge about the marketplace and customer needs. Apple recognized that the home computer needed something new and launched the iMac. Coca-Cola acknowledged that its powerful core brand allowed it to "franchise" and address other thirst needs. *Powerful ideas help express the potential of brands.* They are the vehicles of brand message and value. Powerful ideas are memorable; they provide an emotional context for the customer to bond to the brand.

5. *Message. Messages are not slogans.* Messages are the tools in which brand relevance and value are conveyed. Messages address customers' needs and precede the call to action. Brands can demonstrate their performance if their message taps the customer's intellectual and/or emotional need. When a customer tries the brand, you "show your stuff" and impact behavioral change. Test your message and make sure it's consistent and holds true for all audience segments.

6. *Buy-In. Completed your research, identified your customer targets, gained insight, and honed the "big idea"? Now get buy-in from your internal stakeholders.* As illustrated by

continues

Exhibit 14–1 continued

the Scripps example, "There can never be too much attention given to how the effort will affect the organization internally." A great brand is consistent in its vision. Otherwise, customers will not be certain of when and where to access the brand. Brand building takes time. Brand building requires consistency. Everyone needs to know that brands speak with one voice. Management and the team need to be on board before the effort begins.

7. ***Channels. Advertising professionals think about ads.*** PR pros think about media relationships. Event planners think events. Video production companies produce VHS cassettes. Your message must be conveyed with consistency through all of these channels to be consistent among the audiences those channels reach. The brand is the ultimate integrator of the tools or channels you select. Make sure that the message is uniform and the tools are value-added to the customer.

8. ***Details.*** According to the highly recommended monthly business magazine *Fast Company*, life comprises projects. ***A great idea must be executed flawlessly, just as a great brand must deliver time and time again flawlessly.*** Projects comprise details. If the image and identity campaign is misunderstood by an affiliate, or the customer service phone lines go unanswered, or the health-screening program is inconvenient to attend, your brand is impacted. People respond by punishing the brand.

9. ***Consistency. Performance is where customers assess whether "this brand works for me."*** Consistency is vital in everything we do. Nordstrom is known for its consistent service. Wal-Mart is beloved by its customers for its consistent value. Health institutions have special challenges, for it's not always possible to "consistently" save a life threatened by illness. Information, service, kindness, relevance, and honesty are all part of the expectations of consumers. Be consistent in your message and its delivery.

10. ***Evaluation.*** If your customers demonstrate repeat trial, if the customer satisfaction surveys come back glowing and the media analyses convey consistency of message reported and understood, you are on track. How will you know? Evaluate. The American Cancer Society does this by conducting a biannual image tracking study. Businesses have instituted an era of 360° personnel evaluations. United States Navy Commander Michael Abrashoff relayed this adage in an interview with *Fast Company*: "When a monkey leader looks down at the other monkeys in the same tree he sees their smiling faces. When the monkeys in the tree look up, they have another view." ***Strong brands need to know their status among customers and in the marketplace.*** If the evaluation is great, continue to support your efforts. If you need to address issues, don't wait. Megabrands aspire only to true smiles and greatness.

Index

About the Authors

Gil Bashe has always been driven by the personal side of the business and has long been involved in patient, pharmaceutical, and provider health care issues. His passion for health care dates back to his days as a "non-com" in the army, where he was named "Outstanding Combat Medic" prior to joining his airborne unit.

Bashe, a counselor to industry leaders, is CEO of GTCR-sponsored Health!Quest Global Communication Partners. He has served as group company CEO of Common-Health, the world's largest health care communications company, and as worldwide director of Hill

and Knowlton's Health and Pharmaceutical Practice. Prior to joining Hill and Knowlton, he was president of Medicus Group International's public relations enterprise. *Inside PR* named him a "Health and Medical All-Star" in 1993.

A graduate of Fairleigh Dickinson University with a bachelors degree in humanities, Bashe today serves on the University's board of trustees as well as the boards of the American Heart Association Heritage Chapter, American Federation for Aging Research, and Leukemia Society of Northern New Jersey.

With his knowledge in the core disciplines of health care communications and a cultural sensitivity developed on three continents over the years, Bashe champions treating the emotive rather than just the consumptive needs of the health care consumer as a key to the long-term well-being of the industry.

Bashe sees consumer empowerment and brands as the best ways to reach "end-users" and evolve them into eager participants toward better health. What makes people feel better today holds promise for making the industry function better tomorrow.

For questions about this book and health care communications, you can reach Gil Bashe at gilbashe@aol.com.

Nancy J. Hicks is a Senior Managing Director of Hill and Knowlton and Co-Director of the Healthcare Provider Practice. She has supervised major health care accounts throughout the United States, including Bard Urological Division, the Bausch & Lomb Oral Care Division, the American Cancer Society, the Robert Wood Johnson Foundation, and the American Podiatric Medical Association. In addition, Hicks has worked with numerous health systems and health plans including Blue Cross Blue Shield and Cigna. Hicks specializes in strategic communications planning, the development of national positioning programs for health care clients, and the management of crisis situations.

Prior to joining Hill and Knowlton, Ms. Hicks was manager of public relations for US Health Care Development, the acquisition division of American Medical International in Atlanta, director of public relations for Virginia Mason Medical Center in Seattle, and public relations representative for the Fred Hutchinson Cancer Research Center in Seattle. Hicks has served as a freelance writer, editor, and teacher.

An accredited member of the Public Relations Society of America (PRSA), Hicks has earned several awards from this society for her work in the health care field. She is a board member of the PRSA Health Academy. She publishes articles on health care marketing in national trade journals and is a regular speaker at national health care conferences. Hicks studied literature and history in London and is a liberal arts graduate of the University of Washington.

You can reach Nancy Hicks at nhicks@hillandknowlton.com.